NEW TESTAMENT II

# MARK

EDITED BY

## THOMAS C. ODEN AND
## CHRISTOPHER A. HALL

GENERAL EDITOR

## THOMAS C. ODEN

IVP Academic

An imprint of InterVarsity Press
Downers Grove, Illinois

*InterVarsity Press*
*P.O. Box 1400, Downers Grove, IL 60515-1426*
*ivpress.com*
*email@ivpress.com*

©1998 by the Institute of Classical Christian Studies (ICCS), Thomas C. Oden and Christopher A. Hall. Retypeset with corrections 2005.

*InterVarsity Press® is the book-publishing division of InterVarsity Christian Fellowship/USA®, a movement of students and faculty active on campus at hundreds of universities, colleges, and schools of nursing in the United States of America, and a member movement of the International Fellowship of Evangelical Students. For information about local and regional activities, visit intervarsity.org.*

*Scripture quotations, unless otherwise noted, are from the Revised Standard Version of the Bible, copyright 1946, 1952, 1971 by the Division of Christian Education of the National Council of the Churches of Christ in the U.S.A., and are used by permission.*

*The following translations of patristic works, signified in the footnotes by their respective abbreviations, have been used with permission:*

*FC Selected excerpts from The Fathers of the Church, 86 volumes. Copyright ©1947-. Used by permission of Catholic University of America Press.*

*FGFR Selected excerpts from Faith Gives Fullness to Reasoning: The Five Theological Orations of Gregory Nazianzen. Intro. and commentary by Frederick W. Norris, trans. Lionel Wickham and Frederick Williams. Copyright ©1991. Used by permission of E. J. Brill.*

*HOG Selected excerpts from Bede the Venerable. Homilies on the Gospels. 2 volumes. Trans. Lawrence T. Martin and David Hurst OSB. Copyright ©1991. Used by permission of Cistercian Publications.*

*JFB Selected excerpts from Journey with the Fathers, Year B. Ed. Edith Barnecut. Copyright ©1993 New City Press. Reprinted by permission of New City Press of the Focolare Movement.*

*JSSS2 Saint Ephrem's Commentary on Tatian's Diatessaron: An English Translation of Chester Beatty Syriac MS 709. Trans. and ed. C. McCarthy. Journal of Semitic Studies Supplement 2. Copyright ©1993. Used by permission of Oxford University Press.*

*LCC 1 Selected excerpts from Early Christian Fathers. Library of Christian Classics 1. Ed. Cyril C. Richardson. Copyright ©1953. Used by permission of Westminster John Knox Press.*

*LCC 3 Selected excerpts from Christology of the Later Fathers. Library of Christian Classics 3. Ed. Edward Hardy. Copyright ©1954. Used by permission of Westminster John Knox Press.*

*LCC 4 Selected excerpts from Cyril of Jerusalem and Nemesius of Emesa. Library of Christian Classics 4. Ed. William Telfer. Copyright ©1955. Used by permission of Westminster John Knox Press.*

*SSGF Selected excerpts from The Sunday Sermons of the Great Fathers. 4 volumes. Trans. and ed. M. F. Toal. Copyright ©1996. Used by permission of Preservation Press.*

*Cover design: David Fassett*
*Images: gold texture background: © Katsumi Murouchi / Getty Images*
  *stained glass cathedral window: © elzauer / Getty Images*
  *gold texture: © Katsumi Murouchi / Getty Images*
  *abstract marble pattern: © NK08gerd / iStock / Getty Images Plus*

*ISBN 978-0-8308-4353-4 (paperback)*
*ISBN 978-0-8308-1418-3 (hardcover)*
*ISBN 978-0-8308-9743-8 (digital)*

*Printed in the United States of America ∞*

**Library of Congress Cataloging-in-Publication Data**

*A catalog record for this book is available from the Library of Congress.*

| P | 32 | 31 | 30 | 29 | 28 | 27 | 26 | 25 | 24 | 23 | 22 | 21 | 20 | 19 | 18 | 17 | 16 | 15 | 14 | 13 | 12 | 11 | 10 | 9 | 8 | 7 | 6 | 5 | 4 | 3 | 2 | 1 |
| Y | 47 | 46 | 45 | 44 | 43 | 42 | 41 | 40 | 39 | 38 | 37 | 36 | 35 | 34 | 33 | 32 | 31 | 30 | 29 | 28 | 27 | 26 | 25 | 24 | 23 | 22 | 21 | 20 | 19 |

# Contents

# INTRODUCTION TO MARK

This introduction is meant to prepare the way for readers to explore Mark through the eyes of the ancient Christian writers. Our first task is to examine Markan authorship as viewed by his earliest interpreters. Next we will explore the unique and honored status of Mark among earliest apostolic texts. Finally we will account for our specific method of investigation into early interpreters of Mark. Then we will discuss modern problems in reading the fathers.

## How Early Christian Writers Viewed the Authorship of Mark

Our purpose here is not to establish the Petrine fountain of Mark's Gospel on the basis of a critical evaluation of the historical evidence. Rather, more modestly, we are asking how the early church reasoned and what it consensually concluded about the authorship and authority of Mark on the basis of all the evidence they had available. This is an underlying premise of this whole series: We are not here trying to *correct* the ancient Christian writers from the viewpoint of modern historical criteria, but rather to *listen* to them reason out of their own premises on such questions as the authorship of Mark.

The early church widely regarded the author of Mark's Gospel as the authentic voice and interpreter of Peter. This view was early stated, largely uncontroverted during the early Christian centuries and ecumenically received by the church. The primary textual evidence for this viewpoint is strong and ancient, as we will show.

The earliest evidence of Markan authorship is set forth by Papias (c. 60-130), the bishop of Hieropolis in Phrygia, in the vicinity of the New Testament churches of Colossae and Laodicea. We find this testimony in a primitive Christian fragment preserved by Eusebius:

> But now we must add to the words of his [Papias] which we have already quoted *the tradition which he gives in regard to Mark*, the author of the Gospel. It is in the following words: "This also John the Presbyter[1] said: Mark, having become the *interpreter of Peter*, wrote down accurately, though not indeed in order, whatever he remembered of the things said or done by Christ. For he neither heard the Lord nor accompanied him, but afterward, as I said, he was in company with Peter, who used to offer teaching as necessity demanded, but with no intention of giving a

---

[1]Eusebius thought that Papias distinguished between two Johns: First, the apostle who is numbered among the "apostles whose witness belonged to the past and was related by their hearers; the second is called presbyter and a disciple of the Lord like Aristion, whose witnesses are given in person" (Papias 5, EEC 449; TLG 2018.002, 3.39.5.1-6.1).

connected account of the Lord's discourses. So Mark committed no error in thus writing some single points as he remembered them. For upon one thing he fixed his attention: to leave out nothing of what he had heard and to make no false statements in them." (Fragments of Papias, from Eusebius *Ecclesiastical History* 3.39.14-15)[2]

Papias is remembered by Irenaeus as a man of primitive age, "the hearer of John, and a companion of Polycarp."[3] Born around A.D. 60 (about the time Paul first preached in Rome), Papias was quite possibly a contemporary of John. In any case he had the privilege of hearing at least the second generation and possibly the first generation of apostolic preaching, and passed on the Johannine tradition that he had received. Papias lived in a region where the gospel tradition flourished quite early, as is evident from Paul's missionary itinerary reported in Acts 16:6 and 18:23.[4] And we read of persons from Phrygia being present in Jerusalem on the day of Pentecost (Acts 2:10). Papias understood himself to be simply passing along a tradition already solidly established. There is no evidence to suggest that Papias was reconfiguring the tradition or inventively reshaping it.

This earliest Phrygian tradition attests to five key points of ancient tradition regarding Markan authorship:

☐ Mark interpreted Peter accurately
☐ Peter was Mark's chief access to the recollections of Jesus
☐ Mark did not record the tradition "in order"
☐ Peter presented the Lord's teaching as the situation demanded, but with no intention of giving a connected account of the Lord's discourses
☐ Nothing crucial was distorted or omitted

Within decades after the death of Papias, Clement of Alexandria (c. 150-215) is found in an entirely different locale, in Egypt, reconfirming the tradition that Mark was the reliable interpreter of the narrative of the Lord attested by Peter. The implication is that the tradition of the earliest presbyters of Alexandria known to Clement assumed that Mark had been associated with Peter over a long period of time, that Peter was aware that Mark had written down Peter's narrative, and that Peter had no objection to his doing so, although Peter did not directly promote or prompt it. Mark is portrayed as responding to the requests of many believers to write out Peter's widely recognized and authoritative public teaching about Christ while Peter was at Rome.

These assumptions were in place as an established, received tradition in Alexandria. There it was steadily held that Mark had preached in Egypt and founded the African church in Alexandria (Euse-

---

[2]TLG 2018.002, 3.39.14.4-15.9; NPNF 2 1:172-73*, italics added (cf. Kirsopp Lake translation, *Eusebius: The Ecclesiastical History* [LCL 153 Cambridge, Mass.: Harvard University Press, 1926] 1:297; also ANF 1:154).

[3]*Against Heresies* 5.33.4; TLG 1447.008, 28.1-2; ANF 1:563.

[4]The antiquity of Phrygian Christianity is evidenced in a note by Eusebius, *Ecclesiastical History* 8.11, who reported that as early as the time of Diocletian there was a city in Phrygia in which every soul was Christian.

bius *Ecclesiastical History* 2.16, 24). Here are the words of Clement as recited by Eusebius:

> Again, in the same books, Clement gives the tradition of the earliest presbyters,[5] as to the order of the Gospels, in the following manner: "The Gospels containing the genealogies, he says, were written first. The Gospel according to Mark had this occasion. As Peter had preached the Word publicly at Rome, and declared the Gospel by the Spirit, many who were present requested that Mark, who had followed him for a long time and remembered well what he had said, should write them out. And having composed the Gospel he gave it to those who had requested it. When Peter learned of this, he neither directly hindered nor encouraged it." (Fragments of Clement, Eusebius *Ecclesiastical History* 6.14.5-7)[6]

Far from Phrygia (Papias), Alexandria (Clement) and Caesarea (Eusebius), the second-century tradition in southern Gaul about Mark was similarly recalled by Irenaeus (c. 115-202). He also taught that the most ancient guardians of the canonical tradition valued Mark as the disciple and interpreter of Peter, and that he recorded his Gospel *after* Peter's death.[7] Irenaeus's testimony should be understood in the light of his cherished remembrance of Polycarp, who himself had been directly acquainted with the apostle John and thus mediated the tradition of the first generation after the apostles. Irenaeus left a written record of the Smyrnean tradition he had received about Mark's identity. The terms echo the traditions of Phrygia and Alexandria, as we read the record in Eusebius:

> Since, in the beginning of this work, we promised to give, when needful, the words of the ancient presbyters and writers of the church, in which they have declared those traditions which came down to them concerning the canonical books, and since Irenaeus was one of them, we will now give his words and, first, what he says of the sacred Gospels: "Matthew published his Gospel among the Hebrews in their own language, while Peter and Paul were preaching and founding the church in Rome. After their departure Mark, the disciple and interpreter of Peter, also transmitted to us in writing those things which Peter had preached." (Fragments of Irenaeus, Eusebius *Ecclesiastical History* 5.8.1-3)[8]

Origen (c. 185-c. 254), who had wide firsthand acquaintance with the Palestinian, Alexandrian and Roman traditions, also confirmed this assumption that Mark reliably wrote according to Peter's gospel, and Origen believed that Peter himself had instructed Mark to write it. These traditions, according to Origen, assumed that Mark was the same individual commended by the apostle in 1 Peter 5:13 as "my son."

Among the four Gospels, which are the only indisputable ones in the church of God under

---

[5]Of Alexandria.
[6]TLG 2018 002, 6.14.5.1-7.2; NPNF 2 1:261, cf. *Ecclesiastical History* 2.15.1-2.
[7]Literally, his departure.
[8]TLG 2018.002, 5.8.1.1-3.3; NPNF 2 1:222.

heaven, I have learned by tradition that the first was written by Matthew, who was once a publican, but afterwards an apostle of Jesus Christ, and it was prepared for the converts from Judaism, and published in the Hebrew language. The second is by Mark, who composed it according to the instructions of Peter, who in his Catholic epistle acknowledges him as a son, saying, "The church that is at Babylon[9] elected together with you, salutes you, and so does Mark, my son." (Fragments of Origen, Eusebius *Ecclesiastical History* 6.25.4-5)[10]

Thus by an extraordinary coalescence of diverse testimony from widely diverse arenas we have reliable textual evidence that the second and third generation of Christian teachers viewed Mark as echoing the narrative voice of Peter.

## From Eusebius to Augustine

The Palestinian tradition argued specifically for the trustworthiness of Mark's transmission of Peter's gospel. Eusebius of Caesarea (c. 263-c. 339), who had access to the best library in Palestine, thought that there was sufficient internal evidence in the text of Mark's Gospel to confirm Mark's reliability:

Mark writes thus, and through him Peter bears witness, for the whole of Mark is said to be a record of Peter's teaching. Note how scrupulously the disciples refused to record those things that might have given the impression of their fame. Note how they handed down in writing numerous slanders against themselves to unforgetting ages, and accusations of sins, which no one in later years would ever have known about unless hearing it in their own voice. By thus honestly reporting their own faults, it is reasonable to view them as relatively void of false speaking and egoism. This habit gives plain and clear proof of their truth-loving disposition. As for those who imagine the disciples invented and lied, and slandered themselves as deceivers, ought such critics not to become a laughing-stock? They thereby convict themselves already as accomplices of envy and malice, as enemies of truth-telling itself. For they demean those who have already exhibited in their own lives credible proof of their integrity, whose absolutely sincere character and trustworthiness shines through their very words. Meanwhile their detractors imagine that the Evangelists are rascals and clever sophists who merely fantasized things that never took place. How could believers of such character ascribe falsely to their own Lord things he never did?

This is why I think it has been rightly said that "One must put complete confidence in the disciples of Jesus, or none at all." For *if we are to distrust those of such unimpeachable character, we reasonably must also distrust all ancient writers on the same principle.* We must distrust any who at any time have compiled, either in Greece or anywhere, lives and histories and records of persons of

---

[9]Probably Rome, but it should also be remembered that the ancient church in the old city of Cairo was in a fortress area called Babylon.
[10]TLG 2018.002, 6.25.4.1-5.4; NPNF 2 1:273.

their own times, celebrating their noble achievements. Otherwise we would be considering it as reasonable to have greater confidence in those of lesser character, and have lesser confidence in those of greater character. And that would clearly be tendentious. How could it be that these would falsify the account of his death? What would be their motive in writing down deeds he never did? Were all these things and everything like them in the Gospels merely dreamed up by counterfeit disciples? Or take another twisted hypothesis, that we should distrust the more glorious and lofty parts of the report, yet credit only the ordinary parts of the report as truthful? How could they do so and doubt these candid reports of ignominious actions? How could they reasonably support such an unreasonable type of selectivity? To say that the same witnesses spoke the truth and at the same time lied is to predict contraries about the same people at the same time. They report his hands and feet being pierced, his being given vinegar to drink, struck on the cheek with a reed, and reviled by those who looked upon him. Were these things and all else like them in the Gospels simply by dubious witnesses—the insults and blows to his face, the scourging of his back, the crown of acanthus set on his head in a demeaning way, and finally his carrying of his own cross, and his being nailed to it! If it was their aim to deceive, and to adorn their master with false words, they would never have written these demeaning accounts of his pain and agony, that he was disturbed in spirit, and that they themselves forsook him and fled, or that Peter the apostle and disciple who was chief of them all, denied him three times, unless they had an extraordinarily high standard of truth-telling. (*POG* 3.5, italics added)[11]

Eusebius thought he had good cause to conclude that Mark was "a written monument of the doctrine which had been [by Peter] orally communicated to them" (*Ecclesiastical History* 2.15).[12] Accordingly, Mark's Gospel early and steadily received ecumenical sanction to speak with apostolic authority so as to be read in Lord's Day services in the churches everywhere.

A tradition so widely disseminated as Rome, Palestine, Antioch, Constantinople, Gaul, Phrygia and Alexandria could hardly have been easily invented or subsequently fabricated. It is unlikely that Clement in Alexandria was relying on Papias in Phrygia, or that Irenaeus in Gaul was relying on the Alexandrian tradition. Rather these traditions were more likely widely separated, and perhaps independent traditions reporting the same view of the authorship of Mark as directly dependent on the preaching of Peter. Athanasius wrote: "Mark the Gospel writer . . . uses the same voice [as Peter did in his confession of Jesus as Messiah], speaking in harmony with the blessed Peter" (*Sermon on the Nativity of Christ*, 28).[13]

Hence there is little doubt that a general ecumenical consensus existed on Markan authorship quite

---

[11]TLG 2018.005, 3.5.95.1-100.10; POG 140-41*.
[12]TLG 2018.005, 3.6.2.5-6; NPNF 2 1:116.
[13]TLG 2035.089, 28.968.15-17.

early, possibly in the first century among the elders of Alexandria and Phrygia, and doubtless in the early second century in Asia, and soon thereafter in most other places.

The philologically adept and textually critical Latin writer Jerome, who was widely acquainted with the traditions of Rome, Dalmatia, Gaul, Antioch, Constantinople and Palestine, thought the ancient consensus was clear and confirmable that

> Mark the disciple and interpreter of Peter wrote a short Gospel at the request of the brethren at Rome embodying what he had heard Peter tell. When Peter had heard this, he approved it and published it to the churches to be read by his authority, as Clement in the sixth book of his Hypotyposes, and Papias, bishop of Hierapolis, record. Peter also mentions this Mark in his first epistle, figuratively indicating Rome under the name of Babylon: "She who is in Babylon elect together with you salutes you and so does Mark my son." So, taking the Gospel which he himself composed, he went to Egypt and first preaching Christ at Alexandria he formed a church so admirable in doctrine and continence of living that he constrained all followers of Christ to this example. Philo, most learned of the Jews, seeing the first church at Alexandria[14] still Jewish in a degree, wrote a book on their manner of life as something creditable to his nation telling how, as Luke says, the believers had all things in common at Jerusalem, so he recorded what he saw was done at Alexandria, under the learned Mark. He died in the eighth year of Nero and was buried at Alexandria, Annianus succeeding him. *(Lives of Illustrious Men 8)*[15]

Jerome not only accepted the early tradition that Mark was Peter's disciple and interpreter, but further argued, beyond Clement, that Peter had inspected and approved Mark's report, and that Mark took Peter's gospel to Alexandria and died there as first bishop of Alexandria. Elsewhere Jerome goes so far as to ascribe the Gospel of Mark essentially to Peter *(Lives of Illustrious Men 1)*.[16]

Thus by the time of Augustine (354-430) it had become a long-standing ecumenical tradition (three centuries old) that the Holy Spirit had supervised the accurate transmission of the gospel tradition from the eyewitness apostles to the consenting church through Mark and Luke who

> credibly received accounts with which they had become acquainted in a trustworthy manner through the instrumentality of actual followers of the Lord as he manifested himself in the flesh, and lived in the company of those disciples who were attending him. Divine providence, through the agency of the Holy Spirit, has taken care that they who were intimate associates of the first apostles should be given authority to preach the gospel, and also to compose an account of it in writing. Apart from these four Evangelists, all those other individuals who have attempted or

---

[14]Jerome made the erroneous assumption that Philo was referring to Christian, not Jewish, communities. But that some of these Jewish communities were in various stages of transition toward Christianity is likely.

[15]Cetedoc 0616, 8.12.10; NPNF 2 3:364.

[16]Cetedoc 0616, 1.6.34; NPNF 2 3:361: "Then too the Gospel according to Mark, who was his [Peter's] disciple and interpreter, is ascribed to him [Peter]."

dared to offer a written record of the acts of the Lord or the apostles, failed to commend themselves in their own times as persons of the character which would induce the church to yield them its confidence, and to admit their compositions to the level of canonical authority of holy writ. These spurious accounts were written by persons who could make no legitimate claim to be credited in their narrations. In a deceitful manner they introduced into their writing certain matters which are condemned at once by the catholic and apostolic rule of faith, and by sound doctrine. . . . But the fact is that just as [these four] each received the gift of inspiration, they abstained from adding to their various narratives any superfluous or synthesized compositions. For Matthew is understood to have taken it in hand to construct the record of the incarnation of the Lord according to the royal lineage, and to give an account of a great deal of his deeds and words as they stood in relation to this present life of men. Mark follows him closely, and looks like his associate and epitomizer. For in Mark's narrative he gives nothing in concert with John apart from the others. . . . Taken by himself, Mark has relatively little exclusively to record, and taken in conjunction with Luke even less. In concurrence with Matthew, Mark has a greater number of passages. Frequently he narrates in words almost numerically and identically the same as those used by Matthew. (*Harmony of the Gospels* 1.2)[17]

We have already seen Eusebius relate the testimony of Clement that Mark was the first to establish the church in Alexandria.[18] He further confirms this tradition:

And they say that this Mark was the first that was sent to Egypt, and that he proclaimed the Gospel which he had written and first established churches in Alexandria. And the multitude of believers, both men and women, that were collected there at the very outset, and lived lives of the most philosophical and extreme asceticism, was so great, that Philo thought it worthwhile to describe their pursuits, their meetings, their entertainments, and their whole manner of life. (*Ecclesiastical History* 2.16.1-2)[19]

But did Philo actually meet Peter in Rome or regard Mark as the disciple of Peter in Alexandria? According to a highly questionable but nonetheless intriguing tradition reported by Jerome:

They say that under Caius Caligula he [Philo] ventured to Rome, where he had been sent as legate of his nation, and that when a second time he had come to Claudius, he spoke in the same city with the apostle Peter and enjoyed his friendship, and for this reason also adorned the adherents of Mark, Peter's disciple at Alexandria, with his praises. (*Lives of Illustrious Men* 11)[20]

Jerome may have confused Philo's commendation of the Therapeutae at Alexandria with early Christian communities. Philo (c. 20 B.C.-A.D. 50) was still alive in A.D. 41. Eusebius (260-339) had

---

[17]Cetedoc 0273, 1.1.2.2.12; NPNF 1 6:77-78*.

[18]And quite probably, in our view, in all Africa.

[19]TLG 2018.002, 2.16.1.1-2.5; NPNF 2 1:116.

[20]Cetedoc 0616, 11.14.19; NPNF 2 3:365

fantasies that the Jewish ascetics described in Philo's *Contemplative Life*, the Therapeutae, were Christian groups.[21] While Philo was doubtless describing a Jewish community in Alexandria, Eusebius and Jerome thought he was describing the church in Alexandria, of which Mark, according to tradition, was the founder.

We are here trying to establish what the ancient consensual tradition considered factual concerning the authorship of Mark. The speculations about Philo are less crucial to settle here than that the Palestinian tradition regarded a highly honored and independent source, Philo, as confirming the already-existing ecumenical tradition concerning the reliability of Mark. These later texts, which reflect a growing tendency to assimilate Philo into proto-Christian piety, merely say that Philo mentioned an ascetic group, that this group was Christian and that Mark was thought to have founded the group.[22]

Ancient tradition preserved in Eusebius's *Ecclesiastical History* agrees with the reckoning of Jerome[23] in placing the death of Mark in Alexandria in about the year 62: "When Nero was in the eighth year of his reign, Annianus succeeded Mark the evangelist in the administration of the parish of Alexandria" (*Ecclesiastical History* 2.24.1).[24]

## The Unique and Honored Place of Mark Among Early Apostolic Texts

We find early Christian texts quoting the Gospel of Mark in literature originating in every locale of the early church's missionary and pastoral activity—Africa, Asia and throughout the northern Mediterranean. The evidence points to Mark's Gospel being a normative part of the early Christian corpus of liturgical sources. At an early date the church received it into the canon of New Testament writings by wide (and apparently unanimous) agreement. From the beginning of the worldwide Christian witness, Mark has been listed as a part of every preacher's armamentarium of sources for knowing Jesus Christ.[25]

---

[21]Eusebius writes that Philo "has this to say about the churches in the area of [Alexandria]: 'In every house there is a holy chamber called a sanctuary or "monastery," where they celebrate in seclusion the mysteries of the sanctified life'" (*Ecclesiastical History* 2.17.8-9; TLG 2018.002, 2.17.8.7-9.3; HCCC 91).

[22]Cf. David T. Runia, *Philo in Early Christian Literature: A Survey* (Minneapolis: Fortress, 1993).

[23]*Lives of Illustrious Men*, NPNF 2 3:361.

[24]TLG 2018.002, 2.24.1.1-3; NPNF 2 1:128.

[25]Why were there four and only four Gospels? The second-century church reasoned about this not by allegory but by analogy to the four winds that cover the earth, and the four pillars or corners of a building. Irenaeus passed on this symmetrical reasoning grounded in his missiology: "It is not possible that the Gospels can be either more or fewer in number than four. For, since there are four zones [directions], encompassing all, leaving out none [north, south, east and west] of the world in which we live, and four principal winds [the allusion here is to "four catholic spirits," or the whole of all winds viewed universally], while the church is scattered throughout all the world, and the "pillar and ground" [1 Tim 3:15] of the church is the gospel and the spirit of life; it is fitting that she should have four pillars, offering imperishable inspiration on all sides, and vivifying all humanity ever afresh" (*Against Heresies* 3.11.8, ANF 1:428; TLG 1447.002, 11.1-12). In this way the idea that there are four received Gospels was intrinsically connected with the worldwide mission of preaching. It was thus grounded in scriptural typology and missiology, and not merely a frivolous observation based on numerology.

---

Eusebius argued that Mark's "work obtained the sanction of [Peter's] authority for the purpose of being *used in the churches*" (*Ecclesiastical History* 2.16, based on Clement's testimony).[26] Jerome agreed that Peter had "approved it and *published it to the churches to be read by his authority*" (*Lives of Illustrious Men* 8).[27] No Gospel was earlier or more clearly or consensually received as designated for use in public worship than Mark.

Augustine maintained that Mark, who was not one of the Twelve, was chosen by the Holy Spirit, like Luke, to demonstrate that the fountain of grace had not dried up with the twelve apostles. "The Holy Spirit willed to choose for the writing of the Gospel two [Mark and Luke] who were not even from those who made up the Twelve, so that it might not be thought that the grace of evangelization had come only to the apostles and that in them the fountain of grace had dried up" (*Sermon* 239.1).[28]

Did Mark write in Hebrew? So thought John Chrysostom who, in arguing that Matthew "composed his Gospel in the language of the Hebrews," added: "And Mark too, in Egypt, is said to have done this self-same thing at the entreaty of the disciples" (*Homilies on the Gospel of St. Matthew* 1.7).[29]

It had always been evident that Mark presented a *shorter* version of the gospel than Matthew, but the premise of literary *dependency* was not generally recognized. The view that Matthew and Luke directly relied on Mark did not develop in full form until the nineteenth century, and while it holds the majority opinion among source-critical scholars today, it is still debated and there are notable proponents of the dependence of Mark on Matthew.

## Reading Scripture with the Church Fathers

The purpose of this commentary is not to resolve the debate between the merits of ancient and modern exegesis. It is to present the comments of the ancient interpreters with as little interference as possible. We leave it to others to discuss the merits of ancient versus modern methods of exegesis. But this cannot be done adequately without first examining the patristic texts themselves. And until now we have not had easy access to these texts. This is what this series intends to provide.

The purpose of exegesis in the patristic period was to seek the truth the Scriptures convey. It was not offered to those who were as yet unready to put it into practice. In these respects modern exegesis is different: It does not always assume the truth of Scripture as divine revelation, and it does not require that readers intend to practice it as a premise of truly hearing it.

Today's readers should not impose on ancient Christian exegesis modern assumptions about valid reading of Scripture. The ancient writers offer a constant challenge to these silent modern assumptions. If one begins by assuming modern critical methods as normative and judges the ancient writers

---

[26]TLG 2018.002, 2.15.1-3; NPNF 2 1:116.
[27]Cetedoc 0616, 8.12.12; NPNF 2 3:364, italics added.
[28]Cetedoc 0284, 239.38.1127.9; FC 38:244.
[29]TLG 2062.152, 57.17.34-9; NPNF 1 10:3-4.

uncritically by these standards alone, they are always going to come off looking witless or weak, or in some instances comic or quaint or even atrocious, unjust and oppressive.

With few exceptions, the patristic models of exegesis do not conform to common modern assumptions about what a commentary should be. Our contemporary assumptions tend to resist or rule out chains of scriptural reference, which are often demeaned as appalling proof-texting. But in the view of the ancient Christian writers such chains of biblical reference were crucial in thinking about the text in relation to the whole testimony of sacred Scripture. Utilizing the analogy of faith, they constantly compared sacred text with sacred text. This ancient procedure is neither fundamentalism nor biblical literalism. It is analogical textual reasoning.

We ought not to force the assumptions of twentieth-century fundamentalism or of nineteenth-century naturalistic reductionism, historicism or egalitarianism on the ancient Christian writers. They knew nothing of these assumptions. Their method was not "fundamentalist," because they were not reacting against modern naturalistic reductionism. They were constantly protesting a mere literal or plain-sense view of the text, almost always searching for its spiritual and moral meaning. Modern fundamentalism is a defensive movement understandable only within modernity, a movement which indeed often looks far more like modern historicism than ancient typological reasoning. This makes liberal and fundamentalist exegesis much more like each other than either is like that of the ancient Christian writers, because they both appeal to historicist assumptions invented in the Enlightenment, over a thousand years after the last of the ancient commentators had passed away.[30]

Ancient Christian exegetes characteristically weaved many sacred texts together. They seldom limited themselves to comment on a single text, as some modern exegetes insist, but constantly related one text to another by analogy, using typological reasoning, as was so characteristic of the rabbinic midrashim of the same period. While modern exegesis advocates allowing the Hebrew Bible to speak for itself without the intrusion of New Testament assumptions, ancient exegesis constantly delights in viewing Old Testament events and characters as anticipating fulfillment in the New. Hebraic figures and events are often seen from the point of view of their having been fulfilled in Jesus Christ.

The despairing modern attempt to read the New Testament while ruling out the liturgical, evangelical and missional assumptions that prevailed in the ancient community of faith would have seemed a very thin enterprise indeed to those who early shared those assumptions and were willing to die for them. When we today try to make sense of the New Testament while ruling out the plausibility of the Incarnation and resurrection which was held firm by those who wrote it, the effort is too hard and senseless not to be found discouraging. The ancient exegetes proceeded by allowing the texts their own premises.

---

[30]For further discussion of this anomaly, see T. Oden, *After Modernity . . . What?* (Grand Rapids, Mich.: Zondervan, 1989).

## Discovering Patristic Comment on Mark

It should be kept in mind that some passages of Mark are accompanied by an extensive commentary or homiletic tradition, while others have little or none. We have selected an average of about two patristic comments per Markan verse, or about a dozen selections per pericope. This is a broad average, for in many cases we have selected as many as a half-dozen patristic comments for a single crucial verse and none for those on which comment was insufficient. We have tried not to slacken our criteria in instances where a meager patristic commentary tradition is to be found.

In executing our computer searches of patristic material (see the appendix), some of the most important commentary on Mark was found embedded in Origen's, Chrysostom's or Augustine's commentaries or homilies on Matthew or John, not just on Mark. This illustrates the prevailing principle in ancient Christian exegesis: each text is illumined by other sacred texts and by the whole gist of the history of revelation. Hence we find in patristic comments on a given text many other subtexts interwoven in order to illumine that text. A patristic writer is often commenting on Mark while focusing on a passage in one of the other three Gospels.

Mark presents a special problem for the history of exegesis. Whereas Matthew, Luke and John have all benefited from being the subject of several line-by-line patristic commentaries, there are no complete commentaries of Mark that have survived the patristic period. There is a manuscript by one Victor, a presbyter of Antioch (c. A.D. 500) who is wrongly identified as the author of a brief commentary on Mark, but this "commentary" is itself an early catena whose main sources are the homilies on Matthew by Chrysostom, Origen, Cyril of Alexandria, Titus of Bostra and Theodor of Heraclea.[31] Aside from short works by Jerome, Dionysius and Bede, there is nothing extensive on Mark as such.

Hence if we are to reconstruct what the early Christian writers had to say about Mark, we must do so from the various references found scattered in homilies, letters and treatises. This makes this volume on Mark a more daunting challenge in some ways than any of the other three Gospels. The same problems will face ACCS volume editors who work on texts such as Samuel and Kings which have almost no cohesive commentary tradition. We have had to rely on computer searches of all possible sources commenting on Mark, and then we have sifted and gathered the results.

## Reflecting the Consensual Tradition

We have sought to select those passages that best convey the consensual tradition of early Christian exegesis, not fixating on problematic edges or controverted points but looking for those comments that would be most widely received by the whole church, East and West.

This is not to suggest or imply that all patristic writers agree. Upon reading these selections, readers will easily grasp that within the boundaries of orthodoxy there are many views possible about a given

---

[31]Referenced here as Pseudo-Victor of Antioch, PG, cf. M. Geerard, CPG 3:§§6529; cf. LTK 10, 791; EC 12:1540.

text or narrative and that these different views may be strongly affected by varied social environments and contexts. Critical study of the history of exegesis has often focused on the conflicting views and varieties of interpretations to such an extent that it has eclipsed any interpretive cohesion. But the fact that patristic interpretation was accompanied by enormous cultural variety does not imply that it was characterized by counter-apostolic doctrine. The selections in this volume show much more consensuality than difference even among those commentators from the most distant cultural settings—for example, Ephrem the Syrian and Augustine of Hippo. On the other hand, we have not avoided selections showing alternative interpretations. These examples show how extensive is the room for variable interpretation under the ecumenical umbrella.

### Empathizing with the Allegorical Imagination

There is a prevailing modern Protestant stereotype that ancient Christian exegesis is so saturated with fanciful allegory as to make it almost useless. The selections in this commentary demonstrate that in both Alexandrian and Antiochene traditions of exegesis we will find an interest in the plain sense as well as in the spiritual, moral and mystical senses. These selections show that it is wrong to assume that the Alexandrians had little or no interest in the plain sense, or that the Antiochenes had minimal interest in the spiritual sense.

After making our selections on the basis of our criteria, we were ourselves surprised at the limited extent of protracted allegorical passages.[32] While allegory is an acceptable model of exegesis for the ancient Christian writers, especially those of the Alexandrian school, it does not turn out to be a dominating and ecumenical feature of ancient exegesis of Mark.

Some may wish we had rejected allegory altogether. But suppose we had arbitrarily eliminated all allegorical reasoning on the grounds of its offensiveness to contemporary readers. Would this have been fair to patristic exegesis or a realistic expression of it? Others, on the other hand, who are particularly intrigued by allegory may complain that we have included far too little of it.

### The Case for Renewing the Catena Tradition

The style of this Ancient Christian Commentary on Mark is very much along the lines of the catena tradition, that ancient style of commentary in which a chain of excerpts from patristic exegesis was used to elucidate a scriptural text. Some may object to the very concept of a catena. It might be argued that the catena form itself is not only antiquated but unsatisfactory as a genre. If so, it falls to those of us who are deeply committed to recovering the catena tradition to show its usefulness and serviceability.

It is conceivable that some might see this commentary as a scotchtaped melange of excerpts with no

---

[32]In seeking to determine the proportion of our selections with a decisive allegorical dimension, we made a statistical count and found less than 5 percent were allegorical.

cohesion and no attempt at contextualizing diverse quotations. We point out in response that we have utilized the footnotes precisely for those passages that require further clarification of the context or contain textual problems. We have preferred not to select excerpts that intrinsically require heavy or intricate contextualization. And we have used overviews and headings to assist readers in glimpsing the cohesion of patristic comment on a particular pericope.

In the case of Mark's Gospel, there are practically no line-by-line patristic commentaries (excepting the brief catena under the name of one unknown Victor of Antioch). It would have been easier to have omitted those biblical books for which there are few if any line-by-line commentaries—e.g., Samuel, Chronicles, Kings, Haggai and Mark—but this flies in the face of the fact that there are extensive patristic remarks and homilies on Mark as well as these other texts of Scripture. We think the more laborious approach of digitally searching documents far beyond the range of formal commentaries is well justified by the result. We leave it to the patristic texts themselves to show that these various literary genres contribute significantly to classical Christian Scripture interpretation. The poetry of Ephrem the Syrian or Prudentius brightly illuminates the biblical text, but it would have been ruled out on the basis of modern ideas of what a commentary should include.

Further, it must be kept in mind that the catena is not intended to supplant historical exegesis, but to give a voice to the earliest primary layers of interpretation without overburdening those voices with heavy additional layers of secondary modern interpretation. Our task is not to protect readers against the voice of the ancient Christian interpreter, even if some exegetical misjudgments might have been made, but to allow that interpreter a voice. Where the Fathers interpret Scripture ineptly, we do not want to hide their lapses or rush foolishly to their defense, but rather to reveal accurately and make accessible what they in fact are doing in their own words as they encounter the text. We might say that we will let them stand or fall on the plausibility of their own exegetical proficiencies, but from their point of view, exegetical proficiency took a second place to the power of the Holy Spirit to elicit consensus in the worshiping community. We see no good reason to overload this collection, however, with the worst examples of their least helpful interpretations.

Some may object even more radically that it is ill-advised to refer to any patristic quotation without placing it deliberately and even elaborately in its historical, social and philological context. Those who focus more on context than on what the text itself says have a different relation to the text than do the ancient Christian writers. The temptation to contextualize infinitely has itself a vaudevillian outcome. If no one can quote anything without first placing it in context, then no one can quote anything. Even the apodictic imperative to contextualize must itself be placed in a context. Taking this argument to extremes, the Scripture itself could not legitimately be quoted without an elaborate word study on each word and a detailed sociological study of each passage. That of course would be a nonstarter for preaching and spiritual formation, which is the primary interest of the ancient Christian writers. Such a procedure might keep historians busy, but it would hardly serve the worshiping, proclaiming community. At least it is clear from the historical evidence that this is not the way the early Christian community read Scripture or quoted it or understood its function within the worshiping community.

Classic Christian commentaries, such as those of Origen, Ambrosiaster, Jerome, Augustine, Cyril of Alexandria and Theodoret of Cyr, focus on the moral and spiritual meaning of the text for preaching and spiritual formation, and not simply on the plain or historical sense of the text. After a line-by-line commentary tradition had several centuries of development, there appeared the catena format, which offered catena, or chains, of classic comments on the text. From the fifth century to the modern period, the classic Christian concept of a "commentary" on Scripture largely consisted of a collection of the comments from the most respected writers of the exegetic tradition on that sacred text.

Some might argue that this is not in the modern sense a commentary at all, but merely an expository exercise with little interest in historicity. Here it must be pointed out that there are two competing definitions of what a commentary is. There are classic versus modern historicist conceptions of the very nature of a commentary. As the title of this series indicates, this work is not intended to be mistaken for a modern commentary. It has no claim or desire to be a commentary in the typical modern sense but only in its ancient sense. Nor is it a modern commentary on the ancient Christian exegetes. Rather it is a rare opportunity for the ancient Christian exegetes to speak for themselves on each text, an opportunity which they have largely not been given by biblical scholars.

Modern historicism has a consuming interest in what the patristic writers called the plain or historical sense of Scripture, and only secondarily in the spiritual and moral meaning of the text. Hence it lacks persuasive power to conclude too abruptly, or without examining the evidence, that the modern conception of the commentary is always prima facie superior and thus should rule absolutely over the classic definition of a Scripture commentary. The ancient Christian exegetes continue to challenge the uncritical basis of the assumptions of modern superiority.

The modern historicist conception of a commentary is entirely different. It has as its primary objective the placing of each text in context, the discussion of philological and textual difficulties, the identification of authorship, and speculations on how the text was transmitted—all interesting and significant questions, but not questions that the classic exegetes would allow to displace their primary interest in the revelation of God through the sacred text by the power of the Spirit.

We are not opposing historical-critical inquiry. We invite it and encourage it, but not as if patristic exegesis did not exist or is not worthy to be investigated on its own terms. Our interest is in allowing the primary patristic loci to surface in a convenient form, much as would the texts of the Talmud or the commentaries of Thomas Aquinas.

This Ancient Christian Commentary on Mark is founded on the conviction that the ancient idea of a commentary is still a valid and viable enterprise and that the church and its preaching perennially needs to have ready access to the best and most trustworthy comment in the history of exegesis. It is in this spirit that the following commentary is offered to readers at the dawning of the third millennium.

# THE GOSPEL ACCORDING TO MARK

## 1:1-5 THE BEGINNING OF THE GOSPEL

$^1$*The beginning of the gospel of Jesus Christ, the Son of God.*$^a$
$^2$*As it is written in Isaiah the prophet,*$^b$
*"Behold, I send my messenger before thy face,*
*who shall prepare thy way;*
$^3$*the voice of one crying in the wilderness:*
*Prepare the way of the Lord,*
*make his paths straight—"*
$^4$*John the baptizer appeared*$^c$ *in the wilderness, preaching a baptism of repentance for the forgiveness of sins.* $^5$*And there went out to him all the country of Judea, and all the people of Jerusalem; and they were baptized by him in the river Jordan, confessing their sins.*

a Other ancient authorities omit *the Son of God*  b Other ancient authorities read *in the prophets*  c Other ancient authorities read *John was baptizing*

**OVERVIEW:** The beginning of the gospel is intrinsically connected with the prophetic promises of Hebrew Scripture (ORIGEN). The two Testaments do not announce first one God and then another but the one true God who works through a developing history of revelation (IRENAEUS, CYRIL OF JERUSALEM). Marcion's view that the two covenants are separable is directly countered by Mark's beginning point (AUGUSTINE), in which the prophetic voices of Isaiah and Malachi blend (ORIGEN, JEROME). No prophet is greater than John (CYRIL OF JERUSALEM), the solitary messenger from the desert prophesied by Malachi (TERTULLIAN, EUSEBIUS), who was called to prepare the way for Christ (TERTULLIAN), whose voice blended judgment and mercy, repentance and faith (MAXIMUS OF TURIN). John's baptism prepared the way for the baptism that would be more fully expressed in the future remission of sins that came with the death of the one he baptized (TERTULLIAN, JEROME). The power of John's baptism was in accord with the justice of a just man, yet still of a mere man, although one who had received grace from the coming Lord (AUGUSTINE). The Lord incarnate did not shrink from identifying himself with sinners who need regeneration (CYPRIAN).

## 1:1a The Beginning

**PREPARING THE HEART.** ORIGEN: The way of the Lord must be prepared within the heart; for great and spacious is the heart of man, as if it were a whole world. But see its greatness, not in bodily quantity, but in the power of the mind which enables it to encompass so great a knowledge of the truth. Prepare, therefore, in your hearts the way of the Lord, by a worthy manner of life. Keep straight the path of your life, so that the words of the Lord may enter in without hindrance. HOMILIES ON LUKE 21.5.7.[1]

**THE BEGINNING POINT.** AUGUSTINE: Note that Mark mentions nothing of the nativity or infancy or youth of the Lord. He has made his Gospel begin directly with the preaching of John. HARMONY OF THE GOSPELS 2.6.18.[2]

## 1:1b The Gospel

**OLD AND NEW TESTAMENTS BRIDGED.** ORIGEN: The gospel is primarily concerned with Christ Jesus, who is the head of the whole body of those who are being saved.[3] Mark conveys this point when he says, "The beginning of the gospel concerning Christ Jesus." ... In its unfolding the gospel has a beginning, a continuing middle and an end. The beginning can be viewed either as the entire Old Testament, with John the Baptist being its summarizing type, or (because he stands at the juncture of the new with the old) the final stages of the old covenant. This runs counter to those[4] who would assign the two covenants to two different Gods. COMMENTARY ON JOHN 1.14.[5]

**THE RELATION OF GOSPEL AND LAW.** ORIGEN: Those who deepen in the knowledge of Christianity do not treat the things written in the law with disrespect. ... In saying: "The beginning of the gospel of Jesus Christ, as it is written in the prophet Isaiah," Mark shows that the beginning of the gospel is intrinsically connected with the Old Testament.[6] AGAINST CELSUS 2.4.[7]

**THE INAUGURATOR OF THE NEW TESTAMENT.** CYRIL OF JERUSALEM: With baptism the old covenant ends and the new begins. This is seen in the fact that the inaugurator of the New Testament is John the Baptist. "Among those born of women there is none greater than John."[8] He is the crown of all the prophetic tradition: "For all the prophets and the law prophesied until John."[9] Of the gospel dispensation he was the firstfruits, for we read "the beginning of the gospel of Jesus Christ" and after some words "John did baptize in the wilderness."[10] THE CATECHETICAL LECTURES 3.6.[11]

## 1:2 My Messenger

**THE VOICE OF ONE CRYING.** IRENAEUS: How plainly does the beginning of the gospel focus

---

[1]*SSGF* 1:75*; PG 13:1856. [2]Cetedoc 0273, 2.6.18.113.20; NPNF 1 10:70-71; cf. NPNF 1 6:113. [3]Cf. Eph 4:15; Col 1:18. [4]Such as Marcion. [5]TLG 2042.005, 1.13.79.1-5, 80.1-6, 82.1-1.14.82.3; cf. AEG 1:279; ANF 9:304. Marcion's view that the two covenants are separable is countered by Mark's beginning point for the gospel. This comment on Mark occurs in Origen's *Commentary on John*. For an explanation of why excerpts from commentaries on other Gospels have been included in this catena on Mark, see the heading "Discovering Patristic Comment on Mark" in the introduction. [6]The issue is whether Mark's Gospel can be meaningfully read apart from the history of the people of Israel. [7]TLG 2042.001, 2.4.15-17, 25-31; cf. ANF 4:431. [8]Lk 7:28. [9]Mt 11:13. [10]Mk 1:1, 4. [11]TLG 2110.003, 3.6.1-6; LCC 4:93**. The Baptist is the crown of the prophetic tradition, and the baptism of repentance is the pivot of the coming age.

upon the expectations of the holy prophets. At once it points out that the One whom they confessed as God and Lord, the Father of our Lord Jesus Christ, who had also made promise to him, would send his messenger before his face. This was John, crying in the wilderness, in "the spirit and power of Elijah,"[12] "Prepare the way of the Lord, make his paths straight."[13] For the prophets did not announce first one God and then another,[14] but one and the same God under complementary aspects, and with many various names. AGAINST HERESIES 3.10.5.[15]

**WHY JOHN WAS VIEWED AS AN ANGELIC MESSENGER.** TERTULLIAN: Now he called him an "angel"[16] on account of the great consequence of the mighty deeds which he was to accomplish, comparable to those mighty deeds of Joshua the son of Nun about whom you have read. John served in the office of a prophet to announce God's will, as the forerunner of the Anointed One. The Spirit, speaking in the voice of the Father, called John an "angel" in accord with the promise declared by Malachi: "Behold, I send my messenger to prepare the way before me."[17] It is not a novelty that the Holy Spirit would call those he has appointed ministers of his power "angels." AN ANSWER TO THE JEWS 9.[18]

**HIS SUDDEN APPEARANCE.** EUSEBIUS: He emerged from the desert clothed in a strange garment, refusing all ordinary social intercourse. He did not even share their common food. For it is written that from childhood John was in the deserts until the day of his public appearance to Israel. Indeed, his clothing was made of camel's hair! His food locusts and wild honey![19] . . . It is understandable that they should have been alarmed when they saw a man with the hair of a Nazarite of God,[20] and a divine face, suddenly appearing from the lonely wilderness dressed in bizarre clothing, who after preaching to them, he disappeared again into the wilderness, without eating or drinking or mingling with the people? Must they not have suspected that he was a little more than human? For how could a human being go without food? And so they understood him to be a divine messenger, the very angel foretold by the prophet. PROOF OF THE GOSPEL 9.5.[21]

**THE AUTHORITY OF JOHN'S BAPTISM.** AUGUSTINE: The efficacy of John's baptism is attested by the holy way he lived as a person. His baptism was in accord with the justice of a just man, yet still a mere man, but one who had received extraordinary grace from the Lord, a grace so great that he was deemed worthy to precede the final Judge of history, and to point him out with his finger, and to fulfill the words of that prophecy: "The voice of one crying out in the desert, prepare the way for the Lord."[22] TRACTATE ON THE GOSPEL OF JOHN 5.6.2.[23]

## 1:3a *The Voice of One Crying*

**THE VOICE AND THE CRY IN JOHN'S PREACHING.** MAXIMUS OF TURIN: Voice and crying go together: the voice preaches faith; the cry calls for repentance; the voice, comfort; the cry, dan-

---

[12]Lk 1:17. [13]Mk 1:3. [14]Again, countering the Marcionitic tendency to pit the God of the New Testament against the God of the Old. [15]AHR 2:39; ANF 1:426**. [16]Messenger. [17]Mal 3:1; cf. Mt 11:10; Lk 7:27. [18]Cetedoc 0033, 9.163; ANF 3:163**. John was the messenger or "angel" prophesied by Malachi. [19]Lk 1:80; Mt 3:4. [20]A member of a group in Israel who demonstrated devotion to God through specific signs such as the growth of hair and abstention from alcoholic beverages (see Num 6:1-21). The apostle Paul observed a Nazarite vow for a specific length of time (see Acts 18:18; 21:22-26). [21]TLG 2018.005, 9.5.10.7-11.4, 12.7; POG 2:162-63**. Such an ascetic, holy, solitary figure from the desert appeared to transcend natural occurrences. [22]Mt 3:3; Mk 1:3; Lk 3:4. [23]Cetedoc 0278, 5.6.10; FC 78:113*.

ger; the voice sings mercy; the cry announces judgment. SERMON 6.[24]

## 1:3b *Prepare the Way of the Lord*

**THE SOURCES OF MARK'S PROPHETIC REFERENCE.** ORIGEN: Mark took two prophecies spoken in different places by two prophets and conflated them into one, so as to declare: "As it is written in Isaiah the Prophet . . ." "The voice of one crying in the wilderness,"[25] which is indeed recorded immediately after the narrative about Hezekiah's recovery from his sickness.[26] This is then conflated with "Behold I send my messenger to prepare the way before me," from Malachi.[27] Both John and Mark compress in various ways the quotation from Isaiah, Mark by reading "His paths" for "the paths of our God" and by omitting "before me." COMMENTARY ON JOHN 6.24.[28]

**THE BLENDING OF PROPHETIC VOICES.** JEROME: The quotation is made up from two prophets, Malachi and Isaiah. From the first part: "Behold I send my messenger to prepare the way before me," occurs at the close of Malachi.[29] But the second part: "The voice of one crying," etc., we read in Isaiah.[30] On what ground then has Mark in the very beginning of his book set the words: "As it is written in the prophet Isaiah, Behold I send my messenger," when, as we have said, it is [in part] not written in Isaiah at all, but in Malachi, the last of the twelve prophets? Let ignorant presumption solve this nice question if it can. I will ask pardon for being in the wrong. . . . The apostle has not rendered his original word for word, but using a paraphrase, he has given the sense in different terms.[31] LETTER 57, TO PAMMACHIUS 9.[32]

## 1:4 *The Baptism of Repentance for the Forgiveness of Sins*

**THE BAPTISM OF REPENTANCE.** TERTULLIAN: John called for the baptism of repentance to prepare the way for the Lord. He himself led in that way by means of the sign and seal of repentance for all whom God was calling through grace to inherit the promise surely made to Abraham. . . . He called us to purge our minds of whatever impurity error had imparted, whatever contamination ignorance had engendered, which repentance would sweep and scour away, and cast out. So prepare the home of your heart by making it clean for the Holy Spirit. ON REPENTANCE 2.[33]

**MAKING READY FOR ANOTHER.** TERTULLIAN: Those who sought the baptism of repentance[34] were dealt with as if candidates preparing for the baptismal remission and sanctification that were soon to follow in the ministry of Christ. When John preached baptism *for* "the remission of sins,"[35] the declaration was made with reference to a *future* remission. If so, John's call to repentance is to lead the way, and actual remission is to follow. This is what is meant by "preparing the way."[36] But one who prepares does not himself perfect, but rather makes ready for

---

[24]Cetedoc 0219a, 6.35. Justice and mercy were fused in John's preaching. [25]Is 40:3. [26]Cf. Is 38:10-20. [27]Mal 3:1. [28]TLG 2042.005, 6.24.129.6-8, 130.2-131.9; cf. AEG 1:279-80. [29]Mal 3:1. [30]Is 40:3. [31]Jerome writes this to defend his approach to translation: "I render sense for sense, not word for word." Letter 57.5, NPNF 1 6:113. He is arguing that both classic and Christian writers have followed this procedure. He then turns to similar examples that show that Mark did not employ a literal approach (cf. Mk 2:25-26) on plucking heads of grain on the sabbath. [32]Cetedoc 0620, 57.54.9.518.15; NPNF 2 6:116-17**. Mark did not feel compelled to reference these quotes in precise detail but freely conflated the salient sense of the two prophetic voices. [33]Cetedoc 0010, 2.14; ANF 3:658*. [34]Acts 19:4. [35]Mk 1:4. [36]Lk 1:76.

another to perfect. On Baptism 10.[37]

**The Baptizer and the Baptized.** Cyprian: The Lord was baptized by his servant. The holy One who was destined to grant remission of sins did not himself disdain to submit his body[38] to be cleansed with the water of regeneration.[39] The Good of Patience 6.[40]

**Preparing for Pardon.** Chrysostom: Since the Victim had not been offered, nor had the Holy Spirit yet descended, of what kind was this remission of sins? . . . Fittingly therefore, when he had said that he came "preaching the baptism of repentance," he adds, "for the remission of sins"; as if to say: he persuaded them to repent of their sins, so that later they might more easily receive pardon through believing in Christ. For unless brought to it by repentance, they would not seek for pardon. His baptism therefore served no other end than as a preparation for belief in Christ. The Gospel of St. Matthew, Homily 10.2.[41]

## 1:5 They Were Baptized in the River Jordan

**The Future Remission of Sins.** Jerome: The baptism of John did not so much consist in the forgiveness of sins as in being a baptism of repentance for the remission of sins, that is, for a future remission, which was to follow through the sanctification[42] of Christ. The Dialogue Against the Luciferians 7.[43]

**Types of Baptism.** Gregory Nazianzen: Let us here treat briefly of the different kinds of baptism. Moses baptized, but in water, in the cloud and in the sea; but this he did figuratively. John also baptized, not indeed in the rite of the Jews, not solely in water, but also for the remission of sins; yet not in an entirely spiritual manner, for he had not added: "in the spirit." Jesus baptized, but in the Spirit; and this is perfection. There is also a fourth baptism, which is wrought by martyrdom and blood, in which Christ himself was also baptized, which is far more venerable than the others, in as much as it is not soiled by repeated contagion. There is yet a fifth, but more laborious, by tears; with which David each night bedewed his bed, washing his couch with tears. Oration 39, On the Holy Lights.[44]

---

[37]Cetedoc 0008, 10.32; ANF 3:674**. John's baptism prepared for the baptism that is perfected in the one whom John baptized. John's baptism of repentance is looking toward the remission of sins, while baptism by the Holy Spirit indeed subsequently effects that remission. [38]His body, being undefiled, needed no cleansing. [39]Baptism implied the need for a purification before entering into the presence of the holy. Needing no purification, he nonetheless submitted himself to this radical identification with sinners. Cf. Mt 3:13-17; Lk 3:21-23. [40]Cetedoc 0048, 6.112; FC 36:268**. [41]SSGF 1:74; cf. TLG 2062.152, 57.185.57-61. [42]The setting apart of Christ on the cross for his vocation as Redeemer; cf. 1 Cor 1:30. [43]Cetedoc 0608, 7.170.30; NPNF 2 6:323. John's baptism promised and anticipated a future, full remission of sins. [44]TLG 2022.047, 36.353.37-356.7; SSGF 1:74-75; cf. Ps 6:7.

# 1:6-8 THE PROCLAMATION
# OF JOHN THE BAPTIST

*⁶Now John was clothed with camel's hair, and had a leather girdle around his waist, and ate locusts and wild honey. ⁷And he preached, saying, "After me comes he who is mightier than I, the thong of whose sandals I am not worthy to stoop down and untie. ⁸I have baptized you with water; but he will baptize you with the Holy Spirit."*

**OVERVIEW:** The repentance called for by John was like a snake shedding its old skin by pushing through a narrow place; so do those preparing for baptism ready themselves by repentance (CYRIL OF JERUSALEM). John, clothed in contrition and simplicity of life, savored the sweet and spiritual food of the desert to prepare for the lowly ministry of the Lord (CLEMENT OF ALEXANDRIA). The prophets before John were given grace to foretell the coming of Christ, but to John it was given both to foretell him in his absence and to behold him in his presence (AUGUSTINE). John's baptism offered repentance, while Christ's baptism offered grace (BASIL, AMBROSE). A powerful model of ascetic discipline stems from John's mission, according to the type of Elijah (JEROME). By relinquishing his ancestral right to the priesthood, John became the herald and precursor of God's own priestly self-giving (BEDE). In John the law is beheld clothed in the penitent hair of the desert camel; the coming grace would be clothed in the tunic of the lamb (JEROME). The text, however, does not offer a comparison of the ministries of John and Jesus, for John himself says that they are not comparable (CHRYSOSTOM). Although the mystery of baptism eludes our human language, we cannot therefore cease to attempt to speak of it (BASIL).

## 1:6a *Clothed with Camel's Hair*

**SPIRITUAL FOOD IN THE DESERT.** CLEMENT OF ALEXANDRIA: The blessed John disdained hair obtained from flocks of sheep as smelling of luxury. Instead he chose camel's hair, making his life's pattern one of simplicity and frugality. For he also "ate locusts and wild honey,"[1] sweet and spiritual food, preparing for the humble and self-controlled ways of the Lord. How could John have possibly worn a purple robe? He was one who avoided all false pretenses of the city and lived a calm existence in the desert apart from all frivolous pursuits, from anything ignoble or mean. CHRIST THE EDUCATOR 2.11.[2]

**THE EFFECT OF JOHN'S PREACHING ON CHRISTIAN DISCIPLINE.** JEROME: John the Baptist had a religious mother and his father was a priest. Yet neither his mother's affection nor his father's affluence could induce him to live in his parents' house at the risk of the world's temptations. So he lived in the desert. Seeking Christ with his eyes, he refused to look at anything else. His rough garb, his girdle made of skins, his diet of locusts and wild honey were all alike designed to encourage virtue and continence. Later the spiri-

---

[1]Mk 1:6; Mt 3:4. [2]TLG 0555.002, 2.10—112.1-24; cf. ANF 2:266.

tual descendants of the prophets, who were the monks of the Old Testament, would build for themselves huts by the waters of Jordan and forsaking the crowded cities live in these on pottage and wild herbs.[3] As long as you are at home, make your cell your paradise, gather there the varied fruits of Scripture, let them be your favorite companions, and take its precepts to your heart.[4] LETTER 125, TO RUSTICUS 7.[5]

### PRECURSOR OF A HIGHER PRIESTHOOD. BEDE:

He esteemed the high priestly garment woven of gold cloth of less value than a garment made of camel's hair, girded with a leather belt.[6] Why? Was it not that he who, by reason of a more perfect justice, had received for himself authority to preach, that he might show, even by the neglect of his ancestral right to the high priesthood, how certainly he was the herald and precursor of a more excellent high priesthood?[7] HOMILIES ON THE GOSPELS 2.19.[8]

## 1:6b *A Leather Girdle Around His Waist*

### FOR HEAVY LABOR. CHRYSOSTOM: You may

ask, why did he wear a leather girdle? . . . Elijah also was so clothed, and likewise many others among holy men, either because they were engaged in heavy labor, or were upon a journey, or in any other necessity that involved labor, and because they despised ornament, and followed an austere way of life. . . . Let us, putting away all excess, and drinking the healthy cup of moderation, live in a manner that is becoming and temperate. Let us give ourselves in earnest to prayer. And if we do not receive that for which we pray, let us persevere that we may receive it. And if we do receive it, then let us persevere all the more for what we have received. For it is not his will to withhold the gift we ask for, but in his wisdom, to encourage

our perseverance by delaying it. THE GOSPEL OF ST. MATTHEW, HOMILY 10.[9]

### ELIJAH AND JOHN. JEROME: John, too, wears a

leather girdle about his loins; and there was nothing soft or effeminate in Elijah, but every bit of him was hard and virile. He, too, certainly was a shaggy man.[10] HOMILY 91, ON THE EXODUS.[11]

## 1:6c *He Ate Locusts and Wild Honey*

### FREEDOM FROM NEED. CHRYSOSTOM: It was

necessary that the precursor of the One who was to undo the age-long burdens of men, such as toil, malediction, pain and sweat, should in his own person give some token of the gifts to come, so as to stand above these tribulations. And so it was that he neither tilled the earth, nor plowed the furrow, nor did he eat bread of his own sweat, for his table was easily prepared, and his clothing more easily than his table, and his dwelling more easily than his clothing. For he had need neither of roof, nor bed, nor table, nor any such thing. But even while still within this flesh of ours he lived an almost angelic life. His clothing was put together from the hair of camels, so that even from his garments he might teach us that we free ourselves of human needs, and need not be bound to this earth, but that we may return to the pristine dignity in which Adam first lived, before he had need of garments or of clothing. THE GOSPEL OF ST.

---

[3]Cf. 2 Kings 4:38-39; 6:1-2. [4]Cf. Ps 119:69. [5]Cetedoc 0620, 125.56.7.125.4; NPNF 2 6:246*. Having seen Christ with his eyes, he refused to look at anything else. [6]The issue is why John refused the ancestral right to high priesthood. [7]Cf. Heb 3:1; 4:14; 5:10; 6:20. [8]Cetedoc 1367, 2.19.36; *HOG* 2:190**. [9]SSGF 1:87*; TLG 2062.152, 57.189.9-10, 14-20; 191.34-41. [10]2 Kings 1:8. [11]Cetedoc 0601, 111; FC 57:240.

MATTHEW, HOMILY 10.[12]

**SHEDDING SKIN THROUGH A NARROW PASSAGE.** CYRIL OF JERUSALEM: He fed on locusts to make his soul grow wings. Sated with honey, the words he spoke were sweeter than honey and of more profit. Clothed in a garment of camel's hair, he exemplified in his own person the holy life. . . . For every snake puts off its signs of age by pushing through some narrow place, and gets rid of its old apparel by squeezing it off. From then on it is young again in body. So "enter in at the straight and narrow gate,"[13] squeeze yourself through by fasting, break yourself away from perishing, "put off the old nature with its deeds."[14] THE CATECHETICAL LECTURES 3.6.[15]

## 1:7a Mightier Than I

**NONE GREATER THAN JOHN.** CYRIL OF JERUSALEM: Even though Elijah the Tishbite was taken up to heaven,[16] he was not greater than John. Enoch too was translated[17] but was not greater than John. Moses was the greatest of lawgivers and all the prophets were admirable, but none greater than John. It is not I who would dare to compare prophet with prophet, but their Master and ours who himself declared "Among those born of women there is none greater than John."[18] Not "born of virgins," observe! but "born of women."[19] THE CATECHETICAL LECTURES 3.6.[20]

**THE BAPTISM OF JOHN AND CHRISTIAN BAPTISM.** AMBROSE: Neither repentance avails without grace, nor grace without repentance; for repentance must first condemn sin, that grace may blot it out. So then John, who was a type of the law, came baptizing for repentance, while Christ came to offer grace. EPISTLE 84.[21]

**THE PROLOGUE TO BAPTISM.** JEROME: As he himself bodily preceded Christ as his forerunner, so also his baptism was the prologue to the Lord's baptism. THE DIALOGUE AGAINST THE LUCIFERIANS 7.[22]

**THE HAIR OF THE CAMEL AND THE TUNIC OF THE LAMB.** JEROME: "One mightier than I is coming after me, the thong of whose sandals I am not worthy to stoop down and untie."[23] The meaning of the words: "He must increase, I must decrease,"[24] is that the gospel must increase, but I, the law, must decrease. John, that is, the law in John, was clothed, therefore, in the hair of a camel, for he could not wear a tunic of the lamb of whom it is said: "Behold the lamb of God who takes away the sin of the world;"[25] and again: "He is led like a lamb to the slaughter."[26] In the law, we cannot wear a tunic from that Lamb. HOMILY 75.[27]

**MORE THAN A PROPHET.** AUGUSTINE: John therefore was a foreteller of Christ, nearer to him in time than all who went before him. And because all the righteous ones and prophets of former times desired to see the fulfillment of what, through the revelation of the Spirit, they foresaw should come to pass—so also the Lord himself says that "many prophets and righteous men have desired to see those things

---

[12]TLG 2062.152, 57.188.26-42; SSG⁻ 1:86*. [13]Mt 7:13-14; Lk 13:24. [14]Eph 4:22; Col 3:9. [15]TLG 2110.003, 36.18-21; 7.12-17; LCC 4:93-94. By his way of life he displayed the seriousness of his preaching. [16]2 Kings 2:11. [17]Cf. Gen 5:24. [18]Lk 7:28. [19]Cyril defines the position of John in the history of salvation with precision: greater than Moses, less than Christ; culminating the law and prophets yet awaiting the anointed one to whom they point; greater than others born of women; lesser than the one born of the virgin. [20]TLG 2110.003, 3.6.7-14; LCC 4:93**. That there is none greater born of woman than John does not imply that John's greatness exceeds that of the Lord himself, who was born of a virgin. [21]Cetedoc 0160, 9.68.7.82.2.172.69; FC 26:470*. [22]Cetedoc 0608, 7.170.40; NPNF 2 6:323**. [23]Mk 1:7. [24]Jn 3:30. [25]Jn 1:29. [26]Is 53:7. [27]Cetedoc 0594, 1.107; FC 57:125.

which you see, and have not seen them; and to hear those things which you hear, and have not heard them."[28] Therefore it was said of John that he was more than a prophet, and that among all that were born of women there was none greater than he,[29] because to the righteous who went before him it was only granted to foretell the coming of Christ, but to John it was given both to foretell him in his absence and to behold him in his presence, so that it should be found that to him was made manifest what the others had desired. ANSWER TO THE LETTERS OF PETILIAN, THE DONATIST 2.37.[30]

### 1:7b The Thong of Whose Sandals I Am Not Worthy to Stoop Down and Untie

**THEIR INCOMPARABILITY.** CHRYSOSTOM: John was setting forth the anticipatory and ancillary value of his own baptism, showing that it had no other purpose than to lead to repentance. He did not say he baptized with water of forgiveness, but of repentance. He pointed toward Christ's baptism, full of inexpressible gifts. John seems to be saying: "On being told that he comes after me, you must not think lightly of him because he comes later. When you understand the power of Christ's gift, you will see that I said nothing lofty or noble when I said 'I am unworthy to untie the thong of his sandal.' When you hear, 'He is mightier than I,' do not imagine that I said this by way of comparison. For I am not worthy to be ranked so much as among Christ's servants, no, not even the lowest of his servants, nor to receive the least honored portion of his ministry." Therefore John did not simply say, "his sandals," he said "the thong of his sandals," the part counted the least of all.[31] THE GOSPEL OF ST. MATTHEW, HOMILY 11.5.[32]

### 1:8a Baptized with Water

**WHETHER JESUS BAPTIZED.** ORIGEN: The Messiah therefore does not baptize in water, but his disciples do. He reserves for himself the baptism in the Holy Spirit and fire. COMMENTARY ON JOHN 6.23.[33]

**BAPTISM UNDER MOSAIC LAW COMPARED WITH JOHN'S BAPTISM.** BASIL: The baptism which was handed down through Moses recognized, first, a distinction among sins, for the grace of pardon was not accorded all transgressions. It also required various sacrifices, laid down precise rules for purification, and segregated for a time those who were in a state of impurity and defilement. It appointed the observance of days and seasons, and only then baptism was received as the seal of purification. The baptism of John was far more excellent: It recognized no distinction of sins, nor did it require a variety of sacrifices, nor did it appoint strict rules for purification or any observance of days or seasons. Indeed, with no delay at all, anyone who had confessed his sins, however numerous or grave, had access at once to the grace of God and his Christ. CONCERNING BAPTISM 31.2.[34]

### 1:8b With the Holy Spirit

**STAMMERING BEFORE THE MYSTERY OF BAPTISM.** BASIL: The baptism of the Lord, however, surpasses all human powers of comprehension. It contains a glory beyond all that

---

[28]Mt 13:17. [29]Mt 11:9, 11; Lk 7:28. [30]Cetedoc 0333, 2.37.87.71.15; NPNF 1 4:552-53*. [31]Cf. Lk 3:16; Jn 1:27; 3:28-30. [32]TLG 2062.152, 57.196.46-62; NPNF 1 10:71; cf. 110:19. [33]TLG 2042.005, 6.23.125.11-12. Jesus did not himself baptize, but sent the Holy Spirit to baptize. [34]TLG 2040.052, 31.1533.11-26; FC 9:355*. The penitent with sins great and small were offered immediate access to the grace of repentance in the coming of Christ.

humanity hopes or prays for, a preeminence of grace and power which exceeds the others[35] more than the sun outshines the stars. More than this, if the words of the righteous are recalled to mind, they prove even more conclusively its incomparable superiority. Yet, we must not therefore refrain from speaking of it, but, using the very utterances of our Lord Jesus Christ as our guides, we grope along the way, as with a mirror, or through the maze of an enigma. We must speak, not so as to diminish the greatness of the subject, by an exposition made in weakness of body and with the aid of a form of reasoning that is set at naught. We must speak to magnify the greatness and the long-suffering benevolence of the good God in tolerating our stammering attempts to speak about the prodigies of his love and grace in Christ Jesus. CONCERNING BAPTISM 31.2.[36]

**THE DISTINCTION BETWEEN WATER AND SPIRIT.** JEROME: He is drawing a comparison, therefore, between the law and the gospel. Farther, he says: "I have baptized you with water," that is, the law; "but he will baptize you with the Holy Spirit,"[37] that is the gospel. HOMILY 76.[38]

**THE PERFECTION OF BAPTISM.** JEROME: No baptism can be called perfect except that which depends on the cross and resurrection of Christ. THE DIALOGUE AGAINST THE LUCIFERIANS 7.[39]

---

[35]Baptism under Mosaic law and under John's preaching. [36]FC 9:356*; TLG 2042.052, 31.1533 [37]Mk 1:8. [38]Cetedoc 0594, 2.45; FC 57:133. The baptism of repentance with water is the last act under the dispensation of the law, and the baptism of the Spirit is the first act under the dispensation of the gospel. [39]Cetedoc 0608, 7.171.6; NPNF 2 6:323**.

---

# 1:9-11 THE BAPTISM OF JESUS

[9]*In those days Jesus came from Nazareth of Galilee and was baptized by John in the Jordan.* [10]*And when he came up out of the water, immediately he saw the heavens opened and the Spirit descending upon him like a dove;* [11]*and a voice came from heaven, "Thou art my beloved Son;[d] with thee I am well pleased."*

d Or *my son, my* (or *the*) *Beloved*

---

**OVERVIEW:** The dove, wholly benign, injuring nothing, symbolizes innocence (CHRYSOSTOM), simplicity (BEDE) and grace (AUGUSTINE). Those who study the habits of the dove learn peace (BEDE). After the flood, by which the iniquity of the old world was cleansed away (after, so to speak, the baptism of the world), the dove proclaimed to the earth the tempering of the wrath of heaven (TERTULLIAN). The dove points to Jesus as the new Noah, the pilot of the nature that is everywhere in shipwreck (GREGORY THAUMATURGUS). In the opening of heaven a reconciliation is taking place between Creator and creation through the Redeemer by the testimony of the Holy Spirit (HIPPOLYTUS). In the baptism of Jesus, the Father bore witness, the Son received witness and the Holy Spirit gave confirmation—thus in the Jordan the triune mystery began to be disclosed (ORIGEN), the Son appearing as a man and the Spirit as a dove (AUGUSTINE). Jesus did not become Son only at his baptism, for he is eternally the Son of the Father (ORIGEN) in an abiding sonship that our temporal minds can approach only with wonder and awe (AMBROSE). Though the eternal Son had no external need of baptism, he freely submitted to John's baptism (GREGORY NAZIANZEN, AMBROSE, AUGUSTINE).

### 1:9 Baptized by John in the Jordan

**THE HALLOWING OF WATER.** GREGORY NAZIANZEN: As man he was baptized,[1] but he absolved sins as God.[2] He needed no purifying rites himself—his purpose was to hallow water. ORATION 29, ON THE SON.[3]

### 1:10a The Heavens Opened

**THE DIVINE-HUMAN RECONCILIATION.** HIPPOLYTUS:[4] Do you see, beloved, how many and how great blessings we would have lost if the Lord had yielded to the exhortation of John and declined baptism? For the heavens had been shut before this.[5] The region above was inaccessible. We might descend to the lower parts, but not ascend to the upper. So it happened not only that the Lord was being baptized—he also was making new the old creation. He was bringing the alienated under the scepter of adoption.[6] For straightway "the

heavens were opened to him." A reconciliation took place between the visible and the invisible. The celestial orders were filled with joy, the diseases of earth were healed, secret things made known, those at enmity restored to amity. For you have heard the word of the Evangelist, saying, "The heavens were opened to him," on account of three wonders.[7] At the baptism of Christ the Bridegroom, it was fitting that the heavenly chamber should open its glorious gates.[8] So when the Holy Spirit descended in the form of a dove, and the Father's voice spread everywhere, it was fitting that "the gates of heaven should be lifted up."[9] THE DISCOURSE ON THE HOLY THEOPHANY 106.[11]

**THE NEW NOAH.** GREGORY THAUMATURGUS: And stretching forth slowly his right hand, which seemed both to tremble and to rejoice, John baptized the Lord. Then his detractors who were present, with those in the vicinity and those from a distance, connived together, and spoke among themselves asking: "Was John then superior to Jesus? Was it without cause that we thought John greater, and does not his very baptism attest this? Is not he who baptizes presented as the greater, and he who is baptized as the less important?" But just as they, in their ignorance of the mystery of the

---

[1]Mt 3:16; Lk 3:21. [2]Jn 1:29; Mt 9:2. [3]TLG 2022.009.20.1-20.2; FGFR 258. [4]The authorship is uncertain, but it is attributed to Hippolytus. [5]Due to the rejection of sin by the holy God. [6]Those lost from the family of God are reincluded by adoption; cf. Rom 8:15. [7]Father, Son and Holy Spirit all appear at the theophany of Jesus' baptism. [8]A reconciliation is taking place between the Creator and creation through the Redeemer by the testimony of the Holy Spirit. The bride is welcoming the groom into the bridal chamber. Those alienated from the family of God are being reincluded by adoption. [9]Ps 24:7. [10]Appearance of God, in this case at his baptism. [11]TLG 2115.026, 6.1-16; ANF 5:236; cf. AEG 1:303.

divine economy,[12] babbled about with each other, the holy One who alone is Lord spoke. He who by nature is the Father of the only begotten (who alone was begotten in unblemished fashion) instantly rectified their blunted imaginations. He opened the gates of the heavens and sent down the Holy Spirit in the form of a dove, lighting upon the head of Jesus, pointing him out right there as the new Noah, even the maker of Noah, and the good pilot of the nature[13] which is in shipwreck. And he himself calls with clear voice out of heaven, and says: "This is my beloved Son,"[14]—Jesus, not John: the One baptized, and not the one baptizing; the One who was begotten of me before all time, and not the one who was begotten of Zechariah; the One who was born of Mary after the flesh, and not the one who was brought forth by Elizabeth beyond all expectation; the One who was the fruit of the virginity which he yet preserved intact, not the one who was the shoot from a sterility removed; the One who had his encounter with you, and not the one brought up in the wilderness. This is my beloved Son, in whom I am well pleased: my Son, of the same substance with myself, and not of a different; of the same essence with me according to what is unseen, and of the same essence with you according to what is seen, yet without sin. THE FOURTH HOMILY, ON THE HOLY THEOPHANY, OR OF CHRIST'S BAPTISM.[15]

## 1:10b *The Spirit Descending upon Him*

**THE DESCENT OF THE SPIRIT.** AMBROSE: John, who baptized, stood by, and behold, the Holy Spirit descended as a dove. Not a dove descended, but "as a dove.". . . Descended for what reason? Not that the Lord Jesus himself might seem to be in need of the mystery of sanctification, but that he himself might sanc-

tify, that the Spirit also might sanctify. THE SACRAMENTS 1.6.[16]

**JOHN'S BAPTISM AND CHRIST'S.** AUGUSTINE: Those who receive the baptism of Christ need not seek the baptism of John. Those who received the baptism of John did indeed seek the baptism of Christ. . . . No baptism was necessary for Christ, but he freely received the baptism of a servant ( John) to draw us toward his baptism. TRACTATE ON JOHN 5.5.3, 4.[17]

## 1:10c *Like a Dove*

**THE IMAGE OF INNOCENCE.** ORIGEN: A dove—a tame, innocent and simple bird. Hence we are taught to copy the innocence of doves. HOMILIES ON LUKE, HOMILY 27.[18]

**THE ABSENCE OF GALL.** TERTULLIAN: The Holy Spirit came in the form of a dove in order that the nature of the Holy Spirit might be made plain by means of a creature of utter simplicity and innocence. For the dove's body has no gall in it. So after the deluge, by which the iniquity of the old world was purged away, after, so to speak, the baptism of the world, the dove as herald proclaimed to the earth the tempering of the wrath of heaven—sent forth from

---

[12]Thomas Torrance describes the divine economy as "the patristic expression for the orderly way in which God communicates himself to us within the structures of space and time, in which he remains what he is eternally in himself while communicating himself to us really and truly and without reserve in Jesus Christ and in his Spirit." In John Thompson, ed., *Modern Trinitarian Perspectives* (New York: Oxford University Press, 1994), 25. [13]Of humanity. [14]Mt 3:17; 17:5; Mk 1:11; 9:7; Lk 9:35. [15]PG 10.1188; ANF 6:70-71**. The authorship of this work is disputed. It has also been attributed to Gregory of Antioch cf. ANF 10:326; 331. [16]Cetedoc 0154(M), 1.5.17.22.33; FC 44:274-75*. Christ was baptized not because he was needy but that he might be set apart for the messianic ministry. [17]Cetedoc 0278, 5.5.25; FC 78:112**. [18]TLG 2042.016, 27.160.6-8; AEG 1:307.

the ark and returning with an olive branch,[19] which is a sign of peace among the nations. ON BAPTISM 8.[20]

**THE GENTLE DELIVERANCE.** CHRYSOSTOM: But why in the form of a dove? The dove is a gentle and pure creature. Since then the Spirit, too, is "a Spirit of gentleness,"[21] he appears in the form of a dove, reminding us of Noah, to whom, when once a common disaster had overtaken the whole world and humanity was in danger of perishing, the dove appeared as a sign of deliverance from the tempest, and bearing an olive branch, published the good tidings of a serene presence over the whole world.[22] All these things were given as a type of things to come. . . . In this case the dove also appeared, not bearing an olive branch, but pointing to our Deliverer from all evils, bringing hope filled with grace. For this dove does not simply lead one family out of an ark, but the whole world toward heaven at her appearing.[23] And instead of a branch of peace from an olive tree, she conveys the possibility of adoption[24] for all the world's offspring in common. THE GOSPEL OF ST. MATTHEW, HOMILY 12.3.[25]

**THE VISIBLE WORD.** AUGUSTINE: Why did the Son of God appear as a man and the Holy Spirit as a dove?[26] Because the Son of God came to show humanity a pattern for living, whereas the Holy Spirit made his appearance to bestow the gift which enables excellent living.[27] Moreover, both appearances surely came in a visible manner for the sake of carnal eyes. For we must pass by degrees through the visible sacraments from those things which are seen with the physical eyes to those things which are understood spiritually by the mind. For human words make a sound and then pass away. But when the divine Word is expressed, that which is signified by the words does not pass away.[28] QUESTIONS, QUESTION 43.[29]

**THE GIFT.** AUGUSTINE: The dove is not for sale; it is given gratis. Hence it is called grace. TRACTATE ON JOHN 10.6.3.[30]

**A STRANGER TO MALICE.** BEDE: The image of a dove is placed before us by God so that we may learn the simplicity favored by him. So let us meditate on the nature of the dove, that from each one of its features of innocence we may learn the principles of a more becoming life. The dove is a stranger to malice. So may all bitterness, anger and indignation be taken away from us, together with all malice. The dove injures nothing with its mouth or talons, nor does it nourish itself or its young on tiny mice or grubs, as do almost all smaller birds. Let us see that our teeth are not weapons and arrows.[31] HOMILIES ON THE GOSPELS 1.12.[32]

### 1:11a A Voice from Heaven

**THE TRIUNE WITNESS.** ORIGEN: In the Jordan the Trinity was manifested to humanity. The Father bore witness, the Son received witness, and the Holy Spirit gave confirmation. FRAGMENTS ON MATTHEW 58.[33]

---

[19]Cf. Gen 8:11. [20]Cetedoc 0008, 8.12; AEG 1:304*. [21]Cf. Gal 5:22, which lists the fruit of the Spirit. [22]Cf. Gen 8:11. [23]The dove of Noah led one family to deliverance, while the dove of Jesus' baptism led the whole family of God throughout the world to eternal peace. [24]Adoption is into the family of God by faith. [25]NPNF 1 10:77**, TLG 2062.152, 57. 205.25-35, 41-47; cf. GMI 15. The same phrase, "like a dove," appears in Matthew, Mark and Luke. [26]Mt 3:16; Mk 1:10; Lk 3:22; Jn 1:32. [27]Cf. Rom 8:2, 10; Gal 6:8. [28]Cf. Is 55:11. [29]Cetedoc 0289, 43.1; FC 70:74-75*. [30]Cetedoc 0278, 10.6.24; FC 78:217. [31]Ps 57:4 (LXX 56:5). [32]Cetedoc 1367, 1.12.197; HOG 1:120**. [33]GLCS 41.1.38; AEG 307. Origen remarks in his Homilies on Genesis: "Then for the first time the mystery of the Trinity began to be disclosed" (Homily 2.5, FC 71:84).

**THE TRIUNE PRESENCE.** AUGUSTINE: The Trinity appears very clearly: the Father in the voice, the Son in the man, the Spirit in the dove. TRACTATE ON JOHN 6.5.1.[34]

**THREE IN ONE.** AUGUSTINE: In the Scripture many details are mentioned distinguishably of each of the triune Persons individually, such as cannot be said of them jointly, even though they are inseparably together, as when they are made manifest by corporeal sounds. So in certain passages of Scripture and through certain created beings they are shown separately and successively, as the Father in the voice which is heard: "Thou art my Son,"[35] and the Son in the human nature which he took from the Virgin,[36] and the Holy Spirit in the physical appearance of a dove.[37] These are mentioned distinguishably, it is true, but they do not prove that the Three are separated. To explicate this, we take as an example the unity of our memory, our understanding, our will. Although we list these distinguishably, individually and in their various functions, there is nothing we do or say which proceeds from one of them without the other two.[38] However, we are not to think that these three faculties are compared to the Trinity so as to resemble it at every point, for a comparison is never given such importance in an argument that it exactly fits the thing to which it is compared. Besides, when can any likeness in a created being be applied to the Creator? LETTER 169, TO EUODIUS.[39]

## 1:11b My Beloved Son

**THE FATHER'S VOICE.** HIPPOLYTUS:[40] For this reason did the Father send down the Holy Spirit from heaven upon the One who was baptized. . . . For what reason? That the faithfulness of the Father's voice might be made known. . . . Listen to the Father's voice: "This is my beloved Son, in whom I am well pleased." This is he who is named the son of Joseph, who according to the divine essence is my only begotten. "This is my beloved Son," yes, none other than the One who himself becomes hungry, yet feeds countless numbers. He is my Son who himself becomes weary, yet gives rest to the weary.[41] He has no place to lay his head,[42] yet bears up all things in his hand. He suffers, yet heals sufferings. He is beaten, yet confers liberty upon the world.[43] He is pierced in his side,[44] yet repairs the side of Adam. THE DISCOURSE ON THE HOLY THEOPHANY 7.[45]

**ONE WITHOUT BEGINNING.** ORIGEN: This is spoken to him by God, with whom all time is today. For there is no evening with God, as I see it, and there is no morning—nothing but time that stretches out, along with his unbeginning and unseen life. The day is today with him in which the Son was begotten. Thus the beginning of his birth is not to be found, as neither is the day of it.[46] COMMENTARY ON JOHN 1.32.[47]

**THE ETERNAL RELATION.** AMBROSE: These words are not to be understood, when we speak of God, as when we speak of bodies. The generation of the Son is incomprehensible,[48] the Father begets without changing his nature. Yet

---

[34]Cetedoc 0278, 6.5.11; FC 78:133. [35]Cf. Ps 2:7; Mt 3:17; Mk 1:11; Lk 3:22; Acts 13:33; Heb 5:5. [36]Mt 1:23, 25; Lk 2:7. [37]Mt 3:16; Mk 1:10; Lk 3:22; Jn 1:32. [38]As memory, understanding and will are three and can be conceived distinguishably, nothing we do or say proceeds from one of them without the other two. In this way God is three yet one. [39]Cetedoc 0262, 169.44.2.615.5; FC 30:54-55. [40]The authorship is uncertain. [41]Cf. Mt 11:28-29. [42]Cf. Mt 8:20; Lk 9:58. [43]Heb 1:3; cf. Lk 4:18; 2 Cor 3:17. [44]Jn 19:34. [45]ANF 5:236*; TLG 2115.026, 7.5-6, 9-10, 12-20. The paradox of his sonship is that under the conditions of the incarnation he must endure suffering, hunger and oppression. [46]The Word did not become Son only at a specific time, such as his baptism, for he was eternally the Son of the Father. [47]TLG 2042.005, 1.29.204.3-8; ANF 9:314*. [48]Within the categories of the temporal.

this begotenness is of himself. In ages inconceivably remote the true God has begotten one who is truly God. EXPOSITION OF THE CHRISTIAN FAITH 1.10.67.[49]

### 1:11c *With Thee I Am Well Pleased*

**THE WATERS SANCTIFIED.** EPHREM THE SYRIAN: Today the Source of all the graces of baptism comes himself to be baptized in the river Jordan, there to make himself known to the world. Seeing him approach, John stretches out his hand to hold him back, protesting: Lord, by your own baptism you sanctify all others; yours is the true baptism, the source of perfect holiness. How can you wish to submit to mine? But the Lord replies, I wish it to be so. Come and baptize me. Do as I wish, for surely you cannot refuse me. Why do you hesitate, why are you so afraid? Do you not realize that the baptism I ask for is mine by every right? By my baptism the waters will be sanctified, receiving from me fire and the Holy Spirit. . . . See the hosts of heaven hushed and still, as the all-holy Bridegroom goes down into the Jordan. No sooner is he baptized than he comes up from the waters, his splendor shining forth over the earth. The gates of heaven are opened, and the Father's voice is heard: "This is my beloved Son in whom I am well pleased." All who are present stand in awe as they watch the Spirit descend to bear witness to him. O come all you peoples, worship him! Praise to you, Lord, for your glorious epiphany which brings joy to us all! The whole world has become radiant with the light of your manifestation. HYMNS ON NATIVITY (EPIPHANY) 14.[50]

**VARIED TERMS CONVEY THE SAME MEANING.** AUGUSTINE: Whichever of the Evangelists may have preserved for us the words as they were literally uttered by the heavenly voice, the others[51] have varied the terms only with the object of setting forth the same sense more familiarly, so that what is thus given by all of them might be understood as if the expression were: In You I have set my good pleasure; that is to say, by You I am doing what is my pleasure. HARMONY OF THE GOSPELS 2.14.31.[52]

---

[49] Cetedoc 0150, 1.10.49; NPNF 2 10:212**. His begotenness is eternal, not in time. [50]CSCO 186-187:218-224; JF B 28-29. [51]The other Evangelists. Augustine is asking whether the voice said "with Thee" (Mk 1:11), "with whom" (Mt 3:17) or "in Thee" (Lk 3:22). [52]Cetedoc 0273, 2.14.31.132.11; NPNF 2 6:119-20*. Here we are taught not to be too literalistic in reading the Gospels, for all three Evangelists mean substantially the same thing.

## 1:12-13 THE TEMPTATION OF JESUS

[12]*The Spirit immediately drove him out into the wilderness.* [13]*And he was in the wilderness forty days, tempted by Satan; and he was with the wild beasts; and the angels ministered to him.*

**OVERVIEW:** The setting of Jesus' temptation, like that of Eve's, is the wilderness, with its loneliness and vulnerability (CHRYSOSTOM). Baptism is accompanied by prayer and fasting and is followed by earnest perseverance (BEDE). The dynamics of temptation proceed first by suggestion, then by taking delight in the suggestion, then by consent (GREGORY THE GREAT).

## 1:12 The Spirit Drove Him Out into the Wilderness

**THE WILDERNESS SETTING.** CHRYSOSTOM: You see how the Spirit led him, not into a city or public arena, but into a wilderness. In this desolate place, the Spirit extended the devil an occasion to test him, not only by hunger, but also by loneliness, for it is there most especially that the devil assails us, when he sees us left alone and by ourselves. In this same way did he also confront Eve in the beginning, having caught her alone and apart from her husband. THE GOSPEL OF ST. MATTHEW, HOMILY 13.1.[1]

## 1:13 Tempted by Satan

**SUGGESTION, DELIGHT, CONSENT.** GREGORY THE GREAT: Temptation is brought to fulfillment by three stages: suggestion, delight, consent. And we in temptation generally fall through delight, and then through consent; for being begotten of the sin of the flesh we bear within us that through which we suffer conflict. But God, incarnate in the womb of a virgin, came into the world without sin, and so suffers no conflict within himself. He could therefore be tempted by suggestion, but the delight of sin could never touch his mind. So all these temptations of the devil were from without, not from within Him. ON THE GOSPEL OF THE SUNDAY SERMON 16.[2]

**THE SUCCESSION OF TEMPTATIONS.** BEDE: Soon after he had been baptized, he performed a fast of forty days by himself,[3] and he taught and informed us by his example that, after we have received forgiveness of sins in baptism, we should devote ourselves to vigils, fasts, prayers and other spiritually fruitful things, lest when we are sluggish and less vigilant the unclean spirit expelled from our heart by baptism may return, and finding us fruitless in spiritual riches, weigh us down again with a sevenfold pestilence, and our last state would then be worse than the first.[4] Let us be wary that we do not relight the fires of old obsessions which would wreck us on our new voyage. Whatever sort of flaming sword it is that guards the doorway of paradise has been already effectively extinguished for each of the faithful in the font of baptism. For the unfaithful, however, the gate remains always formidable, and also for those falsely called faithful though they have not been chosen, since they have no fear of entangling themselves in sins after baptism. It is as though the same fire put out in baptism has been rekindled after it had been once extinguished. HOMILIES ON THE GOSPELS 1.12.[5]

---

[1]TLG 2062.152, 57.209.28-36; NPNF 1 10:80*. The theme of temptation alone in the wilderness appears similarly in Matthew, Mark and Luke. [2]Cetedec 1711, 1.16.1.23; SSGF 2:3. [3]Mt 4:2; Mk 1:13; Lk 4:2. [4]Mt 12:43-45; Lk 11:24-26. [5]Cetedec 1367, 1.12.174; HOG 1:119-20**.

## 1:14-20 THE CALL OF THE FIRST DISCIPLES

[14]*Now after John was arrested, Jesus came into Galilee, preaching the gospel of God,* [15]*and saying, "The time is fulfilled, and the kingdom of God is at hand; repent, and believe in the gospel."* [16]*And passing along by the Sea of Galilee, he saw Simon and Andrew the brother of Simon casting a net in the sea; for they were fishermen.* [17]*And Jesus said to them, "Follow me and I will make you become fishers of men."* [18]*And immediately they left their nets and followed him.* [19]*And going on a little farther, he saw James the son of Zebedee and John his brother, who were in their boat mending the nets.* [20]*And immediately he called them; and they left their father Zebedee in the boat with the hired servants, and followed him.*

**OVERVIEW:** The Lord thought it better to use the most rustic and common persons as ministers of his own design, so as to underscore that this is a work of divine grace (ORIGEN, EUSEBIUS). It is preposterous from the world's point of view that those without education could be used to instruct the nations (EUSEBIUS). There must have been something divinely compelling in the Savior's guileless countenance that persons, merely upon seeing him, could trust (JEROME). The disciples could no longer be concerned with anything pertaining to this earthly life insofar as it might run counter to the calling of the Lord (BASIL). All worldly resources are to be left behind in response to the coming reign of God (TERTULLIAN). The joy of faith makes up for whatever bitterness may accompany repentance (JEROME).

### 1:15 *Repent and Believe*

**THE MINGLING OF JOY AND SORROW.** JEROME: The sweetness of the apple makes up for the bitterness of the root. The hope of gain makes pleasant the perils of the sea. The expectation of health mitigates the nauseousness of medi-

cine. One who desires the kernel breaks the nut. So one who desires the joy of a holy conscience swallows down the bitterness of penance.[1] COMMENTARY ON THE GOSPELS.[2]

### 1:16 *They Were Fishermen*

**COMMON MEN ON AN UNCOMMON MISSION.** EUSEBIUS: Reflect on the nature and grandeur of the one Almighty God who could associate himself with the poor of the lowly fisherman's class.[3] To use them to carry out God's mission baffles all rationality. For having conceived the intention, which no one ever before had done, of spreading his own commands and teachings to all nations, and of revealing himself as the teacher of the religion of the one Almighty God to all humanity, he thought good to use the most unsophisticated and common people as minis-

---

[1] Jerome, like most early Christian writers, viewed penance—concrete acts demonstrating repentance and sorrow over postbaptismal sin—as an integral aspect of genuine conversion. Later Protestant critics such as Luther would critique late medieval distortions of earlier medieval penitential doctrine. Cf. EEC 667-669; MLSW, 249-53. [2] GC 3:370. [3] It is an irony of providence that such an extraordinary mission should depend upon such ordinary men.

ters of his own design. Maybe God just wanted to work in the most unlikely way. For how could inarticulate folk be made able to teach, even if they were appointed teachers to only one person, much less to a multitude? How should those who were themselves without education instruct the nations? . . . When he had thus called them as his followers, he breathed into them his divine power, and filled them with strength and courage. As God himself he spoke God's true word to them in his own way, enabling them to do great wonders, and made them pursuers of rational and thinking souls, by empowering them to come after him, saying: "Come, follow me, and I will make you fish for people."[4] With this empowerment God sent them forth to be workers and teachers of holiness to all the nations, declaring them heralds of his own teaching. PROOF OF THE GOSPEL 3.7.[5]

### 1:17 Follow Me, and I Will Make You Fishers of Men

**ON CHOOSING THE UNLETTERED.** ORIGEN: Now we can see how in a short time this religion has grown up, making progress through the persecution and death of its adherents and through their endurance of confiscation of property and every kind of bodily torture. And this is particularly remarkable since the teachers themselves were neither very skillful nor very numerous. For in spite of all, this word is being "preached in all the world,"[6] so that Greeks and barbarians, wise and foolish now are adopting the Christian religion.[7] Hence there can be no doubt that it is not by human strength or resources that the word of Christ comes to prevail with all authority and convincing power in the minds and hearts of all humanity. ON FIRST PRINCIPLES 4.1.2.[8]

**THE RESISTANCE OF THE UNLETTERED.** EUSEBIUS: "But how can we do it?" the disciples might reasonably have answered. "How can we preach to Romans? How can we argue with Egyptians? We are brought up to use the Syrian[9] tongue only. What language shall we speak to Greeks? How shall we persuade Persians, Armenians, Chaldeans, Scythians, Indians and other scattered nations to give up their ancestral gods and worship the Creator of all? What abilities in speaking have we to depend upon in attempting such work as this? And what hope of success can we have if we dare to proclaim laws directly opposed to the laws about their own gods that have been established for ages among all nations? By what power shall we ever survive our daring attempt?" The PROOF OF THE GOSPEL 3.7.[10]

### 1:18 Immediately They Left Their Nets

**WHAT IS TO BE LEFT BEHIND.** TERTULLIAN: Do you hesitate about your business and professions for the sake of your children and parents? It has been demonstrated to us in Scripture that any too dear relations, crafts and trades are to be quite left behind for the Lord's sake. For James and John, called by the Lord, immediately leave quite behind both father and ship.[11] Matthew is roused from the toll-booth.[12] Even burying a father was too tardy a business for faith![13] None of those whom the Lord chose to him said, "I have no

---

[4]Mk 1:17 NRSV; Mt 4:19. [5]TLG 2018.005, 3.7.4.1-6.2; 8.1-8; POG 1:156**. The Lord used the most rustic and common persons as ministers of his own design, to underscore that this is entirely a work of grace. [6]Mt 24:14. [7]Cf. Rom 1:14. [8]TLG 2042.002, 4.1.2.1-9; OFP 259. Humble fishermen were chosen to put the focus upon the power of God. [9]Aramaic. [10]TLG 2018.005, 3.7.10.1-11..8; POG 1:157*. [11]Mt 4:21-22; Mk 1:19-20; Lk 5:10-11. [12]Mt 9:9; Mk 2:14; Lk 5:28. [13]Lk 9:59-60.

means to live." ON IDOLATRY 12.[14]

**MAKING A PLACE FOR HIM.** AUGUSTINE: And from that day they adhered to him so resolutely that they did not depart. . . . Let us, also, ourselves build a house in our heart and make a place where he may come and teach us. TRACTATE ON JOHN 7.9.2, 3.[15]

### 1:20 They Left Their Father in the Boat

**HIS COMPELLING CALL.** JEROME: There must have been something divinely compelling in the face of the Savior. Otherwise they would not have acted so irrationally as to follow a man whom they had never seen before. Does one leave a father to follow a man in whom he sees nothing more than he sees in his father? They left their father of the flesh to follow the Father of the spirit. They did not leave a father; they found a Father. What is the point of this digression? To show that there was something divine in the Savior's very countenance that men, seeing, could not resist. HOMILY 83.[16]

**DETACHING ALL.** BASIL: A beginning is made by detaching oneself from all external goods:

property, self-importance, social class and useless desire, following the holy example of the Lord's disciples. James and John left their father Zebedee and the very boat upon which their whole livelihood depended.[17] Matthew left his counting house and followed the Lord, not merely leaving behind the profits of his occupation, but also paying no heed to the dangers which were sure to befall both himself and his family at the hands of the magistrates because he had left the tax accounts unfinished.[18] Paul speaks of the whole world being crucified to him, and he to the world.[19] Thus, those who are strongly seized with the desire of following Christ can no longer be concerned with anything pertaining to this life, not even with the love of their parents or other relatives insofar as this runs counter to the calling of the Lord. THE LONG RULES, QUESTION 8.[20]

---

[14]Cetedoc 0023, 43.16; ANF 3:68**. [15]Cetedoc 0278, 7.9.12; FC 78:162-63. [16]Cetedoc 0594, 9.37; FC 57:180**. [17]Mk 1:20. [18]Mt 9:9. [19]Gal 6:14. "But far be it from me to glory except in the cross of our Lord Jesus Christ, by which the world has been crucified to me, and I to the world." [20]TLG 2040.048.31.936.39-937.5; FC 9:254*.

## 1:21-28 JESUS IN THE SYNAGOGUE AT CAPERNAUM

[21]*And they went into Capernaum; and immediately on the sabbath he entered the synagogue and taught.* [22]*And they were astonished at his teaching, for he taught them as one who had authority, and not as the scribes.* [23]*And immediately there was in their synagogue a man*

*with an unclean spirit;* [24]*and he cried out, "What have you to do with us, Jesus of Nazareth? Have you come to destroy us? I know who you are, the Holy One of God."* [25]*But Jesus rebuked him, saying, "Be silent, and come out of him!"* [26]*And the unclean spirit, convulsing him and crying with a loud voice, came out of him.* [27]*And they were all amazed, so that they questioned among themselves, saying, "What is this? A new teaching! With authority he commands even the unclean spirits, and they obey him."* [28]*And at once his fame spread everywhere throughout all the surrounding region of Galilee.*

**OVERVIEW:** The demonic powers were the first to be confronted by the Lord (BEDE). Even if the demons confessed Christ, without charity that meant nothing (CHRYSOSTOM, AMBROSE, AUGUSTINE). While Peter's confession sounded almost the same verbally as the demonic confession, the crucial difference was that Peter confessed out of love, the demons out of fear (AUGUSTINE). So we are not to believe the demonic powers, even when they tell the truth (AMBROSE). Jesus silenced the demons because he did not wish that the truth should proceed from an unclean mouth (ATHANASIUS). It was fitting that the truth should become a means of judgment not only for the salvation of those who believe but also for the condemnation of those who do not believe, that all should be fairly judged (IRENAEUS).

### 1:24a What Have You to Do with Us, Jesus of Nazareth?

**THE EARLIEST INTIMATION OF HIS IDENTITY.** BEDE: It was appropriate, since death first entered into the world through the devil's envy,[1] that the healing medicine of salvation should first operate against him. . . . The presence of the Savior is the torment of the devils. EXPOSITION ON THE GOSPEL OF MARK 1.1.25.[2]

### 1:24b Have You Come to Destroy Us?

**TOWARD HASTY DESTRUCTION.** AUGUSTINE: Unclean spirits knew that Jesus Christ would come. They had heard it from the angels, they had heard it from the prophets, so they were expecting him to come. For if not, why did they cry out, "What have we to do with you? Have you come to destroy us before the time? We know who you are, the holy one of God."[3] TRACTATE ON JOHN 7.6.2.[4]

### 1:24c I Know Who You Are, the Holy One of God

**DEMONIC RECOGNITION.** IRENAEUS: Even the demons cried out, on beholding the Son: "I know who you are, the Holy One of God."[5] Later the devil looking at him and tempting him, would say: "If you are the Son of God."[6] All of these thus recognized the Son and the Father, yet without believing. So it was fitting that the truth should receive testimony from all, and should become a means of judgment for the salvation not only of those who believe, but also for the condemnation of those who do not believe. The result is that all

---

[1]Gen 3:15. [2]Cetedoc 1355, 1.1.406, 409 ; *GMI* 29. Cf. *HOG* 1:121; *HOG* 1:122; *GC* 1:370. As death first came by the demonic, so salvation first came by Christ binding up the demonic. [3]Mt 8:29; Mk 1:24; Lk 4:34. [4]Cetedoc 0278, 7.6.10; FC 78:159*. [5]Mk 1:24. [6]Mt 4:3; Lk 4:3.

should be fairly judged, and that the faith in the Father and Son should be a matter of decision for all, so that one means of salvation should be established for all, receiving testimony from all, both from those belonging to it who were its friends, and by those having no connection with it who were its enemies. For that evidence is most trustworthy and true which elicits even from its adversaries striking testimonies on its behalf. AGAINST HERESIES 4.6.6-7.[7]

**FORCED NOTICE.** CHRYSOSTOM: Does no demon call upon God's name? Did not the demons say, "We know who you are, O Holy One of God?"[8] Did they not say to Paul: "these men are the servants of the Most High God?"[9] They did, but only upon scourging, only upon compulsion, never of their own will, never without being trounced. HOMILIES ON FIRST CORINTHIANS 29.3.[10]

**UNWILLING TESTIMONY.** AMBROSE: I do not accept the devil's testimony but his confession. The devil spoke unwillingly, being compelled and tormented. LETTER 22, TO HIS SISTER.[11]

**HOW THE DEMONS' CONFESSION DIFFERED FROM PETER'S.** AUGUSTINE: Call to mind with me the time when Peter was praised and called blessed. Was it because he merely said, "You are the Christ, the Son of the living God"?[12] No, he who pronounced him blessed regarded not merely the sound of his words, but the affections of his heart. Compare that with the words of the demons who said almost the same thing: "We know who you are, the Son of God,"[13] just as Peter had confessed him as "Son of God." So what is the difference? Peter spoke in love, but the demons in fear. . . . So tell us how faith is to be defined, if even the devils can believe and tremble? Only the faith that works by love is faith. SER-

MONS ON NEW TESTAMENT LESSONS 40.8.[14]

**KNOWING WITHOUT LOVING.** AUGUSTINE: Those words show clearly that the demons had much knowledge, but entirely lacked love. They dreaded receiving their punishment from him. They did not love the righteousness that was in him. He made himself known to them to the extent he willed; and he willed to be made known to the extent that was fitting. But he was not made known to them as he is known to the holy angels, who enjoy participation in his eternity, in that he is the Word of God. To the demons he is known as he had to be made known, by striking terror into them, for his purpose was to free from their tyrannical power all who were predestined for his kingdom and glory, which is eternally true and truly eternal. Therefore, he did not make himself known to the demons as the life eternal, and the unchangeable light which illuminates his true worshipers, whose hearts are purified by faith in him so that they see that light. He was known to the demons through certain temporal effects of his power, the signs of his hidden presence, which could be more evident to their senses, even those of malignant spirits, than to the weak perception of human beings. CITY OF GOD 9.21.[15]

**THE CONFESSION THAT LACKED LOVE.** AUGUSTINE: Faith is mighty, but without love it profits nothing. The devils confessed Christ, but lacking charity it availed nothing. They

---

[7]AHR 2:161; ANF 1:469*. [8]Mk 1:24; Lk 4:34. [9]Acts 16:17. [10]TLG 2062.156, 61.243.6-12; NPNF 1 12:170*. [11]Cetedoc 0160, 10.7.22.82/3.139.221; NPNF 2 10:440. [12]Mt 16:16. [13]Mt 8:29; Mk 1:24; Lk 8:28. [14]Cetedoc 0284, 90.38.564.12; cf. WSA 3 3:453, Sermon 90.8; NPNF 1 6:395*. [15]Cetedoc 0313, 47.9.21.3; CG 367*; cf. FC 14:108-9. Jesus let himself be known by the demons. The demons knew enough to fear his punishment, but for his holiness they had no love. [16]Mk 1:24.

said, "What have we to do with you?" They confessed a sort of faith, but without love. Hence they were devils. Do not boast of that faith that puts you on the same level with the devils. TRACTATE ON JOHN 6.21.[16]

### 1:25 Be Silent!

**BRIDLING THE MOUTH.** ATHANASIUS: He put a bridle in the mouths of the demons that cried after him from the tombs. For although what they said was true, and they did not lie when they said, "You are the Son of God" and "the Holy One of God,"[17] yet he did not wish that the truth should proceed from an unclean mouth, and especially from such as

those who under pretense of truth might mingle with it their own malicious devices.[18] TO THE BISHOPS OF EGYPT 1.3.[19]

**CHASTISING THE TONGUE.** BEDE: The devil, because he had deceived Eve with his tongue, is punished by the tongue, that he might not speak. EXPOSITION ON THE GOSPEL OF MARK 1.1.25.[20]

---

[16]Cetedoc 0278, 6.21.6; NPNF 1 7:46*. The devils confessed Christ, but lacking love their confession availed nothing. [17]Mt 8:29; Mk 1:24; Lk 8:28. The issue is whether truth can be told by deceivers. [18]Cf. Paul's exorcism of the young slave girl in Acts 16:16-21. [19]TLG 2035.041, 25.544.13-20; NPNF 2 4:224*. Truth mingled with demonic malice is only a pretense of truth. [20]Cetedoc 1355, 1.1.409; CCL 120:447; GC 1:373; cf. HOG 1:116. Thus the devil is chastised in a fitting way.

---

## 1:29-45 JESUS HEALS AT SIMON'S HOUSE AND DEPARTS FROM CAPERNAUM, HEALING A LEPER

[29]*And immediately he[e] left the synagogue, and entered the house of Simon and Andrew, with James and John.* [30]*Now Simon's mother-in-law lay sick with a fever, and immediately they told him of her.* [31]*And he came and took her by the hand and lifted her up, and the fever left her; and she served them.*

[32]*That evening, at sundown, they brought to him all who were sick or possessed with demons.* [33]*And the whole city was gathered together about the door.* [34]*And he healed many who were sick with various diseases, and cast out many demons; and he would not permit the demons to speak, because they knew him.*

[35]*And in the morning, a great while before day, he rose and went out to a lonely place, and there he prayed.* [36]*And Simon and those who were with him pursued him,* [37]*and they found him and said to him, "Every one is searching for you."* [38]*And he said to them, "Let us go on to the next towns, that I may preach there also; for that is why I came out."* [39]*And he went throughout all Galilee, preaching in their synagogues and casting out demons.*

⁴⁰*And a leper came to him beseeching him, and kneeling said to him, "If you will, you can make me clean." ⁴¹Moved with pity, he stretched out his hand and touched him, and said to him, "I will; be clean." ⁴²And immediately the leprosy left him, and he was made clean. ⁴³And he sternly charged him, and sent him away at once, ⁴⁴and said to him, "See that you say nothing to any one; but go, show yourself to the priest, and offer for your cleansing what Moses commanded, for a proof to the people."ᶠ ⁴⁵But he went out and began to talk freely about it, and to spread the news, so that Jesusᵍ could no longer openly enter a town, but was out in the country; and people came to him from every quarter.*

e Other ancient authorities read *they*   f Greek *to them*   g Greek *he*

**OVERVIEW:** Believers are in a position analogous to that of Simon's mother-in-law: They pray for the Lord to grasp their hands and lift them up. Since Jesus stands in their midst, beckoning them to health, offering himself immediately to them, it is absurd that they would remain in bed in his presence ( JEROME). Scripture constantly attests Jesus as a man of prayer (ORIGEN). To the pure in heart, whose hearts are made pure by faith, nothing is impure (CHRYSOSTOM). The momentary concealing of the truth of revelation was commanded temporarily but not permanently (BEDE). The variable order of presentation of events in the Gospel narratives is not to be considered a deficit in the memory of the Holy Spirit (AUGUSTINE).

### 1:30 Now Simon's Mother-in-Law Lay Sick with a Fever

**THE ROTTEN ODOR OF SIN BECOMES THE PERFUME OF REPENTANCE.** JEROME: Can you imagine Jesus standing before your bed and you continue sleeping? It is absurd that you would remain in bed in his presence. Where is Jesus? He is already here offering himself to us. "In the middle," he says, "among you he stands, whom you do not recognize."[1] "The kingdom of God is in your midst."[2] Faith

beholds Jesus among us. If we are unable to seize his hand, let us prostrate ourselves at his feet. If we are unable to reach his head, let us wash his feet with our tears.[3] Our repentance is the perfume of the Savior. See how costly is the compassion of the Savior. Our sins give off a terrible odor; they are rottenness. Nevertheless, if we repent of our sins, they will be transformed into perfume by the Lord. Therefore, let us ask the Lord to grasp our hand. "And at once," he says, "the fever left her."[4] Immediately as her hand is grasped, the fever flees. TRACTATE ON MARK'S GOSPEL 2.[5]

### 1:35 He Went Out to a Lonely Place, and There He Prayed

**THE HABIT OF PRAYER.** ORIGEN: Jesus prayed and did not pray in vain, since he received what he asked for in prayer when he might have done so without prayer. If so, who among us would neglect to pray? Mark says that "in the morning, a great while before day, he rose and went out to a lonely place, and there he prayed."[6] And Luke says, "He was praying in a certain place, and when he ceased, one of his disciples

---

[1]Cf. Jn 1:26. [2]Mk 1:15. [3]Cf. Lk 7:38. [4]Mk 1:31. [5]Cetedoc 0594, 2.375. [6]Mk 1:35.

said to him, 'Lord, teach us to pray,' "[7] and else-where, "And all night he continued in prayer to God."[8] And John records his prayer, saying, "When Jesus had spoken these words, he lifted up his eyes to heaven and said, 'Father, the hour has come; glorify your Son that the Son may glorify you.' "[9] The same Evangelist writes that the Lord said that he knew "you hear me always."[10] All this shows that the one who prays always is always heard. On Prayer 13.1.[11]

### 1:40 A Leper Came to Him Beseeching Him

**The Gospel Writers' Memory.** Augustine: It is not in one's own power, however admirable and trustworthy may be the knowledge one has of the facts, to determine the order in which he will recall them to memory.[12] For the way in which one thing comes into one's mind before or after another proceeds not as we will, but simply as it occurs to us. It is reasonable enough to suppose that each of the Evangelists believed it to have been his duty to relate what he had to relate in that order in which it had pleased God to suggest it to his recollection. Harmony of the Gospels 21.51.[13]

### 1:41 He Touched Him

**Why Did He Touch the Leper?** Origen: And why did he touch him, since the law for-bade the touching of a leper? He touched him to show that "all things are clean to the clean."[14] Because the filth that is in one person does not adhere to others, nor does external uncleanness defile the clean of heart. So he touches him in his untouchability, that he might instruct us in humility; that he might teach us that we should despise no one, or abhor them, or regard them as pitiable, because of some wound of their

body or some blemish for which they might be called to render an account. . . . So, stretching forth his hand to touch, the leprosy immedi-ately departs. The hand of the Lord is found to have touched not a leper, but a body made clean! Let us consider here, beloved, if there be anyone here that has the taint of leprosy in his soul, or the contamination of guilt in his heart? If he has, instantly adoring God, let him say: "Lord, if you will, you can make me clean." Fragments on Matthew 2.2-3[15]

**The Sign of Touching.** Chrysostom: He did not simply say, "I will, be cleansed," but he also "extended his hand, and touched him"— an act we do well to analyze. If he cleansed him merely by willing it and by speaking it, why did he also add the touch of his hand? For no other reason, it seems to me, than that he might sig-nify by this that he is not under the hand of the law, but the law is in his hands. Hence to the pure in heart, from now on, nothing is im-pure.[16] . . . He touched the leper to signify that he heals not as servant but as Lord. For the lep-rosy did not defile his hand, but his holy hand cleansed the leprous body. The Gospel of St. Matthew, Homily 25.2.[17]

### 1:43 Show Yourself to the Priest

**The Law and the Leper.** Ephrem the Syr-

---

[7]Lk 11:1. [8]Lk 6:12. [9]Jn 17:1. [10]Jn 11:42. [11]TLG 2042.008, 13.1.1-14; CWS 104-5. Scripture constantly attests Jesus as a man of prayer. [12]Augustine is asking why this narrative is located in a different sequence in Mark than in the other Gospels. [13]Cetedoc 0273, 2.21.51.152.19; NPNF 1 6:127. The variable order of presen-tation of events is not to be considered a deficit in the memory of the Holy Spirit but a normal aspect of recollective consciousness. [14]Tit 1:15. [15]GCS 41.1:248-9; SSGF 1:301-02*. [16]Cf. Tit 1:15. [17]TLG 2062.152, 57.329.7.13, 17-21; NPNF 1 10:173**; His touch conveyed his lordship over the law, and his holiness, which cannot be defiled.

IAN: "'If you are willing, you can cleanse me.' So he stretched out his hand."[18] In this stretching out of his hand he seemed to be abrogating the law. For [it is written] in the law that whoever approaches a leper becomes impure.... He showed that nature was good in that he repaired its defect. Because he sent him to the priests, he thereby upheld the priesthood. He also ordered him to make an offering for his cleansing.[19] Did he not thus uphold the law, as Moses had commanded? There were many prescriptions concerning leprosy. But they were unable to procure any benefit. Then the Messiah came, and, with his word, bestowed healing and abolished these many precepts which the law had reckoned should exist for leprosy. COMMENTARY ON TATIAN'S DIATESSARON.[20]

### 1:44 See That You Say Nothing to Anyone

**UNSPOKEN BENEFITS.** BEDE: In the performance of this miracle Jesus requested silence.[21] Yet it did not remain concealed in silence for long. So it is with the called people of God— while following his precepts and example, they may prefer their responsible actions to remain unspoken, yet for the benefit of others providence may allow them to become known contrary to their own wishes. EXPOSITION ON THE GOSPEL OF MARK 1.1.45.[22]

---

[18]Mt 8:2-3; cf. Mk 1:40-41; Lk 5:12-13. [19]Mt 8:4; Mk 1:44; Lk 5:14. [20]JSSS 2:203*. [21]The issue is whether good deeds are made better by remaining unspoken. [22]Cetedoc 1355, 1.1.603; CCL 120:452; GMI 29*; cf. HOG 1:111.

---

## 2:1-12 HEALING OF THE PARALYTIC

[1]*And when he returned to Capernaum after some days, it was reported that he was at home.* [2]*And many were gathered together, so that there was no longer room for them, not even about the door; and he was preaching the word to them.* [3]*And they came, bringing to him a paralytic carried by four men.* [4]*And when they could not get near him because of the crowd, they removed the roof above him; and when they had made an opening, they let down the pallet on which the paralytic lay.* [5]*And when Jesus saw their faith, he said to the paralytic, "My son, your sins are forgiven."* [6]*Now some of the scribes were sitting there, questioning in their hearts,* [7]*"Why does this man speak thus? It is blasphemy! Who can forgive sins but God alone?"* [8]*And immediately Jesus, perceiving in his spirit that they thus questioned within themselves, said to them, "Why do you question thus in your hearts?* [9]*Which is easier, to say to the paralytic, 'Your sins are forgiven,' or to say, 'Rise, take up your pallet and walk'?* [10]*But that you may know that the Son of man has authority on earth to forgive sins"—he said to the paralytic—* [11]*"I say to you, rise, take up your pallet and go home."* [12]*And he rose, and immediately took up the pallet and went out before them all; so that they were all amazed and glorified God, saying, "We never saw anything like this!"*

**OVERVIEW:** Jesus charged the paralytic to perform an action of which health was the necessary condition (AMBROSE). One need not be paralyzed bodily, however, to be paralyzed inwardly (AUGUSTINE). The healing of body and soul occurs interconnectedly (CLEMENT OF ALEXANDRIA). The ministry of forgiveness is not the exercise of an independent power or right but points to God's own saving work (AMBROSE). The administration of forgiveness, which according to the scribes is the office of God alone, acutely raised the question of Jesus' identity. Being God incarnate, of the same nature as God, he had authority on earth to act as God (CHRYSOSTOM). If Christ forgives sins, he must be truly God, for no one can forgive sins but God (IRENAEUS, NOVATIAN).

### 2:7a It Is Blasphemy!

**THE SCRIBES' ENTANGLEMENT.** CHRYSOSTOM: They persecuted Jesus not only because he broke the Sabbath but also because he said that God was his Father, making himself equal with God,[1] which is a far more drastic declaration. He confirmed this through his own actions. . . . The scribes themselves had devised this definition.[2] They themselves had introduced the precept. They themselves had interpreted the law. But he proceeded to entangle them in their own words. In effect he said: It is you yourselves who have confessed that forgiveness of sins is given to God alone. THE PARALYTIC LET DOWN THROUGH THE ROOF 6.[3]

### 2:7b Who Can Forgive Sins but God Alone?

**ONLY GOD FORGIVES SIN.** IRENAEUS: How can sins be rightly remitted unless the very One

against whom one has sinned grants the pardon?[4] AGAINST HERESIES 5.17.1.[5]

**THE IMPLICATION OF HIS ACT OF FORGIVING.** NOVATIAN: If Christ forgives sins, Christ must be truly God because no one can forgive sins but God alone.[6] THE TRINITY 13.[7]

**THE MINISTRY OF FORGIVENESS.** AMBROSE: In their ministry of the forgiveness of sin, pastors do not exercise the right of some independent power. For not in their own name but in the name of the Father and the Son and the Holy Spirit do they forgive sins. They ask, the Godhead forgives. The service is enabled by humans, but the gift comes from the Power on high. THE HOLY SPIRIT 3.18.137.[8]

### 2:8 Why Do You Question Thus in Your Hearts?

**DISCERNING SECRETS OF THE HEART.** CHRYSOSTOM: The scribes asserted that only God could forgive sins, yet Jesus not only forgave sins, but showed that he had also another power that belongs to God alone: the power to disclose the secrets of the heart. THE GOSPEL OF ST. MATTHEW, HOMILY 29.1.[9]

### 2:9 Which Is Easier to Say?

**HEALING THE WHOLE PERSON.** CLEMENT OF ALEXANDRIA: The physician's art, according to

---

[1]Jn 5:16-18. [2]That only God can forgive. [3]TLG 2062.063, 51.59.19-23,35-39; NPNF 1 9:218**. [4]1 Sam 2:25. [5]AHR 2:370; GMI 45*. The issue is who has the right to forgive sin. [6]Mt 9:2; Mk 2:5; Lk 5:20-21. [7]Cetedoc 0071, 13.37; FC 67:54*. His act of forgiveness implies that he indeed is God. [8]Cetedoc 0151, 3.18.137.208.44; FC 44:202-03**, cf. NPNF 2 10:154. Ministers of the Eucharist do not of themselves have the autonomous power to forgive. [9]TLG 2062.152, 57.359.53-57; JF B 82; NPNF 1 10:196.

Democritus, heals the diseases of the body; wisdom frees the soul from its obsessions. But the good Instructor, Wisdom, who is the Word of the Father who assumed human flesh, cares for the whole nature of his creature. The all-sufficient Physician of humanity, the Savior, heals both body and soul conjointly. "Stand up," he commanded the paralytic; "take the bed on which you lie, and go home"; and immediately the paralytic received strength.[10] CHRIST THE EDUCATOR 1.4.[11]

### 2:10 Authority on Earth

**ACTING UPON HIS OWN AUTHORITY.** CHRYSOSTOM: Whenever there was need to punish or to honor, to forgive sins or to make laws, Christ was fully authorized to do it.[12] Whenever Christ had to do any of these much greater things, you will not characteristically find him praying or calling on his Father for assistance. All these things, as you discover in the text, he did on his own authority. ON THE INCOMPREHENSIBLE NATURE OF GOD, HOMILY 10.19.[13]

### 2:11 Take Up Your Pallet

**REVERSE YOUR RELATION WITH SICKNESS.** PETER CHRYSOLOGUS: Take up your bed. Carry the very mat that once carried you. Change places, so that what was the proof of your sickness may now give testimony to your soundness. Your bed of pain becomes the sign of healing, its very weight the measure of the strength that has been restored to you. HOMILY 50:6.[14]

**THE CHARGE TO PERFORM AN ACT OF WHICH HEALTH IS A NECESSARY CONDITION.** AMBROSE: He charged the man to perform an action of which health was the necessary condition, even while the patient was still praying for a remedy for his disease. . . . It was our Lord's custom to require of those whom he healed some response or duty to be done.[15] ON THE CHRISTIAN FAITH 4.8.54-55.[16]

**INWARD PARALYSIS.** AUGUSTINE: You have been a paralytic inwardly. You did not take charge of your bed. Your bed took charge of you. ON THE PSALMS 41.4.[17]

---

[10]Mk 2:11. [11]TLG 0555.002, 1.2.6.2.1-3.3; ANF 2:210**. [12]Cf. Mt 28:18. [13]TLG 2062.018, 48.787.44-48; FC 72:251**. Jesus had full authority on earth to act as God. [14]Cetedoc 0227, 24.50.98; SSGF 4:191**; cf. PL 52:339. [15]Jn 5:8; 8:11. [16]Cetedoc 0150, 4.5.37; GMI 48.* [17]Cetedoc 0283, 38.40.5.10; NPNF 1 8:129. One can be paralytic inwardly without bodily paralysis.

## 2:13-17 THE CALL OF LEVI

[13]*He went out again beside the sea; and all the crowd gathered about him, and he taught them.* [14]*And as he passed on, he saw Levi the son of Alphaeus sitting at the tax office, and he said to him, "Follow me." And he rose and followed him.*

*[15]And as he sat at table in his house, many tax collectors and sinners were sitting with Jesus and his disciples; for there were many who followed him. [16]And the scribes of[h] the Pharisees, when they saw that he was eating with sinners and tax collectors, said to his disciples, "Why does he eat[i] with tax collectors and sinners?" [17]And when Jesus heard it, he said to them, "Those who are well have no need of a physician, but those who are sick; I came not to call the righteous, but sinners."*

h Other ancient authorities read *and*   i Other ancient authorities add *and drink*

**OVERVIEW:** Following Jesus is not so much a motion of the feet as of the heart (BEDE). To blame Jesus for mingling with sinners would be like blaming a physician for associating closely with sick people (GREGORY NAZIANZEN). Just as surgery gives a sharp pain to the body, so must there be some anguish in the recovering soul (GREGORY OF NYSSA). Health requires the reversal of behaviors that caused illness (IRENAEUS). The obsessive sinner is like one who imagines himself to be in such good health that he pounces upon the physician (AUGUSTINE). Matthew's corrupt past was spent amid those occupied compulsively with overreaching one another (EUSEBIUS). That righteousness for which we pray we must first know about and wish it to be; we then pray for the grace of the Spirit to empower our wills to receive it (AUGUSTINE). Christ, who willed to save the things that were perishing, did a far greater work by establishing those things that are falling than by holding up those things that were standing (PSEUDO-CLEMENT, JEROME).

### 2:14a *The Tax Office*

**THE MILIEU OF COMPULSIVE ACQUISITIVE-NESS.** EUSEBIUS: The Apostle Matthew, if you consider his former life, did not leave a holy occupation, but came from those consumed with tax-gathering and overreaching one another.[1] PROOF OF THE GOSPEL 3.5.[2]

**A NEW NAME FOR LEVI.** BEDE: Jesus found him sitting in the tax collector's place, with his stubborn intellect avid for temporal gain. His new name was Matthew, the gospel says. The name Matthew in Hebrew means "granted" in Latin, a name aptly corresponding to one who received the favor of heavenly grace. HOMILIES ON THE GOSPELS 1.21.[3]

### 2:14b *Follow Me*

**THE GIFT OF FOLLOWING.** BEDE: By "follow" he meant not so much the movement of feet as of the heart, the carrying out of a way of life. For one who says that he lives in Christ ought himself to walk just as he walked,[4] not to aim at earthly things, not to pursue perishable gains, but to flee base praise, to embrace willingly the contempt of all that is worldly for the sake of heavenly glory, to do good to all, to inflict injuries upon no one in bitterness, to suffer patiently those injuries that come to oneself, to ask God's forgiveness for those who oppress, never to seek one's own glory but always God's,[5] and to uphold whatever helps one love

---

[1]Mt 9:9; Lk 5:27.   [2]TLG 2018.005, 3.5.81.1-3; POG 1:137*.
[3]Cetedoc 1367, 1.21.30; HOG 1:206*.   [4]Cf. 1 Pet 2:21; 1 Jn 2:6.
[5]Cf. Jn 7:18.

heavenly things. This is what is meant by following Christ. In this way, disregarding earthly gains, Matthew attached himself to the band of followers of One who had no riches. For the Lord himself, who outwardly called Matthew by a word, inwardly bestowed upon him the gift of an invisible impulse so that he was able to follow. HOMILIES ON THE GOSPELS 1.21.[6]

## 2:16 Eating with Sinners and Tax Collectors

**NO PHYSICIAN CAN AVOID THE ARENA OF SICKNESS.** GREGORY NAZIANZEN: When Jesus is attacked for mixing with sinners, and taking as his disciple a despised tax collector, one might ask: What could he possibly gain by doing so?[7] Only the salvation of sinners. To blame Jesus for mingling with sinners would be like blaming a physician for stooping down over suffering and putting up with vile smells in order to heal the sick. ORATION 45, ON HOLY EASTER 26.[8]

## 2:17a Those Who Are Well Have No Need of a Physician

**THE REVERSAL OF PREVIOUS BEHAVIOR.** IRENAEUS: What competent doctor, when asked to cure a sick person, would simply follow the desires of the patient, and not act in accordance with the requirements of good medicine? The Lord himself testified that he came as the physician of the sick, saying, "Those who are well have no need of a physician, but those who are sick; I came not to call the righteous, but sinners." How, then, are the sick to be made strong? How are sinners to repent? Is it by merely holding fast to what they are presently doing? Or, on the contrary, by undergoing a great change and reversal of their previous

behavior, by which they had brought upon themselves serious illness and many sins? Ignorance, the mother of intractability, is driven out by knowing the truth. Therefore the Lord imparted knowledge of the truth to his disciples, by which he cured those who were suffering, and restrained sinners from sin. So he did not speak to them in accordance with their previous assumptions, nor answer according to the presumptions of inquirers, but according to sound teaching, without any pretense or pandering. AGAINST HERESIES.[9]

**THE TEMPORARY HARM DONE BY SURGERY.** GREGORY OF NYSSA: They who use the knife or heat to remove certain unnatural growths in the body, such as cysts or warts, do not bring to the person they are serving a method of healing that is painless, though certainly they apply the knife without any intention of injuring the patient. Similarly whatever material excrescences are hardening on our souls, which have been made carnal by collusion with inordinate passions, will be, in the day of the judgment, cut and scraped away by the ineffable wisdom and power of him who, as the Gospel says, "healed those that were sick." For as he says, "they who are well have no need of the physician, but they that are sick." Just as the excision of the wart gives a sharp pain to the skin of the body, so then must there be some anguish in the recovering soul which has had a strong bent to evil. THE GREAT CATECHISM 8.[10]

**THE DELIRIOUS ATTACK ON THE PHYSICIAN.** AUGUSTINE: By those who are well he means

---

[6]Cetedoc 1367, 1.21.57; HOG 1:207**. [7]Cf. Lk 15:2. [8]TLG 2022.052, 36.660.20-26; NPNF 2 7:433**. [9]AHR 2:19-20; LCC 1:377**. [10]TLG 2017.046, 8.96-108; NPNF 2 5:483-84**. God's saving action sometimes requires the enduring of pain.

those being made righteous. Sinners are compared to those who are ill. Let the sick man, then, not presume on his own strength, because "he shall not be saved by his great strength."[11] The strength of self-deceivers is not that strength that well people enjoy, but like those in delirium. They are like those out of their minds, who imagine themselves in such good health that they do not consult a physician, and even fall upon him with blows as if he were an intruder! In the same way, these delirious people, with their mad pride, fall upon Christ with blows, so to speak, because they have felt no need of his kindly help to those who seek to be just according to the prescriptions of the law. Let them, then, put away this madness. Let them understand, as far as they are able, that they have free will, and that they are called not to despise the Lord's help with a proud heart, but to call upon him with a contrite heart. The free will then will be free in proportion as it is sound, and sound in proportion as it is submissive to divine mercy and grace. LETTER 157, TO HILARIUS.[12]

## 2:17b Not to Call the Righteous but Sinners

RESCUE THE PERISHING. PSEUDO-CLEMENT: It is a greater work to establish those things that are falling than those that still stand. Thus also did Christ desire to save those who are perishing. He has saved many by coming and calling us just when we were hastening to destruction. 2 CLEMENT.[13]

THE CALL TO SINNERS. JEROME: There are two ways of interpreting the saying "I came not to call the righteous, but sinners." The first is by analogy with the accompanying phrase: "Those who are well have no need of a physician, but those who are sick." The other way is to put a more literal construction on the statement, like this: Since no one is perfectly righteous, Christ has not come to call those who are not there, but the multitudes of sinners who are there, with whom the world is filled, remembering the Psalm which says "Help, O Lord, for there is no longer any one who is godly."[14] AGAINST THE PELAGIANS 2.12.[15]

THE GRACE TO PRAY FOR RIGHTEOUSNESS. AUGUSTINE: Pray for us that we may be saved by that salvation of which it is said: "They that are in health need not a physician, but they that are ill; for I am not come to call the just but sinners."[16] Pray, then, for us that we may be made upright. This is indeed something which one cannot do unless he knows and wishes it; and he will become so as constantly as he wishes it fully—but it will not be through his own effort that he is able, unless he is healed and helped by the grace of the Spirit. LETTER 145, TO ANASTASIUS.[17]

---

[11]Ps 33:16. [12]Cetedoc 0262, 157.44.2.453.15; FC 20:323**. [13]TLG 1271.002, 2.6.1-7.2; AF 69**; cf. ANF 7:517. [14]Ps 12:1. [15]Cetedoc 0615, 2.12.15; FC 53:313**. The second interpretation focuses upon the assumption that since no one is righteous, Christ came for the salvation of more, not fewer. [16]Cf. Mt 9:12-13. [17]Cetedoc 0262, 145.44.8.273.9; FC 20:168-69*.

# 2:18-22 THE QUESTION ABOUT FASTING

<sup>18</sup>*Now John's disciples and the Pharisees were fasting; and people came and said to him, "Why do John's disciples and the disciples of the Pharisees fast, but your disciples do not fast?"* <sup>19</sup>*And Jesus said to them, "Can the wedding guests fast while the bridegroom is with them? As long as they have the bridegroom with them, they cannot fast.* <sup>20</sup>*The days will come, when the bridegroom is taken away from them, and then they will fast in that day.* <sup>21</sup>*No one sews a piece of unshrunk cloth on an old garment; if he does, the patch tears away from it, the new from the old, and a worse tear is made.* <sup>22</sup>*And no one puts new wine into old wineskins; if he does, the wine will burst the skins, and the wine is lost, and so are the skins; but new wine is for fresh skins."*<sup>j</sup>

j Other ancient authorities omit *but new wine is for fresh skins*

**OVERVIEW:** New wine symbolizes the good news that cannot be compressed into the prevailing categories of the previous history of revelation (TERTULLIAN). The new wine of the kingdom expresses itself through faith active in love (BEDE). Those who continue to wear the old garment of self-indulgence have not yet understood servanthood, which is the defining garment of the new era (CHRYSOSTOM). The mystical marriage for which this new wine is an accompanying symbol is that time and occasion when, through the mystery of the incarnation, Christ joins the church to himself; during that treasured moment it would be unfitting to weep while God is dwelling among us in the flesh (GREGORY NAZIANZEN). Truly to fast is to refrain from vice (PSEUDO-BASIL). It is not whether one eats and drinks, but whether one does so in moderation or excess, that indicates one's good temperament within the reign of God (PALLADIUS).

## 2:18 Your Disciples Do Not Fast

**TRUE FASTING.** BASIL: Take heed that you do not make fasting to consist only in abstinence from meats. True fasting is to refrain from vice. Shred to pieces all your unjust contracts. Pardon your neighbors. Forgive them their trespasses. HOMILY 1, ON FASTING.[1]

### 2:19 Can the Wedding Guests Fast While the Bridegroom Is with Them?

**NOT BY BREAD ALONE.** PSEUDO-BASIL[2]: True death is not a result of hunger for bread nor a result of thirst for this tangible water, but as a result of a hunger for hearing the word of the Lord. True death arises in the souls of those who do not hear. For one does "not live by bread alone, but by every word coming out through the mouth of God."[3] This is why . . . the attendants of the bridegroom cannot fast as long as the bridegroom is with them. COMMENTARY ON THE PROPHET ISAIAH.[4]

---

[1]TLG 2040.020, 31.181.17-21; *GMI* 52*. [2]Doubtful authorship. [3]Cf. Mt 4:4; Lk 4:4. [4]TLG 2040.009, 5.165.29-33, 37-38.

**THE BLESSING OF MODERATION.** PALLADIUS: It is better to drink wine in moderation than to drink water in excess. Some who are holy drink wine in moderation. Some who squander water immoderately may be depraved and pleasure-loving. So it appears to me. Do not therefore ascribe blame or praise to the eating of food as such, or to the drinking of wine, but rather to those who make proper or improper use of food and drink. Recall Joseph who in patriarchal times drank wine with the Egyptians and was in no way injured in his judgment, having taken heed to the admonitions of his conscience. But then compare the sorrier examples of Pythagoras, Diogenes and Plato, and with them also the Manichaeans, and other sects of philosophers, who did not heed these admonitions. Some of them came to such a pitch of sensuality or pride that they even forgot the God of the universe and worshiped lifeless images. So the blessed Apostle Peter and those who were with him did not hesitate to receive wine and make use of it. It was just because of this that our Lord's detractors actively reproached the redeemer of all and their teacher, and made complaints against him, saying, "Why do not your disciples fast like John?"[5] LAUSIAC HISTORY.[6]

**NO TIME TO MOURN.** GREGORY NAZIANZEN: Can the children of the bridechamber fast while the bridegroom is present?[7] Why should they keep a bodily fast who are effectively cleansed by the Word, who came in bodily form as visible Word? The time of his sojourning among us was not one of mourning, but gladness. ORATION 30, ON THE SON 10.[8]

**THE PRESENCE OF THE BRIDEGROOM.** BEDE: From the time that the incarnation of our Sav-ior was first promised to the patriarchs, it was always awaited by many upright souls with tears and mourning—until he came. From that time when, after his resurrection, he ascended to heaven, all the hope of the saints hangs upon his return. It was at the time when he was keeping company with humanity that his presence was to be celebrated. Then it would have been unfitting to weep and mourn. For like the bride, she had him with her bodily whom she loved spiritually. Therefore the bridegroom is Christ, the bride is the church, and the friends of the bridegroom[9] and of the marriage are each and every one of his faithful companions. The time of his marriage is that time when, through the mystery of the incarnation, he is joining the holy church to himself.[10] Thus it was not by chance, but for the sake of a certain mystical meaning that he came to a marriage ceremony on earth in the customary fleshly way,[11] since he descended from heaven to earth in order to wed the church to himself in spiritual love. His nuptial chamber was the womb of his virgin mother. There God was conjoined with human nature. From there he came forth like a bridegroom to join the church to himself. HOMILIES ON THE GOSPELS 1.14.[12]

### 2:21 Unshrunk Cloth on an Old Garment

**RESISTANCE TO SERVANTHOOD.** CHRYSOSTOM: The souls of some are like an old garment, an old wineskin—not as yet renewed by faith. Not yet renovated in the grace of the Spirit, they remain weak and earthly. All their affec-

---

[5]Mt 9:14; Mk 2:18; Lk 5:33. [6]TLG 2111.001, 10.4-11.9; *PHF* 1:85\*\*. [7]Cf. Mt 9:15; Lk 5:34. Is it fitting to mourn in the presence of the living Word? [8]TLG 2022.210, 10.10-14; LCC 3:183\*. [9]Mt 9:15; Lk 5:34. [10]Cf. Rev 19:7. [11]Cf. Jn 2:1-12. [12]Cetedoc 1367, 1.14.24; *HOG* 1:135\*\*.

tions are turned toward this life, fluttering after worldly show, loving a glory that is ephemeral. If such a soul should incidentally hear that if he became a Christian he would immediately become like a servant, as if he had a manacle on his foot, he would recoil with indignity and horror from the word as preached. CONCERNING THE STATUES, HOMILY 16.9.[13]

**INWARD AND OUTWARD GLADDENING.** BEDE: By wine we are refreshed inwardly. By a garment we are outwardly covered. Both relate to the dynamics of spiritual life. The garment indicates good works performed outwardly in order to shine in the sight of the world. By wine and new wine we mean that fervor of faith, hope and love by means of which, in the sight of our maker, our souls are recovered inwardly to newness of spirit. EXPOSITION ON THE GOSPEL OF MARK 1.2.24.[14]

### 2:22 The New Wine in New Wineskins

**THE NEW CONDITIONS OF GRACE.** TERTULLIAN: He has prescribed for his new disciples of the New Testament a new form of prayer. For this it was fitting that new wine be stored in new wine skins and that a new patch be sewed upon a new garment.[15] What had prevailed in days gone by was either abolished, like circumcision, or completed, like the rest of the law, or fulfilled, like the prophecies, or brought to its perfection, like faith itself. Everything has been changed from carnal to spiritual by the new grace of God which, with the coming of the gospel, has wiped out the old era completely. ON PRAYER 1.[16]

---

[13]TLG 2062. 024, 49.167.10-18; NPNF 1 9:449*. [14]Cetedoc 1355, 1.2.955; CCL 120:462; *GMI* 53-54*. The inward wine of newness of spirit expresses itself in the outward garment of faith active in works. [15]Mt 9:16-17; Mk 2:21-22; Lk 5:36-38. [16]Cetedoc 0007, 1.2; FC 40:157-58*.

# 2:23-28 PLUCKING EARS OF GRAIN ON THE SABBATH

[23]*One sabbath he was going through the grainfields; and as they made their way his disciples began to pluck heads of grain.* [24]*And the Pharisees said to him, "Look, why are they doing what is not lawful on the sabbath?"* [25]*And he said to them, "Have you never read what David did, when he was in need and was hungry, he and those who were with him:* [26] *how he entered the house of God, when Abiathar was high priest, and ate the bread of the Presence, which it is not lawful for any but the priests to eat, and also gave it to those who were with him?"* [27]*And he said to them, "The sabbath was made for man, not man for the sabbath;* [28]*so the Son of man is lord even of the sabbath."*

**OVERVIEW:** The God-man had a body and a soul like ours. As it is unintelligible to imagine him eating without a body, so it is impossible to think of him hungering without a soul (AUGUSTINE). As the Lord of the sabbath is truly God, so he is truly human. As Son of David so he is the Lord of David. Belonging to the children of Abraham, yet before Abraham he was (NOVATIAN).

## 2:25 What David Did When He Was Hungry

**THE HUNGER OF JESUS.** AUGUSTINE: It is foolish to believe the Evangelist's account that he ate and not to believe that he was really hungry. Yet it does not follow that everyone who eats is hungry. For we read that even an angel ate,[1] but we do not read that he was hungry. Nor does it follow that everyone who is hungry eats. He may either restrain himself due to some obligation or lack food or the means to eat. . . . Now, just as the fact that Jesus ate food is unintelligible without a body, so the fact that he felt hunger is impossible without a soul. AGAINST THE APOLLINARIANS, QUESTION 80.[2]

## 2:28 Lord of the Sabbath

**THE SEVENTH DAY.** UNKNOWN GREEK AUTHOR: Now every week has seven days. Six of these God has given to us for work, and one for prayer, rest, and making reparation for our sins, so that on the Lord's Day we may atone to God for any sins we have committed on the other six days. Therefore, arrive early at the church of God; draw near to the Lord and confess your sins to him, repenting in prayer and with a contrite heart. Attend the holy and divine liturgy; finish your prayer and do not leave before the dismissal. Contemplate your master as he is broken and distributed, yet not consumed. If you have a clear conscience, go forward and partake of the body and blood of the Lord. SERMON 6, 1-2.[3]

**SON OF DAVID, DAVID'S LORD.** NOVATIAN: In the same manner that he, according to his humanity, is like Abraham,[4] even so, according to his divinity, he is before Abraham.[5] As he is, according to his humanity, the Son of David,[6] so is he also, as God, the Lord of David.[7] As he is, according to his humanity, born under the law,[8] so is he as God, the Lord of the sabbath.[9] THE TRINITY 11.[10]

---

[1]Gen 18:8. [2]Cetedoc 0289, 80.103; FC 70:210-11*. The incarnate Lord had a body and a soul like ours, for he could hardly eat without a body, and he could hardly be hungry without a soul. Some heretical voices were denying that he had a body, others a soul. [3]JF B 86-87; PG 86/1, 416. According to Migne, the Greek text belongs to Eusebius of Alexandria. [4]Mt 1:1. [5]Jn 8:58. [6]Mt 20:31; 22:42. [7]Mt 22:43-45. [8]Gal 4:4. [9]Mt 12:8; Mk 2:28; Lk 6:5. [10]Cetedoc 0071, 11.53; FC 67:48-49**. As Lord of the sabbath he is truly God, as truly human he was born under the law, paradoxically of Abraham yet before Abraham, both Son of David and Lord of David.

# 3:1-6 THE HEALING OF THE MAN
## WITH THE WITHERED HAND

¹*Again he entered the synagogue, and a man was there who had a withered hand.* ²*And they watched him, to see whether he would heal him on the sabbath, so that they might accuse him.* ³*And he said to the man who had the withered hand, "Come here."* ⁴*And he said to them, "Is it lawful on the sabbath to do good or to do harm, to save life or to kill?" But they were silent.* ⁵*And he looked around at them with anger, grieved at their hardness of heart, and said to the man, "Stretch out your hand." He stretched it out, and his hand was restored.* ⁶*The Pharisees went out, and immediately held counsel with the Herodians against him, how to destroy him.*

**OVERVIEW:** The intent of Christ's detractors was to discredit him. They had little interest in seeing the sufferer made whole. Jesus' mission was to soften their harshness (CHRYSOSTOM). Even by the measure of the law, doing good to preserve life would have been permitted on the sabbath. Without touching the man, Jesus openly healed merely through speaking, so as to avoid the charge of working on the sabbath (ATHANASIUS). When we see Jesus' anger, directed to its proper object, we learn that all forms of anger are not vice (AUGUSTINE). Just as the incarnate Lord had a body, he had a soul with the whole range of emotions that characterize the human body-soul relationship (AUGUSTINE). The recipient of grace is neither allowed to so completely relax as to leave everything to God nor to imagine that by one's own exertions the whole work is achieved by human effort (CHRYSOSTOM).

### 3:4 Is It Lawful on the Sabbath to Do Good?

**WITHERED HANDS, WITHERED MINDS.**

ATHANASIUS:[1] In the synagogue of the Jews was a man who had a withered hand. If he was withered in his hand, the ones who stood by were withered in their minds. And they were not looking at the crippled man nor were they expecting the miraculous deed of the one who was about to work. But before doing the work, the Savior ploughed up their minds with words. For knowing the evil of the mind and its bitter depth, he first softened them up in advance with words so as to tame the wildness of their understanding, asking: "Is it permitted to do good on the sabbath or to do evil; to save a life or to destroy one?" For if he had said to them, "Is it permitted to work?" immediately they would have said, "You are speaking contrary to the law." Then he told them what was intended by the law, for he spoke as the One who established the laws concerning the sabbath, adding,[2] "except this: that which will be done for the sake of a life." Again if a person falls into a hole on a sabbath, Jews are permit-

---

[1] Attributed to Athanasius. [2] Adding to the imperative that no work is permitted.

ted to pull the person out.[3] This not only applies to a person, but also an ox or a donkey. In this way the law agrees that things relating to preservation may be done, hence Jews prepare meals on the sabbath. Then he asked them about a point on which they could hardly disagree: "Is it permitted to do good?"[4] But they did not even so much as say, "Yes," because by then they were not in a good temper. HOMILIES 28.[5]

**THE INTENT TO DISCREDIT.** CHRYSOSTOM: Jesus said to the man with the withered hand, "Come here." Then he challenged the Pharisees as to whether it would be lawful to do good on the sabbath. Note the tender compassion of the Lord when he deliberately brought the man with the withered hand right into their presence.[6] He hoped that the mere sight of the misfortune might soften them, that they might become a little less spiteful by seeing the affliction, and perhaps out of sorrow mend their own ways. But they remained callous and unfeeling. They preferred to do harm to the name of Christ than to see this poor man made whole. They betrayed their wickedness not only by their hostility to Christ, but also by their doing so with such contentiousness that they treated with disdain his mercies to others. GOSPEL OF ST. MATTHEW, HOMILY 40.1.[7]

### 3:5a He Looked at Them with Anger

**PUTTING ANGER TO GOOD USE.** AUGUSTINE: If angry emotions which spring from a love of what is good and from holy charity are to be labeled vices, then all I can say is that some vices should be called virtues. When such affections as anger are directed to their proper objects, they are following good reasoning, and

no one should dare to describe them as maladies or vicious passions. This explains why the Lord himself, who humbled himself to the form of a servant,[8] was guilty of no sin whatever as he displayed these emotions openly when appropriate. Surely the One who assumed a true human body and soul would not counterfeit his human affections. Certainly, the Gospel does not falsely attribute emotions to Christ when it speaks of him being saddened and angered by the lawyers because of their blindness of heart. THE CITY OF GOD, BOOK 14.[9]

### 3:5b Grieved at Their Hardness of Heart

**THE DIVERSITY OF HIS FEELINGS.** AUGUSTINE: Feelings cannot exist in anything but a living soul. These events show that just as Jesus had a human body he had a human soul. We read about the diversity of his feelings in the reports of the same Evangelists [who attested his divinity]: Jesus was astonished,[10] was angered,[11] was grieved,[12] was elated,[13] and similar emotive responses without number. Likewise it is clear that he experienced the ordinary fully human experience of interconnectedness between his body and his soul. He was hungry;[14] he slept;[15] he was tired from his journey.[16] AGAINST THE APOLLINARIANS 80.[17]

---

[3]Mt 12:11. [4]Mk 3:4; Lk 6:9. [5]Athanasius *Homilia de semente* 28; cf. TLG 2035.069, 28.165.8-29; PG 28:165; cf. E. A. W. Budge, *Coptic Homilies in the Dialect of Upper Egypt* (London: British Museum, 1910). [6]Lk 6:8. [7]TLG 2062.152, 57.439.3-4, 6-17; NPNF 1 10:259*. [8]Phil 2:7. [9]Cetedoc 0313, 48.14.9.59; FC 14:368-69*. [10]Mt 8:10. [11]Mk 3:5. [12]Cf. Jn 11:33-35. [13]Cf. Heb 12:2. [14]Mt 4:2; Lk 4:2. [15]Mt. 8:24; Mk 4:38; Lk 8:23. [16]Jn 4:6. [17]Cetedoc 0289, 80.84; FC 70:210-11**.

### 3:5c Stretch Out Your Hand

**COOPERATING WITH GRACE.** CHRYSOSTOM: I exhort you that you not carelessly slumber so as to leave everything to God. Nor, when diligent in your endeavors, imagine that by your own exertions the whole work is achieved. God does not will that we should be indolent. For God does not do the whole work by himself by fiat. Nor is it his will that we should be entirely self-sufficient. For God does not commit the whole work to us alone.[18] THE GOSPEL OF ST. MATTHEW, HOMILY 82.[19]

### 3:5d His Hand Was Restored

**STRETCH OUT YOUR HAND FOR THE POOR.** ATHANASIUS:[20] But Jesus, deeply grieved in heart at the hardness of their hearts, said in effect: "Let the ones who see continue to see. Let the ones who refuse to hear do what they want to do. Let the ones who are hard in heart become stone. But let your right hand become full and tender. Rise, beg no longer."[21] . . . In effect Jesus was saying: "Do not continue to beg because of having a withered hand, but after you finally have received it healthy and whole and have begun to work, stretch out your hand to the poor.[22] Rise up and stand in their midst. Become a marvel to those who see. In you the struggle concerning the sabbath is finally being contested. Stand in their midst, so that the ones who are lame in their

legs might stand. . . . Stretch out your hand. I am not touching you so that they may not bring a charge against me. I am speaking with a speech so that they may not think that touching is an act of work. God did not say, 'Do not speak on the sabbath.' But if speech becomes an act of work, let the one who has spoken be an object of amazement. Stretch out your hand." . . . While the withered hand was restored, the withered minds of the onlookers were not. For they went out and immediately, according to the reading,[23] were debating what they would do to Jesus. Are you debating what you will do? Worship him as God. Worship the wonder worker. Worship one who worked good things on behalf of another.[24] He did not add plasters; he was not tenderizing with lotions. He did not apply medical ointments. He did this work openly, standing in their midst, and not in a hidden way, so that some might retort: "He applied a plant; he added a plaster." HOMILIES 28.[25]

---

[18]Cf. Ps 146:5; Is 41:10; 50:7; Acts 26:22. [19]TLG 2062.152, 58.742.57-743.5; GMI 59*. Neither should we leave everything to God as if God required nothing of ourselves, nor should we leave everything to ourselves as if God did not supply grace for the will. [20]Attributed to Athanasius. [21]Cf. Mt 13:15. [22]Cf. Mk 3:5. [23]Cf. Mk 3:6. [24]As Jesus worked openly to heal, so we are to show forth our healing openly through our worship. [25]TLG 2035.069, 28.165.37-44; 165.48-168.1; 168.2-24. cf. PG 28.144-68; Budge, Coptic Homilies. The withered minds of the beholders remained untouched by the miracle.

---

## 3:7-12 JESUS HEALS THE MULTITUDES

[7]*Jesus withdrew with his disciples to the sea, and a great multitude from Galilee followed; also from Judea* [8]*and Jerusalem and Idumea and from beyond the Jordan and from about Tyre*

*and Sidon a great multitude, hearing all that he did, came to him. ⁹And he told his disciples to have a boat ready for him because of the crowd, lest they should crush him; ¹⁰for he had healed many, so that all who had diseases pressed upon him to touch him. ¹¹And whenever the unclean spirits beheld him, they fell down before him and cried out, "You are the Son of God." ¹²And he strictly ordered them not to make him known.*

**OVERVIEW:** Far better, Augustine maintains, to touch him by faith than to touch him with the hand alone. Note that even when beholding and confessing Christ verbally, the demonic powers were evidencing no love. The devils may believe and tremble, but they do not respond in love (AUGUSTINE).

### 3:10 They Pressed upon Him to Touch Him

**TOUCHING HIM BY FAITH.** AUGUSTINE: It is by faith that we touch Jesus. And far better to touch him by faith than to touch or handle him with the hands only and not by faith. It was no great thing to merely touch him manually. Even his oppressors doubtless touched him when they apprehended him, bound him, and crucified him, but by their ill-motivated touch they lost precisely what they were laying hold of. O worldwide church! It is by touching him faithfully that your "faith has made you whole."[1] SERMONS, ON EASTER 148.[2]

### 3:11 The Unclean Spirits Fell Down Before Him and Cried Out, "You Are the Son of God"

**THE ABSENCE OF CHARITY IN DEMONIC CONFESSION.** AUGUSTINE: Both the devils and the

faithful confessed Christ. "Thou art Christ, the Son of the living God,"[3] said Peter. "We know who thou art. Thou art the Son of God,"[4] said the devils. I hear a similar confession, but I do not find a similar charity. In one there is love, in another fear. He is lovely to those who are sons. He is terrible to those who are not sons. ON THE PSALMS 50.2.[5]

**FAITH WORKS BY LOVE.** AUGUSTINE: The "faith that works by love,"[6] is not the same faith that demons have. "For the devils also believe and tremble,"[7] but do they love? If they had not believed,[8] they would not have said: "You are the holy one of God" or "You are the Son of God."[9] But if they had loved, they would not have said: "What have we to do with you?"[10] LETTER 194, TO SIXTUS.[11]

---

[1]Cf. Is 1:10-18; Mt 9:22; Mk 5:34; 10:52; Lk 8:48; Jn 20:29. [2]Cetedoc 0284, 246.116.300.83; *GMI* 61-62**. To touch him with the hand but without faith is of no avail; but with faith to touch him is healing. [3]Mt 16:16. [4]Mk 3:11; Lk 4:41. [5]Cetedoc 0283, 38.49.2.40; NPNF 1 8:178. Even when beholding and confessing Christ, the demonic powers lacked charity. The devils may believe and tremble, but they do not respond in love. [6]Gal 5:6. [7]Jas 2:19. [8]The demons believed in the sense that they believed that he was Son of God, yet not so as to trust in his grace. [9]Mk 3:11-12; Lk 4:34, 41. [10]Mt 8:29; Mk 5:7; Lk 8:28. [11]Cetedoc 0262, 194.57.3.185.5; FC 30:308-9*.

# 3:13-19 THE CALL OF THE TWELVE

[13]*And he went up on the mountain, and called to him those whom he desired; and they came to him.* [14]*And he appointed twelve,[k] to be with him, and to be sent out to preach* [15]*and have authority to cast out demons:* [16]*Simon whom he surnamed Peter;* [17]*James the son of Zebedee and John the brother of James, whom he surnamed Boanerges, that is, sons of thunder;* [18]*Andrew, and Philip, and Bartholomew, and Matthew, and Thomas, and James the son of Alphaeus, and Thaddaeus, and Simon the Cananaean,* [19]*and Judas Iscariot, who betrayed him.*

k Other ancient authorities add *whom also he named apostles*   x Other ancient authorities read *demons.* [16]*So he appointed the twelve: Simon*

**OVERVIEW:** As the Lord renamed the patriarchs when they passed through certain trials, so Jesus renamed the disciples as they journeyed with him (CHRYSOSTOM). The very physiology of thunder exhibits the explosiveness of the lives of those claimed by the gospel, as seen in those Jesus called "sons of thunder" (BASIL), whose preaching was made thunderous by divine power (EUSEBIUS). The renaming of persons implies a reversal of identity (BEDE). Meanwhile the eternal does not change (ORIGEN).

## 3:16 Simon Whom He Surnamed Peter

**THE ALTERING OF NAMES.** ORIGEN: A name[1] is a designation that sums up and describes the particular character of the one named. . . . For when the character of "Abram" was changed, he was called "Abraham."[2] So when "Simon" was changed, he was called "Peter."[3] And when "Saul" stopped persecuting Christ, he was named "Paul."[4] In the case of God, however, whose character is eternally unchangeable and always remains unaltered, there is always a single name. It is that spoken of him in Exodus: "I am."[5] ON PRAYER 24.2.[6]

## 3:17 Sons of Thunder

**THE SHOUTING OF HEAVEN.** EUSEBIUS: Thunder here refers to the preaching of the gospel. For as a heavenly shout occurs like a voice of thunder, surpassing all human power, in the same way also the preaching of the gospel, which is a heavenly happening, does not consist of human strength. The gospel did not fill the world by human planning, but by divine power. COMMENTARY ON PSALMS 23.[7]

**THE EXPLOSIVENESS OF LIVES CLAIMED BY THE GOSPEL.** BASIL: Thunder[8] is produced when a dry and violent wind, closed up in the hollows of a cloud and violently hurled around in the cavities of the clouds, seeks a passage to the outside. The clouds, offering resistance under the excessive pressure, produce that harsh sound from the friction of the wind. But when,

---

[1]As viewed in ancient times.  [2]Gen 17:5.  [3]Mk 3:16; Jn 1:42.  [4]Acts 13:9.  [5]Ex 3:14.  [6]TLG 2042.008, 24.1-2, 9-15; CWS 129*.  [7]TLG 2018.034, 23.897.31-38; Ps 77:18 (76:19 LXX).  [8]What follows is both a scientific explanation of thunder, in Basil's view, and a metaphorical exploration of what it means poetically.

like bubbles distended by the air, they are unable to resist and endure any longer, but are violently torn apart and give the air a passage to the outer breeze, they produce the noises of the thunder. And this normally causes the flash of lightning. It is the Lord who is upon the waters and who arouses the mighty noises of the thunder, causing such an exceedingly great noise through the delicate medium of air.[9] The eloquent teaching which leads from baptism to sanctification is like thunder to the soul. That the gospel is like thunder is made evident by the disciples who were given a new name by the Lord: sons of thunder.[10] HOMILY 13.3.[11]

**RENAMING ELICITS A PERPETUAL MEMORY.** CHRYSOSTOM: James and John his brother he called "sons of thunder."[12] Why? To show that he was the same One who, in giving the old covenant, altered names, who called Abram "Abraham,"[13] and Sarai "Sarah"[14] and Jacob "Israel."[15] . . . It was also a custom of the patriarchs to give descriptive names to persons, as Leah did.[16] This is not mere arbitrariness, but in order that they may have a hallmark to remind them of the goodness of God. By this means, a perpetual memory of the prophecy conveyed by the name sounds forth in the ears of those who receive it. HOMILIES ON ST. JOHN, HOMILY 19.[17]

## 3:18 And Matthew

**THE RENAMING OF MATTHEW.** BEDE: We must not pass over the fact that Matthew had two names, for he was also called Levi, and that name too bears witness to the grace granted to him. Levi means "added"[18] or "taken up," signifying that he was "taken up" through being chosen by the Lord, and "added" to the number of the apostolic band. Mark and Luke generously chose to use this name alone, so as to not make glaringly conspicuous his former way of life, for he was now their companion in the work of the gospel.[19] In setting down the list of the twelve apostles, they simply called him Matthew, not mentioning Levi.[20] Matthew himself, on the other hand (in accord with what is written, "The just man is the first accuser of himself; his friend came and searched him out"),[21] calls himself by his ordinary name when telling of being called from his tax-collector's place, but adds pointedly "the publican"[22]—"Thomas," he says, "and Matthew the publican." In this way he offers to publicans and sinners greater confidence in securing their salvation. HOMILIES ON THE GOSPELS 1.21.[23]

---

[9]Cf. Is 29:6. [10]Mk 3:17. [11]TLG 2040.018, 29.289.49-292.21; FC 46:200-201*. [12]Mk 3:17. [13]Cf. Gen 17:5. [14]Cf. Gen 17:15. [15]Cf. Gen 32:28. [16]Cf. Gen 29:32; 30:11, 13, 18, 20. [17]TLG 2062.153, 5.9.122.24-29, 34-39; NPNF 1 14:68*. Like Yahweh, who renamed the patriarchs when they passed through certain trials, Jesus renamed the disciples as a perpetual memorial of his presence. This renaming motif echoes pivotal transformations in the history of salvation. [18]Or "a joining." [19]Mk 2:14; Lk 5:27. [20]Mk 3:18; Lk 6:15. [21]Prov 18:17. [22]Mt 10:3. [23]Cetedoc 1367, 1.21.34; HOG 1:206-07**. Mark's report of Matthew generously avoided the disreputable term *publican*, which Matthew penitently applied to himself.

## 3:19-27 ACCUSATIONS AGAINST JESUS

*[19]Then he went home; [20]and the crowd came together again, so that they could not even eat. [21]And when his family heard it, they went out to seize him, for people were saying, "He is beside himself." [22]And the scribes who came down from Jerusalem said, "He is possessed by Beelzebul, and by the prince of demons he casts out the demons." [23]And he called them to him, and said to them in parables, "How can Satan cast out Satan? [24]If a kingdom is divided against itself, that kingdom cannot stand. [25]And if a house is divided against itself, that house will not be able to stand. [26]And if Satan has risen up against himself and is divided, he cannot stand, but is coming to an end. [27]But no one can enter a strong man's house and plunder his goods, unless he first binds the strong man; then indeed he may plunder his house."*

**OVERVIEW:** It was necessary within the economy of salvation that Satan be bound up with the same chains with which he had bound humanity (IRENAEUS, AUGUSTINE). Satan had willfully led humanity by deceit into bondage of the will (IRENAEUS). The God-man had to act fairly to bind up the will of the strong man. For this purpose Christ came to plunder the strong man's goods—the devil's hold upon the ungodly. The demonic purpose was not just to enter into the body or senses as such but to strike at the innermost volitional center of the self to make it yield to idolatry. Hence the one guilty of no sin loosed the grip of the devil upon sinners who were being held in bondage to sin. In this way the devil was conquered precisely at the point at which he seemed to be conquering (AUGUSTINE). In his struggle against demonic powers, even his family wondered if Jesus had gone berserk (JEROME). The indwelling Spirit brings into unity those who had been divided against themselves (AUGUSTINE).

### 3:21 When His Family Heard It, They Went Out to Seize Him, for People Were Saying, "He Is Beside Himself"

**HIS WORRIED KINFOLK.** JEROME: In the gospel we read that even his kinsfolk desired to bind him as one of weak mind. His opponents also reviled him saying, "You are a Samaritan and have a devil."[1] LETTER 108, TO EUSTOCHIUM.[2]

### 3:23 How Can Satan Cast Out Satan?

**THE DEMONIC INTENT TO DOMINATE THE WILL.** AUGUSTINE: Now as for the Lord's saying: "Satan cannot drive out Satan,"[3] lest perhaps anyone using the name of some of the lowest powers when driving out a demon should think this opinion of the Lord's to be false, let him understand the point of this saying: Satan does spare the body or the senses of the body, but he tempts the senses for the pur-

---

[1]Jn 8:48. [2]Cetedoc 0620, 108.55.19.333.20; NPNF 2 6:205. Even his family thought Jesus may have gone berserk as he was attracting great numbers from far away to be cured. [3]Mk 3:23.

pose of dominating the will of the man in question, in a triumph of greater import, through the error of impiety. Satan does not strike for the body as such, but rather for the innermost self in order to work in him in the manner described by the apostle: "according to the prince of the power of this air, who is now active in the sons of disobedience."[4] For Satan was not troubling and tormenting the senses of their bodies, nor was he battering their bodies, but he was reigning in their wills, or better, in their covetousness. EIGHTY-THREE DIFFERENT QUESTIONS, QUESTION 79.2.[5]

### 3:25 A House Divided Against Itself

**THE SPIRIT UNITES THOSE DIVIDED AGAINST THEMSELVES.** AUGUSTINE: Mention has been made of the unclean spirit whom the Lord shows to be divided against himself.[6] The Holy Spirit, however, is not divided against himself. Rather he makes those whom he gathers together undivided against themselves, by dwelling within those who have been cleansed, that they may be like those of whom it is written in the Acts of the Apostles, "The multitude of them that believed were of one heart and of one soul."[7] SERMONS ON THE NEW TESTAMENT LESSONS 21.35.[8]

### 3:27a The Strong Man's House

**THE DEVIL'S GOODS.** AUGUSTINE: The "strong man" in this passage means the devil who was able to hold the human race in bondage. By his "goods," which Christ was coming to plunder, the devil was keeping for himself those who would in time become faithful, but had remained in the clutches of ungodliness and various sins. It was for the purpose of binding up this strong man that John, in the Apocalypse, saw "an angel coming down from heaven, having the key of the abyss and a great chain in his hand. And he laid hold on the dragon, the ancient serpent, who is the devil and Satan, and bound him for a thousand years."[9] The angel checked and repressed his power to seduce and possess those destined to be set free. THE CITY OF GOD 20.7.[10]

**WEAKNESS MADE STRONG.** AUGUSTINE: He conquered the devil first by righteousness, and then by power. First by righteousness, because he who had no sin[11] was slain by him most unjustly. But then by power, because having been dead he lived again, never afterwards to die.[12] For Christ was crucified, not through immortal power, but through the weakness which he took upon him in mortal flesh.[13] Of this weakness the apostle nevertheless says, "God's weakness is stronger than human strength."[14] ON THE TRINITY 13.14.15.[15]

**CROSS AS VICTORY.** AUGUSTINE: It is not difficult, therefore, to see how the devil was conquered when he, who was slain by him, rose again.[16] But there is something greater and more profound of comprehension: to see how the devil was conquered precisely when he was thought to be conquering, namely, when Christ was crucified. For at that moment the blood of him who had no sin at all, was shed for the

---

[4]Eph 2:2. [5]Cetedoc 0289, 79.54; FC 70:202*. Satan's purpose is not just to enter into the body or senses as such, but to attach the innermost part of the self for the purpose of dominating the will to yield to idolatry. [6]The issue being discussed is how the Holy Spirit unites those who have been inwardly divided by the demonic. [7]Acts 4:32. [8]Cetedoc 0284, 71.75.104.808; NPNF 1 6:330; Dominican ed. Sermon 71.35, WSA 3 3:258. [9]Cf. Rev 20:1-2. [10]Cetedoc 0313, 48.20.7.44; FC 24:266*. [11]Cf. 2 Cor 5:21. [12]Rom 6:9. [13]Cf. 2 Cor 13:4. [14]Cf. 1 Cor 1:25. [15]Cetedoc 0329, 50A.13.14.35; NPNF 1 3:177**. He conquered the devil by that righteousness which, having no sin, was slain; and by the power of his resurrection. [16]The issue is how the devil was conquered precisely at the point where he seemed to be conquering.

remission of our sins.[17] The devil deservedly held those whom he had bound by sin to the condition of death. So it happened that One who was guilty of no sin freed them justly from this condemnation.[18] The strong man was conquered by this paradoxical justice and bound by this chain, that his vessels[19] might be taken away. Those vessels which had been vessels of wrath were turned into vessels of mercy.[20] ON THE TRINITY 13.15.19.[21]

### 3:27b Then Indeed He May Plunder His House

**THE SAME CHAINS.** IRENAEUS: The adversary enticed humanity to transgress our maker's law, and thereby got us into his clutches.[22] Yet his power consisted only in tempting the human will toward trespass and apostasy. With these chains he bound up the human will.[23] This is why in the economy of salvation it was necessary that he be bound with the same chains by which he had bound humanity.[24] It would be through a man that humanity would be set free to return to the Lord,[25] leaving the adversary in those bonds by which he himself had been fettered, that is, sin. For when Satan is bound, man is set free; since "none can enter a strong man's house and spoil his goods, unless he first bind the strong man himself."[26] It is in this way that he became exposed as the opposer of the Word who made all things, and subdued by his command. The new man showed him to be a fugitive from the law, and an apostate from God. He then was securely bound as a fugitive, and his goods[27] hauled away. These goods are those who had been in bondage, whom he had unjustly used for his own purposes. So it was a just means by which he was led captive, who had led humanity into captivity unjustly. In this way humanity was rescued from the clutches of its possessor by the tender mercy of God the Father, who had compassion on his own handiwork, and gave to it salvation, restoring it by means of the Word, Christ, in order that humanity might learn from this actual event that they receive incorruptibility not of themselves, but by the free gift of God.[28] AGAINST HERESIES 5.21.3.[29]

---

[17]Cf. Mt 26:28; 1 Jn 3:5.. [18]Cf. Heb 2:14. [19]Booty. [20]Rom 9:22-23. [21]Cetedoc 0329, 50A.13.15.1; FC 45:396-97. [22]Cf. Gen 3:1-6. [23]At issue is why in the plan of salvation it was necessary that the devil be bound up by one truly human. [24]Namely, through his own twisted willing. [25]Cf. Rom 5:18. [26]Mt 12:29; Mk 3:27. [27]Humanity in bondage. [28]Cf. Rom 5:16. [29]AHR 2:383-84; ANF 1:550**. As Satan had unfairly led humanity into bondage of the will, so the God-man had fairly bound up the will of the strong man.

## 3:28-30 BLASPHEMY AGAINST THE HOLY SPIRIT

[28]"Truly, I say to you, all sins will be forgiven the sons of men, and whatever blasphemies they utter; [29]but whoever blasphemes against the Holy Spirit never has forgiveness, but is guilty of an eternal sin," [30]for they had said, "He has an unclean spirit."

**OVERVIEW:** The Spirit dwells in those who live by faith. But those who once having been counted worthy to share in the Holy Spirit and then having finally and decisively turned their backs from grace are by this act said to have blasphemed against the Holy Spirit (ORIGEN). Contempt of the Holy Spirit is defiance of the ground of the Christian faith and life, for it is the Spirit who offers testimony to Christ (NOVATIAN). The Holy Spirit is God himself enabling our faith. God the Spirit is not only the one whom we worship but the one by whom we worship (GREGORY NAZIANZEN). The text does not suggest that blasphemy makes repentance impossible (AUGUSTINE).

### 3:28 Whoever Blasphemes Against the Holy Spirit

**TURNING AWAY FROM FAITH.** ORIGEN: The power of God the Father and God the Son is at work in the whole of creation.[1] The saints are those who are fully receiving life in the Holy Spirit.[2] Accordingly it is said, "No man can say that Jesus is the Lord except in the Holy Spirit."[3] However unworthy the apostles might have been, they were told: "You shall receive power when the Holy Spirit is come upon you."[4] This is what is referred to by the phrase, "he who has sinned against the Son of Man is worthy of forgiveness."[5] Even if one at times ceases to live according to this divine word, even if one falls into ignorance or folly, the way is not blocked to true penitence and forgiveness. But one who has once been counted worthy to share in life in the Holy Spirit and then finally turns back again in apostasy is by this very act and deed said to have blasphemed against the Holy Spirit.[6] ON FIRST PRINCIPLES 1.3.7.[7]

**THOSE SO INDWELT WOULD NOT CURSE JESUS.** NOVATIAN: No one who is indwelt by the Holy Spirit can imagine saying "anathema" to Jesus.[8] No one in the Spirit would deny that Christ is the Son of God, or reject God as Creator. No believer would utter such things contrary to Scriptures, or substitute alien or sacrilegious ordinances contrary to moral principles. But if anyone shamelessly blasphemes against this same Holy Spirit, he "does not have forgiveness, either in this world or in the world to come."[9] For it is the Spirit who through the apostles offers testimony to Christ,[10] who in the martyrs manifests unwavering faith, and who in the lives of the chaste embraces the admirable continence of sealed chastity.[11] It is the Spirit who, among the whole church, guards the laws of the Lord's teaching uncorrupted and untainted, destroys heretics, corrects those in error, reproves unbelievers, reveals impostors, and corrects the wicked.[12] THE TRINITY 29.[13]

**THE SPIRIT IS GOD.** GREGORY NAZIANZEN: He[14] is the subject, not the object, of hallowing, apportioning, participating, filling, sustaining. We share in him; he shares in nothing.[15] He is our inheritance, he is glorified, counted together with Father and Son. He is a dire warning to us, the "finger of God."[16] The Spirit is, like God, a "fire."[17] This means that the Holy

---

[1]Cf. Rom 1:20. [2]Cf. Rom 8:10; Gal 6:8. [3]1 Cor 12:3. [4]Acts 1:8. [5]Mt 12:32. [6]Mt 12:31-32; Mk 3:29. [7]OBP 176; OFP 36-37**. [8]1 Cor 12:3. [9]Cf. Mt 12:32; Lk 12:10. [10]Cf. Eph 3:5. [11]For further reference to voluntary continence as a form of asceticism, particularly in response to pagan eroticism, see EEC 930 and EEC 161. [12]2 Cor 11:2. [13]Cetedoc 0071, 29.98; FC 67:104**. For this reason the indwelling Holy Spirit is pivotal to every aspect of the Christian life. [14]At issue in this oration is whether the Holy Spirit is the object of our worship or the subject who makes our worship possible. [15]In the sense that nothing external is necessary for his being. [16]Cf. Lk 11:20. [17]Cf. Acts 2:3.

Spirit is of the same essential nature as the Father.[18] The Spirit is the very One who created us and creates us anew through baptism and resurrection. The Spirit knows all things,[19] teaches all things,[20] moves where and when and as strongly as he wills.[21] He leads,[22] speaks,[23] sends,[24] and separates those who are vexed and tempted. He reveals,[25] illumines,[26] gives life, or better said, he is himself light and life.[27] He makes us his temple,[28] he sanctifies,[29] he makes us complete.[30] He both goes before baptism and follows after it.[31] All that the Godhead actively performs, the Spirit performs. ORATION 31, ON THE HOLY SPIRIT 29.[32]

**REPENTANCE FOR BLASPHEMY.** AUGUSTINE: It is not that this was a blasphemy which under no circumstances could be forgiven, for even this shall be forgiven if right repentance follows it. SERMONS ON NEW TESTAMENT LESSONS 21.35.[33]

---

[18]The Holy Spirit is truly God, of the same nature as God.  [19]Cf. Rom 8:26; Eph 3:4-5.  [20]Cf. Neh 9:20; Is 11:2; Jn 14:26.  [21]Cf. Jn 3:8.  [22]Cf. Ps 143:10; Jn 16:13.  [23]Cf. 2 Sam 23:2; Ezek 11:5; Mt 10:20; Mk 13:11; Jn 16:13; 1 Tim 4:1.  [24]Cf. Is 61:1; Acts 13:4.  [25]Cf. 1 Cor 2:10; Eph 3:5.  [26]Cf. Joel 2:28.  [27]Cf. Job 27:3; 33:4; Ps 104:30; Dan 5:14; Eph 2:1-10.  [28]Cf. 1 Cor 3:16.  [29]Cf. 1 Cor 6:11; 1 Thess 5:23; 2 Thess 2:13; 1 Pet 1:2.  [30]Cf. Is 11:2; 32:15.  [31]Cf. Mk 1:8, 10.  [32]TLG 2022.011, 29.17-29; FGFR 296-97**. The Holy Spirit is God himself enabling our faith: not merely the object of our worship but the one by whose power and inspiration we worship.  [33]Cetedoc 0284, 71.75.104.808; NPNF 1 6:330*; Dominican ed., Sermon 71:35; WSA 3 3:268. Assuming a right repentance, even this blasphemy can be forgiven.

---

## 3:31-35 WHO ARE MY MOTHER AND MY BROTHERS?

[31]*And his mother and his brothers came; and standing outside they sent to him and called him.* [32]*And a crowd was sitting about him; and they said to him, "Your mother and your brothers[1] are outside, asking for you."* [33]*And he replied, "Who are my mother and my brothers?"* [34]*And looking around on those who sat about him, he said, "Here are my mother and my brothers!* [35]*Whoever does the will of God is my brother, and sister, and mother."*

1 Other early authorities add *and your sisters*

---

**OVERVIEW:** Mary was more blessed in receiving the faith of Christ than in conceiving the flesh of Christ. She was blessed because she kept the Word of God, not merely because she gave birth. Mary's closeness to Jesus as a natural mother would have been little help for her salvation if she had not borne Christ in her heart. From this passage we learn to view earthly kinship in relation to heavenly kinship (AUGUSTINE). To the Lord's family belong all who do the will of the Father (PSEUDO-CLEMENT).

### 3:32 *His Mother and His Brothers Came*

**ORDERING THE RELATION TO FAMILY.** AUGUS-TINE: It is he who said that no one belongs to his family except those who do the will of his Father. To be sure, he graciously included Mary herself in this number, for she was doing the will of his Father. Thus he spurned the earthly name of his mother in comparison to heavenly kinship. . . . Do not be ungrateful, pay your duty of gratitude to your mother, repay earthly favors by spiritual ones, temporal by eternal ones. LETTER 243, TO LAETUS.[1]

### 3:34 *Here Are My Mother and My Brothers!*

**BELONGING TO THE FAMILY.** PSEUDO-CLEM-ENT: Let us then praise him, not with the mouth only, but from the heart, so that he may accept us as sons. For the Lord said, "My brothers are those who do the will of my Father."[2] So let us do the will of the Father who called us, that we may live peaceably within this family, where our inclination[3] shall be the pursuit of virtue. 2 CLEMENT 9.10-10.1.[4]

### 3:35 *Whoever Does the Will of God Is My Brother, Sister, Mother*

**WHETHER MARY WAS CLOSER TO HIM AS PARENT OR BELIEVER.** AUGUSTINE: What else does he here teach us, than to prefer to kinship "after the flesh" our descent "after the Spirit."[5] He teaches that persons are united by nearness

of spirit to those who are just and holy, and that by obeying and following they cleave to their teaching and conduct. Therefore Mary is more blessed in receiving the faith of Christ than in conceiving the flesh of Christ. For to the one who said, "Blessed is the womb, which bore you!" he himself answered: "Blessed are they who hear the Word of God and keep it."[6] Concerning his own brothers, his own relatives after the flesh, who at first did not believe in him,[7] he found dubious advantage in being their kin. As for Mary, her nearness as a mother would have been little help for her salvation if she had not borne Christ in her heart in a more blessed manner than in the flesh.[8] ON VIRGINITY 3.[9]

**THE GROUND OF MARY'S BLESSEDNESS.** AU-GUSTINE: She did the Father's will. It was this in her that the Lord magnified, not merely that her flesh gave birth to flesh. . . . When he said, "Blessed are they who hear the Word of God and keep it,"[10] he was in effect saying: "My mother whom you have called blessed is blessed for the reason that she keeps the Word of God, not that the Word was made flesh in her and dwelt among us,[11] but that she keeps the very Word of God through which she was made and which was made flesh in her." TRACTATE ON JOHN 10.3.2.[12]

---

[1]Cetedoc 0262, 243.57.9.576.3; FC 32:224-25**. [2]Mt 12:50; Lk 8:21. [3]Above all earthly commitments, including domestic duties. [4]TLG 1271.002, 9.10.1-10.1.2; LCC 1:197**. [5]Cf. Rom 8:1-5; Gal 4:29. [6]Lk 11:27-28. [7]Jn 7:4. [8]Mt 3:8-10; Lk 11:27-28; Rom 9:1-8. [9]Cetedoc 0300, 3.237.5; GMI 74**. [10]Lk 11:28, in response to the exclamation "Blessed is the womb that bore you, and the breasts that nursed you." [11]Jn 1:14. [12]Cetedoc 0278, 10.3.8; FC 78:214**.

## 4:1-9 THE PARABLE OF THE SOWER

[1]*Again he began to teach beside the sea. And a very large crowd gathered about him, so that he got into a boat and sat in it on the sea; and the whole crowd was beside the sea on the land.* [2]*And he taught them many things in parables, and in his teaching he said to them:* [3]*"Listen! A sower went out to sow.* [4]*And as he sowed, some seed fell along the path, and the birds came and devoured it.* [5]*Other seed fell on rocky ground, where it had not much soil, and immediately it sprang up, since it had no depth of soil;* [6]*and when the sun rose it was scorched, and since it had no root it withered away.* [7]*Other seed fell among thorns and the thorns grew up and choked it, and it yielded no grain.* [8]*And other seeds fell into good soil and brought forth grain, growing up and increasing and yielding thirtyfold and sixtyfold and a hundredfold."* [9]*And he said, "He who has ears to hear, let him hear."*

**OVERVIEW:** Those who obsess about riches are like fields of thistles and thorns that do not allow the seeds of the kingdom to grow (THE SHEPHERD OF HERMAS). Though God is everywhere, he comes especially near to us in our human nature by sowing the seed of his Word through the incarnation in the ground of our human souls (CLEMENT OF ROME). The seed was lost not through the fault of the sower but through the unreadiness of the soil to receive it (CHRYSOSTOM). Mark withheld elaborate analytical exposition of the parables because the things signified by them were beyond the power of ordinary words to express (ORIGEN).

### 4:2 He Taught Them Many Things in Parables

**PARABLES INEXHAUSTIBLE.** ORIGEN: We try to think in a general way about every parable,[1] the elaborate interpretation of which has not been recorded by the Evangelists, remembering that Jesus explained all things to his own disciples privately.[2] The writers of the Gospels have withheld any detailed exposition of the parables, because the things signified by them were beyond the power of words to express. Not even the whole world itself could contain the books that might be written to fully clarify and develop the parables. But it may happen that a receptive heart will grasp something of them. Purity of intent enables greater discernment of the parables, that they might become written on the heart by the Spirit of the living God.[3] But someone might then reply that we act with impiety when we want to give the parables symbolic meaning, as if we had the authority to expound what is secret and mystical. This is sometimes claimed even in cases where one might suppose that we had some reasonable knowledge of their meaning. But to this we must respond that, if there are those who have obtained some gift of accurate apprehension of these things, they know what they ought to do. But as for us, we readily acknowledge that we

---

[1]For a helpful survey of patristic interpretation of the parables, see EEC 2:648-49. [2]Mk 4:34. [3]Cf. 2 Cor 3:3.

fall short of the ability to see into the depth of the things here signified. We do better not to venture to commit to writing those things of which, even after much examination and inquiry, we have only some crass perception, whether by grace or by the power of our own minds. But some basic things, for the sake of our own intellectual discipline, and that of those who may chance to read them, we are permitted to some extent to set forth. COMMENTARY ON MATTHEW 14.12.[4]

## 4:3 A Sower Went Out to Sow

**THE BURIAL OF THE SEED.** CLEMENT OF ROME: Think of the various ways, dear friends, by which the master points us toward the coming resurrection, by which the Lord Jesus Christ was made the firstfruit when he raised him from the dead.[5] Let us observe, dear friends, how something like resurrection is so often anticipated in the course of nature. Day and night, for example: the night falls asleep, and day arises; day departs, and night returns. Or consider the planting of crops: How and in what manner does the sowing take place? The sower goes forth and casts into the earth each of the seeds.[6] They fall into the dry and bare ground and decay. Then out of their decay the majesty of God's providence raises them up, and from being one seed, many grow up and bring forth fruit. Even more dramatically, recall that remarkable wonder which has been reported in eastern regions in the vicinity of Arabia, of a bird named Phoenix.[7] This bird is said to be a unique species, living perhaps five hundred years. When the time of its dissolution and death arrives, it makes for itself a coffinlike nest of frankincense and myrrh and the other spices, into which, its time being completed, it enters and dies. But as the flesh decays, a certain worm is born, which is nourished by the juices of the dead bird and eventually grows wings. Then, when it has grown strong, it takes up that coffinlike nest containing the bones of its parent, and carrying them away, makes its way from the country of Arabia to Egypt, to the city of Heliopolis. There, in broad daylight in the sight of all, it flies to the altar of the sun and deposits them there, and then sets out on its return, which the priests who examine records think occurs at the end of the five hundredth year. With all these indications in nature, why should it surprise us that the creator of the universe might bring about the resurrection of those who have served him with holiness in the assurance of a good faith,[8] seeing that he shows to us even by a bird the magnificence of his promise? I CLEMENT 24.1-26.1.[9]

**GOING OUT TO SOW.** CHRYSOSTOM: What is the meaning of this parable? He went out to sow his seed. From where could he "go out"

---

[4]TLG 2042.030, 14.12.17-57; cf. ANF 9:502. Those who interpret do well readily to acknowledge that they themselves fall short of the ability to see into the depth of what the parables signify, and in any event not everything one seems to grasp should be committed to writing. [5]Cf. 1 Pet 1:3. [6]Cf. Mt 13:3-9; Mk 4:3-9; Lk 8:5-8. [7]"The story of the phoenix, well known in antiquity, was widely used (with varying levels of credulity) by early Christian writers; sanction for this usage was found in Ps 92:12 (91:13 LXX), AF 43n. Paul Finney notes that the story of the phoenix probably originated in Asia, but in later editions of the legend Syria and Egypt play an important role. It was a legend "adopted by many cultures throughout the ancient world, from the Mediterranean to China." As in Clement's letter to the Corinthians, many early Christians "saw in the phoenix a pagan anticipation of Christianity." The image of the phoenix occurs on early Christian sarcophagi, mosaics and paintings (see EEC 732). [8]Cf. Lk 14:14; Jn 5:29. [9]TLG 1271.001, 24.1-26.1; AF 24*. Like the turning of night to day, as in the primeval story of the phoenix, we are taught the resurrection, as when seeds are buried, decay, rise and bring forth fruit. So nature in some ways providentially reflects and anticipates the miracle of the resurrection of the body.

who is present everywhere, and fills all places? He went out, not into a place, but into a life and into a historic dispensation wherein he saved us, being brought close to us by reason of assuming our flesh. Since we could not enter in, for our sins had shut the door to us, he came out to us. . . . He came to till and to take care of the earth: to sow the word of compassion. For here he calls his teaching seed, the souls of men a ploughed field, and himself the sower. ON TEMPERANCE.[10]

## 4:4 Some Seed Fell Along the Path

INDISCRIMINATE SOWING. CHRYSOSTOM: As the sower fairly and indiscriminately disperses seed broadly over all his field, so does God offer gifts to all,[11] making no distinction between rich and poor, wise and foolish, lazy or diligent, brave or cowardly. He addresses everyone, fulfilling his part, although knowing the results beforehand. . . . Why then, tell me, was so much of the seed lost? Not through the sower, but through the ground that received it—meaning the soul that did not listen. . . . Even though more seed would be lost than survive, the disciples were not to lose heart. For it is the way of the Lord never to stop sowing the seed, even when he knows beforehand that some of it will not respond. But how can it be reasonable, one asks, to sow among the thorns, or on the rock, or alongside the road? Maybe it is not reasonable insofar as it pertains only to seeds and earth, for the bare rock is not likely to turn into tillable soil, and the roadside will remain roadside and the thorns, thorns. But in the case of free wills and their reasonable instruction, this kind of sowing is praiseworthy. For the rocky soul can in time turn into rich soil. Among souls, the wayside may come no longer to be trampled by all that pass, and

may become a fertile field. The thorns may be destroyed and the seed enjoy full growth. For had this not been impossible, this sower would not have sown. And even if no change whatever occurs in the soul, this is no fault of the sower, but of those who are unwilling to be changed. He has done his part. THE GOSPEL OF ST. MATTHEW, HOMILY 44.5.1.[12]

## 4:6 Since It Had No Root It Withered Away

THE ROOT OF CORRUPTION IN THE WILL. CHRYSOSTOM: And if the young shoots of the wheat wither, that is not because of the heat, for he did not say that it withered because of the heat, but "because it had no roots."[13] And if that which he has taught us is choked, neither is it the fault of the thorns, but of those who allow them to grow. For you can, if you will, oppose their evil growth, and make fitting use of your resources. For this reason he says not "the world," but "the care of this world"; not "riches," but "the deceitfulness of riches." Let us put blame, not on created things, but on the corrupted will. ON TEMPERANCE.[14]

THE CAUSE OF WITHERING AWAY. CHRYSOSTOM: Now pay particular attention. There is not one single way of destruction. Rather there are various ways that differ from one another significantly. Some, like the seed along the roadside, are the coarse-minded, indifferent, and careless. Others, those on the rock, are like people who fail from weakness only. THE GOSPEL OF ST. MATTHEW, HOMILY 44.5.[15]

---

[10]TLG 2062.152, 57.467.26-33; SSGF 1:392*; PG 57.467-72. [11]Cf. Rom 5:15. [12]NPNF 1 10:281-82*; cf. TLG 2062.152, 57.467.53-58, 468.12-14, 23-42. [13]Mt 13:6; Mk 4:6. [14]TLG 2062.152, 57.469.2-12; SSGF 1:394. [15]NPNF 1 10:282*; TLG 2062.152, 57.468.43-47.

### 4:7 The Thorns Grew Up and Choked It, and It Yielded No Grain

**CHOKING OUT FRUITFULNESS.** THE SHEPHERD OF HERMAS: The thistles are the rich, and the thorns are those obsessed with business deals. They tend not to remain long with the servants of God. They wander away, choked by commercial preoccupations.[16] The rich cleave only with great difficulty to the servants of God, fearing lest someone might ask something of them. Such people, therefore, will enter the kingdom of God only with difficulty. You know how hard it is to walk through thistles with bare feet? Just that hard it will be for them to enter the kingdom of God.[17] THE SHEPHERD OF HERMAS 3.9.20.[18]

### 4:8 Yielding Thirtyfold and Sixtyfold and a Hundredfold

**READINESS TO RECEIVE.** CHRYSOSTOM: Why did one soil bear a hundred, one sixty, one thirty? The difference is the readiness of the ground, for even where the ground is good, differences remain in the readiness of soils. The fault lies not in the farmer or the seed, but in the condition of the land itself, its disposition to receive. THE GOSPEL OF ST. MATTHEW, HOMILY 44.6.[19]

**VARIED GIFTS.** CYRIL OF ALEXANDRIA: Note that Christ has recounted three ways of disaster, and that three likewise are the grades of glory. For the seed that fell upon the wayside was seized by the birds. That which sprang up on stony ground quickly perished. That which grew amid the thorns was choked. But the desirable good earth brought forth fruit, and with a threefold difference, as I have said; some a hundredfold, some sixty, and some thirtyfold. As the most learned Paul writes: "Everyone has his proper gift from God," one after this manner, another after that.[20] And we don't find the good actions of holy men to be all of equal merit. But it behooves us to strive earnestly after their better actions, and rise above the less worthy; so shall we be rewarded bountifully by Christ, to whom, with the Father and the Holy Ghost, be praise and glory for ever. Amen. COMMENTARY ON THE GOSPEL OF LUKE 8.5.9.[21]

---

[16]Cf. 1 Tim 6:9.  [17]Cf. Mt 19:23-24; Mk 10:23-25; Lk 18:25.  [18]TLG 1419.001, 97.1.1-3.1; ANF 2:50**; cf. AF 278.  [19]TLG 2062.152, 57.469.26-31; NPNF 1 10:282**. The readiness of the soil decisively affects the yield.  [20]1 Cor 7:7.  [21]SSGF 1:399; PG 72.628.

---

## 4:10-20 THE PURPOSE OF PARABLES

[10]And when he was alone, those who were about him with the twelve asked him concerning the parables. [11]And he said to them, "To you has been given the secret of the kingdom of God, but for those outside everything is in parables; [12]so that they may indeed see but not perceive, and may indeed hear but not understand; lest they should turn again, and be forgiven." [13]And he said to them, "Do you not understand this parable? How then will you understand all the para-

bles? ¹⁴*The sower sows the word.* ¹⁵*And these are the ones along the path, where the word is sown; when they hear, Satan immediately comes and takes away the word which is sown in them.* ¹⁶*And these in like manner are the ones sown upon rocky ground, who, when they hear the word, immediately receive it with joy;* ¹⁷*and they have no root in themselves, but endure for a while; then, when tribulation or persecution arises on account of the word, immediately they fall away.*ᵐ ¹⁸*And others are the ones sown among thorns; they are those who hear the word,* ¹⁹*but the cares of the world, and the delight in riches, and the desire for other things, enter in and choke the word, and it proves unfruitful.* ²⁰*But those that were sown upon the good soil are the ones who hear the word and accept it and bear fruit, thirtyfold and sixtyfold and a hundredfold."*

m Or *stumble*

**OVERVIEW:** Parables are grasped with the eyes of the mind (CYRIL OF ALEXANDRIA). By making speech visual, the parables facilitate easy recollection. Each parable is best read in relation to the whole fabric of Scripture (CHRYSOSTOM). The Word becomes effective in us by its own power (CLEMENT OF ALEXANDRIA). In this parable, believers are called to work seasonally to become good soil (AUGUSTINE). Readiness for the indwelling Spirit requires a rigorous weeding out of inordinate desires (EVAGRIUS). By careful cultivation one may reside in this world and not be choked with its cares (CHRYSOSTOM). Only with diligence and grace can the assaults of the enemy be deflected (IRENAEUS). Those without spiritual roots will fall away amid tribulation (ATHANASIUS). God may heal by delaying healing, lest a premature recovery should render one incurable (ORIGEN). Jesus treated warily those who sought to find a pretense for criminal charges against him (AUGUSTINE).

### 4:10 They Asked Him Concerning the Parables

**FIXING MEMORY.** CHRYSOSTOM: He speaks in parables that he may also make his discourse more vivid, and fix the memory of it in them more perfectly, and bring the things before their sight, as did the prophets also. THE GOSPEL OF ST. MATTHEW, HOMILY 44.3.[1]

**THE ORGANIC UNITY OF HOLY SCRIPTURE.** CHRYSOSTOM: Suppose a physician excised a portion from the side of an organism, even in that small part you would find all the elements out of which the whole is composed—nerves and veins, bones, arteries and blood, and a sample, as one might say, of the whole lump. So likewise with regard to the organic unity of the Scriptures. In each distinct portion of what is written, one may see the connection with the whole clearly appearing. THE GOSPEL OF ST. MATTHEW, HOMILY 1.8.[2]

### 4:11 For Those Outside Everything Is in Parables

**THOSE UNREADY TO HEAR.** ORIGEN: Sometimes it does not turn out to be an advantage

---

[1]TLG 2062.152, 57.467.21-25; NPNF 1 10:281*. [2]TLG 2062.152, 57.18.3-10; NPNF 1 10:4*. The whole gist of Scripture may be found implicitly in a single parable.

for one to be healed quickly or superficially, especially if the disease by this means becomes even more shut up in the internal organs where it rages more fiercely. Therefore God, who perceives secret things and who knows all things before they come to be, in his great goodness delays the healing of such persons and defers the remedy to a later time. If I may speak paradoxically, God heals them by not healing them, lest a premature recovery of health should render them incurable. This pertains to those whom our Lord and Savior addressed as "those outside," whose hearts and reins[3] he searches out. Jesus covered up the deeper mysteries of the faith in veiled speech to those who were not yet ready to receive his teaching in straightforward terms. The Lord wanted to prevent the unready from being too speedily converted and only cosmetically healed. If the forgiveness of their sins were too easily obtained, they would soon fall again into the same disorder of sin which they imagined could be cured without any difficulty. ON FIRST PRINCIPLES 3.1.7.[4]

## 4:12 See but Not Perceive

**AN OPEN UTTERANCE PARTIALLY VEILED.**
AUGUSTINE: Jesus did not ordinarily assume that his teaching would remain hidden. He expected it to be proclaimed openly in every direction. Yet it is possible, in defensive circumstances, to utter something openly and yet veiled at the same time. Something may be said not strictly in secret, but in a secret way. Note that it was not in secret that Jesus said "they may indeed see but not perceive."[5] If this had not been spoken openly, there would have been no sense to the phrase "not seeing." The same hearer may not perceive the level on which something is spoken openly, yet on another

level secretly understood. The very things which his detractors had heard without understanding were such as could not with justice or truth be turned into a criminal charge against him. As often as they tried by their questions to find something by which to accuse him, he gave them such replies as utterly confounded all their plots and left no ground for the calumnies they devised. TRACTATES ON JOHN 113.[6]

**THE EYES OF THE MIND.** CYRIL OF ALEXANDRIA: Parables are word pictures not of visible things, but rather of things of the mind and the spirit. That which cannot be seen with the eyes of the body, a parable will reveal to the eyes of the mind, informing the subtlety of the intellect by means of things perceivable by the senses, and as it were tangible. COMMENTARY ON THE GOSPEL OF LUKE 8.5.4.[7]

## 4:13 Do You Not Understand This Parable?

**THE WORD IS MADE EFFECTIVE BY ITS OWN POWER.** CLEMENT OF ALEXANDRIA: At times our Savior spoke the Word to the apostles by means of mysterious sayings. For prophecy says of him: "He will open his mouth in parables, and will declare things kept secret from the foundation of the world."[8] . . . The efficacy of the Word itself, being strong and powerful,[9] gradually draws into itself secretly and invisibly everyone who receives it. STROMATEIS 5.12.[10]

---

[3]Deepest thoughts and feelings. [4]OFP 190-191* (from the Latin version); cf. TLG 2042.002, 3.1.17.1-16. "Those outside" are those unready to hear. [5]Mk 4:12. [6]Cetedoc 0278, 113.3.38; NPNF 1 7:419**; cf. FC 92:12-13. [7]TLG 4090.108, 72.624.41-8; SSGF 1:398*. [8]LXX: "I will open my mouth in parables; I will utter dark sayings which have been from the beginning" (Ps 78:2; [77:2 LXX]). [9]Cf. Heb 4:12. [10]TLG 0555.004, 5.12.80.7.1-8.1, 9.3-5; cf. ANF 2:463.

## 4:14 The Sower Sows the Word

**THE SEED SOWED IN ALL CULTURES.** CLEMENT
OF ALEXANDRIA: The Greek culture, along
with its philosophy, was preparatory. By this it
is made clear how obliquely, not with a straight
direction, gifts have come from God to humanity—in that miscellaneous way that showers
fall down on the good land, and on the dung-
hill, and on the houses. Then both grass and
wheat sprout. Both figs and reckless trees grow
on sepulchers. These things are like a figure of
the truth disclosing itself. All enjoy the same
influence of the rain.[11] But they do not have the
same grace as those which spring up in rich
soil, inasmuch as they are withered or plucked
up. And here we are aided by the parable of the
sower, which the Lord interpreted. Finally
there is only one cultivator of the soil of the
human soul. It is the One who from the beginning, from the foundations of the world, has
been sowing living seeds by which all things
grow. In each age the Word has come down
upon all like rain. But the times and places
which received these gifts account for the differences which exist. . . . Some cultures have
rightly sought out the word of truth through
understanding. "But Abraham was not justified
by works, but by faith."[12] It is therefore of no
advantage to them after the end of life, even if
they do good works now, if they do not have
faith. STROMATEIS 1.7.[13]

## 4:15 Satan Immediately Comes and Takes Away the Word Which Is Sown in Them

**THE WORD TAKEN AWAY.** IRENAEUS: While
we are sleeping, the enemy is sowing weeds.
This is why the Lord commanded his disciples
to be always on the outlook. Those who are not
actively bringing forth fruits of righteousness

are quickly covered over and lost among the
brambles. Yet if they exercise diligence and
receive the word of God as a graft into themselves, they may again recover the pristine
nature of humanity, created after the image and
likeness of God.[14] AGAINST HERESIES 5.10.1.[15]

## 4:17 When Tribulation or Persecution Arises, They Fall Away

**THE ROOTLESS AMID TRIBULATION.** ATHANA-
SIUS: Let us, therefore, following the faith of the
apostles, hold frequent communion with our
Lord. For the world is like the sea to us, beloved,
of which it is written, "There go the ships, and
Leviathan that you[16] formed to sport in it."[17] We
float upon this sea, like wind, with everyone
directing his own course with his own free will.
Under the pilotage of the Word, one may safely
approach the port. But, if possessed by wayward
inclinations, one is in peril by storm and may
suffer shipwreck. For as in the ocean there are
storms and waves, so in the world there are
many afflictions and trials. The unbelieving
therefore, "have no root in themselves, but
endure for a while; then, when tribulation or
persecution arises on account of the word,
immediately they fall away,"[18] just as the Lord
said. They are not likely to endure the complica-
tions which arise from afflictions, if they are
fixed upon the temporal and not confirmed in
the faith. LETTER 19.7, EASTER A.D. 347.[19]

---

[11]Cf. Mt 5:45. [12]Rom 4, passim. [13]TLG 0555.004, 1.7.37.1.1-3.1; 1.7.38.1.2-3.1; ANF 2:308**; cf. FC 85:48. It is by grace, not works of understanding, that faith grows in every human culture. [14]Cf. Gen 1:26. [15]AHR 2:346; ANF 1:536*. [16]God. [17]Ps 104:26. [18]Mk 4:17. [19]PG 26:1428 (the Latin version only); NPNF 2 4:547**. Athanasius intensified the metaphor of rootlessness by adding to it the metaphor of the pilotless ship on troubled waters: With the Word we have a pilot in this sea. But those who are with-out direction or spiritual roots will fall away amid tribulation.

### 4:18 *Sown Among Thorns Which Choke the Word*

**WEEDING OUT THE UNDERGROWTH OF THE SOUL.** EVAGRIUS: Allow the Spirit of God to dwell within you; then in his love he will come and make a habitation with you; he will reside in you and live in you.[20] If your heart is pure you will see him and he will sow in you the good seed of reflection upon his actions and wonder at his majesty. This will happen if you take the trouble to weed out from your soul the undergrowth of sporadic desires, along with the thorns and tares of bad habits.[21] ADMONITION ON PRAYER.[22]

**HOW RICHES CHOKE THE WORD.** CHRYSOSTOM: When the Word is choked, it is not merely due to the thorns as such, but to the negligence of those allowing them to spring up. There is a way, if there is a will, to hinder evil growth and use wealth appropriately. For this reason he warned not of "the world" but of the "care of the world"; not "riches" as such but "the deceitfulness of riches." Let us not place the blame on what we possess, but on our own corrupt mind. For it is possible to be rich and not be deceived. It is possible to be in this world, and not be choked with its cares. For indeed riches have two contrary disadvantages; one, anxiety over them, wearing us out, and spreading darkness over us; and the other, luxury, which makes us soft.... Do not marvel at his calling our luxuries "thorns." If you are intoxicated in your sense you may not be aware of this. One is in sound health who knows that luxury pricks sharper than any thorn. Luxury wastes the soul away even worse than anxiety. It causes more grievous pains both to body and soul. For no one is as seriously harmed by anxiety as by immoderate indulgence.... It brings on premature old age, dulls the senses, darkens our reasoning, blinds the keen-sighted mind, and makes the body flabby. THE GOSPEL OF ST. MATTHEW, HOMILY 44.7.[23]

### 4:20 *The Good Soil*

**BECOMING GOOD SOIL.** AUGUSTINE: Work diligently the soil while you may. Break up your fallow with the plough. Cast away the stones from your field, and dig out the thorns. Be unwilling to have a "hard heart," such as makes the Word of God of no effect.[24] Be unwilling to have a "thin layer of soil," in which the root of divine love can find no depth in which to enter. Be unwilling to "choke the good seed" by the cares and the lusts of this life, when it is being scattered for your good. When God is the sower and we are the ground, we are called to work to be good ground.[25] SERMONS ON NEW TESTAMENT LESSONS 73.3.[26]

**THE PERPETUAL STREAM.** EPHREM THE SYRIAN: The fields have but one season of harvest; but from the Scripture there gushes forth a stream of saving doctrine. The field when reaped lies idle, and at rest, and the branches when the vine is stripped lie withered and dead. The Scriptures are garnered each day, yet the years of its interpreters never come to an end; and the clusters of its vines, which in it are those of hope, though are gathered each day, are likewise without end. COMMENTARY ON TATIAN'S DIATESSARON, PROEM.[27]

---

[20]Cf. Rom 8:9. [21]Cf. Mt. 13:22; Lk 8:14. [22]CS 101:68. [23]NPNF 1 10:283; TLG 2062.152, 57.469.4-16; 470.20-26, 34-37. [24]Cf. Ps 95:8; Prov 28:14; Mk 16:14. [25]Is 1:19-20; Hos 10:12; Lk 6:47-48. [26]Cetedoc 0284, 73.38.471.25; *GMI* 83\*\*; cf. NPNF 1 6:334. [27]*SSGF* 2:44-45; Vossio, St. Ephraem 686 (Cologne, 1616); Proem to Mark 9.

## 4:21-25 A LAMP UNDER A BUSHEL BASKET

²¹And he said to them, "Is a lamp brought in to be put under a bushel, or under a bed, and not on a stand? ²²For there is nothing hid, except to be made manifest; nor is anything secret, except to come to light. ²³If any man has ears to hear, let him hear." ²⁴And he said to them, "Take heed what you hear; the measure you give will be the measure you get, and still more will be given you. ²⁵For to him who has will more be given; and from him who has not, even what he has will be taken away."

**OVERVIEW:** Goodness rejoices in being recognized as what it is (TERTULLIAN). The purpose of the lamp of wisdom is not to be set under a bed but to be used and seen (CLEMENT OF ALEXANDRIA).

### 4:21 A Lamp Under a Bed

**WHEN WISDOM LIES UNUSED.** CLEMENT OF ALEXANDRIA: A well, when pumped regularly, produces purer water. If neglected, and no one uses it, it changes into a source of pollution. Use keeps metal brighter, but disuse produces rust. For, in a word, exercise produces a healthy condition both in souls and bodies. So "No one lights a candle and puts it under a bowl, but upon a candlestick, that it may give light."[1] For of what use is wisdom, if it fails to make those who hear it wise? STROMATEIS 1.1.[2]

### 4:22 There Is Nothing Hid, Except to Be Made Manifest

**HIDING GOOD WORKS.** TERTULLIAN: Why does the Lord call us the light of the world? Why has he compared us to a city on a hill?[3] Are we not called to shine in the midst of darkness, and stand up high for those most sunk down? If you hide your lamp beneath a bushel,[4] you will soon notice that you yourself will be in the dark. You will find others bumping into you. So what can you do to illumine the world? Let your faith produce good works. Be a reflection of God's light. The good is not preoccupied with darkness. It rejoices in being seen.[5] It exults over the very pointings which are made at it. Christian modesty not only wishes to be modest, but also it wishes to be beheld as what it actually is. ON THE APPAREL OF WOMEN 2.13.[6]

---

[1]Mt 5:15; Mk 4:21; Lk 8:16. [2]TLG 0555.004, 1.1.12.2.1-3.4; ANF 2:302**. [3]Mt 5:14. [4]Mt 5:15; Lk 8:16; 11:33. [5]Jn 3:21. [6]Cetedoc 0011, 2.13.7; ANF 4:25*.

# 4:26-29 THE PARABLE OF THE SEED GROWING SECRETLY

²⁶And he said, "The kingdom of God is as if a man should scatter seed upon the ground, ²⁷and should sleep and rise night and day, and the seed should sprout and grow, he knows not how. ²⁸The earth produces of itself, first the blade, then the ear, then the full grain in the ear. ²⁹But when the grain is ripe, at once he puts in the sickle, because the harvest has come."

**OVERVIEW:** The kingdom grows silently (AMBROSE). When the corn is fully ripe, it is like matured righteousness (GREGORY THE GREAT). In four stages righteousness has grown within history after the fall: primitive natural dread, consciousness of the law, the righteousness revealed in the gospel and the mature age of the Holy Spirit (TERTULLIAN).

## 4:28a First the Blade, Then the Ear

**GROWTH IN THE KINGDOM.** AMBROSE: While you are asleep, O man, and without your being aware of it, the earth of itself is producing its fruits. SIX DAYS OF CREATION 3.[1]

**PATTERNS OF INCREASE.** TERTULLIAN: Observe how the created order has advanced little by little toward fruitfulness. First comes the grain, and from the grain arises the shoot, and from the shoot emerges the shrub. From there the boughs and leaves gather strength, and the whole that we call a tree expands. Then follows the swelling of the germen, and from the germen bursts the flower, and from the flower the fruit opens. The fruit itself, primitive for a while, and unshapely, keeping the straight course of its development, is matured, little by little, to the full mellowness of its fla-

vor.[2] In just this way has righteousness grown in history.[3] The proximate righteousness found in the created order is grounded in the holy God whose righteousness first emerged in a rudimentary stage as an undeveloped natural apprehension in the presence of the holy One. Then it advanced through the law and prophets to childhood. At long last through the gospel, God's righteousness has been personally manifested with the vital energies of youth. Now through the paraclete, righteousness is being manifested in its mature stage. ON THE VEILING OF THE VIRGINS 1.[4]

## 4:28b Then the Full Grain in the Ear

**THE FULL CORN.** GREGORY THE GREAT: To produce "the blade" is to hold the first tender beginning of good. The "blade" arrives at maturity when virtue conceived in the mind leads to advancement in good works. The "full corn" fructifies in "the ear" when virtue makes such great progress that it comes into its fullest possible expression. HOMILIES ON EZEKIEL 15.[5]

---

[1]FC 42:101*. [2]Mk 4:28. [3]Cf. Ps 92:12. [4]Cetedoc 0027, 1.39; ANF 4:27-28**. [5]Cetedoc 1710, 2.3.96; GC 1:388.

## 4:30-34 JESUS' USE OF PARABLES

³⁰*And he said, "With what can we compare the kingdom of God, or what parable shall we use for it?* ³¹*It is like a grain of mustard seed, which, when sown upon the ground, is the smallest of all the seeds on earth;* ³²*yet when it is sown it grows up and becomes the greatest of all shrubs, and puts forth large branches, so that the birds of the air can make nests in its shade."* ³³*With many such parables he spoke the word to them, as they were able to hear it;* ³⁴*he did not speak to them without a parable, but privately to his own disciples he explained everything.*

**OVERVIEW:** From the tiny mustard seed, which resists infection and adversity, comes the magnificent tree of the boundless, worldwide community of faith offering its branches to the whole world (CLEMENT OF ALEXANDRIA). This great tree is known by its extension into the whole world and is not adequately embodied by an inwardly turned or detached or separated branch (AUGUSTINE). The mystery of the Word is gradually revealed to us analogically by grace through parables, not by simple analysis of the literal words (ORIGEN). In all things essential Jesus made his identity sufficiently clear to those who were called to proclaim his coming (TERTULLIAN).

### 4:30 With What Can We Compare the Kingdom of God?

**COMPARING THE KINGDOM.** ORIGEN: Now a simile differs from a parable; for it is written in Mark, "With what can we compare the kingdom of God, or what parable shall we use for it?"[1] From this it is plain that there is some logical distinction between a comparison and a parable. The simile seems to be generic, and the parable specific. The simile, which is the highest genus of the parable, contains the parable as one of its species. COMMENTARY ON MATTHEW 10.4.[2]

### 4:31 It Is Like a Grain of Mustard Seed

**SHARP AND PUNGENT.** CLEMENT OF ALEXANDRIA: The word which proclaims the kingdom of heaven is sharp and pungent as mustard. It represses bile (anger) and checks inflammation (pride). From this word flows the soul's true vitality and fitness for eternity. To such increased size did the growth of the word come that the tree which sprang from it (that is the Church of Christ now being established over the whole earth) filled the world, so that the birds of the air (that is, holy angels and lofty souls) dwelt in its branches. FRAGMENTS FROM THE CATENA OF NICETAS, BISHOP OF HERACLEA 4.[3]

### 4:32 Puts Forth Large Branches

**THE BRUISED SEED.** AMBROSE: Its seed is in-

---

[1]Mk 4:30. [2]ANF 9:416*; TLG 2042.029, 10.4.21-28. [3]ANF 2:578*; PG 9:744.

deed very plain, and of little value; but if bruised or crushed it shows forth its power. So faith first seems a simple thing; but if it is bruised by its enemies it gives forth proof of its power, so as to fill others who hear or read of it with the odor of its sweetness. Our martyrs, Felix, Nabor and Victor, possessed the sweet odor of faith; but they dwelt in obscurity. When the persecution came, they laid down their arms, and bowed their necks, and being stricken by the sword they diffused to all the ends of the earth the grace of their martyrdom. . . . The Lord himself is the grain of mustard seed. He was without injury; but the people were unaware of him as a grain of mustard seed of which they took no notice. He chose to be bruised, that we might say: "For we are the good odor of Christ unto God." Exposition on the Gospel of Luke 7.178-79.[4]

**Little Branch, Great Tree.** Augustine: In the same manner,[5] then, the catholicity of our mother[6] becomes palpable when others who are not her sons make war on her. It is a fact that this little branch of worshipers in Africa[7] has been broken off from the great tree[8] which embraces the whole world in the spreading of its branches. She is in labor with them in charity, that they may return to the root without which they cannot have true life. Letter 32.[9]

**The Spreading Tree.** Peter Chrysologus: It is up to us to sow this mustard seed in our minds and let it grow within us into a great tree of understanding reaching up to heaven and elevating all our faculties; then it will spread out branches of knowledge, the pungent savor of its fruit will make our mouths burn, its fiery kernel will kindle a blaze within us inflaming our hearts, and the taste of it will dispel our unenlightened repugnance. Yes, it is true: a

mustard seed is indeed an image of the kingdom of God. Christ is the kingdom of heaven. Sown like a mustard seed in the garden of the virgin's womb, he grew up into the tree of the cross whose branches stretch across the world. Crushed in the mortar of the passion, its fruit has produced seasoning enough for the flavoring and preservation of every living creature with which it comes in contact. As long as a mustard seed remains intact, its properties lie dormant; but when it is crushed they are exceedingly evident. So it was with Christ; he chose to have his body crushed, because he would not have his power concealed. . . . Christ became all things in order to restore all of us in himself. The man Christ received the mustard seed which represents the kingdom of God; as man he received it, though as God he had always possessed it. He sowed it in his garden, that is in his bride, the Church. The Church is a garden extending over the whole world, tilled by the plough of the gospel, fenced in by stakes of doctrine and discipline, cleared of every harmful weed by the labor of the apostles, fragrant and lovely with perennial flowers: virgins' lilies and martyrs' roses set amid the pleasant verdure of all who bear witness to Christ and the tender plants of all who have faith in him. Such then is the mustard seed which Christ sowed in his garden. When he promised a kingdom to the patriarchs, the seed took root in them; with the prophets it sprang up; with the apostles it grew tall; in the Church it became a great tree putting forth innumerable branches

---

[4]Cetedoc 0143, 7.1948; SSGF 1:349; CSEL 32:360-66; cf. Phil 4:18. [5]When the Donatists were severed from the wholeness of the church, it suggested to Augustine this metaphor. [6]The universal church spread over the whole world. [7]The Donatists. [8]The kingdom of God is here being compared to the great tree of which the universal church in time is a proximate expression. [9]Cetedoc 0262, 185.57.8.29.19; FC 30:172-73*.

laden with gifts. And now you too must take the wings of the psalmist's dove, gleaming gold in the rays of divine sunlight, and fly to rest for ever among those sturdy, fruitful branches. No snares are set to trap you there; fly off, then, with confidence and dwell securely in its shelter. SERMON 98.[10]

### 4:34 Privately He Explained Everything

**THE ILLUMINATION OF THE DISCIPLES.** TERTULLIAN: Christ Jesus our Lord clearly declared himself as to who he was while he lived on earth. . . . Who then of sound mind can possibly suppose that those whom the Lord ordained to be leaders and teachers were ignorant of anything essential to salvation? Who could suppose that he who kept them, as he did, so close to himself in their daily attentiveness, in their discipline, in their companionship, to whom, when they were alone, he used to expound all things[11] which were obscure, telling them that "to them it was given to know those mysteries,"[12] which it was not permitted the people to understand—now would he leave them ignorant? PRESCRIPTION AGAINST HERETICS 20, 22.[13]

---

[10]Cetedoc 0027+, 98.25; JF B 90-91;  [11]Mk 4:34.  [12]Mt 13:11.  [13]Cetedoc 0005, 20.1, 22.9; ANF 3:252-53**. Christ did not leave his disciples ignorant with respect to any matter essential to salvation.

---

## 4:35-41 THE STILLING OF THE STORM

[35]On that day, when evening had come, he said to them, "Let us go across to the other side." [36]And leaving the crowd, they took him with them in the boat, just as he was. And other boats were with him. [37]And a great storm of wind arose, and the waves beat into the boat, so that the boat was already filling. [38]But he was in the stern, asleep on the cushion; and they woke him and said to him, "Teacher, do you not care if we perish?" [39]And he awoke and rebuked the wind, and said to the sea, "Peace! Be still!" And the wind ceased, and there was a great calm. [40]He said to them, "Why are you afraid? Have you no faith?" [41]And they were filled with awe, and said to one another, "Who then is this, that even wind and sea obey him?"

---

**OVERVIEW:** While the ship was quietly bearing Jesus' humanity, the power of his Godhead was wonderfully carrying the ship itself (EPHREM THE SYRIAN). The mystery of the God-man is seen in that he who is the rest of the weary himself grew tired (GREGORY NAZIANZEN). His explicit use of the terms of personal authority teaches us of his divine identity as eternal Son (BASIL). In the stilling of the storm, the prophecies of Habakkuk and Nahum were fulfilled

(TERTULLIAN). The Lord of the sea, eliciting faith through temporal events, exhibited his awesome power in the storm (ATHANASIUS). Only the author of the deep could still its storm and walk its sea (PRUDENTIUS). His sleep had the purpose of maturing their faith (ORIGEN, CYRIL OF ALEXANDRIA). Amid our temptations we may awaken the sleeping Christ in us (AUGUSTINE).

### 4:36 The Boat Was Already Filling

**TESTING THE DISCIPLES.** ATHANASIUS: Even while he was asleep on the pillow, the Lord was testing his disciples,[1] when a miracle was wrought that was calculated especially to put even the wicked to contrition. For when he arose, and rebuked the sea, and silenced the storm, he plainly disclosed two things: that the storm of the sea was not simply from winds, but from the fear of the Lord who walked upon it;[2] and that the Lord who rebuked it was not a creature, but rather its creator. LETTER 29.[3]

**THE WORD SAILED WITH THEM.** ATHANASIUS: They awakened the Word, who was sailing with them, and immediately the sea became smooth at the command of its Lord, and they were saved. They became proclaimers and teachers at the same time, attesting the miracles of our Savior, and also teaching us to imitate their example. LETTER 19.6, EASTER A.D. 347.[4]

### 4:38 Asleep on the Cushion, They Awoke Him

**THE BARK OF THE CHURCH.** ORIGEN: For as many as are in the little ship of faith are sailing with the Lord; as many as are in the bark of holy church will voyage with the Lord across this wave-tossed life; though the Lord himself may sleep in holy quiet, he is but watching your patience and endurance: looking forward to the repentance, and to the conversion of those who have sinned. Come then to him eagerly, instant in prayer. FRAGMENTS ON MATTHEW 3.3.[5]

**WHO WAS ASLEEP?** GREGORY NAZIANZEN: He was tired[6]—yet he is the "rest" of the weary and the burdened.[7] He was overcome by heavy sleep[8]—yet he goes lightly over the sea, rebukes the winds, and relieves the drowning Peter.[9] ORATION 29, ON THE SON 20.[10]

**SHARPENING THEIR PERCEPTIONS.** CYRIL OF ALEXANDRIA: And so he sleeps, leaving them in fear, in which their senses would be sharpened to perceive the significance of what was to come. For no one feels what takes place in another's body as acutely as that which happens in his own. COMMENTARY ON THE GOSPEL OF LUKE 8.5.22.[11]

### 4:39a He Rebuked the Wind

**THE PROPHETS FULFILLED.** TERTULLIAN: When he disperses its waves, Habakkuk's words are fulfilled, where he speaks of the Lord "scattering the waters in his passage."[12] When at his rebuke the sea is calmed, Nahum's prophesy is fulfilled: "He rebukes the sea and makes it dry."[13] AGAINST MARCION 4.20.[14]

---

[1]Mk 4:37-41. [2]Cf. Mt 14:26; Mk 6:48; Jn 6:19. [3]NPNF 2 4:550; PG 26:1435. [4]NPNF 2 4:547*, PG 26:1428. [5]GCS 41.1:260; SSGF 1:320. [6]Jn 4:6. [7]Mt 11:28. [8]Mt 8:24; Mk 4:38; Lk 8:23. [9]Cf. Mt 8:26; 14:25-32; Mk 4:39; 6:48-51; Lk 8:24; Jn 6:19-21. [10]TLG 2022.003, 20.7-10; FGFR 258-59. This is the God-man, who according to his humanity is able to sleep and according to his divinity is able to still the storm. [11]TLG 4090.108, 72.629.24-30; SSGF 1:324. [12]Hab 3:10 LXX: "as thou dost divide the moving waters." [13]Nahum 1:4. [14]Cetedoc 0014, 4.484.16; ANF 3:379*.

### 4:39b *Peace! Be Still!*

**BY WHOSE AUTHORITY.** BASIL: Pay close attention to the Lord's words; whenever he instructs us about the Father, he knows that by using terms of personal authority, such as "I will; be clean";[15] and "Peace! Be still!"[16] and "But I say to you";[17] and "You deaf and dumb spirit, I command you";[18] and other similar expressions, we will be led to recognize his authority as master and creator. By these encounters we are meeting the Father of the Son, the Father who creates through the Son. This does not insinuate that the Father's creation is imperfect, or that the Son's energy is feeble, but shows their unity of will. ON THE HOLY SPIRIT 8.21.[19]

### 4:41a *Who Then Is This?*

**THE SHIP, HIS HUMANITY AND HIS DIVINITY.** EPHREM THE SYRIAN: The ship carried his humanity, but the power of his Godhead carried the ship and all that was in it. In order that he might show that even his humanity did not require the ship, instead of the planks which a shipwright puts together and fastens, he, like the architect of creation, made the waters firm and joined them together solidly under his feet. So just as the Lord strengthened the hands of Simeon the priest, that his arms might bear up in the temple the strength that was bearing up all,[20] so did he strengthen the feet of Simon the apostle, that they might bear themselves up on the water.[21] So that name which bore the first-begotten in the temple was afterwards borne up by the first-begotten in the sea. HOMILY ON OUR LORD 50.[22]

### 4:41b *Wind and Sea Obey Him*

**AWAKENING THE CHRIST ASLEEP IN YOU.**

AUGUSTINE: When you have to listen to abuse, that means you are being buffeted by the wind. When your anger is roused, you are being tossed by the waves. So when the winds blow and the waves mount high, the boat is in danger, your heart is imperiled, your heart is taking a battering. On hearing yourself insulted, you long to retaliate; but the joy of revenge brings with it another kind of misfortune—shipwreck. Why is this? Because Christ is asleep in you. What do I mean? I mean you have forgotten his presence. Rouse him, then; remember him, let him keep watch within you, pay heed to him. . . . A temptation arises: it is the wind. It disturbs you: it is the surging of the sea. This is the moment to awaken Christ and let him remind you of those words: "Who can this be? Even the winds and the sea obey him." SERMONS 63.1-3.[23]

**THE AUTHOR OF THE DEEP.** PRUDENTIUS:

His power and miracles proclaim him God.
I see the wild winds suddenly grow calm
When Christ commands; I see the storm-
    tossed sea
Grow smooth, with tranquil surface bright,
At Christ's behest; I see the waves grow firm
As the raging flood sustains his treading
    feet.
He walks dry-shod upon the flowing tide
And bears upon the flood with footsteps
    sure.
He chides the winds and bids the tempest
    cease.

---

[15]Mt 8:3; Mk 1:41; Lk 5:13. [16]Cf. Mk 4:39. [17]Mt 5:22. [18]Mk 9:25. [19]OHS 41-42; TLG 2040.003, 8.21.10-23; cf. NPNF 2 8:14-15. [20]Cf. Lk 2:25-35. [21]As the Lord bore up the hands of Simeon as he was praying in the temple, so did he bear up the feet of Simon Peter as he was walking in the water; cf. Mt 14:31. [22]CSCO 270-71:49; NPNF 2 13:328*. [23]Cetedoc 0284, 63.38.424.20; Mt 8:27; Mk 4:41; Lk 8:25; JF B 92-93; PL 38. 424-25; cf. WSA 3 3:173-74.

Who would command the stormy gales:
    "Be still,
Your strongholds keep and leave the bound-
    less sea,"
Except the Lord and maker of the winds? . . .
Who on the sea could walk, who with firm
    step
Upon the flood could without sinking tread
That path with soles upborne and feet
    unwet,

Except the author of the deep, the
    Spirit,
Poured from the Father's lips, that moved
    across
The waves, not yet hemmed in by solid
    shores?
A HYMN ON THE TRINITY, LINES 649-79.[24]

[24]Cetedoc 1439, 646; FC 52:27.

## 5:1-20 THE GERASENE DEMONIAC

[1]*They came to the other side of the sea, to the country of the Gerasenes.*[n] [2]*And when he had come out of the boat, there met him out of the tombs a man with an unclean spirit,* [3]*who lived among the tombs; and no one could bind him any more, even with a chain;* [4]*for he had often been bound with fetters and chains, but the chains he wrenched apart, and the fetters he broke in pieces; and no one had the strength to subdue him.* [5]*Night and day among the tombs and on the mountains he was always crying out, and bruising himself with stones.* [6]*And when he saw Jesus from afar, he ran and worshiped him;* [7]*and crying out with a loud voice, he said, "What have you to do with me, Jesus, Son of the Most High God? I adjure you by God, do not torment me."* [8]*For he had said to him, "Come out of the man, you unclean spirit!"* [9]*And Jesus[o] asked him, "What is your name?" He replied, "My name is Legion; for we are many."* [10]*And he begged him eagerly not to send them out of the country.* [11]*Now a great herd of swine was feeding there on the hillside;* [12]*and they begged him, "Send us to the swine, let us enter them."* [13]*So he gave them leave. And the unclean spirits came out, and entered the swine; and the herd, numbering about two thousand, rushed down the steep bank into the sea, and were drowned in the sea.*

[14]*The herdsmen fled, and told it in the city and in the country. And people came to see what it was that had happened.* [15]*And they came to Jesus, and saw the demoniac sitting there, clothed and in his right mind, the man who had the legion; and they were afraid.* [16]*And those who had seen it told what had happened to the demoniac and to the swine.* [17]*And they began to beg Jesus[p] to depart from their neighborhood.* [18]*And as he was getting into the boat, the man who had been possessed with demons begged him that he might be with him.* [19]*But he refused,*

*and said to him, "Go home to your friends, and tell them how much the Lord has done for you, and how he has had mercy on you." ²⁰And he went away and began to proclaim in the Decapolis how much Jesus had done for him; and all men marveled.*

n Other ancient authorities read *Gergesenes*, some *Gadarenes*    o Greek *he*    p Greek *him*

**OVERVIEW:** It was for the greater good of attesting God's power and eliciting faith that the swine were slain by the agency of demons (JEROME, CHRYSOSTOM). The glory of humanity made in the image of God has freely fallen to the depths under the power of unclean spirits (PRUDENTIUS). These fallen spiritual creatures were first to recognize the Son as holy, sovereign God (ATHANASIUS, PETER CHRYSOLOGUS, PRUDENTIUS). It is one who is truly man and truly God that the demons instantly recognize with dread (GREGORY NAZIANZEN). Even if a whole army of demons takes up residence in a single body, the redeemer can transform human misery into soundness (LACTANTIUS, EPHREM THE SYRIAN). Limited powers are temporarily permitted to the demonic to test faith (TERTULLIAN). The church continues to petition God to deliver the faithful from demonic powers (APOSTOLIC CONSTITUTIONS, EPHREM THE SYRIAN). The demonic powers are not originally and directly willed by God but are only permitted by God under the conditions of sin, and as a consequence of taking freedom seriously, they play a role in drawing forth a greater good. They are already being bound up by the anointed one (JOHN OF DAMASCUS). The faithful today attest the same cleansing grace (GREGORY THE GREAT).

### 5:1 The Country of the Gerasenes

**GERASA OR GADARA OR GERGESA?** ORIGEN: One who aims at fuller understanding of the holy Scriptures must not neglect the careful examination of the proper names in it. Concerning Palestinian place names the Greek copies are often incorrect, and one might be misled by them. The displacement of the swine, who were driven down a steep place by the demons and drowned in the sea, is said to have taken place in the country of the Gerasenes.[1] Now, Gerasa is a town of Arabia, and has no sea or lake near it. The Evangelists would not have made a statement so obviously and demonstrably false; for they were men who informed themselves carefully of all matters connected with Judea. But in a few copies we have found, "into the country of the Gadarenes." On this reading, Gadara is described as a town of Judea. In its neighborhood are the well-known hot springs. There is no lake there with overhanging banks, nor any sea. But Gergesa, from which the name Gergesenes is taken, is an old town in the neighborhood of the lake now called Tiberias. On the edge of it there is a steep place bordering on the lake, from which the pigs could have been driven down by the demons. Now, the meaning of Gergesa is the "dwelling of the one who drives out," and may contain a prophetic reference to the response of the citizens toward the Savior. They "begged him to depart out of their coasts."[2] COMMENTARY ON JOHN 6.24.[3]

---

[1]Cf. Lk 8:26-37.  [2]Mt 8:34; Mk 5:17; Lk 8:37.  [3]TLG 2042.005, 6.40.207.6-6.41.211.7; ANF 9:371**. This passage shows the great care that Origen took to identify place names accurately and to check the Greek against the Aramaic. The text could have referred to Gerasa or Gadara, but the geographical evidence may suggest Gergesa.

### 5:3 One Who Lived Among the Tombs

**FALLEN TO THE DEPTHS.** PETER CHRYSOLO-GUS: Behold where is he, who was promised all the glories of this world, found to dwell— where? —in the tombs![4] Compassed about with the putrid rottenness of dead bodies. SERMONS 17.[5]

**BEREFT OF REASON.** PRUDENTIUS:
> Then a man bereft of reason,
>     dwelling in sepulchral caves,
> Bound with cruel and grinding fetters and
>     with raging frenzy torn,
> Rushes forth and kneels in worship, as the
>     saving Christ draws near.[6]

HYMN 9.[7]

### 5:4 No One Had the Strength to Subdue Him

**TRANSFORMING THE DEPTHS.** LACTANTIUS: "Neither could anyone tame him."[8] Give me a reprobate who is impetuous, foul-mouthed and overbearing. With few words the Lord will render him as gentle as a lamb. Give me one who is covetous, avaricious, grasping. The Lord will restore him to liberality, and he will dispose of his resources bountifully of his own hand. Show me one who trembles at the idea of pain and of death, and soon I will show you one who has learned to disdain crosses, flames and the bull of Perillus.[9] Even one who is sensual, adulterous and gluttonous can be made sober, chaste and abstinent.[10] DIVINE INSTITUTES 3.26.4.[11]

### 5:7 What Have You to Do with Me?

**THE INSTANT RECOGNITION.** ATHANASIUS: Obviously he would not be expelling evil spirits and pillaging idols if he were impotent, for the evil spirits would not obey one who was impo-tent. If, on the other hand, the very naming of him drives them forth, he clearly is not powerless. The spirits especially see through what is unseen by human eyes. They could tell if Christ was vulnerable and refuse him any obedience at all. As it is, what human disbelief doubts, the evil spirits see clearly: that he is God. For that reason they flee from him and fall at his feet, still crying out even as they once cried when he was in the body, "We know who you are, the holy one of God,"[12] and, "Ah, what have I in common with you, Son of God? I implore you, do not torment me."[13] INCARNATION OF THE WORD 32.4.5.[14]

**THE GOD-MAN BEHELD.** GREGORY NAZIAN-ZEN: Yes, he is recognized by demons,[15] drives out demons,[16] drowns deep a legion of spirits[17] and sees the prince of demons falling like light-ning.[18] He is stoned, yet not hit;[19] he prays yet he hears prayer.[20] He weeps,[21] yet he puts an end to weeping.[22] He asks where Lazarus is[23]— he was man; yet he raises Lazarus[24]—he was God. ORATION 29, ON THE SON 20.[25]

---

[4]Cf. Mk 5:3; Lk 8:27. [5]Cetedoc 0227, 17.38; *GMI* 97. What has become of the glory of humanity made in the image of God? In the person of the demoniac, humanity seems to have fallen to the depths under the power of the demonic. [6]Mk 5:2-6; Lk 8:28. [7]Cetedoc 1438, 9.52; FC 43:63. The redeemer was recognized even by one whose reasoning had become demonically enslaved. [8]Mk 5:4. [9]Perillus was an Athenian artist, who designed the hollow brazen bull in which people could be roasted alive. Phalaris (c. 570-549 B.C.), the tyrant of Agrigentum, Sicily, who commissioned the bull, decided to make Perillus its first victim. [10]Cf. Is 55:13; 1 Cor 6:9-11. [11]Cetedoc 0085, 3.26.4; CSEL 19:260.4; cf. ANF 7:128. Are the demonic powers untamable? The redeemer can transform the worst. [12]Mk 1:24; Lk 4:34. [13]Mk 5:7; Lk 8:28. [14]TLG 2035.002, 32.4.1-5.5; cf. NPNF 2 4:53; LCC 3:86. The demons recognized him instantly as sovereign God. The unclean spirits could see what human eyes could not. [15]Cf. Lk 4:33-34; Mk 1:23-24. [16]Cf. Mt 8:16; Mk 1:34. [17]Cf. Mt 8:32; Mk 5:9, 13; Lk 8:30, 33. [18]Cf. Lk 10:18. [19]Cf. Jn 8:59; 10:31, 39. [20]Cf. Mt 8:13; Mk 1:35. [21]Cf. Jn 11:35. [22]Cf. Lk 7:13; 8:52; 23:28. [23]Cf. Jn 11:34. [24]Cf. Jn 11:43-44. [25]FGFR 259; TLG 2022.009, 20.12-17. The demons instantly recognize one who is at once truly a man and truly God.

## 5:9 My Name Is Legion

**THE SUPPLICATION.** EPHREM THE SYRIAN:
Look too at Legion:[26] when in anguish he
begged, our Lord permitted the demons to enter
into the herd. He asked for respite, without
deception, in his anguish, and our Lord in his
kindness granted this request. His compassion
for the demoniac is a rebuke to the demons,
showing how much anguish his love suffers in
desiring that humans should live. Encouraged by
the words I had heard, I knelt down and wept
there, and spoke before our Lord: "Legion
received his request from you without any tears.
Permit me, with my tears, to make my request."
HYMNS ON PARADISE 12.8-9.[27]

**GOD'S ANTECEDENT AND CONSEQUENT WILL-
ING.** JOHN OF DAMASCUS: One should also bear
in mind that God antecedently wills all to be
saved and to attain to his kingdom.[28] For he did
not form us to be chastised, but to share his
goodness, because he is incomparably good.
Yet, because he is just, it is required that sin be
punished. So, the first form of the will of God
is called his antecedent will and blessing, which
has God as its cause. The second is called
God's consequent will and permission, of
which we are a participating cause. What God
wills as a consequence of our sinning is twofold: either that which God permits to continue by his gracious dispensation for our
instruction and salvation, or that which God
finally abandons to certain chastisement.
These, however, belong to those things which
do not depend upon us. As to the things which
do depend upon us, whatever is good God wills
antecedently and blesses. Whatever is evil he
neither wills antecedently nor consequently,
but permits them to the free will. If something
is done under compulsion, it cannot be a virtu-

ous act or according to reason, since virtue
must be chosen. In these ways God provides
for all creation. Through all creation God does
good and teaches, and he may even use the
demons themselves for this purpose of instruction, as he did in the case of Job and in the gospel narrative of the swine.[29] THE ORTHODOX
FAITH 2.29.[30]

## 5:13a The Unclean Spirits Came Out and Entered the Swine

**THE TEMPORARY POWER TO TEST FAITH.** Tertullian: The devil's legion would not have had
power over the herd of swine[31] unless they had
gotten it from God. Thus they are far from
having power over the sheep of God. Even the
bristles of the swine were counted by God, just
as were the hairs of the heads of the just.[32] The
devil, it must be admitted, seems indeed to
have power—in this case really his own—over
those who do not belong to God. In relation to
God the idolatrous nations are all counted as a
drop in the bucket, as dust on the threshing
floor, as spittle in the mouth,[33] and so thrown
open to the devil as if they were a free possession. But the devil has no power over those
who belong to the household of God, and cannot treat them as if they were his own. The
cases marked out in Scripture show when and
for what reasons he may touch the faithful.
Indeed to vindicate faith, the power of trial of a
believer is sometimes temporarily granted to

---

[26]Cf. Mk 5:9; Lk 8:30. [27]CSCO 174-175:51-52; HOP 163**. We
still pray for the same cleansing. [28]Cf. 1 Tim 2:4; 2 Pet 3:9. [29]Cf.
Mk 5:13. [30]TLG 2934.004, 43.67-81; FC 37:262-63**. The
demonic powers are not from the beginning (antecedently) willed
by God but are permitted by God (consequently) under the conditions of sin to play a role in drawing forth a greater good. [31]Cf. Mk
5:11-13. [32]Cf. Mt 10:30; Lk 12:7. [33]Cf. Is 40:15 LXX; 4 Ezra
6:56.

the devil to test and challenge faith.[34] Or to elicit repentance the sinner may be temporarily handed over to the devil as though he were an executioner to whom belonged the inflicting of punishment, as we see in the case of Saul.[35] On Flight During Persecution.[36]

**Why Swine Were Destroyed.** Jerome: It need not disturb anyone that by the Lord's command two thousand swine were slain by the agency of demons, since those who witnessed the miracle would not have believed that so great a multitude of demons had gone out of the man unless an equally vast number of swine had rushed to ruin, showing that it was a legion that impelled them. The Life of St. Hilarion 32.[37]

### 5:13b Two Thousand Swine

**Was This Just?** Jerome: Was it just that two thousand swine perished so one soul might be saved? One seeking purity of heart had best not become preoccupied with the natural prerogative of the demonic legion or animals. It is better that each single reader reflect upon his own soul, his own way of life, and the rarity of true excellence. Remember when the whole of Judea was led into captivity when Nebuchadneser came, and thousands were displaced into Babylonia as prisoners[38]— Jeremiah alone was left praising God. And they threw him into a muddy cistern.[39] Nevertheless, the soul of this one man was more decisive for the destiny of Israel[40] than all the rest. Homily 54.[41]

**Whether Demons Take Up Space.** Ephrem the Syrian: I asked this too, whether Paradise was sufficient in size for all the righteous to live there. I asked about what is not written in

Scripture, but my instruction came from what is written there: "Consider the man in whom there dwelt a legion of all kinds of demons.[42] They were there although not apparent, for their army is of a stuff finer and more subtle than the soul itself. That whole army dwelt in a single body. A hundred times finer and more subtle are the bodies of the righteous when they are risen at the resurrection.[43] They resemble the mind that is able, if it so wills, to stretch out and expand, or, should it wish, to contract and shrink, so as either to focus on one place or to expand to encompass all places. Listen and learn: A lamp with thousands of rays can exist in a single house. Ten thousand scents can exist in a single blossom. Though located in a small space, they have ample room to extend themselves. So it is with Paradise: though full of spiritual beings, it is amply spacious for their habitation." Hymn 5.[44]

### 5:13c And They Were Drowned

**Why Drowned?** Chrysostom: He did this so that you might know that the demons would have done the same thing to human beings and would have drowned them if God had allowed them to do so. But he restrained the demons, stopped them, and allowed them to do no such

---

[34]Cf. Job 1:12. [35]Cf. Acts 9:1-2. [36]Cetedoc 0025, 2.52; ANF 4:117*. Limited powers are temporarily given to the demonic to test faith or elicit repentance. [37]Cetedoc 0618, 106.14.20; NPNF 2 6:309. It was for the good of attesting God's power that the swine were slain by the agency of demons. [38]Cf. 2 Chron 36:20. [39]Cf. Jer 38:6. [40]Within the scheme of the history of salvation. [41]Cetedoc 0592, 143.267; FC 48:390**. One godly human soul may make more difference than an unclean multitude of animals. Each believer must look to his or her own soul to ferret out the legion of unclean spirits. [42]Mk 5:9; Lk 8:30. [43]Cf. 1 Cor 15:42. [44]HOP 104-5*. So different from ours is the relation of demonic powers to space that a whole legion can take up residence in a single human body.

thing. When their power was transferred to the swine, it became clear to all witnesses what they would have done to persons. From this we learn that if the demons had the power to possess swine, they also could have possessed humans. DISCOURSES AGAINST JUDAIZING CHRISTIANS 8.6.[45]

**INTO THE MUDDY WATERS.** PRUDENTIUS:

> Driven forth, the wily demons, legion
>     named that evil scourge,
> Seize upon the sordid foulness of a herd of
>     filthy swine
> And into the muddy waters plunge them-
>     selves with maddened beasts.[46]

HYMN 9.[47]

### 5:15 Clothed and in His Right Mind

**THE PETITION FOR EXORCISM.** APOSTOLIC CONSTITUTIONS: After this, let the deacon say: Go out, catechumens,[48] in peace. And after they have gone out, let him say: You energumens,[49] afflicted with unclean spirits, pray, and let us all earnestly pray for them, that God, the lover of humankind, through Christ, may rebuke the unclean and wicked spirits, and deliver the faithful from the dominion of the adversary. May he that rebuked the legion of demons, and the devil, the prince of wickedness, even now rebuke these demons which have turned away from piety. May God deliver his own workmanship from their power, and cleanse those creatures which he has with great wisdom created. CONSTITUTIONS OF THE HOLY APOSTLES 8.2.6.[50]

### 5:19 Tell Them How Much the Lord Has Done

**ATTESTING DELIVERANCE.** GREGORY THE GREAT: A legion of demons has been, as I believed, cast out of me. I would prefer merely to forget all of this that I have known and simply to rest at the feet of the Savior. But lo it is said to me, so strongly as to compel me against my will, "Go home to your friends, and tell them how much the Lord has done for you, and how he has had mercy on you."[51] EPISTLE 5.[52]

### 5:20 All Marveled

**MELTING THE CALLOUS HEART.** PRUDENTIUS:

> Behold, a legion hurls headlong the swine
> Of Gerasenes, and once enchained in tombs,
> It loudly grunts with pain. From lips
>     possessed
> It had cried out: "O Jesus, Son of God,
> Offspring of David's royal line, we know
> Who you are and why you have come, what
>     power
> Expels us, at your coming filled with
>     dread."[53]
> Has not this voice, Judea, reached your
>     ears?
> True, but it has not pierced your darkened
>     mind
> And, driven back, has from the threshold
>     fled.[54]

---

[45]TLG 2062.021, 48.940.39-45; FC 68:236-27**. God justly allowed brute creatures to be drowned to show how the demonic power over human souls might be broken. [46]Cf. Mk 5:13. [47]Cetedoc 1438, 9.55; FC 43:64. [48]A candidate for baptism; Tertullian *Prescription Against Heretics* 41; Hippolytus *Apostolic Tradition* 16-20; EEC 151; EECy 185. [49]An individual believed to be possessed or inhabited by a demon. [50]PG 1:1080; ANF 7:483-84*. The worshiping community is authorized to petition God to deliver the faithful from demonic powers. [51]Mk 5:19. [52]Cetedoc 1714, 140.1.5.38; NPNF 2 11:75*. The faithful even today may experience the same cleansing grace and are called to attest its power. [53]Mk 5:1-13; Lk 8:26-33. [54]Under the law we hear of the coming of the Savior but resist it.

Now sets the evening sun, where he who
   beholds
The rosy dawn beholds the Lord's advent.
The fervent gospel word
Has thawed the Scythian frosts and
   Hyrcanian snows,
So that Rhodopeian Hebrus, freed from
   ice,[55]

Flows from Caucasian cliffs, a gentler
   stream.
A HYMN ON THE TRINITY.[56]

---

[55]The frost, snow and ice refer to the rigidity of the life lived in bondage to the law, which the gospel melts. [56]Cetedoc 1439, 414; FC 52:19**. How warmly does the love of God melt the callous, frozen heart and wash away the ingrained residues of sin.

## 5:21-43 JAIRUS'S DAUGHTER AND THE WOMAN WITH A HEMORRHAGE

[21]And when Jesus had crossed again in the boat to the other side, a great crowd gathered about him; and he was beside the sea. [22]Then came one of the rulers of the synagogue, Jairus by name; and seeing him, he fell at his feet, [23]and besought him, saying, "My little daughter is at the point of death. Come and lay your hands on her, so that she may be made well, and live." [24]And he went with him.

And a great crowd followed him and thronged about him. [25]And there was a woman who had a flow of blood for twelve years, [26]and who had suffered much under many physicians, and had spent all that she had, and was no better but rather grew worse. [27]She had heard the reports about Jesus, and came up behind him in the crowd and touched his garment. [28]For she said, "If I touch even his garments, I shall be made well." [29]And immediately the hemorrhage ceased; and she felt in her body that she was healed of her disease. [30]And Jesus, perceiving in himself that power had gone forth from him, immediately turned about in the crowd, and said, "Who touched my garments?" [31]And his disciples said to him, "You see the crowd pressing around you, and yet you say, 'Who touched me?'" [32]And he looked around to see who had done it. [33]But the woman, knowing what had been done to her, came in fear and trembling and fell down before him, and told him the whole truth. [34]And he said to her, "Daughter, your faith has made you well; go in peace, and be healed of your disease."

[35]While he was still speaking, there came from the ruler's house some who said "Your daughter is dead. Why trouble the Teacher any further?" [36]But ignoring[q] what they said, Jesus said to the ruler of the synagogue, "Do not fear, only believe." [37]And he allowed no one to fol-

*low him except Peter and James and John the brother of James.* ³⁸*When they came to the house of the ruler of the synagogue, he saw a tumult, and people weeping and wailing loudly.* ³⁹*And when he had entered, he said to them, "The child is not dead but sleeping."* ⁴⁰*And they laughed at him. But he put them all outside, and took the child's father and mother and those who were with him, and went in where the child was.* ⁴¹*Taking her by the hand he said to her, "Talitha cumi"; which means, "Little girl, I say to you, arise."* ⁴²*And immediately the girl got up and walked (she was twelve years of age), and they were immediately overcome with amazement.* ⁴³*And he strictly charged them that no one should know this, and told them to give her something to eat.*

q  Or *overhearing.* Other ancient authorities read *hearing*

**OVERVIEW:** Faith has powerful evidences, as seen in the new life that it creates (APHRAHAT). By healing and raising from the dead, Jesus showed compassion and demonstrated his messianic identity (PRUDENTIUS). It was not the mere manual touching of the Lord that healed, but touching the Lord with simple faith (BEDE). She who was perceived as being dead was given new life simply through the divine address (AMBROSE). The cry of anquish was itself a primitive form of faith (JEROME). She ate to confirm the authenticity of her resurrection (JEROME, THEODORET OF CYR). When we are made children of God by faith, life is restored (JEROME). The sole requisite to receiving new life is faith (AUGUSTINE, BEDE). If she were a witness to his divinity, he in turn was a witness to her faith (EPHREM THE SYRIAN). The one whose hands formed her from nothing in creation reformed her from what had perished (PETER CHRYSOLOGUS).

### 5:23 Lay Your Hands on Her

**WHOSE HANDS?** PETER CHRYSOLOGUS: Those who are sick do not lay down the conditions of how they are to be cured. They only want to be made well. But this man was a ruler of the syn-

agogue, and versed in the law. He had surely read that while God created all other things by his word, man had been created by the hand of God. He trusted therefore in God that his daughter would be recreated, and restored to life by that same hand which, he knew, had created her.... He who laid hands on her to form her from nothing, once more lays hands upon her to reform her from what had perished. SERMON 33.3.[1]

### 5:27 She Touched His Garment

**THE CRY OF ANGUISH.** JEROME: The woman with the hemorrhage had spent all that she had on doctors. Hungering and thirsting, her spirit had died within her. Having lost everything she possessed, because her life was wasting away within her, she cried out to the Lord in anguish. Her touch on the hem of his garment was the cry of a believing heart. In this she is the figure of the assembly of God gathered from all nations. HOMILY 33.[2]

**DRAWING NEAR TO THE PHYSICIAN.** PETER

[1]Cetedoc 0227+, 33.37; SSGF 4:323**; CCL 24:188.  [2]Cetedoc 0.592, 106.88; FC 48:241**.

CHRYSOLOGUS: No seas were ever so troubled by the ebb and flow of the tide, as the mind of this woman, pulled to and fro by the sway of her thoughts. After all the hopeless strivings of physicians, after all her outlay on useless remedies, after all the usual but useless treatment, when skill and experience had so long failed, all her substance was gone. This was not by chance, but divinely ordered, that she might be healed solely through faith and humility, whom human knowledge had failed through so many years. At a little distance apart from him stood this woman, whom nature had filled with modesty, whom the law had declared unclean, saying of her: She shall be unclean and shall touch no holy thing.[3] She fears to touch, lest she incur the anger of the religious leaders, or the condemnation of the law. For fear of being talked about, she dares not speak, lest she embarrass those about her, lest she offend their ears. Through many years her body has been an arena of suffering. Everyday, unceasing pain she can endure no more. The Lord is passing by so quickly. The time is short to think what she must do, aware that healing is not given to the silent, nor to the one who hides her pain. In the midst of her conflicting thoughts, she sees a way, her sole way of salvation. She would secure her healing by stealth, take in silence what she dares not ask for, guarding her respect and modesty. She who feels unworthy in body, draws near in heart to the physician. In faith she touches God. With her hand she touches his garment, knowing that both healing and forgiveness may be bestowed on this stratagem, undertaken due to the demands of modesty, and not as she otherwise would have preferred. She knew the gain she sought by stealth would cause no loss to him from whom she took it. . . . In an instant, faith cures where human skill had failed through twelve years. SERMON 33.4.[4]

**IRONIES OF HER HEALING.** EPHREM THE SYRIAN: Glory to you, hidden Son of God, because your healing power is proclaimed through the hidden suffering of the afflicted woman. Through this woman whom they could see, the witnesses were enabled to behold the divinity that cannot be seen. Through the Son's own healing power his divinity became known. Through the afflicted woman's being healed her faith was made manifest. She caused him to be proclaimed, and indeed was honored with him. For truth was being proclaimed together with its heralds. If she was a witness to his divinity, he in turn was a witness to her faith. . . . He saw through to her hidden faith, and gave her a visible healing. COMMENTARY ON TATIAN'S DIATESSARON.[5]

### 5:33 She Told Him the Whole Truth

**FAITH AND TRUTH.** JEROME: Note the separate stages; mark the progress. As long as she was hemorrhaging, she could not come into his presence. She was healed by faith and then came before him. She fell at his feet. Even then she did not yet dare to look up into his face. As long as she had been cured, it was enough for her to cling to his feet. She "told him all the truth."[6] Christ himself is the truth. She was giving praise to the truth. She had been healed by the truth. HOMILY 77.[7]

---

[3]Cf. Lev 15:25. [4]Cetedoc 0227+, 33.70; SSGF 4:324**; CCL 24:189-90. [5]Leloir 1990:88; JSSS 2:129**. [6]Mk 5:33. [7]Cetedoc 0594, 3.9; FC 57:148*.

### 5:34a Daughter, Your Faith Has Made You Well

**WHETHER PROXIMITY ELICITS FAITH.** AUGUS-
TINE: Few are they who by faith touch him;
multitudes are they who throng about him.[8]
SERMON 62.4.[9]

**TOUCHING IN DOUBT.** BEDE: Some "seeing see
not, and hearing do not hear."[10] So also some
who touch, touch not, when they approach the
Lord not in simplicity of soul, but in doubt or
in duplicity. EXPOSITION ON THE GOSPEL OF
MARK 2.5.[11]

### 5:34b Be Healed of Your Disease

**THE WAY OF HEALING.** APOSTOLIC CONSTITU-
TIONS: Provide remedies suitable to every
patient's case. Cure them, heal them by all means
possible. Restore them soundly to the church.
Feed the flock, "not with insolence and contempt,
as lording it over them,"[12] but as a gentle shepherd,
"gathering the lambs into your bosom, and gently
leading those which are with young."[13] CONSTI-
TUTIONS OF THE HOLY APOSTLES 2.3.20.[14]

**THE HEALING IMPERATIVE.** PRUDENTIUS:
    Members filled with leprous ulcers,
        flesh corrupted and decayed,
    "Go and wash them, I command you";
        what he ordered then is done;
    Wounds are healed by pious cleansing,
        swollen flesh grows smooth again.[15]

    Now on eyes, by lifelong darkness,
        shrouded from the light of day
    Thou dost spread a clay of healing, made
        with nectar from thy lips;
    Soon the blinded orbs are opened and
        rejoice in late-found sight.[16]

    Thou dost chide the angry tempest
        and the savage hurricane,
    Which upheave the tossing billows
        and beset the fragile boat;
    At thy bidding winds are subject,
        and the rolling waves are stilled.[17]

    Then a woman, weak and timid, touched
        his sacred garment's hem:
    Instant was the blessed healing, and
        the pallor left her cheek,
    As the hemorrhage she had suffered
        through so many years was stopped.[18]

    Lazarus for four days buried, hidden in
        the sunless tomb,
    He restores to life and vigor, giving
        power to breathe again,
    And the soul returning, enters flesh
        now crumbling to decay.[19]
HYMN 9.[20]

### 5:36 Do Not Fear, Only Believe

**THE SOLE REQUISITE TO RECEIVING NEW
LIFE.** APHRAHAT: When the chief of the synagogue asked him about his daughter, Jesus said
to him: "Only firmly believe and your daughter
shall live."[21] He believed and so his daughter
lived and arose. Similarly when Lazarus died,
our Lord said to Martha, "If you believe, your
brother shall rise." Martha said to him, "Yes,
Lord, I believe."[22] And he raised him after four

---

[8]Cf. Is 1:11. [9]Cetedoc 0284, 62.38.416.48; *GMI* 111. [10]Mt 13:13.
[11]Cetedoc 1355, 2.5.360; *GMI* 111*; cf. *WSA* 3 3:158. It was not the
mere manual touching of the Lord itself that healed but touching the
Lord in simplicity of soul. [12]Cf. Ezek 34:4; Mt 20:25. [13]Cf. Is 40:11.
[14]PG 1:637; ANF 7:405. The healing ministry of the church is
adapted to each particular adversity confronted. [15]Mt 8:2-3. [16]Cf. Jn
9:1-7. [17]Cf. Mt 8:24-26. [18]Cf. Mt 9:20-22; Mk 5:25-34; Lk 8:43-48.
[19]Cf. Jn 11:38-44. [20]Cetedoc 1438, 9.31; FC 43:62-63. [21]Cf. Mk
5:35-36. [22]Cf. Jn 11:23-27.

days.... So let us draw near then, my beloved, to faith, since its powers are so many. For faith raised up [Enoch] to the heavens[23] and conquered the deluge.[24] Faith causes the barren to sprout forth.[25] It delivers from the sword.[26] It raises up from the pit.[27] It enriches the poor.[28] It releases the captives. It delivers the persecuted.[29] It brings down the fire.[30] It divides the sea.[31] It cleaves the rock, and gives to the thirsty water to drink.[32] It satisfies the hungry.[33] It raises the dead, and brings them up from Sheol.[34] It stills the billows.[35] It heals the sick.[36] It conquers hosts.[37] It overthrows walls.[38] It stops the mouths of lions,[39] and quenches the flame of fire.[40] It humiliates the proud, and brings the humble to honor.[41] All these mighty works are wrought by faith. Now this is faith; when one believes in God the Lord of all, Who made the heavens and the earth and the seas and all that is in them. He made Adam in his image. He gave the law to Moses. He sent his Spirit upon the prophets. Moreover he sent his Christ into the world, that we should believe in the resurrection of the dead; and should also trust in the efficacy of our baptism. This is the faith of the church of God. So distance yourselves from all divinations and sorceries and Chaldean arts and magic, and superficial prayers and rites and moons and seasons, from fornication and lewd music, from vain doctrines which are instruments of the adversary, from the allure of honeyed words, from blasphemy and from adultery. Do not bear false witness or speak with a double tongue. DEMONSTRATION 4.17-19.[42]

## 5:37 He Allowed No One to Follow Except Peter, James and John

**WHY ONLY THREE?** JEROME: Someone may wonder or ask: Why are these three apostles always chosen and the others sent away? Even when he was transfigured on the mountain, these three were with him.[43] Yes, these three were chosen: Peter, James and John. But why only three? First there is the mystery of the Trinity embedded in this number, a number sacred in itself. Second, according to Moses, Jacob set three peeled branches in the watering troughs.[44] Finally, it is written: "A three-ply cord is not easily broken."[45] Peter is chosen as one upon whom the church would be built.[46] James is the first of the apostles to be crowned with martyrdom.[47] John is the beloved disciple[48] whose love prefigures the state of virginity. HOMILY 77.[49]

## 5:39 The Child Is Not Dead but Sleeping

**THE AWAKENING VOICE OF THE LORD.** AMBROSE: And what shall I say about the daughter of the ruler of the synagogue, at whose death the people were mourning and the flute players were playing their music?[50] On the assumption that she was indeed dead, solemn funeral services were already being performed. But her spirit returned immediately at the voice of the Lord. She arose with revived body and partook of food to furnish proof that she was alive.[51] ON HIS BROTHER, SATYRUS 2.82.[52]

---

[23]Cf. Gen 5:24; Heb 11:5. [24]Cf. Gen 7:1—8:22; Heb 11:7. [25]Cf. Gen 21:1-3; Heb 11:11-12. [26]Cf. Gen 22:1-19; Heb 11:17, 34. [27]Cf. Gen 37:28. [28]Cf. Mk 12:42-44. [29]Cf. Heb 11:27-29. [30]Cf. 1 Kings 18:38. [31]Cf. Ex 14:21. [32]Cf. Ex 17:6. [33]Cf. Ex 16:15. [34]Cf. Heb 11:35. [35]Cf. Mt 8:26. [36]Cf. Mt 9:2, 22; Mk 2:5. [37]Cf. Heb 11:34. [38]Cf. Heb 11:30. [39]Cf. Heb 11:33. [40]Cf. Heb 11:34. [41]Cf. Heb 11:26; Jas 4:6. [42]NPNF 2 13:351-52**. [43]Cf. Mt 17:1-3; Mk 9:2-4; Lk 9:28-30. [44]Gen 30:38; to stimulate the animals to reproductive activity. [45]Eccles 4:12. [46]Cf. Mt 16:18. [47]Cf. Acts 12:2. [48]The beloved disciple, whose love anticipates the tradition of sexual chastity in apostolic ministry. Cf. Jn 19:26; 20:2; 21:7, 20. [49]Cetedoc 0594, 3.31; FC 57:149*. Within this inner circle we find the prefiguring of the apostolate, of martyrdom and of purity of heart. [50]Cf. Mt 9:23. [51]Cf. Mk 5:38-43; Lk 8:52-55. [52]Cetedoc 0157, 2.82.294.1; FC 22:233*. Cf. Ambrose *On Belief in the Resurrection* 2, NPNF 2 10:187. She who was perceived as being irrevocably dead was given new life simply through the voice of the Lord.

**WHETHER THE CHILD WAS DEAD.** AUGUSTINE: He comes to the house, and finds the customary funeral rites already underway, and he says to them, "Why do you make a tumult and weep? The child is not dead, but sleeping."[53] He spoke the truth. She was in a certain sense asleep—asleep, that is, in respect of him, by whom she could be awakened. So awakening her, he restored her alive to her parents. SERMON ON NEW TESTAMENT LESSONS 48.[54]

**THE LONG-SUFFERING OF PARENTS.** PETER CHRYSOLOGUS: Let us, if it is pleasing to you, speak for a moment of the pains and anxieties which parents take upon themselves and endure in patience out of love and affection for their children. Here, surrounded by her family and by the sympathy and affection of her relations, a daughter lies upon her bed of suffering. She is fading in body. Her father's mind and spirit are worn with grief. She is suffering the inward pangs of her sickness. He, unwashed, unkempt, is absorbed wholly in sorrow. He suffers and endures before the eyes of the world. She is sinking into the quiet of death. . . . Alas! why are children indifferent to these things! Why are they not mindful of them? Why are they not eager to make a return to their parents for them? But the love of parents goes on nevertheless; and whatever parents bestow upon their children, God, the parent of us all, will

duly repay. SERMON 33.2.[55]

### 5:43 Give Her Something to Eat

**AVOIDING DELUSION.** JEROME: For whenever he raised anyone from the dead[56] he ordered that food should be given him to eat, lest the resurrection should be thought a delusion. And this is why Lazarus after his resurrection[57] is described as being at the feast with our Lord. AGAINST JOVINIANUS 2.17.[58]

**VALIDATING THE RESURRECTION.** THEODORET OF CYR: For since eating is appropriate for those living this present life, the Lord necessarily demonstrated this by means of eating and drinking, thus proving the resurrection of the flesh to those who did not think it real. This same course he pursued in the case of Lazarus and of Jairus' daughter. For when he had raised up the latter he ordered that something should be given her to eat.[59] DIALOGUE 2, THE UNCONFOUNDED.[60]

---

[53]Mark 5:39. [54]Cetedoc 0284, 98.38.593.16; NPNF 1 6:414**; cf. WSA 3 4:45, Sermon 98.4. Her assumed death and sleeping in relation to him is seen in the light of her awakening to him. [55]Cetedoc 0227+, 33.13; SSGF 4:322-23*. [56]Cf. Mk 5:43; Lk 8:55. [57]Cf. Jn 12:2. [58]Cetedoc 0610, 2.17.325.13; NPNF 2 6:401. [59]Cf. Mk 5:43. [60]TLG 4089.002, 147.15-20; NPNF 2 3:198. Eating by those raised demonstrates their return to actual life, thus validating the reality of the resurrection.

## 6:1-6 REJECTED AT NAZARETH

[1]He went away from there and came to his own country; and his disciples followed him. [2]And on the sabbath he began to teach in the synagogue; and many who heard him were astonished, saying, "Where did this man get all this? What is the wisdom given to him? What

*mighty works are wrought by his hands!* [3]*Is not this the carpenter, the son of Mary and brother of James and Joses and Judas and Simon, and are not his sisters here with us?" And they took offense[r] at him.* [4]*And Jesus said to them, "A prophet is not without honor, except in his own country, and among his own kin, and in his own house."* [5]*And he could do no mighty work there, except that he laid his hands upon a few sick people and healed them.* [6]*And he marveled because of their unbelief.*

*And he went about among the villages teaching.*

r Or *stumbled*

---

**Overview:** Jesus blessed by his own labor the unpretentious vocation of carpentry (Ephrem the Syrian). As a youth he did not separate himself from his synagogue tradition (Origen). At Nazareth Jesus lived an active, common life, identifying with the poor, obedient within the economic order as an ordinary workman (Justin Martyr). Yet as the eternal Son, he came down into our broken humanity as if we were already his own (Peter Chrysologus). As a magnet is drawn toward iron, so faith is drawn toward God's healing power, which may surmount disbelief but works with greater power among those who believe (Origen). Human willing can temporarily thwart God's gifts by its faithless resistance. This is the ironic pseudo-power of unbelief—the refusal of God's gifts (John Cassian). Meanwhile God's gracious purpose is not finally obstructed by the resistance of any particular recipient. Determined not to coerce freedom, God respects even the freedom that resists his promptings (Gregory Nazianzen).

### 6:1 He Came to His Own Country

**He Taught in Synagogue.** Origen: "His own country" refers to Nazareth . . . because of the saying, "he shall be called a Nazarene."[1] . . . In his own country Jesus was not held in honor, but he was held in honor among those who were "strangers from the covenants,"[2] the Gentiles. Only let it be noted that he taught in their synagogue, not separating from it, and not disregarding it.[3] Commentary on Matthew 10. 16.[4]

**How Can One Who Is Everywhere Be Said to "Come to" Some Place?** Peter Chrysologus: How can he be said to go out and to come in, whom no space can enclose? What country can be his, who made, and who possesses the whole universe? In truth, Christ goes out and comes in not of himself, nor for himself, but in you, and on behalf of you, until he recovers you from your exile, and calls you home from your captivity.[5] Sermons 49.[6]

### 6:3 The Carpenter, the Son of Mary

**Common Labor.** Justin Martyr: Jesus came as the son of a carpenter.[7] He was not physically attractive, just as the prophets had predicted of him.[8] He was merely a carpenter,

---

[1]Mt 2:23. [2]Eph 2:12. [3]Cf. Mt 13:54. [4]TLG 2042.029, 10.16.32-34, 44-45, 49-50; ANF 9:424. He was less honored by those in the covenant than by those outside. In seeking his own, his own received him not. [5]Gen 3:8; Ps 24:1; Mt 9:13; 18:11; Lk 15:4. [6]Cetedoc 0227+, 49.8; GMI 119*. The eternal Son comes to our broken humanity as if our banishment from our native unfallen humanity were a breach to be overcome. [7]Cf. Mt 13:55. [8]Cf. Is 53:2.

making ploughs and yokes, and instructing us by such symbols of righteousness to avoid an inactive life. DIALOGUE WITH TRYPHO 7.9.[9]

**CARPENTRY A BLESSED OCCUPATION.** EPHREM THE SYRIAN: The ordinary workmen will come to the son of Joseph singing:

> "Blessed be your coming,[10] O master of
> workers everywhere.
> The imprint of your labor is seen in the
> ark,[11]
> And in the fashioning of the tabernacle[12]
> Of the congregation that was for a time
> only!
> Our whole craft praises you, who are our
> eternal glory.
> Make for us a yoke that is light, even easy,
> for us to bear.[13]
> Establish that measure in us in which there
> can be no falseness."

HYMNS ON THE NATIVITY 6.[14]

## 6:5a He Could Do No Mighty Work There

**WHAT DOES "COULD NOT" MEAN IN GOD'S CASE?** GREGORY NAZIANZEN: One meaning of "could not" is simply the limits of some human will. Take, for example, the point that Christ "could not" fulfill any signs in Nazareth was due to disbelief on their part.[15] Something essential for healing is required on both sides—faith on the part of the patients, power on that of the healer. So one side without its counterpart "could not," so to speak, perform them. As this can be seen in medical care, it can also be seen in moral transformation. Similarly involving the limits of the will are the texts: "The world cannot not hate you" and "How can you[16] speak good, being evil?"[17] The metaphor of "impossibility" here must mean free refusal by the will. The same idea

applies to those passages which say that what is impossible for humanity is possible for God.[18] Note also those passages that say that a person "cannot" (in one sense) be born a second time[19] and a needle's eye "cannot" let a camel through.[20] What would stop these events happening if God willed them directly?[21] Besides all these there is, as in the case we are presently considering, a "cannot" in the sense of that which is totally inconceivable. We cannot conceive that God can be evil or fail to exist. It is inconceivable that reality cannot exist or two times two is fourteen. So here it cannot be the case that the Son would do anything which the Father would not do. ORATION 30, ON THE SON 10-11.[22]

**IMPEDING GOD'S GIFTS.** JOHN CASSIAN: In some cases he so richly poured forth the mighty work of healing that the Evangelist was led to exclaim: "He healed all their sick."[23] But among others the unfathomable depth of Christ's goodness was so thwarted that it was said: "And Jesus could do there no mighty works because of their unbelief."[24] So the bounty of God is actually curtailed temporarily according to the receptivity of our faith. So it is said to one: "According to your faith may it be to you,"[25] and to another: "Go your way, and as you have believed so let it be to you,"[26] and to another "Let it be to you according as you

---

[9]TLG 0645.003, 88.8.1-7; *GMI* 120*.  [10]Cf. Ps 118:26.  [11]Cf. Ex 25:10-16.  [12]Cf. Ex 26.  [13]Cf. Mt 11:30.  [14]NPNF 2 13:239**. He blessed common labor by his own hands that ordinary workers everywhere might see how he participated in their humble work.  [15]Mt 13:58; Mk 6:5.  [16]Brood of vipers.  [17]Mt 12:34.  [18]Cf. Mt 19:26; Mk 10:27.  [19]Jn 3:4.  [20]Mt 19:24; Mk 10:25; Lk 18:25.  [21]Setting aside human freedom.  [22]TLG 2022.010, 10.13-11.6; *FGFR* 268**; cf. LCC 3:183. The phrase "he could not" implies not that the Savior lacked power but that the recipients of the divine gift lacked the faithfulness to receive divine power.  [23]Mt 8:16; Lk 4:40.  [24]Mt 13:58; Mk 6:6.  [25]Mt 9:29.  [26]Mt 8:13.

will,"[27] and again to another: "Your faith has made you whole."[28] THIRD CONFERENCE OF ABBOT CHAERMEON 15.[29]

### 6:5b Except That He Laid His Hands upon a Few Sick People and Healed Them

DISTINGUISHING GOD'S POWER AND OUR FAITH. ORIGEN: And perhaps, as in the case of metallic substances there exists in some a natural attraction toward some other thing, as in the magnet for iron, and in naphtha for fire, so there is an attraction in such faith toward the divine power according to what Jesus said: "If you have faith as a grain of mustard seed, you shall say unto this mountain, 'Move to another place,' and it shall be moved."[30] Matthew and Mark wished to present the all-surpassing value of that divine power as a power that works even in those who do not believe. But they did not deny that grace works even more powerfully among those who have faith. So it seems to me that they accurately said not that

the Lord did not do *any* mighty works because of their unbelief, but that he did not do *many* there.[31] Mark does not flatly say that he could do no mighty work there at all, and stop at that point, but added, "except that he laid his hands upon a few sick folk and healed them."[32] Thus the power in him overcame even their unbelief. COMMENTARY ON MATTHEW 10.19.[33]

### 6:5c And He Marveled Because of Their Unbelief

THE "POWER" OF UNBELIEF. JOHN CASSIAN: If the faith of those who bring them or of the sick is lacking, it may prevent those who possess the gift of healing from exercising it. SECOND CONFERENCE OF ABBOT NESTEROS 15.1.[34]

---

[27]Cf. Mt 15:28. [28]Mt 9:22; Mk 5:34; 10:52; Lk 8:48; 17:19. [29]Cetedoc 0512, 13.15.390.13; NPNF 2 11:432-33*. Our unreadiness temporarily impedes God's offering us his gifts. [30]Mt 17:20. [31]Cf. Mk 6:5. [32]Mk 6:5. [33]ANF 9:426*; TLG 2042.029, 10.19.19-34. Italics added. [34]Cetedoc 0512, 15.1.426.22; NPNF 2 11:445*; LCC 12:258, *Western Asceticism*, 258.

## 6:7-13 COMMISSIONING THE TWELVE

[7]And he called to him the twelve, and began to send them out two by two, and gave them authority over the unclean spirits. [8]He charged them to take nothing for their journey except a staff; no bread, no bag, no money in their belts; [9]but to wear sandals and not put on two tunics. [10]And he said to them, "Where you enter a house, stay there until you leave the place. [11]And if any place will not receive you and they refuse to hear you, when you leave, shake off the dust that is on your feet for a testimony against them." [12]So they went out and preached that men should repent. [13]And they cast out many demons, and anointed with oil many that were sick and healed them.

**OVERVIEW:** Putting on two coats implies double-mindedness, a burden of deception that a rigorous journey does not need (AUGUSTINE). The apostolic mission must not be weighted down with extravagant wishes or mundane yearnings (PRUDENTIUS). The grace to follow the command to take no money in apostolic ministry is received voluntarily, not as an oppressive regulation of law. It is given to those who are being readied eventually to receive the fullness of sanctifying grace (JEROME). Only those rightly prepared are called to anoint the sick with oil (CYPRIAN).

### 6:8 Take Nothing Except a Staff: No Bread, No Bag, No Money

**TO WHOM ADDRESSED.** JEROME: Are all commanded not to have two coats, nor food in their possession, money in their purse, only a staff in the hand and shoes on the feet?[1] Are all commanded to sell all they possess and give it to the poor, and follow Jesus? Of course not. This command is for those who earnestly desire to respond fully to grace. . . . The Lord says in the Gospel to him who had boasted of having kept the whole law: "If you will be perfect, go and sell all that you have, and give to the poor, and come, follow me."[2] He said this to those who wish to be wholly mature in faith, that he might not seem to be laying a heavy burden on unwilling shoulders. AGAINST JOVINIANUS 2.[3]

**RESOURCES FOR APOSTOLIC MISSION.** PRUDENTIUS:

> To wish for nothing more than need
> demands
> Is rest supreme, with simple food and dress
> To feed and clothe our bodies and to seek
> No more than is prescribed by nature's
> wants.

> When going on a journey, take no purse,[4]
> Nor of a second tunic think, and be
> Not anxious for the morrow,[5] lest for food
> The belly lack. Our daily bread returns
> With every sun. Does any bird take thought
> Of tomorrow, certain to be fed by God?[6]

THE SPIRITUAL COMBAT.[7]

### 6:9 Wear Sandals and Do Not Put On Two Tunics

**ON NOT WEARING TWO COATS.** AUGUSTINE: What is forbidden is neither the carrying nor the possessing of two coats, but more distinctly the wearing of two coats at the same time. The words say: "and not put on two coats." What counsel is conveyed to them by this? They ought to walk not in duplicity, but in simplicity. HARMONY OF THE GOSPELS 2.32.75.[8]

### 6:13 They Anointed with Oil Many That Were Sick

**THOSE RIGHTLY PREPARED TO ANOINT.** CYPRIAN: One who is anointing should be baptized, so that having received the chrism [the anointing], he may be anointed of God, and have in him the grace of Christ. Those to be baptized and anointed with the oil of chrismation, receive the oil sanctified on the altar of the eucharist. But one who has neither an altar nor a church cannot duly consecrate the creature of oil. EPISTLE 69, TO JANUARIUS 2.[9]

---

[1]Cf. Mt 10:9; Mk 6:8. [2]Mt 19:21. [3]Cetedoc 0610, 2.6.307.18; NPNF 2 6:393*. [4]Mt 10:10; Mk 6:8-9; Lk 9:3; 22:35. [5]Mt 6:34. [6]Mt 10:29. [7]Cetedoc 1441, 609; FC 52:100. [8]Cetedoc 0273, 2.30.75.180.12; NPNF 1 6:139*. The picture of not putting on two coats has a hidden meaning in reference to duplicity. [9]COG 2:201; ANF 5:376*. Not just anyone is fit to sanctify the oil, but only those duly called.

## 6:14-29 THE DEATH OF JOHN

[14]*King Herod heard of it; for Jesus'[s] name had become known. Some[t] said, "John the baptizer has been raised from the dead; that is why these powers are at work in him."* [15]*But others said, "It is Elijah." And others said, "It is a prophet, like one of the prophets of old."* [16]*But when Herod heard of it he said, "John, whom I beheaded, has been raised."* [17]*For Herod had sent and seized John, and bound him in prison for the sake of Herodias, his brother Philip's wife; because he had married her.* [18]*For John said to Herod, "It is not lawful for you to have your brother's wife."* [19]*And Herodias had a grudge against him, and wanted to kill him. But she could not,* [20]*for Herod feared John, knowing that he was a righteous and holy man, and kept him safe. When he heard him, he was much perplexed; and yet he heard him gladly.* [21]*But an opportunity came when Herod on his birthday gave a banquet for his courtiers and officers and the leading men of Galilee.* [22]*For when Herodias' daughter came in and danced, she pleased Herod and his guests; and the king said to the girl, "Ask me for whatever you wish, and I will grant it."* [23]*And he vowed to her, "Whatever you ask me, I will give you, even half of my kingdom."* [24]*And she went out, and said to her mother, "What shall I ask?" And she said, "The head of John the baptizer."* [25]*And she came in immediately with haste to the king, and asked, saying, "I want you to give me at once the head of John the Baptist on a platter."* [26]*And the king was exceedingly sorry; but because of his oaths and his guests he did not want to break his word to her.* [27]*And immediately the king sent a soldier of the guard and gave orders to bring his head. He went and beheaded him in the prison,* [28]*and brought his head on a platter, and gave it to the girl; and the girl gave it to her mother.* [29]*When his disciples heard of it, they came and took his body, and laid it in a tomb.*

**s** Greek *his*   **t** Other ancient authorities read *he*

---

**OVERVIEW:** John's life of moral excellence gave plausibility to his rigorous admonitions (CHRYSOSTOM). He was imprisoned for challenging the degenerate moral behavior of the royal family (EUSEBIUS). No prison, however, could take away the freedom to walk the path that leads to God (TERTULLIAN). Herod's lesser sin, his oath, tripped him up in his greater sin, murder. In this way a single act of dissipation may combine and express many accrued forms of vice (AMBROSE, AUGUSTINE). As David was right to take back his oath, Herod was wrong to keep his (AMBROSE, BEDE). By our own words we may needlessly place ourselves under grievous moral necessity, so that Satan snares us through our own words freely spoken. Such tragic misjudgments continue to plague those who become captive to their own appetites (CHRYSOSTOM). A better disposition would have treated words as vessels of sanctification, alert to potential imprudence (AMBROSE). John was righteous in the eyes of the Lord first through his open truth-telling and then through his martyrdom, which resulted directly from his attesting the truth (AMBROSE, BEDE). All of us have a duty of admonition to our fellow human beings when circumstances require it, since they have a right to our good judgment (CHRYSOSTOM).

### 6:17a Herod Seized John and Bound Him in Prison

**THE SOUL IS NOT BOUND.** TERTULLIAN: Set aside for a moment the term "prison." Just call it a temporary retirement. Even though the body is imprisoned, even though the flesh is confined, everything still remains open to the spirit. Walk back and forth, my spirit, not thinking of shady walks or long cloisters, but of the road that leads directly to God. As often as you shall walk in this way in the spirit, so often shall you find yourself not in prison.[1] ON MARTYRDOM 2.[2]

### 6:17b For the Sake of Herodias, His Brother Philip's Wife, Because He Had Married Her

**THE REASON JOHN WAS IMPRISONED.** EUSEBIUS: Not long after this, John the Baptist was beheaded by the younger Herod,[3] as stated in the Gospels.[4] Josephus also records the same fact, mentioning Herodias[5] by name, and stating that, although she was the wife of his brother, Herod made her his own wife after divorcing his former lawful wife, the daughter of Aretas,[6] king of Petra, and separating Herodias from her husband while he was still alive. It was on her account also that he killed John, and waged war with Aretas, because of the disgrace inflicted on the daughter of the latter. Josephus wrote that in this war, when they came to battle, Herod's entire army was destroyed, and that he suffered this calamity on account of his crime against John. ECCLESIASTICAL HISTORY 1.11.[7]

### 6:18 It Is Not Lawful

**WHO SHALL ADMONISH THE KING?** CHRYSOSTOM: John saw a man that was a tyrant overthrowing the divine commands on marriage. With boldness, he proclaimed in the midst of the forum, "It is not lawful for you to have your brother Philip's wife."[8] So we learn from him to admonish our fellow servant as an equal. Do not shrink from the duty of chastising a brother, even though one may be required to die for it. Now do not make this cold reply: "What does it matter to me? I have nothing in common with him." With the devil alone we have nothing in common, but with all humanity we have many things in common. All partake of the same nature with us. They inhabit the same earth. They are nourished with the same food. They have the same Lord. They have received the same laws. They are invited to the same blessings with ourselves. Let us not say then that we have nothing in common with them. CONCERNING THE STATUES 1.32.[9]

### 6:20 Herod Feared John and Heard Him Gladly

**ADMONITION VALUED BY THOSE REPROVED.**

---

[1]Cf. Rom 8:1. [2]Cetedoc 0001, 5.2.1; *Ad Martyras GMI* 129*; ANF 3:694*. [3]Herod Antipas. [4]Mt 14:1-12; Mk 6:17-29. [5]Herodias was a daughter of Aristobulus and granddaughter of Herod the Great. [6]The Aretas mentioned in 2 Cor 11:32. [7]TLG 2018.002, 1.11.1-3.3; NPNF 2 1:97*. [8]Mk 6:18. [9]TLG 2062.024, 49.33.6-9, 16-18, 23-31; NPNF 19:343.

CHRYSOSTOM: Mark says that Herod exceedingly honored the man [John], even when reproved.[10] So great a thing is virtue. THE GOSPEL OF ST. MATTHEW, HOMILY 48.[11]

### 6:22 When Herodias's Daughter Came In and Danced, She Pleased Herod and His Guests

THE INTERWEAVING OF VICES. AMBROSE: Note how varied sins are interwoven in this one vicious action! A banquet of death is set out with royal luxury, and when a larger gathering than usual has come together, the daughter of the queen, sent for from within the private apartments, is brought forth to dance in the sight of all. What could she have learned from an adulteress but the loss of modesty? Is anything so conducive to lust as with unseemly movements to expose in nakedness those parts of the body which either nature has hidden or custom has veiled, to sport with looks, to turn the neck, to loosen the hair? CONCERNING VIRGINS 3.6.27.[12]

CALAMITIES ACCUMULATE. AUGUSTINE: A girl dances, a mother rages, there is rash swearing in the midst of the luxurious feast, and an impious fulfillment of what was sworn. HARMONY OF THE GOSPELS 2.33.[13]

### 6:23 Herod Vowed to Her: Ask Whatever You Wish

THE TRAP. CHRYSOSTOM: So the princess danced and, after the dance, committed another more serious sin. For she persuaded that senseless man to promise with an oath to give her whatever she might ask. Do you see how easily swearing makes one witless? Thus, whatever she asked, he swore to give. What, then, if she were to have asked for *your* head,

Herod? What if she were to have asked for your *whole* kingdom? Yet he took no thought of these things. The devil had set his trap, making it strong, and from the moment the oath was complete, he both cast his snares and stretched his net on every side. The request was abominable, but she persuaded him, and he gave the order to bridle John's holy tongue. But even now it continues to speak. For even today in every church, you can hear John still crying aloud through the Gospels and saying: "It is not lawful for you to have the wife of your brother Philip."[14] He cut off the head, but he did not cut off the voice. He curbed the tongue, but he did not curb the accusation. Do you see what swearing leads to? It cuts off the heads of prophets. You saw the bait. Dread, then, the ruin it brings. BAPTISMAL INSTRUCTIONS 10.26-27.[15]

SLAVERY TO INORDINATE AFFECTIONS. CHRYSOSTOM: So much did he value his kingdom, such a captive was he to his passion, that he would give it to her for her dancing. And why do you wonder that this happened then, when even now, after so much instruction in sound doctrine, many men give away their soul for the dancing of these effeminate young men with no oath needed? They have been made captives by their pleasure and are led around like sheep wherever the wolf may drag them. THE GOSPEL OF ST. MATTHEW, HOMILY 49.[16]

---

[10]Mk 6:20. [11]NPNF 1 10:298*; TLG 2062.152, 58.489.8-10. [12]Cetedoc 0145, 3.6.26.9; NPNF 2 10:385*. [13]Cetedoc 0284, 307.38.1406.7; NPNF 1 6:140*. Cf. GC 1:402-3. A single debauched act may combine and express many accrued forms of vice: murder, lust, immodesty, exhibitionism, adultery, seduction and deception. [14]Mt 14:4; Mk 6:18. [15]TLG 2062.380, 164.21-165.2; 165.11-19; ACW 31:158-59. The devil set the trap by means of a rash oath, but the beheading did not end the accusation. [16]TLG 2062.152, 58.490.46-54; ACW 31:311.

**THE IMPULSIVE OATH.** BEDE: We hear at the same time of three evil deeds done: the inauspicious celebration of a birthday, the lewd dancing of a girl, and the rash oath of a king. This is the judgment to which Herod fell victim, so that he found he either had to break his oath or, to avoid breaking his oath, to commit another shameful act. If it should perhaps happen that we swear carelessly to something which, if carried out, would have most unfortunate consequences, we should be willing to change it in accord with wiser counsel. There is an urgent necessity for us to break our oath, rather than turn to another more serious crime in order to avoid breaking our oath. David swore by the Lord to kill Nabal, a stupid and wicked man, and to destroy all his possessions. But at the first entreaty of the prudent woman Abigail, he quickly took back his threats, put back his sword into its scabbard, and did not feel that he had contracted any guilt by thus breaking his oath in this way.[17] Herod swore that he would give the dancing girl whatever she asked of him, and, to avoid being accused of breaking his oath by those who were at his banquet, he defiled the banquet with blood when he made the reward for the dancing the death of a prophet. EXPOSITION ON THE GOSPEL OF MARK 2.23.[18]

### 6:25 Give Me the Head of John

**WHEN A LESSER SIN ELICITS A GREATER.** BEDE: His love for the woman prevailed. She forced him to lay his hands upon a man whom he knew to be holy and just. Since he was unwilling to restrain his lechery, he incurred the guilt of homicide. What was a lesser sin for him became the occasion of a greater sin. By God's strict judgment it happened to him that, as a result of his craving for the adulteress

whom he knew he ought to refuse, he caused the shedding of the blood of the prophet he knew was pleasing to God. . . . Already holy, John became more holy still when, through his office of spreading the good news, he reached the palm[19] of martyrdom. EXPOSITION ON THE GOSPEL OF MARK 2.23.[20]

### 6:26a The King Was Exceedingly Sorry, but Because of His Oaths and His Guests

**THE PERIL OF SWEARING.** CHRYSOSTOM: It is indeed a haven of safety if we do not swear at all. So whatever storms burst upon us we are in no danger of sinking. Whether it be through anger or insult or passion, be what it may, the soul is stayed securely. Even though one might have vented some chance word that ought not to have been spoken, one is not laying oneself absolutely under necessity or law. . . . For it is indeed a snare of Satan, this swearing. Let us burst these cords. Let us bring ourselves into a condition in which it will be easy not to swear.[21] THE ACTS OF THE APOSTLES, HOMILY 13.[22]

**SHOULD A BAD OATH BE FULFILLED?** AMBROSE: A good disposition ought to be open and straightforward, so that one may utter words without deceit, and possess one's soul with singleness of intent, and not delude another with false words, and not promise anything dishonorable.[23] If he has made such a promise, it is far better for him not to fulfill it, than to fulfill what is shameful. Sometimes people bind themselves by a solemn oath, and,

---

[17]Cf. 1 Sam 25:2-39. [18]Cetedoc 1367, 2.23.89; *HOG* 2:232-33. [19]Reward. [20]Cetedoc 1367, 2.23.74; *HOG* 2:232*. The evil of the murder was disproportionate to the evil of his oath. [21]Cf. Mt 5:34, 36; Jas 5:12. [22]TLG 2062.154, 60.112.17-24, 32-36; PG 60:112; NPNF 1 11:86-87. [23]Cf. Num 30:2.

though they come to know that they ought not to have made the promise, fulfill it in consideration of their oath. This is what Herod did. For he made a shameful promise of reward to a dancer—and then cruelly performed it. DUTIES OF THE CLERGY 3.12.76-77.[24]

### THE SORROW OF THE KING. AMBROSE: When it is said that "the king was sorry,"[25] that does not indicate genuine repentance on the part of the king, but rather a confession of his guilt. Thus, according to the design of divine governance, those who do evil condemn themselves by their own confession. But what was the motive, in this case: "Because of his oath and his guests"! What could be more vile than a murder done to not displease one's guests? CONCERNING VIRGINS 3.6.28.[26]

## 6:26b He Did Not Want to Break His Word with Her

### THE DILEMMA OF THE HASTY OATH. AMBROSE: It was shameful in the first place for a kingdom to be promised for a dance. And it was cruel, in the second place, for a prophet to be sacrificed for the sake of an oath. DUTIES OF THE CLERGY 3.12.77.[27]

## 6:27 He Beheaded Him in the Prison

### THE PASSION ANTICIPATED. PETER CHRYSOLOGUS: For then did the old greedy dragon taste in the head of the servant what he so thirsted after—the passion of the master. SERMONS 174.[28]

## 6:28a They Brought His Head on a Platter

### THE WEAKNESS OF THE TYRANT AND THE

### POWER OF THE BEHEADED. CHRYSOSTOM: Note well the weakness of the tyrant compared to the power of the one in prison. Herod was not strong enough to silence his own tongue. Having opened it, he opened up countless other mouths in its place and with its help. As for John, he immediately inspired fear in Herod after his murder—for fear was disturbing Herod's conscience to such an extent that he believed John had been raised from the dead and was performing miracles![29] In our own day and through all future time, throughout all the world, John continues to refute Herod, both through himself and through others. For each person repeatedly reading this Gospel says: "It is not lawful for you to have the wife of Philip your brother."[30] And even apart from reading the Gospel, in assemblies and meetings at home or in the market, in every place . . . even to the very ends of the earth,[31] you will hear this voice and see that righteous man even now still crying out, resounding loudly, reproving the evil of the tyrant. He will never be silenced nor the reproof at all weakened by the passing of time. ON THE PROVIDENCE OF GOD 22.8-9.[32]

### HIS TONGUE DID NOT REMAIN SILENT. AMBROSE: Look, most savage king, at the spectacle of your feast. Stretch out your right hand and see the streams of holy blood pouring down between your fingers. Nothing is lack-

---

[24]Cetedoc 0144, 2.3.12.76.117.5; NPNF 2 10:80**. [25]Mk 6:25-28. [26]Cetedoc 0145, 3.6.28.7; NPNF 2 10:385-86*. The sorrow was an evidence of guilt, not repentance. [27]Cetedoc 0144, 2.3.12.76.117.11; NPNF 1 10:80**. [28]Cetedoc 0227+, 174.44; *GMI* 138. Satan was greedily anticipating the death of Jesus. [29]Cf. Mk 6:14-16. [30]Mk 6:18. [31]Cf. Ps 48:10; Is 52:10; Mic 5:4; Acts 13:47; Rom 10:18. [32]TLG 2062.087, 22.7.5-9.5, 9.6-11; C. Hall, trans., 376-377, "John Chrysostom's *On Providence*: A Translation and Theological Interpretation" (Ph.D. diss., Drew University, 1991). John's voice proved stronger than Herod's tyranny.

ing in your cruelty. The hunger for such unheard-of cruelty could not be satisfied by banquets, or the thirst by goblets. So as you drink the blood pouring from the still flowing veins of the cut-off head, behold those eyes. Even in death, those eyes are the witnesses of your crime, turning away from the sight of the delicacies. The eyes are closing, not so much owing to death, as to horror of excess. That bloodless golden mouth, whose sentence you could not endure, is silent, and yet it is still dreaded. Meanwhile the tongue, which even after death is apt to observe its duty as when living, continues to condemn the incest with trembling motion. CONCERNING VIRGINS 3.6.30.[33]

### 6:28b He Gave It to the Girl

**THE SUPPOSED "VICTORY" OF HERODIAS.** AMBROSE: His head is presented to Herodias. She rejoices, exults as though she had escaped from a crime, because she has slain her judge. What say you, holy women? Do you see what you ought to teach, and what also to unteach your

daughters? CONCERNING VIRGINS 3.6.30-31.[34]

**DEATH AS A CROWN.** CHRYSOSTOM: In what way, then, was this just man harmed by this demise, this violent death, these chains, this imprisonment? Who are those he did not set back on their feet—provided they had a penitent disposition—because of what he spoke, because of what he suffered, because of what he still proclaims in our own day—the same message he preached while he was living. Therefore, do not say: "Why was John allowed to die?" For what occurred was not a death, but a crown, not an end, but the beginning of a greater life.[35] Learn to think and live like a Christian. You will not only remain unharmed by these events, but will reap the greatest benefits.[36] ON THE PROVIDENCE OF GOD 22.10.[37]

---

[33]Cetedoc 0145, 3.6.30.1; NPNF 2 10:386**. Even in his appalling death the head of the Baptist continued to attest the truth. [34]Cetedoc 0145, 3.6.30.11; NPNF 2 10:386**. Her transient victory is followed by mounting disasters. Thus women are to teach daughters to receive truthful admonition and not to deceive and seduce. [35]Cf. Rev 2:10. [36]Cf. Mt 10:28. [37]TLG 2062.087, 22.10.1-9.

## 6:30-44 FEEDING THE FIVE THOUSAND

[12930]The apostles returned to Jesus, and told him all that they had done and taught. [31]And he said to them, "Come away by yourselves to a lonely place, and rest a while." For many were coming and going, and they had no leisure even to eat. [32]And they went away in the boat to a lonely place by themselves. [33]Now many saw them going, and knew them, and they ran there on foot from all the towns, and got there ahead of them. [34]As he went ashore he saw a great

*throng, and he had compassion on them, because they were like sheep without a shepherd; and he began to teach them many things. [35]And when it grew late, his disciples came to him and said, "This is a lonely place, and the hour is now late; [36]send them away, to go into the country and villages round about and buy themselves something to eat." [37]But he answered them, "You give them something to eat." And they said to him, "Shall we go and buy two hundred denarii[u] worth of bread, and give it to them to eat?" [38]And he said to them, "How many loaves have you? Go and see." And when they had found out, they said, "Five, and two fish." [39]Then he commanded them all to sit down by companies upon the green grass. [40]So they sat down in groups, by hundreds and by fifties. [41]And taking the five loaves and the two fish he looked up to heaven, and blessed, and broke the loaves, and gave them to the disciples to set before the people; and he divided the two fish among them all. [42]And they all ate and were satisfied. [43]And they took up twelve baskets full of broken pieces and of the fish. [44]And those who ate the loaves were five thousand men.*

u The denarius was a day's wage for a laborer

---

**OVERVIEW:** The bread of life is offered in a lonely place (AMBROSE). The God-man who once hungered now feeds the multitude (GREGORY NAZIANZEN, THEODORET OF CYR). The faithful receive the bread of the gospel from the apostles, who first received it from the Lord (BEDE, PRUDENTIUS). By blessing the loaves Jesus teaches us to bless our daily bread (BEDE). Repentance (by fifties) and faith (by hundreds) are symbolically embodied in the companies of halves and wholes who, humbled on lowly grass, are thus prepared to receive the bread of God (ORIGEN).

### 6:31 They Had No Leisure Even to Eat

**HARD WORK.** BEDE: The great happiness of those days can be seen from the hard work of those who taught and the enthusiasm of those who learned. If only in our time such a concourse of faithful hearers would again press round the ministers of the word. EXPOSITION ON THE GOSPEL OF MARK 2.6.[1]

### 6:34 He Began to Teach Them Many Things

**BREAKING OPEN THE WORD.** BEDE: As he broke up the five loaves and two fishes, and distributed them to his disciples, he opened their minds to understand everything that had been written about him in the law of Moses and in the prophets and the psalms.[2] EXPOSITION ON THE GOSPEL OF MARK 2.2.[3]

### 6:35a This Is a Lonely Place

**WHERE BREAD IS OFFERED.** PSEUDO-JEROME: The bread of life is most valued not by the idle, or those who live in crowded cities encompassed with the honors of the world. It is rather most cherished by those who seek Christ "in a desert place."[4] HOMILY ON THE SONG OF SONGS 5.[5]

---

[1]Cetedoc 1355, 2.6.844; JF B 100; CCL 120, 510-11. [2]Lk 24:44-45. [3]Cetedoc 1367, 2.2.136; HOG 2:18. [4]Cf. Mt 14:13; Mk 6:31-35; Lk 4:42; 9:10; Heb 13:13-14. [5]Cetedoc 0194.5.79; GMI 144.

## 6:35b *The Hour Is Now Late*

**THE ONE WHO GIVES TIME.** CHRYSOSTOM: Even though the place is desolate, yet the one who feeds the world is present.[6] And even though the hour is late, yet the one who is not subject to the hour is conversing with you. THE GOSPEL OF ST. MATTHEW 58.[7]

## 6:37 *You Give Them Something to Eat*

**THE ONE WHO HUNGERED FEEDS.** GREGORY NAZIANZEN: As man he was put to the test, but as God he came through victorious[8]—yes, he bids us be of good cheer, because he has conquered the world.[9] He hungered[10]—yet he fed thousands.[11] He is indeed "living, heavenly bread."[12] He thirsted[13]—yet he exclaimed: "Whoever thirsts, let him come to me and drink."[14] Indeed he promised that believers would become fountains.[15] ORATION 29, ON THE SON 20.[16]

**THE GOD-MAN.** THEODORET OF CYR: For if the incarnation was a fantasy, then our salvation is a delusion. The Christ was at the same time visible man and invisible God. He ate as man, quite like ourselves. He possessed from his humanness the same passions we have.[17] He fed the five thousand with five loaves as God.[18] As man he really died.[19] As God he raised the dead on the fourth day.[20] As human he slept in the boat.[21] As God he walked upon the waters.[22] DIALOGUES 2.[23]

## 6:38 *Five Loaves and Two Fish*

**FEEDING UPON THE WORD.** PRUDENTIUS:
Five loaves and fishes two he orders placed[24]
As food before the people thronging round
Their master, by their hunger undeterred,

Who mindful not of food forgot their towns,
Their forts, their markets, hamlets, trading-
posts
And cities, glad to feed upon his words.
The festive gathering swarms upon the plain;
By hundreds they recline in friendly bands,
And round the countless boards they
range themselves
To dine on two small fish and scanty crusts
He multiplies—know now that he is God!
A HYMN ON THE TRINITY.[25]

## 6:39 *Sit Down by Companies upon the Green Grass*

**HUMBLING THE FLESH.** ORIGEN: I believe that he ordered the people to sit down upon the grass because of what is said in Isaiah: "all flesh is grass";[26] that is, to humble the flesh, to make subject the arrogance of the flesh; so that each one may become a partaker of the loaves to which Jesus gave his blessing. COMMENTARY ON MATTHEW 11.3.[27]

## 6:40 *They Sat Down in Groups by Hundreds and by Fifties*

**THE DIVISION BY COMPANIES.** ORIGEN: Since

---

[6]Jn 6:35, 51. [7]TLG 2062.152, 58.497.50-53; cf. NPNF 1 10:304*. The one who made time does not regard the hour as late. [8]Cf. Mt 4:1-11; Mk 1:12-13; Lk 4:1-13. [9]Jn 16:33. [10]Mt 4:2; Lk 4:2. [11]Mt 14:20-21; 15:37-38; Mk 6:42-44; 8:6-9. [12]Jn 6:51. [13]Jn 19:28. [14]Jn 7:37. [15]Jn 7:38. [16]FGFR 258; TLG 2022.009, 20.2-7. The one who will thirst on the cross is he who is making of believers fountains of grace. [17]Cf. Heb 4:15. [18]Cf. Mt 14:17-21; Mk 6:38-44; Lk 9:14-17; Jn 6:10-13. [19]Cf. Mt 27:50; Mk 15:37; Lk 23:46; Jn 19:30. [20]Jn 11:39-44. [21]Cf. Mt 8:24; Mk 4:38; Lk 8:23. [22]Cf. Mt 14:25; Mk 6:48; Jn 6:19. [23]NPNF 2 3:211*; TLG 4089.002, 177.19-26; cf. Cyril of Jerusalem, NPNF 2 7:21. The humbled one, who like us ate, slept and died, is also found offering food to the hungry, walking on water and raising the dead. [24]Mk 6:38-44. [25]Cetedoc 1439, 706; FC 52:28-29. Those who became most forgetful of food fed on his word. [26]Is 40:6. [27]TLG 2042.029, 11.3.28-32; SSGF 2:112.

there are different classes of those who need the food which Jesus supplies, for all are not equally nourished by the same words, on this account I think that Mark has written, "And he commanded them that they should all sit down by companies upon the green grass; and they sat down in ranks by hundreds and by fifties."[28] ... For it was necessary that those who were to find comfort in the food of Jesus should either be in the order of the hundred—the sacred number which is consecrated to God because of its completeness; or in the order of the fifty—the number which symbolizes the remission of sins in accordance with the mystery of the Jubilee which took place every fifty years, and of the feast at Pentecost.[29] COMMENTARY ON MATTHEW 11.3.[30]

### 6:41a He Blessed and Broke the Loaves

GIVING THANKS. BEDE: Nor must we overlook the fact that as he was on the point of refreshing the multitude, he gave thanks. He gave thanks in order to teach us always to give thanks for the favors we have received from heaven, and in order to impress upon us how much he himself rejoices at our spiritual refreshment. EXPOSITION ON THE GOSPEL OF MARK 2.2.[31]

### 6:41b He Gave Them to the Disciples to Set Before the People

THE MOMENT OF CREATION. EPHREM THE SYRIAN: Take note therefore of how his [creative] activity is mixed in with everything. When our Lord took a little bread, he multiplied it in the twinkling of an eye. That which [people] effect and transform in ten months with toil, his ten fingers effected in an instant. For he placed his hands beneath the bread as

though it were earth, and spoke over it as though thunder. The murmur of his lips sprinkled over it like rain, and the breath of his mouth [was there] in place of the sun. [Thus] did he complete in the flash of one tiny moment something which requires a whole lengthy hour. One tiny amount of bread was forgotten, and from the midst of its smallness, abundance came to birth so that it might be like the first blessing, "Give birth and be fruitful and multiply."[32] The loaves of bread, like barren women and women deprived [of children], became fruitful at his blessing, and many were the morsels born from them. COMMENTARY ON TATIAN'S DIATESSARON.[33]

THE BREAD OF LIFE. PRUDENTIUS:

> Thou, our bread, our true refreshment,
>     never failing sweetness art;[34]
> He can nevermore know hunger,
>     who is at thy banquet fed,[35]
> Nourishing not our fleshly nature,
>     but imparting lasting life.[36] ...
> Every sickness now surrenders,
>     every listlessness departs,[37]
> Tongues long bound by chains of silence
>     are unloosed and speak aright,[38]
> While the joyful paralytic
>     bears his pallet through the streets.[39]

HYMNS 9.[40]

THE INSIGNIFICANT MADE SIGNIFICANT. BEDE: By the manifold grace of the Spirit he

---

[28]Mk 6:39-40. [29]Cf. Lev 25:10; Tob 2:1; Acts 2:1. [30]ANF 9:433*; TLG 2042.029, 11.3.33-38, 40-46. [31]Cetedoc 1367, 2.2.163; HOG 2:19*. By blessing the loaves, he teaches us to bless our bread, and in doing so he demonstrates his own joy in our reception of sustaining spiritual food. [32]Gen 1:28. [33]JSSS 2:191. [34]Jn 6:56. [35]Jn 6:35. [36]Jn 6:51-52. [37]Lk 6:18-19. [38]Mk 7:35. [39]Mt 9:6-7; Jn 5:9. [40]Cetedoc 1438, 9.61; FC 43:64-65. This food imparts eternal life, freedom and the healing of our afflictions.

disclosed how matters that seemed insignificant and unworthy of attention might be fruitful, and he handed these things over to be administered to all nations by the apostles and their successors. Hence it is appropriate that the other Evangelists relate how our Lord administered the loaves and fishes to his disciples, and the disciples then administered them to the crowd.[41] Although the mystery of human salvation received its start by being declared by our Lord, it was confirmed in us by those who heard it [from him]. He broke up the five loaves and two fishes, and distributed them to his disciples, as he opened their minds to understand everything that had been written about him in the law of Moses and in the prophets and the psalms.[42] EXPOSITION ON THE GOSPEL OF MARK 2.2.[43]

### 6:43 Twelve Baskets Full of Broken Pieces

THE FEAST OF THE CREATOR. PRUDENTIUS:
The banquet ended, plates still overflow,
And with the crumbs twelve baskets then
  they fill.
The stuffed boy strives with undigested fare,
The waiter groans beneath his heavy load.
Who can a great feast spread from stores
  so few?
Who but the maker of our frame and all
That nurtures it, who shaped the world
  from nought?
Almighty God without the aid of seed
Fashioned the earth, not as the sculptor
  works
To lift the block of bronze from metal fused.
All that now is was nought: that nothing-
  ness
Was into being brought and bidden grow.
Small was the first creation, but it grew
Till it became the mighty universe.

Therefore, when I behold that meager fare
Thus multiplied within the hands of Christ,
Can I doubt that the elemental forms
First made by him from nothing, by degrees
Have grown to that perfection we now see?
Lest fragments should be trodden on and
  lost,
When men had fed, or should become the
  spoil
Of wolves or foxes or of petty mice,
Twelve men were charged to heap in baskets
  full
The gifts of Christ to keep and spread afar.
A HYMN ON THE TRINITY.[44]

### 6:44 Those Who Ate the Loaves Were Five Thousand Men

FIVE THOUSAND. BEDE: The number one thousand, beyond which no calculation of ours[45] extends, ordinarily indicates the fullness of the things which are being treated. By the number five the well-known senses of our body are represented, namely, sight, hearing, taste, smell and touch. The spiritual meaning of the five thousand: Those who act boldly and take courage by living soberly, righteously, and piously, that they may deserve to be renewed by the sweetness of heavenly wisdom, are those implied by the five thousand whom our Lord satisfied by this mystical banquet. EXPOSITION ON THE GOSPEL OF MARK 2.2.[46]

---

[41]Mt 14:19; Mk 6:41; Lk 9:16. [42]Lk 24:44-45. [43]Cetedoc 1367, 2.2.124; HOG 2:18. We receive the bread of the gospel from the apostles, who received it from the Lord. [44]Cetedoc 1439, 712; FC 52:28-29**. The one we meet in the breaking of bread is the creator and redeemer of all. [45]Of the ancient human imagination. [46]Cetedoc 1367, 2.2.155; HOG 2:19*. All five senses of our bodies are being thoroughly nourished and enlivened by the fullness of grace.

## 6:45-56 WALKING ON WATER

⁴⁵*Immediately he made his disciples get into the boat and go before him to the other side, to Bethsaida, while he dismissed the crowd. ⁴⁶And after he had taken leave of them, he went up on the mountain to pray. ⁴⁷And when evening came, the boat was out on the sea, and he was alone on the land. ⁴⁸And he saw that they were making headway painfully, for the wind was against them. And about the fourth watch of the night he came to them, walking on the sea. He meant to pass by them, ⁴⁹but when they saw him walking on the sea they thought it was a ghost, and cried out; ⁵⁰for they all saw him, and were terrified. But immediately he spoke to them and said, "Take heart, it is I; have no fear." ⁵¹And he got into the boat with them and the wind ceased. And they were utterly astounded, ⁵²for they did not understand about the loaves, but their hearts were hardened.*

⁵³*And when they had crossed over, they came to land at Gennesaret, and moored to the shore. ⁵⁴And when they got out of the boat, immediately the people recognized him, ⁵⁵ and ran about the whole neighborhood and began to bring sick people on their pallets to any place where they heard he was. ⁵⁶And wherever he came, in villages, cities, or country, they laid the sick in the market places, and besought him that they might touch even the fringe of his garment; and as many as touched it were made well.*

**OVERVIEW:** It was not through weakness that he made himself vulnerable to suffering (AMBROSE). The wood of the boat prefigured the wood of the cross. The way through the stormy sea was the way of the cross, by whose wood the faithful would be carried to salvation (AUGUSTINE). The shipwrecked poet Prudentius portrayed himself as turning to the saving Lord amid the tumult of his own sin (PRUDENTIUS). Those compulsively protected from risk do not grow strong in faith (ORIGEN). The thought of Jesus passing by evoked a crisis of despair that made the disciples all the more ready to cry out for help (AUGUSTINE).

### 6:45 *Immediately He Made the Disciples Get into the Boat*

**FAITH LEARNED THROUGH RISK.** ORIGEN: The Savior thus compelled the disciples to enter into the boat of testing and to go before him to the other side, so to learn victoriously to pass through difficulties. But when they got in the middle of the sea, and of the waves in the temptation, and of the contrary winds which prevented them from going away to the other side, they were not able, struggling as they were, to overcome the waves and the contrary wind and reach the other side without Jesus. In this way the Word, taking compassion upon those who had done all that was in their power to reach the other side, came to them walking upon the sea, which for him had no waves or wind. COMMENTARY ON MATTHEW 11.5.[1]

## 6:48a For the Wind Was Against Them

TRAINING BY EXERCISE. ORIGEN: But what is the spiritual nuance of the boat into which Jesus constrained the disciples to enter? Is it perhaps the conflict of temptations and difficulties into which any one is constrained by the Word, and goes unwillingly? The Savior wishes to train by exercise the disciples in this boat which is distressed by the waves and the contrary wind. COMMENTARY ON MATTHEW 11.5.[2]

THE ANCHOR'S HOOK UNLOOSED. PRUDENTIUS:

Simon, surnamed Peter,[3]
Chief disciple of Christ the Lord,
On a day at the set of sun
When the evening sky grows red,
Unloosed his anchor's hook,
And filled his sails with the swelling winds,
And made ready to cross the sea.
But night roused up a contrary gale[4]
That stirred up the deeper waves
And buffeted the floundering boat.
Shouts of fishermen struck the sky,
With shrieks and despairing groans
Amid the creak of swaying ropes.
Nor did any have hope of escape
From shipwreck and a watery death,
When the oarsmen all wan with fear
Saw Christ himself not far away
Treading surely upon the surge,
Just as though on the barren shore
He walked over the solid ground.
AGAINST SYMMACHUS 2.[5]

## 6:48b He Meant to Pass by Them

WHY PASS BY THEM? AUGUSTINE: When he walked upon the waters, he seems poised to pass by them. For in what way could they have understood this, were it not that he was really proceeding in a different direction from them, as if minded to pass those persons by like strangers, who were so far from recognizing him that they took him to be a ghost? Who, however, is so obtuse as not to perceive that this bears some spiritual significance? At the same time, too, he came to the help of the men in their agitation and outcry, and said to them, "Be of good cheer, it is I; be not afraid."[6] What is the explanation, therefore, of his wish to bypass those persons whom nevertheless he was prepared to encourage when they were in despair? His intent in passing by them was to serve the purpose of eliciting those outcries in response to which he would then come to bring relief. HARMONY OF THE GOSPELS 2.47.[7]

## 6:50 Have No Fear

HOW EASILY CAN I BE SHIPWRECKED. PRUDENTIUS:

Thus I by my loquacious tongue
From the heaven of silence am led
Into perils unknown and dark.
Not as Peter, disciple true,
Confident in his virtue and faith,
I am as one whose unnumbered sins
Have shipwrecked on the rolling seas. . . .
How easily can I be shipwrecked,

---

[1]TLG 2042.029, 11.5.65-76; ANF 9:435**. [2]ANF 9:434*; TLG 2042.029, 11.5.43-48. They were in training to exercise faith. [3]Cf. Mt 10:2; Acts 10:5. [4]Cf. Mt 14:24-32; Mk 6:45-51; Jn 6:16-21. [5]Cetedoc 1442, 2.1; FC 52:139**. [6]Mt 14:27; Mk 6:50; Jn 6:20. [7]Cetedoc 0273, 2.47.99.206.22; NPNF 1 6:150**.

One untaught in seafaring arts,
Unless you, almighty Christ,
Stretch forth your hand with help divine.[8]
AGAINST SYMMACHUS 2.[9]

### 6:51a Then He Got into the Boat with Them

THE WAY BEHELD UPON THE SEA. AUGUSTINE: But why was he crucified? Because the wood of his lowliness was necessary for you. For you had swollen with pride and had been cast forth far from your homeland. The way has been washed out by the waves of this world, and there is no way to cross over to the homeland unless you are carried by the wood. Ungrateful man, do you ridicule him who has come to you that you may return? He himself became the way, and this through the sea. For this reason he walked on the sea:[10] that he might show you that there is a way upon the sea. But you, who cannot in any way yourself walk on the sea, let yourselves be carried by the ship, be carried by the wood! TRACTATE ON JOHN 2.4.3.[11]

### 6:51b The Wind Ceased, and They Were Utterly Astounded

THE ONE WHO COMMANDS WIND AND SEA. PRUDENTIUS:

O mighty is the power of God,
The power that all things did create,
That calmed the waters of the sea
When Christ upon its surface walked,

So that in treading on the waves,
He moved dry-shod across the deep,
Nor ever did he wet his soles
As light he skimmed the surging flood.
HYMN 5.[12]

### 6:56 That They Might Touch Even the Fringe of His Garment

HIS VULNERABILITY TO SUFFERING NOT THROUGH WEAKNESS BUT STRENGTH. AMBROSE: The Lord of hosts was not signaling weakness as he gave sight to the blind, made the crooked to stand upright, raised the dead to life,[13] anticipated the effects of medicine at our prayers, and cured those who sought after him. Those who merely touched the fringe of his robe were healed.[14] Surely you did not think it was some divine weakness, you speculators, when you saw him wounded. Indeed there were wounds that pierced his body,[15] but they did not demonstrate weakness but strength. For from these wounds flowed life to all, from the One who was the life of all. ON THE CHRISTIAN FAITH 4.5.54-55.[16]

---

[8]Cf. Mt 14:31. [9]Cetedoc 1442, 2.44; FC 52:140-41**. Amid our human shipwreck, we may now turn to the saving Lord amid the tumult of the sea. [10]Cf. Mt 14:22-33; Mk 6:45-51; Jn 6:16-21. [11]Cetedoc 0278, 2.4.29; FC 78:64*. [12]Cetedoc 1443, 5.473; FC 43:164. The Lord of all governs the forces of nature. [13]Mt 11:5. [14]Mk 6:56. [15]Cf. Mt 27:35; Mk 15:24; Lk 23:33; Jn 19:18, 31-37. [16]Cetedoc 0150, 4.5.40; NPNF 2 10:269. He made himself vulnerable to suffering as Lord, not through weakness.

## 7:1-23 THE TRADITION OF THE ELDERS

[1]Now when the Pharisees gathered together to him, with some of the scribes, who had come from Jerusalem, [2]they saw that some of his disciples ate with hands defiled, that is, unwashed. [3](For the Pharisees, and all the Jews, do not eat unless they wash their hands,[v] observing the tradition of the elders; [4]and when they come from the market place, they do not eat unless they purify[w] themselves;[a] and there are many other traditions which they observe, the washing of cups and pots and vessels of bronze.[x]) [5]And the Pharisees and the scribes asked him, "Why do your disciples not live[y] according to the tradition of the elders, but eat with hands defiled?" [6]And he said to them, "Well did Isaiah prophesy of you hypocrites, as it is written,

'This people honors me with their lips,
but their heart is far from me;
[7]in vain do they worship me,
teaching as doctrines the precepts of men.'

[8]You leave the commandment of God, and hold fast the tradition of men."

[9]And he said to them, "You have a fine way of rejecting the commandment of God, in order to keep your tradition! [10]For Moses said, 'Honor your father and your mother'; and, 'He who speaks evil of father or mother, let him surely die' [11]but you say, 'If a man tells his father or his mother, What you would have gained from me is Corban' (that is, given to God)[z] [12]then you no longer permit him to do anything for his father or mother, [13]thus making void the word of God through your tradition which you hand on. And many such things you do."

[14]And he called the people to him again, and said to them, "Hear me, all of you, and understand: [15]there is nothing outside a man which by going into him can defile him; but the things which come out of a man are what defile him."[a] [17]And when he had entered the house, and left the people, his disciples asked him about the parable. [18]And he said to them, "Then are you also without understanding? Do you not see that whatever goes into a man from outside cannot defile him, [19]since it enters, not his heart but his stomach, and so passes on?"[b] (Thus he declared all foods clean.) [20]And he said, "What comes out of a man is what defiles a man. [21]For from within, out of the heart of man, come evil thoughts, fornication, theft, murder, adultery, [22]coveting, wickedness, deceit, licentiousness, envy, slander, pride, foolishness. [23]All these evil things come from within, and they defile a man."

v One Greek word is of uncertain meaning and is not translated   w Other ancient authorities read *baptize*   a Other ancient authorities read *and they do not eat anything from the market unless they purify it*   x other ancient authorities add *and beds*   y Greek *walk*   z Or *an offering*   a Other ancient authorities add verse 16, *If any man has ears to hear, let him hear*   b Or *is evacuated*

**Overview:** God sees straight through our evasions to our deepest inward intention (Clement of Rome, Clement of Alexandria). We are made unclean by what comes out of our lips, not by what goes into our mouth (Origen, Bede). We are called to absorb censure patiently, for one's character cannot be inwardly sullied by external reproaches from others but only by what comes from oneself. The cycle of interpersonal bitterness is broken by forbearance (Tertullian). Sin that is deliberate is more culpable (Basil). Divine judgment penetrates human rationalizations that pretend to follow the tradition of the elders (Irenaeus, Chrysostom, Jerome, John of Damascus).

### 7:4 The Pharisees, Observing the Tradition of the Elders

**Marks of Pharisaic Living.** John of Damascus: Pharisee is a name meaning "those who are set apart." They followed a way of life which they regarded as most perfect. They esteemed their way as superior to others. They affirmed the resurrection of the dead, the existence of angels, and holiness of life.[1] They followed a rigorous way of life, practicing asceticism and sexual abstinence for periods of time and fasting twice a week.[2] They ceremonially cleansed their pots and plates and cups,[3] as did the scribes. They observed the paying of tithes,[4] the offering of first fruits, and the recitation of many prayers.[5] On Heresies 15.[6]

### 7:6 Their Heart Is Far from Me

**Verbal Religion.** Clement of Rome: So let us devote ourselves to those at peace in their devotion to God, and not to those who seek peace through hypocrisy. For he says in one place: "This people honors me with their lips, but their heart is far from me."[7] And again: "They blessed with their mouth, but they cursed in their heart."[8] And again he says: "They flattered him with their mouths; they lied to him with their tongues. Their heart was not steadfast toward him; they were not true to his covenant."[9] 1 Clement 15.1-4.[10]

**God Sees Through to Our Inward Condition.** Clement of Alexandria: God considers our inward thoughts. Remember Lot's wife. All she did was voluntarily to turn her head back toward worldly corruption. She was left a senseless mass, a pillar of salt.[11] Stromateis 2.14.[12]

### 7:8 You Leave the Commandment of God and Hold Fast to the Tradition of Men

**Mixing Water with Wine.** Irenaeus: The Pharisees claimed that the traditions of their elders safeguarded the law, but in fact it contravened the law Moses had given. By saying: Your merchants mix water with the wine, Isaiah shows that the elders mixed their watery tradition with God's strict commandment. They enjoined an adulterated law at cross-purposes with the divine law. The Lord made this clear when he asked them: Why do you transgress God's commandment for the sake of your tradition? By their transgression they not only falsified God's law, mixing water with the wine, but they also set against it their own law, called to

---

[1]Cf. Acts 23:8. [2]Lk 18:12. [3]Mk 7:4. [4]Cf. Mt 23:23; Lk 11:42. [5]Cf. Lk 5:33. [6]TLG 2934.006, 15.1-12; FC 37:115**. This was a caricature, to some extent, as subsequent studies of the Pharisees have shown. See J. Neusner, *From Politics to Piety: The Emergence of Pharisaic Judaism* (Englewood Cliffs, N.J.: Prentice-Hall, 1973). [7]Is 29:13; Mk 7:6. [8]Ps 62:4. [9]Ps 78:36-37. [10]TLG 1271.001, 15.1-4; FC 1:21**. [11]Cf. Gen 19:26. [12]ANF 2:361*; TLG 0555.004, 2.14.61.4.1-5.

this day the Pharisaic law. In this their rabbis suppress some of the commandments, add new ones, and give others their own interpretation, thus making the law serve their own purposes. AGAINST HERESIES 4.12.1-2.[13]

## 7:11 *What You Would Have Gained from Me Is Corban*

**THE DECEPTION EMBEDDED IN THIS LEGALISM.** JEROME: The Lord himself discussed that commandment of the law which says: "Honor thy father and thy mother."[14] He made it clear that it is to be interpreted not as mere words, which, while offering an empty show of honor to parents, might still leave them poor and their necessities unrelieved. Instead the honor of parents should focus on the actual provision of the necessities of life. The Lord commanded that poor parents should be supported by their children who would reimburse them back when they are old for all those benefits which they themselves received in childhood. The scribes and Pharisees instead were teaching children to honor their parents by saying: "It is corban, that is to say, a gift which I have promised to the altar and will present at the temple, where it will relieve you as much as if I were to give it to you directly to buy food."[15] So it frequently happened that while father and mother were destitute, their children were offering sacrifices for the priests and scribes to consume. LETTER 123, TO AGERUCHIA.[16]

## 7:12 *You No Longer Permit Him to Do Anything for His Father or Mother*

**CORRUPTED RELIGION.** BASIL: The condemnation of those who have knowledge yet do not put their knowledge into practice is more severe. Even sin committed in ignorance is not

without risk. THE MORALS 4.[17]

**HOW MAMMON ORCHESTRATES THE POVERTY OF PARENTS.** CHRYSOSTOM: Christ says, "Care for the poor";[18] Mammon says, "Take away even those things the poor possess." Christ says, "Empty yourself of what you have";[19] Mammon says, "Take also what they possess." Do you see the opposition, the strife between them? See how it is that one cannot obey both, but must reject one? . . . Christ says, "None of you can become my disciple if you do not give up all your possessions";[20] Mammon says, "Take the bread from the hungry." Christ says, "Cover the naked";[21] the other says, "Strip the naked." Christ says, "You shall not turn away from your own family,[22] and those of your own house";[23] Mammon says, "You shall not show mercy to those of your own family. Though you see your mother or your father in want, despise them."[24] HOMILIES ON PHILIPPIANS 6.[25]

## 7:15 *The Things Which Come Out of a Man Are What Defile Him*

**THE CYCLE OF BITTERNESS BROKEN BY FORBEARANCE.** TERTULLIAN: Let us, then, his servants, follow our Lord and patiently submit to denunciations that we may be blessed! If, with slight forbearance, I hear some bitter or evil remark directed against me, I may return it,

---

[13]AHR 2:177; JF B 112*; SC 100, 508-14. [14]Cf. Ex 20:12; Deut 5:16; Mt 15:4; 19:19; Mk 7:10; 10:19; Lk 18:20. [15]Mk 7:11. [16]Cetedoc 0620, 123.56.5.78.7; NPNF 2 6:231-32*. In this way religious rules were twisted to allow some to steal from poor parents through their children's piety. So the legalistic rationalizers acquired through cunning what should have gone to poor parents. [17]FC 9:85*; TLG 2040.051, 31.717.38-40. [18]Cf. Mt 19:21; Mk 10:21; Lk 14:13. [19]Cf. Mt 16:24; Mk 8:34; Lk 9:23. [20]Lk 14:33. [21]Cf. Mt 25:34-40; Is 58:7. [22]Is 58:7. [23]1 Tim 5:8; Gal 6:10. [24]Mk 7:11. [25]TLG 2062.160, 62.226.32-38, 49-57; cf. NPNF 1 13:211**.

and then I shall inevitably become bitter myself. Either that, or I shall be tormented by unexpressed resentment. If I retaliate when cursed, how shall I be found to have followed the teaching of our Lord? For his saying has been handed down that one is defiled not by unclean dishes but by the words which proceed from his mouth.[26] On Patience 8.[27]

### 7:19 Thus He Declared All Foods Clean

**The Mouth and the Soul.** Origen: When we read in Leviticus[28] and Deuteronomy[29] of the laws about food as clean and unclean (for the transgression of which we are censured by the legalists and by the Ebionites, who differ from them very little), we are not to think that the scope of the Scripture is found in any superficial understanding of them. For "whatever goes into a person from the outside cannot defile him, since it enters not his heart but his stomach, and so passes on."[30] According to Mark, the Savior "declared all food clean,"[31] so we are not defiled when we eat those things declared to be unclean by those who still desire

to be in bondage to the letter of the law. But we are then defiled when our lips, which ought to be bound with good judgment as we search for correct balance and weight, speak recklessly and discuss matters we ought not. Commentary on Matthew 11.12.[32]

### 7:23 All These Evil Things Come from Within

**Evil Willed.** Bede: This is an answer to those who consider that evil thoughts are simply injected by the devil and that they do not spring from our own will. He can add strength to our bad thoughts and inflame them, but he cannot originate them. Exposition on the Gospel of Mark 2.7.20-21.[33]

---

[26]Mk 7:15. [27]Cetedoc 0009, 8.15; FC 40:207*. Absorb censure patiently, for one's character cannot be inwardly besmirched by external reproaches from others but only by what comes out of oneself. [28]Cf. Lev 11. [29]Cf. Deut 14. [30]Cf. Mt 15:11, 17. [31]Mk 7:19. [32]TLG 2042.029, 11.12.4-17; ANF 9:440**. [33]Cetedoc 1355, 2.7.1331; CCL 120:522; GMI 163*. Evil spins out of willing, not by simple coercion by demonic powers.

---

# 7:24-30 THE FAITH OF
# THE SYROPHOENICIAN WOMAN

[24]And from there he arose and went away to the region of Tyre and Sidon.[c] And he entered a house, and would not have any one know it; yet he could not be hid. [25]But immediately a woman, whose little daughter was possessed by an unclean spirit, heard of him, and came and fell down at his feet. [26]Now the woman was a Greek, a Syrophoenician by birth. And she begged him to cast the demon out of her daughter. [27]And he said to her, "Let the children first be fed, for it is not right to take the children's bread and throw it to the dogs." [28]But she

*answered him, "Yes, Lord; yet even the dogs under the table eat the children's crumbs."* [29]*And he said to her, "For this saying you may go your way; the demon has left your daughter."* [30]*And she went home, and found the child lying in bed, and the demon gone.*

c Other ancient authorities omit *and Sidon*

**OVERVIEW:** The Lord's compassion was awakened by the tenacity of the Syrophoenician woman's supplications (CHRYSOSTOM). The plain sense of "the borders of Tyre" differs from its spiritual sense, which is that sinning after baptismal confession returns one to the outskirts of belief (ORIGEN). In this text the Lord promises to women the same respect and dignity as men (TERTULLIAN). We separate ourselves from the people of God by pretentious attempts to differentiate those who are good from those who are evil (AUGUSTINE). God does not respond inflexibly to our every supplication (AMBROSE). It pleased God that the Word be revealed in Jesus as displaying the ordinary limitations of human willing (JOHN OF DAMASCUS). The bread of the Word is offered to those who are inwardly prepared by the Spirit to receive it, not to the impulsive or the unprepared (CLEMENT OF ALEXANDRIA).

### 7:24a He Withdrew to the Region of Tyre and Sidon

**THE PLAIN SENSE OF THE TEXT.** ORIGEN: He withdrew, perhaps because the Pharisees were offended when they heard that "What comes out of the mouth proceeds from the heart, and this is what defiles."[1] . . . It is probable that he sought to avoid the Pharisees, who were offended at his teaching, while he was waiting for the time of his impending suffering—a time suitably and duly appointed. COMMENTARY ON MATTHEW 11.16.[2]

**A SPIRITUAL INTERPRETATION.** ORIGEN: The Gentiles, those who dwell on the borders, can be saved if they believe. . . . Think of it this way: Each of us when he sins is living on the borders of Tyre or Sidon or of Pharaoh and Egypt. They are on the borders of those who are outside the inheritance of God. COMMENTARY ON MATTHEW 11.16.[3]

### 7:24b He Could Not Be Hid

**WAS JESUS POWERLESS TO KEEP HIS IDENTITY AS GOD-MAN CONCEALED?** JOHN OF DAMASCUS: His divine will was all-powerful, yet it was said that he was unable to conceal himself when he willed to. Why? It was while willing within the limits of his humanity that he was [voluntarily] subject to the limitations of the flesh. As a human he possessed the common human ability to will. . . . The sanctification of his will did not occur by circumventing his natural volition but by uniting his will with the divine and almighty will, as the will of God incarnate. Hence when he wished to be hid, he could not do so of himself,[4] because it pleased God that the Word be revealed in himself as having the limitations of human willing. THE ORTHODOX FAITH 3.17.[5]

---

[1]Mt 15:18. [2]TLG 2042.029, 11.16.6-8, 13-16; ANF 9:444*. He withdrew temporarily to Tyre to avoid offending the Pharisees. [3]TLG 2042.029, 11.16.30-31, 43-46; ANF 9:445*. To sin after confession of faith is to return to the outskirts of belief. [4]Mk 7:24. [5]TLG 2934.004, 58.101-103; 61.24-30; FC 37:300, 317**. Jesus' human will is portrayed as freely uniting with the divine will without changing or replacing its reality as limited human willing (fleshly,

## 7:26a The Woman Was a Greek

**The Same Moral Dignity in Both Genders.** Tertullian: For you, as women, have the very same angelic nature promised[6] as your reward, the very same sexual respect as men. You have the same dignity in making moral judgments. This the Lord promises to women. On the Apparel of Women 1.2.[7]

## 7:26b She Begged Him

**Eliciting the Lord's Compassion.** Chrysostom: Have you not heard of the Syrophoenician woman? By the constancy of her entreaty, she elicited the Lord's compassion. Homily 24, On Ephesians.[8]

## 7:27a Let the Children Be Fed First

**The Equity of Divine Responsiveness.** Ambrose: If God invariably listened to every supplicant equally, he might appear to us to act from some necessity rather than from his own free will. On the Mysteries 1.3.[9]

## 7:27b Not Right to Take the Children's Bread and Throw It to the Dogs

**Diluting the Pure Stream of Divinity.** Clement of Alexandria: Those who possess the Holy Spirit search out "the deep places of God"[10]—in other words, they attain the hidden secrets that surround prophecy. But it is forbidden to share holy things with dogs, as long as they remain wild. It is never appropriate to dilute the pure stream of divinity, the living water,[11] for interests that are full of malice, disturbed persons, still without faith, who are unrestrained in barking at the hunt. Stromateis 2.2.[12]

## 7:28 Even the Dogs Under the Table Eat the Children's Crumbs

**Dangers of Disciplinary Excess.** Augustine: Some people, intent on severe disciplinary precepts, admonish us to rebuke the restless and not to give what is holy to dogs,[13] to consider a despiser of the church as a heathen,[14] to cut off from the unified structure of the body the member who causes scandal.[15] These may so disturb the peace of the church that they try prematurely to separate out the wheat from the chaff[16] before the proper time, and blinded by this pretext, they themselves then become separated from the unity of Christ. Faith and Works 4.6.[17]

## 7:29 The Demon Has Left Your Daughter

**The Mother's Persistence.** Ephrem the Syrian: She was crying out [as] she was following after him, "Have mercy on me." But he did not reply to her.[18] The silence of our Lord elicited an even deeper cry by the Canaanite woman. He who was spurned by Israel spurned her by his silence, but she did not give up. Though neglected, she did not hold back. On the contrary, she again humbled herself and again magnified Israel, by [her words], "Even the dogs eat from their mas-

---

limited, circumscribed willing), and in this sense his humanity "could not be concealed." Hence Jesus was unwilling to conceal his human willing, his subjection to the limitations of the flesh. [6]Mt 22:30; Mk 12:25; Lk 20:35-36; Gal 3:28. [7]Cetedoc 0011, 1.2.43; ANF 4:15. This Gentile woman had the same dignity accorded by God to men. [8]NPNF 1 13:169; TLG 2062.159, 62.172.24-26. So it is with our petitions. [9]Cetedoc 0157, 1.65.242.7; FC 44:6**; cf. GMI 168. [10]1 Cor 2:9-10. [11]Cf. Jn 4:10. [12]FC 85:161*; TLG 0555.004, 2.2.7.3.4-8.1.15. [13]cf. Mt 7:6; 15:26. [14]Mt 18:17. [15]Mt 5:30; 18:8-9; Mk 9:42-48. [16]Mt 13:29-30. [17]Cetedoc 0294, 4.6.41.9; FC 27:227**. [18]Mt 15:22-23.

ters' [crumbs],"[19] as though the Jews were masters of the Gentiles. His disciples therefore drew near and begged him to send her away.[20] . . . She was not ashamed, to her own benefit, of the name of dogs. Therefore [he said], "Great is your faith, O woman."[21] COMMENTARY ON TATIAN'S DIATESSARON.[22]

[19]Mt 15:27. [20]Cf. Mt 15:23. [21]Mt 15:28. [22]JSSS 2:196-97*.

## 7:31-37 HEALING OF THE DEAF MUTE

[31]Then he returned from the region of Tyre, and went through Sidon to the Sea of Galilee, through the region of the Decapolis. [32]And they brought to him a man who was deaf and had an impediment in his speech; and they besought him to lay his hand upon him. [33]And taking him aside from the multitude privately, he put his fingers into his ears, and he spat and touched his tongue; [34]and looking up to heaven, he sighed, and said to him, "Ephphatha," that is, "Be opened." [35]And his ears were opened, his tongue was released, and he spoke plainly. [36]And he charged them to tell no one; but the more he charged them, the more zealously they proclaimed it. [37]And they were astonished beyond measure, saying, "He has done all things well; he even makes the deaf hear and the dumb speak."

**OVERVIEW:** In his ministry of loosing tongues and opening ears, the Lord was pointing to the time when all nations would hear and speak of God's own coming in person (LACTANTIUS, PRUDENTIUS, GREGORY THE GREAT). In preaching the Word today, the minister is symbolically touching human ears that they may be opened to the living Word by the mystery of grace (AMBROSE). The power that may not be handled came down and clothed itself in flesh that could be touched, that all humanity might behold his divinity, which transcends the touch of flesh (EPHREM THE SYRIAN).

### 7:33 He Put His Fingers into His Ears, and He Spat and Touched His Tongue

**THE TOUCH OF THE LORD.** EPHREM THE SYRIAN: That power which may not be handled came down and clothed itself in members that may be touched, that the desperate may draw near to him, that in touching his humanity they may discern his divinity. For that speechless man the Lord healed with the fingers of his body. He put his fingers into the man's ears and touched his tongue. At that moment with fingers that may be touched, he touched the Godhead that may not be touched. Immediately this loosed the string of his tongue,[1] and opened the clogged doors of his ears. For the very architect of the body itself and artificer of all flesh had come personally to him, and with his gentle voice tenderly opened up his obstructed ears. Then his mouth which had been so closed up that it could not give birth to a word, gave birth to praise him who made its barrenness fruitful. The One who immediately had given to Adam speech without teaching, gave speech to him so that he could speak easily a language that is learned only with difficulty.[2] HOMILY ON OUR LORD 10.[3]

**THE FINGER OF GOD.** GREGORY THE GREAT: The Spirit is called the finger of God. When the Lord put his fingers into the ears of the deaf mute, he was opening the soul of man to faith through the gifts of the Holy Spirit. HOMILIES ON EZEKIEL, HOMILY 10.[4]

### 7:34 Be Opened

**THE MYSTERY OF OPENING.** AMBROSE: Every sabbath we witness the "opening up" of a mystery. It is in outline form the type of that liturgical opening when the minister once touched your ears and nostrils.[5] What does this mean? Remember in the Gospel, our Lord Jesus Christ, when the deaf and dumb man was presented to him, touched his ears and his mouth: the ears, because he was deaf; the mouth, because he was dumb. And he said: "Ephphatha," a Hebrew word, which in Latin means *adaperire* [be opened]. In this way the minister is now touching your ears, that your ears may be opened to this sermon and exhortation. ON THE MYSTERIES 1.4.[6]

**PETITION FOR AN OPEN WAY.** AMBROSE: So open your ears and enjoy the good odor of eternal life which has been breathed upon you by the grace of the sacraments. This we pointed out to you as we celebrated the mystery of the opening and said: "Ephphatha," that is, "Be opened," so that everyone about to come to the table of grace might know what he was asked and remember the way he once responded. Christ celebrated this mystery in the Gospel, as we read, when he healed the one who was deaf and dumb. ON THE MYSTERIES 1.3-4.[7]

### 7:35 His Ears Were Opened, His Tongue Released

**THE HEARING OF THE GENTILES.** LACTANTIUS: He thereby declared that it would shortly come to pass, that those[8] who were destitute of the revealed truth would both hear and understand the majestic words of God. Accordingly you may truly call those deaf who do not hear the heavenly things which are true, and worthy of being performed. He loosed the tongues of the dumb. They spoke plainly—a power worthy of admiration[9] even in its ordinary operation. But there was also contained in this display of power another meaning. It would shortly come to pass that those who were previously ignorant of heavenly things, having received the instruction of wisdom, might soon speak God's own truth. DIVINE INSTITUTES 4.26.[10]

---

[1]Mk 7:32-37. [2]Cf. Gen 1:27-28; 2:20. [3]CSCO 270-271:8-9; NPNF 2 13:309**. With Jesus' human fingers that touch, the deaf mute was simultaneously being touched by the Godhead who transcends touch. [4]Cetedoc 1710, 1.10.341; SSGF 4:20**. [5]At baptism and chrismation. [6]Cetedoc 0155, 1.2.15.9; FC 44:269**; cf. NPNF 2 10:317. Listening to the gospel preached in the sabbath service is a recapitulation of the liturgical opening that occurs when the minister touches ears and nostrils in baptismal chrismation. This sort of opening of the ears occurs upon meeting the living Word. [7]Cetedoc 0155, 1.3.90.12; FC 44:6**. [8]Gentiles. [9]Mt 9:33; Mk 7:37. [10]Cetedoc 0085, 4.26.6, 3.78.8; ANF 7:127**.

### 7:36 He Even Makes the Deaf Hear and the Dumb Speak

**TONGUES UNLOOSED.** PRUDENTIUS:

Deafened ears, of sound unconscious,
    every passage blocked and closed,
At the word of Christ responding,
    all the portals open wide,
Hear with joy friendly voices and
    the softly whispered speech.[11]

Every sickness now surrenders,
    every listlessness departs,[12]
Tongues long bound by chains of silence
    are unloosed and speak aright,[13]
While the joyful paralytic
    bears his pallet through the streets.[14]
HYMNS 9.[15]

---

[11]Mk 7:34-35. [12]Lk 6:18-19. [13]Mk 7:35. [14]Mt 9:6-7; Jn 5:9. [15]Cetedoc 1438, 9.64; FC 43:64-65**.

## 8:1-10 THE FEEDING OF THE FOUR THOUSAND

[1]*In those days, when again a great crowd had gathered, and they had nothing to eat, he called his disciples to him, and said to them,* [2]*"I have compassion on the crowd, because they have been with me now three days, and have nothing to eat;* [3]*and if I send them away hungry to their homes, they will faint on the way; and some of them have come a long way."* [4]*And his disciples answered him, "How can one feed these men with bread here in the desert?"* [5]*And he asked them, "How many loaves have you?" They said, "Seven."* [6]*And he commanded the crowd to sit down on the ground; and he took the seven loaves, and having given thanks he broke them and gave them to his disciples to set before the people; and they set them before the crowd.* [7]*And they had a few small fish; and having blessed them, he commanded that these also should be set before them.* [8]*And they ate, and were satisfied; and they took up the broken pieces left over, seven baskets full.* [9]*And there were about four thousand people.* [10]*And he sent them away; and immediately he got into the boat with his disciples, and went to the district of Dalmanutha.*[d]

d Other ancient authorities read *Magadan* or *Magdala*

**OVERVIEW:** The incarnate Lord who himself was hungry in the desert is now seen feeding humanity with the bread of life (AUGUSTINE). The great variety of gifts of the Spirit to the church is indicated anticipatively in this miracle of the feeding of the four thousand. Those who partake and eat more zestily of the written Word have less spiritual hunger remaining (JEROME). The whole church, and not four thousand only, is now being fed by the one who

99

breaks bread (AUGUSTINE, EPHREM THE SYR-IAN).

## 8:6 He Took the Seven Loaves, and Having Given Thanks He Broke Them

**BREAKING THE BREAD.** AUGUSTINE: In expounding holy Scriptures, I am, so to speak, now breaking bread for you. If you hunger to receive it, your heart will sing out with the fullness of praise.[1] And if you are thus made rich in your banquet, why would you then be niggardly in good works and deeds of mercy? What I am distributing to you is not my own. What you feast upon, I also feast upon. SERMONS ON NEW TESTAMENT LESSONS 45.1.[2]

## 8:8a Ate and Were Satisfied

**NATURAL APPETITES FILLED.** EPHREM THE SYRIAN:

Grant, Lord, that I and those dear to me
May together there
Find the very last remnants of your gift!
HYMNS ON PARADISE 9.27, 29.[3]

## 8:8b Seven Baskets Full

**NO FRAGMENTS LOST.** AUGUSTINE: Are you hungry? You too have been given these baskets. For those fragments were not lost. For you, too, belong to the whole church, and they are surely for your benefit. SERMONS ON NEW TESTAMENT LESSONS 45.2.[4]

## 8:9 About Four Thousand Were Present

**WHETHER FOUR OR FIVE THOUSAND.** JEROME:

From the lesser number of men [four thousand[5]], less remains; from the greater number [five thousand[6]], more is left over.[7] Four thousand men—fewer certainly in number, but greater in faith. The one who is greater in faith eats more, and because he does, there is less left over! I wish that we, too, might eat more of the hardy bread of holy writ, so that there would be less left over for us to learn. TRACTATE ON THE GOSPEL OF MARK, HOMILY 78.[8]

## 8:10 The District of Dalmanutha

**WHETHER MARK'S DALMANUTHA IS THE SAME LOCATION AS MATTHEW'S MAGEDAN.** AUGUSTINE: After his account of the miracle of the seven loaves, Mark subjoins the same transition as is given us in Matthew, only with this difference: Matthew's expression for the locality is not Dalmanutha, as is read in certain codices, but Magedan.[9] There is no reason, however, for questioning the fact that it is the same place that is intended under both names. For most codices,[10] even of Mark's Gospel, give no other reading than that of Magedan. HARMONY OF THE GOSPELS 2.51.[11]

---

[1]Ps 138:1. [2]Cetedoc 0284, 95.38.581.15; NPNF 1 6:406**; cf. WSA 3 4:24, Sermon 95.1. [3]CSCO 174-175:42; HOP 146*. [4]Cetedoc 0284, 95.38.581.39; NPNF 1 6:406*; cf. WSA ibid. [5]Cf. Mk 8:9. [6]Cf. Mk 6:44. [7]This spiritual-numerological interpretation was suggested to Jerome as he puzzled over the difference between four and five thousand reported in the varied accounts. [8]Cetedoc 0594, 4.43; FC 57:153*. As less is left over by the greater level of consumption, so those who eat more heartily of the Word have less remaining over which yet to puzzle. [9]Cf. Mt 15:39. [10]It appears that Augustine had access to several distinguishable texts of Mark. [11]Cetedoc 0273, 2.51.106.215.5; NPNF 1 6:153*.

## 8:11-21 THE LEAVEN OF THE PHARISEES

[11]The Pharisees came and began to argue with him, seeking from him a sign from heaven, to test him. [12]And he sighed deeply in his spirit, and said, "Why does this generation seek a sign? Truly, I say to you, no sign shall be given to this generation." [13]And he left them, and getting into the boat again he departed to the other side.

[14]Now they had forgotten to bring bread; and they had only one loaf with them in the boat. [15]And he cautioned them, saying, "Take heed, beware of the leaven of the Pharisees and the leaven of Herod."[e] [16]And they discussed it with one another, saying, "We have no bread." [17]And being aware of it, Jesus said to them, "Why do you discuss the fact that you have no bread? Do you not yet perceive or understand? Are your hearts hardened? [18]Having eyes do you not see, and having ears do you not hear? And do you not remember? [19]When I broke the five loaves for the five thousand, how many baskets full of broken pieces did you take up?" They said to him, "Twelve." [20]"And the seven for the four thousand, how many baskets full of broken pieces did you take up?" And they said to him, "Seven." [21]And he said to them, "Do you not yet understand?"

e Other ancient authorities read *the Herodians*

---

**OVERVIEW:** The Lord wished to avoid any impression that his purpose might be to usurp civil authority. Here leaven signifies a small or hidden thing that may have a vast effect later, as in the touch of zyme put in dough to make it slowly rise. In this way Jesus warned against mendacity among religious leaders. He advocated open correction rather than taciturn indulgence. Friends who trust each other do not require special signs of friendship (CHRYSOSTOM).

### 8:12 Why Does This Generation Seek a Sign?

**THE NEED FOR A SIGN.** CHRYSOSTOM: But for what sign from heaven were they asking? Maybe that he should hold back the sun, or curb the moon, or bring down thunderbolts, or change the direction of the wind, or something like that? . . . In Pharaoh's time there was an enemy from whom deliverance was needed.[1] But for one who comes among friends, there should be no need of such signs. GOSPEL OF ST. MATTHEW, HOMILY 53.3.[2]

### 8:13 He Left Them, and Getting into the Boat Again He Departed

**HIS SPEEDY EXIT.** CHRYSOSTOM: No sign more impressed the crowds than the miracles of the loaves. Not only did they want to follow

---

[1]Cf. Ex 3—15. [2]TLG 2062.152, 58.528.28-30, 57-59; NPNF 1 10:328-29*. The hallmark of Jesus' communication was openness, without special deceptions, as friends talk with friends, where no subversions are required.

him, but also seemed ready to make him a king.[3] In order to avoid all suspicion of usurping civil authority, he made a speedy exit after this wonderful work. He did not even leave on foot, lest they chase after him, but took off by boat. GOSPEL OF ST. MATTHEW, HOMILY 53.2.[4]

### 8:15 Beware of the Leaven of the Pharisees and the Leaven of Herod

HIS WARNING. CHRYSOSTOM: It was not to learn faith that they [the Pharisees] sought him, but to seize him. GOSPEL OF ST. MATTHEW, HOMILY 53.3.[5]

### 8:21 Do You Not Yet Understand?

HIS TRENCHANT REPROOF. CHRYSOSTOM:

Can you hear the intense displeasure in his voice? For nowhere else does he appear to have rebuked them so strongly. Why now? In order to cast out their prejudices about clean foods.[6] . . . For not everywhere is permissiveness a good thing. As he earlier had allowed them to speak freely, now he reproves them. . . . He even reminds them of the specific numbers of loaves and of persons fed, both to bring them to recall the past, and to make them more attentive to the future. GOSPEL OF ST. MATTHEW, HOMILY 53.4.[7]

---

[3]Cf. Jn 6:15. [4]TLG 2062.152, 58.527.60-66; NPNF 1 10:328*. Jesus left the crowd abruptly to avoid any suspicion that he might be willing to usurp civil authority. [5]TLG 2062.152, 58.528.18-19; NPNF 1 10:328. [6]Cf. Mk 7:19. [7]TLG 2062.152, 58.529.35-38, 40-42, 48-51; NPNF 1 10:329-33*.

## 8:22-26 THE BLIND MAN OF BETHSAIDA

[22]*And they came to Bethsaida. And some people brought to him a blind man, and begged him to touch him.* [23]*And he took the blind man by the hand, and led him out of the village; and when he had spit on his eyes and laid his hands upon him, he asked him, "Do you see anything?"* [24]*And he looked up and said, "I see men; but they look like trees, walking."* [25]*Then again he laid his hands upon his eyes; and he looked intently and was restored, and saw everything clearly.* [26]*And he sent him away to his home, saying, "Do not even enter the village."*

---

OVERVIEW: The spittle and mud in the miracle of the blind man are a prototype pointing to the washing away of our sins in baptism (AMBROSE). The blind man was being freed to recognize the otherwise hidden, corrupt condition of his soul. We are urged to pay special attention to the spiritual sense at those points where the literal sense alone may be misleading (JEROME). Thus from Bethsaida, the "house of fishers," fishermen would be sent into the whole world to tell of his coming. When the new law of the Spirit is given, there is no reason to cling blindly to the old law of the letter (JEROME).

## 8:22a They Came to Bethsaida

THE MEANING OF BETHSAIDA. JEROME: They came, then, to Bethsaida, into the village of Andrew and Peter, James and John. Bethsaida means "house of fishers," and, in truth, from this house, hunters and fishermen are sent into the whole world. Ponder the text. The historical facts are clear, the literal sense is obvious. But we must now search into its spiritual message. That he came to Bethsaida, that there was a blind man there, that he departed, what is there remarkable about all that? Nothing, but what he did there is great; striking, however, only if it should take place today, for we have ceased to wonder about such things. HOMILY 79.[1]

## 8:22b They Brought to Him a Blind Man

THE BLINDNESS OF ISRAEL. JEROME: Watch this very carefully. Note exactly what is said. In the home village of the apostles, there is a blind man. In the very place where the apostles were born there is blindness. Do you grasp what I am saying? This blind man in the very home of the apostles is like the lost covenant people of Israel. HOMILY 79.[2]

## 8:23 When He Had Spit on His Eyes

A BAPTISMAL ANALOGY. AMBROSE: So too he placed mud upon you, that is, modesty, prudence, and consideration of your frailty. . . . You went, you washed, you came to the altar, you began to see what you had not seen before.[3] This means: Through the font of the Lord and the preaching of the Lord's passion, your eyes were then opened. You who seemed before to have been blind in heart began to see the light

of the sacraments. THE SACRAMENTS 3.15.[4]

## 8:25 He Laid His Hands upon His Eyes

THE FILM OF SIN. JEROME: Christ laid his hands upon his eyes that he might see all things clearly, so through visible things he might understand things invisible, which the eye has not seen, that after the film of sin is removed, he might clearly behold the state of his soul with the eye of a clean heart.[5] TRACTATE ON THE GOSPEL OF MARK, HOMILY 5.[6]

## 8:26 He Sent Him Away to His Home

THE PLAIN SENSE BEGS FOR FURTHER SPIRITUAL INTERPRETATION. JEROME: How, then, is his house not in Bethsaida? Note the text exactly. If we consider the literal interpretation only, it does not make any sense. If this blind man is found in Bethsaida and is taken out and cured, and he is commanded: "Return to your own house," certainly, he is bid: "Return to Bethsaida." If, however, he returns there, what is the meaning of the command: "Do not go into the village?" You see, therefore, that the interpretation is symbolic. He is led out from the house of the Jews, from the village, from the law, from the traditions of the Jews. He who could not be cured in the law is cured in the grace of the gospel. It is said to him, "Return to your own house" —not into the house that you think, the one from which he came out, but into the house that was also the house of Abraham, since Abraham is the father of those who believe.[7] HOMILY 79.[8]

---

[1]Cetedoc 0594, 5.7; FC 57:154**. [2]Cetedoc 0594, 5.16; FC 57:154-55**. [3]The healing of the blind man recalls the opening of the ears in baptismal chrismation. [4]Cetedoc 0154, 3.2.14.45.52; FC 44:295*. [5]Cf. Is 6:5; 1 Cor 2:9. [6]Cetedoc 0594, 5.97; CCL 78:476; GC 1:414*. [7]Cf. Ex 4:5; Rom 4:3; Gal 3:6; Jas 2:23. [8]Cetedoc 0594, 5.116; FC 57:158*.

## 8:27-30 THE CONFESSION AT CAESAREA PHILIPPI

[27]And Jesus went on with his disciples, to the villages of Caesarea Philippi; and on the way he asked his disciples, "Who do men say that I am?" [28]And they told him, "John the Baptist; and others say, Elijah; and others one of the prophets." [29]And he asked them, "But who do you say that I am?" Peter answered him, "You are the Christ." [30]And he charged them to tell no one about him.

**Overview:** The venerable Bede grasped the subtle irony embedded in this passage: Jesus' human identity was being declared in a divine voice while his divine identity was being declared in a human voice. We become Christians when we are anointed by the same Spirit by whom even the Christ himself was anointed. To be identified as the Christ is to be recognizable as the God-man anointed to save humanity (BEDE).

### 8:27 Who Do People Say That I Am?

**HIS HUMANITY AND DIVINITY FORESHADOWED.** BEDE: We note that the Lord called himself "Son of man,"[1] while Nathanael proclaimed him "Son of God."[2] Similarly is the account in the Gospels where Jesus himself asks the disciples who people say the Son of man is, and Peter answers, "You are the Christ, Son of the living God."[3] This was done under the guidance of the economy of righteousness. It shows that the two natures of the one mediator are affirmed: his divinity and his humanity, and attested both by our Lord himself and by human mouths. By this means the God-man declared the weakness of the humanity assumed by him. Those purely human would themselves declare the power of eternal divinity in him. HOMILIES ON THE GOSPELS 1.17.[4]

### 8:29 You Are the Christ

**WHY BELIEVERS ARE CALLED CHRISTIANS.** BEDE: "Messiah" in the Hebrew language means "Christ" in Greek; in Latin it is interpreted as "the Anointed One." Hence "chrisma" in Greek means "anointing" in Latin. The Lord is named Christ, that is, the Anointed One, because, as Peter says, "God has anointed him with the Holy Spirit and with power."[5] Hence the Psalmist also speaks in his praise, "God, your God, has anointed you with the oil of gladness above your companions."[6] He calls us his companions since we have also been fully anointed with visible chrism for the reception of the grace of the Holy Spirit in baptism, and we are called "Christians" from Christ's name.[7] EXPOSITION ON THE GOSPEL OF MARK 1.16.[8]

---

[1]Cf. Mt 8:20; 9:6; 16:13; Mk 8:31; 14:62; Lk 18:31; 22:48; Jn 5:27. [2]Cf. Jn 1:49. [3]Cf. Mt 16:16. [4]Cetedoc 1367, 1.17.255; *HOG* 1:175**. [5]Acts 10:38. [6]Ps 45:7. [7]Cf. Acts 11:26. [8]Cetedoc 1367, 1.16.111; *HOG* 1:174*.

# 8:31-38 THE FIRST PREDICTION
## OF THE PASSION
## AND CONDITIONS OF DISCIPLESHIP

³¹*And he began to teach them that the Son of man must suffer many things, and be rejected by the elders and the chief priests and the scribes, and be killed, and after three days rise again.* ³²*And he said this plainly. And Peter took him, and began to rebuke him.* ³³*But turning and seeing his disciples, he rebuked Peter, and said, "Get behind me, Satan! For you are not on the side of God, but of men."*

³⁴*And he called to him the multitude with his disciples, and said to them, "If any man would come after me, let him deny himself and take up his cross and follow me.* ³⁵*For whoever would save his life will lose it; and whoever loses his life for my sake and the gospel's will save it.* ³⁶*For what does it profit a man, to gain the whole world and forfeit his life?* ³⁷*For what can a man give in return for his life?* ³⁸*For whoever is ashamed of me and of my words in this adulterous and sinful generation, of him will the Son of man also be ashamed, when he comes in the glory of his Father with the holy angels."*

**OVERVIEW:** A false relationship with this world cannot be the basis for a true relationship with eternity (AUGUSTINE). To love God and the world equally is to love neither God nor the world (PSEUDO-CLEMENT). We provoke God's displeasure when we love God's gifts more than God himself (CAESARIUS OF ARLES). As no one can be a Christian and remain ashamed of Christ (CYPRIAN), so can no one both avoid suffering and confess Christ as Lord. Finally it is one's own cruciform body that becomes a cross (TERTULLIAN). We are not called, however, to become more burdened by our own crosses than by his (AUGUSTINE). The right reordering of our earthly loves is made possible only by grace (CAESARIUS OF ARLES). Believers are made able to fulfill this seemingly heavy requirement because his gifts supply the strength for doing his tasks. Rightly understood, the call to be ready to

lose one's life does not encourage masochistic self-hate (AUGUSTINE). The right enjoyment of things given to us depends upon their virtuous reception (CLEMENT OF ALEXANDRIA). This is the mystery of the incarnation: His glory was hid in his suffering in the flesh and only gradually began to be fully revealed in his resurrection (CYRIL OF ALEXANDRIA). The glory of the Father is beheld in the crucified Son raised from the dead (GREGORY OF NYSSA). The absurdity of the crucifixion shows the radical nature of God's love, proving itself by its very implausibility (TERTULLIAN).

### 8:34a *Let Him Deny Himself*

**WHAT SEEMS HARD, LOVE MAKES EASY.**

[1]Mt 16:24; Mk 8:34; Lk 9:23. The issue is how believers are made able to follow such a weighty, counterintuitive requirement.

AUGUSTINE: How hard and painful does this appear! The Lord has required that "whoever will come after him must deny himself."[1] But what he commands is neither hard nor painful when he himself helps us in such a way so that the very thing he requires may be accomplished. . . . For whatever seems hard in what is enjoined, love makes easy.[2] SERMONS ON NEW TESTAMENT LESSONS 46.1.[3]

**HE HELPS EFFECT WHAT HE COMMANDS.**
CAESARIUS OF ARLES: What he commands is not difficult, since he helps to effect what he commands. . . . Just as we are lost through loving ourselves, so we are found by denying ourselves. Love of self was the ruin of the first man. If he had not loved himself in the wrong order, he would have been willing to be subject to God, preferring God to self. SERMONS 159.[4]

## 8:34b *Take Up His Cross*

**BODY AS CROSS.** TERTULLIAN: "Your cross"[5] means your own anxieties and your sufferings in your own body, which itself is shaped in a way already like a cross. ON IDOLATRY 12.[6]

**BEARING WITH VEXATION.** CAESARIUS OF ARLES: What does this mean, "take up a cross"? It means he will bear with whatever is troublesome, and in this very act he will be following me. When he has begun to follow me according to my teaching and precepts, he will find many people contradicting him and standing in his way, many who not only deride but even persecute him.[7] Moreover, this is true, not only of pagans who are outside the church, but also of those who seem to be in it visibly, but are outside of it because of the perversity of their deeds. Although these glory in merely the title of Christian, they continually persecute faith-

ful Christians. Such belong to the members of the church in the same way that bad blood is in the body.[8] Therefore, if you wish to follow Christ, do not delay in carrying his cross; tolerate sinners, but do not yield to them. Do not let the false happiness of the wicked corrupt you. You do well to despise all things for the sake of Christ, in order that you may be fit for his companionship. SERMONS 159.5.[9]

**SUFFERING MOMENTARILY.** AUGUSTINE: Turn, rather, to these teachings, my very dear friend: take up your cross[10] and follow the Lord. For, when I noticed that you were being slowed down in your divine purpose by your preoccupation with domestic cares, I felt that you were being carried and dragged along by your cross rather than that you were carrying it. What else does the cross mean than the mortality of this flesh? This is our very own cross which the Lord commands us to carry that we may be as well armed as possible in following him. We suffer momentarily until death is swallowed up in victory.[11] Then this cross itself will be crucified. The cross will be nailed to the fear of God. We would hardly be able to carry it now if it forever resisted us with free and unfettered limbs. There is no other way for you to follow the Lord except by carrying it, for how can you follow him if you are not his? LETTER 243, TO LAETUS.[12]

## 8:35 *Whoever Loses His Life*

**DEFLECTING SELF-HATE.** AUGUSTINE: This

---

[2]Cf. Mt 11:29-30. [3]Cetedoc 0284, 96.38.584.48; NPNF 1 6:408*; cf. *WSA* 3 4:29, Sermon 96.1. [4]Cetedoc 1008, 104.159.1.6; FC 47:365-66*. [5]Mt 16:24; Lk 9:23; 14:27. [6]Cetedoc 0023, 43.13; ANF 3:68**. [7]Cf. Mt 5:11. [8]Cf. 2 Pet 2:1-3. [9]Cetedoc 1008, 104.159.5.3; FC 47:368-69**. [10]Mt 16:24; Mk 8:34; Lk 9:23. [11]Is 25:8; Hos 13:14; 1 Cor 15:54-55. [12]Cetedoc 0262, 243.57. 11.578.1; FC 32:226**.

precept by which we are enjoined to lose our life does not mean that a person should kill himself, which would be an unforgivable crime, but it does mean that one should kill that in oneself which is unduly attached to the earthly, which makes one take inordinate pleasure in this present life to the neglect of the life to come.[13] This is the meaning of "shall hate his life" and "shall lose it." Embedded in the same admonition, he speaks most openly of the profit of gaining one's life when he says: "He that loses his life in this world shall find it unto life eternal."[14] LETTER 243, TO LAETUS.[15]

**WALKING REQUIRES TWO FEET.** CAESARIUS OF ARLES: When the Lord tells us in the Gospel that anyone who wants to be his follower must renounce himself, the injunction seems harsh; we think he is imposing a burden on us.[16] But an order is no burden when it is given by one who helps in carrying it out. To what place are we to follow Christ if not where he has already gone? We know that he has risen and ascended into heaven; there, then, we must follow him. There is no cause for despair—by ourselves we can do nothing, but we have Christ's promise. . . .

One who claims to abide in Christ ought to walk as he walked. Would you follow Christ? Then be humble as he was humble. Do not scorn his lowliness if you want to reach his exaltation. Human sin made the road rough. Christ's resurrection leveled it. By passing over it himself, he transformed the narrowest of tracks into a royal highway. Two feet are needed to run along this highway; they are humility and charity. Everyone wants to get to the top—well, the first step to take is humility. Why take strides that are too big for you—do you want to fall instead of going up? Begin with the first step, humility, and you will already be climbing. SERMONS 159, 1.4-6.[17]

### 8:36 What Does It Profit One to Gain the Whole World?

**THE ENJOYMENT OF EARTHLY GOODS.** CLEMENT OF ALEXANDRIA: Those who neglect good works may fail to grasp just how much the good work of God has benefited them. Hence they are less capable of praying fittingly so as to receive good things from God. And even if they receive them, they will likely be unaware of what has been given them. And even if they enjoy them, they will not enjoy worthily what they have not understood. For from their lack of knowledge they will not grasp how to use the good things given them. And from their impulsiveness they will remain ignorant of how to avail themselves of the divine gifts offered. STROMATEIS 6.14.[18]

**INORDINATE LOVE OF THE WORLD.** PSEUDO-CLEMENT: This world talks of adultery and corruption and love of money and deceit, but that world[19] says farewell to these things. We cannot, then, be friends equally of both, but we must say farewell to this to possess the other. We think that it is better to despise the things below, for they are small and passing and perishable, and to love the things which are truly there, things good and imperishable. 2 CLEMENT 6.4-6.[20]

**ON RIGHTLY LOVING THE WORLD.** CAESARIUS OF ARLES: While there is much in the world to love, it is best loved in relation to the One who made it. The world is beautiful, but much fairer is the One who fashioned it. The world is glorious, but more delightful is the One by whom

---

[13]Rightly understood, this precept does not tend inadvertently to encourage self-hate. [14]Jn 12:25. [15]Cetedoc 0262, 243.57.5.572.11; FC 32:222**. [16]Cf. Mt 16:24; Mk 8:34; Lk 9:23. [17]Cetedoc 1008, 159.1.3, and 159.4.1; JF B 116; CCL 104, 650.652-54*. [18]TLG 0555.004, 6.14.112.4.1-8; ANF 2:506*. [19]When viewed from the vantage point of faith. [20]FC 1:68-69*; TLG 1271.002, 6.4.1-6.6.2.

the world was established. Therefore, let us labor as much as we can, beloved, that love of the world as such may not overwhelm us, and that we may not love the creature more than the creator. God has given us earthly possessions in order that we may love him with our whole heart and soul.[21] But sometimes we provoke God's displeasure against us when we love his gifts more than God himself. The same thing happens in human relationships. Suppose someone gives a special gift to his protégé. But the protégé then begins to despise the giver, and loves the gift more than the one who gave. Suppose he comes to think of the giver no longer as friend but enemy. Just so it is with our relationship with God. We love more those who love us for ourselves rather than our gifts. So God is known to love those who love him more than the earthly gifts he gives. SERMONS 159.6.[22]

### 8:38a Whoever Is Ashamed of Me

**THE CONTEMPT OF SHAME.** TERTULLIAN: The faithful are not ashamed that the Son of God was crucified. Hence they are shameless in a good sense through their contempt of shame, and foolish in a happy sense. The crucifixion was indeed a shameful event, viewed humanly. Yes, the Son of God died![23] This is to be believed precisely amid its being an offense to humanity. The Son was buried![24] He rose from the dead![25] This fact is made all the more poignant by seeming all the more absurd.[26] But how could any of this be true if he himself was not truly the One[27] he made himself known to be? ON THE FLESH OF CHRIST 5.[28]

**FACING PERSECUTION.** TERTULLIAN: If I avoid suffering, I am ashamed to confess: "Blessed are they who suffer persecution for my name's sake."[29] Unhappy, therefore, are they who, by

running away, refuse to suffer as God at times requires. "He who shall endure to the end shall be saved."[30] How then, when you ask me to flee, would I be enduring to the end? FLIGHT IN TIME OF PERSECUTION 7.[31]

**ON BEING UNASHAMED.** CYPRIAN: Does he think himself a Christian who is either ashamed or fears to be a Christian? How can he be with Christ, who either blushes or fears to belong to Christ? THE LAPSED 28.[32]

### 8:38b When He Comes in the Glory of His Father

**THE GLORY OF GOD HID IN SUFFERING.** CYRIL OF ALEXANDRIA: He who as God was beyond suffering, suffered in his own flesh as a human being. When he became flesh, being God, he did not in any way cease to be God. Precisely as he entered into the created order, he remained above creation. He remained as giver of the law when he came to serve "under the law."[33] He retained the inviolable divine dignity precisely when he took on "the form of a slave."[34] It was precisely as only begotten Son that he became "the firstborn among many brothers,"[35] while still remaining the only begotten. So why should it seem so strange that he should suffer in the flesh according to his humanity, even while transcending suffering according to his divinity? Thus the ever astute Paul says that the Word himself who is "in the form of God"[36]

---

[21]Cf. Deut 10:12; Mt 22:37. [22]Cetedoc 1008, 104.159.5.16; FC 47:369**. [23]Cf. Mt 27:50; Mk 15:37; Lk 23:46; Jn 19:30. [24]Cf. Mt 27:60; Mk 15:46; Lk 23:53; Jn 19:42. [25]Cf. Mt 28:6; Mk 16:6; Lk 24:5; Jn 20:16. [26]This is the famous sentence sometimes translated: "It is by all means to be believed just because it is such an offense to reason," or "I believe because it is absurd." [27]Truly God, truly human. [28]Cetedoc 0018, 5.24; cf. ANF 3:525**. [29]Mt 5:10-11. [30]Mt 10:22. [31]Cetedoc 0025, 7.12; ANF 4:120*. [32]Cetedoc 0042, 28.557; FC 36:82. [33]Gal 4:4. [34]Phil 2:7. [35]Rom 8:30. [36]Phil 2:6.

and equal to God the Father "became obedient even unto death, death of the cross."[37] LETTER 55, TO ANASTASIUS AND THE MONKS.[38]

**HIS UNDIVIDED GLORY.** GREGORY OF NYSSA: The Son does not divide the glory with the Father, but receives the glory of the Father in its entirety, even as the Father receives all the glory of the Son.[39] AGAINST EUNOMIUS 2.6.[40]

---

[37]Phil 2:8. [38]TLG 5000.001, 1.1.4.58.26-37; FC 77:30-31*. The glory of God was hidden in his suffering but revealed in his resurrection. [39]Cf. Jn 17:5. [40]TLG 2017.031, 41.6-9; NPNF 2 5:107.

---

## 9:1-8 THE TRANSFIGURATION

[1]*And he said to them, "Truly, I say to you, there are some standing here who will not taste death before they see that the kingdom of God has come with power."* [2]*And after six days Jesus took with him Peter and James and John, and led them up a high mountain apart by themselves; and he was transfigured before them,* [3]*and his garments became glistening, intensely white, as no fuller on earth could bleach them.* [4]*And there appeared to them Elijah with Moses; and they were talking to Jesus.* [5]*And Peter said to Jesus, "Master,[f] it is well that we are here; let us make three booths, one for you and one for Moses and one for Elijah."* [6]*For he did not know what to say, for they were exceedingly afraid.* [7]*And a cloud overshadowed them, and a voice came out of the cloud, "This is my beloved Son,[g] listen to him."* [8]*And suddenly looking around they no longer saw any one with them but Jesus only.*

f Or Rabbi    g Or my Son, my (or the) Beloved

---

**OVERVIEW:** The transfiguration points symbolically beyond itself and toward the final resurrection, when the garments of the faithful will become white as snow when they are purified in heaven (BEDE). In this transfiguration the divine glory is adapting itself unpretentiously to the disciples' capacity to receive it (EPHREM THE SYRIAN). Patristic commentary on the text focuses upon the motif of brilliance in the purifying light. Jesus' splendor was manifested not merely as earthly light but as the sun of righteousness to the children of light (ORIGEN). The sun's glory and the snow's purity are only faintly to be compared with his more brilliant glory and purity (CHRYSOSTOM). The best of human wisdom is bleached and purified by his coming (ORIGEN). Jesus' identity as beloved Son is declared in pivotal moments of the Gospel narratives, of which this is a definitive instance (AMBROSE). The three beloved disciples present at the transfiguration glimpsed the glory of God dwelling among humankind (CHRYSOSTOM).

Since Moses and Elijah were servants of the Lord, anticipating his own coming, three booths would have been a misleading equation suggesting their commensurability to Christ. Besides, Peter's proposal was premature, for the time had not yet come for the Lord's full glory to be revealed (ORIGEN, JEROME). Through holy contemplation one can become united with the trans-figured Lord (PSEUDO-DIONYSIUS). Jesus is beheld according to his divinity by all those who ascend above the earthly to be ready to receive spiritual knowledge (ORIGEN).

### 9:2a After Six Days

**WHY SIX?** ORIGEN: In six days (the very number denoting perfect fulfillment)[1] the whole world, this perfect work of art, was made.[2] But there is One who transcends all the things of the world, all that belongs to the "six days." Being eternal, this One beholds not only what is seen in time, but what is not seen and is eternal. If therefore any one of us wishes to be taken by Jesus, and led up by him into the high mountain, and be deemed worthy to witness his transfiguration apart, let him pass beyond the six days, because he no longer beholds the things which are seen, nor longer loves the world, nor the things in the world.[3] COMMENTARY ON MATTHEW 12.36.[4]

**THE RECKONING OF DAYS.** AUGUSTINE: Leaving out of their calculation the day on which Jesus spoke these words, and the day on which he exhibited that memorable spectacle on the mount, they have regarded simply the intermediate days, and have used the expression, "after six days." But Luke, reckoning in the extreme day at either end, that is to say, the first day and the last day, has made it "after eight days,"[5] in accordance with that mode of speech in

which the part is put for the whole. HARMONY OF THE GOSPELS 2.56.[6]

### 9:2b He Took with Him Peter, James and John and Led Them Up a High Mountain Apart

**HE ADAPTED TO OUR EYES THE SIGHT OF HIMSELF.** EPHREM THE SYRIAN:

The Lord who is beyond measure
    measures out nourishment to all,
adapting to our eyes the sight of himself,
    to our hearing his voice,
His blessing to our appetite,
    His wisdom to our tongue.

HYMNS ON PARADISE 9.27.[7]

**WHAT WAS DISCLOSED.** CHRYSOSTOM: He disclosed, it is said, a glimpse of the Godhead. He manifested to them the God who was dwelling among them.[8] EUTROPIUS, AND THE

---

[1]The interest of early Christian authors in the symbolism of numbers frequently strikes modern readers as strange and often forced. Yet, as A. Quacquarelli comments, there "is no early Christian author who does not, directly or indirectly, mention the symbolism of numbers." Augustine, for example, contends that the mystical and metaphorical aspects of Scripture would remain a mystery for those unfamiliar with the language of numbers. This interest in numbers was an integral aspect of the culture of the times and is not limited to the Fathers. "The flexing of the fingers [in counting] produced images that attributed definite values to biblical numbers. A typical example is the 100 (martyrs), 60 (widows) and 30 (married people) of the parable of the sower. The digital representation of 100 (a circle formed by the right thumb and index finger) developed images that become a possession of the spirit, i.e., it was the crown of martyrdom. . . . The symbolism of numbers is a vital part of patristics and must be studied in order to understand a method of research based on the culture of the time. The theology of the Fathers had no wish to detach itself from the popular mind." See *EEC* 605-6. [2]Cf. Gen 1:31; Ex 20:11; 31:17. [3]Cf. 1 Jn 2:15. [4]TLG 2042.030, 12.36.20-40, cf. ANF 9:469. To behold the eternal redeemer transfigured, we must be led beyond the visible, earthly, created order. [5]Cf. Lk 9:28. [6]Cetedoc 0273, 2.56.113.219.8; NPNF 1 6:155. [7]HOP 146. Divine revelation generously adapts itself to our limited capacity to receive it. [8]Cf. Ps 68:18.

VANITY OF RICHES, HOMILY 2.[9]

### 9:2c He Was Transfigured Before Them

IN THEIR PRESENCE. ORIGEN: Listen spiritually that it is not said simply, "he was transfigured," but with a certain necessary addition, which Matthew and Mark have recorded; for, according to both, "he was transfigured before them"[10] [in the presence of Peter, James and John]. The text suggests that it would be possible for Jesus to be transfigured before some of his disciples, and not before others. But if you wish to see the transfiguration of Jesus as seen by those who went up into the lofty mountain apart from the others, view with me the Jesus in the Gospels. Remember that Jesus was more literally apprehended by those below "according to the flesh"[11]—by those who did not go up to the lofty mountain of wisdom, who did not go up through words and deeds that are uplifting. But there were others by whom he became known no longer after the flesh, but in his divinity. To this all the Gospels attest. He was beheld in the form of God according to their spiritual knowledge.[12] It was before these who ascended and in their presence that Jesus was transfigured, not to those who remained below. COMMENTARY ON MATTHEW 12.37.[13]

### 9:3a His Garments Became Glistening

MANIFESTED TO THE CHILDREN OF LIGHT. ORIGEN: But when he is transfigured, his face also shines as the sun that he may be manifested to the children of light who have put off the works of darkness and put on the armor of light,[14] and are no longer the children of darkness or night but have become the sons of day, and walk honestly as in the day.[15] Being mani-

fested, he will shine unto them not simply as the sun, but as demonstrated to be the sun of righteousness.[16] COMMENTARY ON MATTHEW 12.37.[17]

AS SUN TO THE EYES. AUGUSTINE: What this sun is to the eyes of the flesh, that is the Lord to the eyes of the heart. SERMONS ON NEW TESTAMENT LESSONS 28.[18]

### 9:3b Intensely White As No Fuller on Earth Could Bleach Them

THE FULLERS (CLEANERS, PURIFIERS). ORIGEN: Perhaps the "fullers upon the earth" refers to the wise men of this world who cultivate the art of rhetoric. They imagine that their own poor thoughts might appear bright and clean because of their speech, adorned as it is with verbal bleaching. But the One who shows his own garments glistening to those who have ascended, and even brighter than any bleaching could ever make them, is the Word, who exhibits in the expression of the Scriptures (which are despised by many) the glistening of his thoughts, when the raiment of Jesus becomes white and dazzling.[19] COMMENTARY ON MATTHEW 12.39.[20]

LIMITS OF THE ANALOGIES OF SNOW AND SUN. CHRYSOSTOM: How did he shine? Tell me. Exceedingly. And how do you express this? He shone as the sun.[21] As the sun, you say? Yes. Why the sun? Because I do not know any

---

[9]TLG 2062.142, 52.404.53-55; NPNF 1 9:258*. [10]Mt 17:2; Mk 9:2. [11]Cf. 2 Cor 10:2. [12]Cf. Phil 2:6. [13]ANF 9:470*; TLG 2042.030, 12.37.10-40. [14]Cf. Jn 12:36; Rom 13:12; Eph 5:8. [15]Cf. Rom 13:13; 1 Thess 5:5. [16]Cf. Mal 4:2; Wis 5:6. [17]ANF 9:470*; TLG 2042.030, 12.37.40-53. He is manifested not merely as earthly light but as the sun of righteousness to the children of light. [18]Cetedoc 0284, 78.38.490.53; NPNF 1 6:347*; cf. WSA 3 3:340, Sermon 78.2. [19]Cf. Lk 9:29. [20]ANF 9:470-71*; TLG 2042.030, 12.39.20-37; GCS 40. [21]Cf. Mt 17:2.

other luminary more brilliant. And he was white, you say, as snow?[22] Why as snow? Because I do not know any other substance which is whiter. But he did not strictly speaking shine merely as the sun shines daily. This is proved by what follows: the disciples fell to the ground.[23] If he had shone as the sun daily shines, the disciples would not have fallen, for they saw the sun every day, and did not fall. But inasmuch as he shone more brilliantly than the sun or snow, they, being unable to bear the splendor, fell to the earth. EUTROPIUS, AND THE VANITY OF RICHES, HOMILY 2.10-11.[24]

**THE GARMENTS OF THE FAITHFUL.** BEDE: If anyone asks what the Lord's garments, which became white as snow, represent typologically, we can properly understand them as pointing to the church of his saints [who] . . . at the time of the resurrection will be purified from every blemish of iniquity and at the same time from all the darkness of mortality.[25] Concerning the Lord's garments the Evangelist Mark remarks that "they became as bright as snow, such as no bleacher on earth can make them white."[26] It is evident to everyone that there is no one who can live on earth without corruption and sorrow. So it is evident to all who are wise, although heretics deny it, that there is no one who can live on earth without being touched by some sin. But what a cleansing agent (that is, a teacher of souls or some extraordinary purifier of his body) cannot do on earth, that the Lord will do in heaven. He will purify the church, which is his clothing, "from all defilement of flesh and spirit,"[27] renewing [her] besides with eternal blessedness and light of flesh and spirit. EXPOSITION ON THE GOSPEL OF MARK 1.24.[28]

## 9:4 There Appeared to Them Elijah with Moses

**WHY ELIJAH? WHY MOSES?** ORIGEN: When the Son of God in his transfiguration is so understood and beheld as if his face were a sun, and his clothes white as the light itself, immediately it will appear to those who behold Jesus in this way that he is conversing with Moses (the law) and Elijah (the prophets). By means of the device of synecdoche[29] he is holding conversation not with one prophet only, but symbolically with all the prophets. COMMENTARY ON MATTHEW 12.38.[30]

**BOTH HAD WITHSTOOD A TYRANT.** CHRYSOSTOM: For both the one and the other had courageously withstood a tyrant: one the Egyptian, the other Ahab; and this on behalf of a people who were both ungrateful and disobedient. . . . And both were simple unlearned men. One was slow of speech and weak of voice.[31] The other a rough countryman. And both were men who had despised the riches of this world. For Moses possessed nothing. And Elijah had nothing but his sheepskin. GOSPEL OF ST. MATTHEW, HOMILY 56.[32]

**POINTING TOWARD THE FINAL RESURREC-**

---

[22]Cf. Mt 28:3. [23]Cf. Mt 17:6. [24]TLG 2062.142, 52.405.5-15; NPNF 1 9:258**. According to the analogy of faith, the sun's glory is grasped by comparing it with God's, not God's glory grasped by comparing it with the sun's. The snow is the purest white we know, but its purity is grasped in relation to God's purity. The sun's glory is to be compared to Jesus' more brilliant glory and the purity of the snow compared to his purity. [25]Cf. 1 Cor 15:42-44. [26]Mk 9:3. [27]2 Cor 7:1. [28]Cetedoc 1367, 1.24.121; HOG 1:238-39*. The church will be purified in heaven. [29]A figure of speech by which the whole of a thing is put for a part or a part for the whole. [30]ANF 10:470*; TLG 2042.030, 12.38.28-36. The law's requirement and the prophets' expectations are fulfilled in Christ. [31]Cf. Ex 4:10. [32]TLG 2062.152, 58.551.17-19, 22-27; SSGF 2:54.

TION. BEDE: Moses and Elijah, who talked with the Lord on the mountain, and spoke about his passion and resurrection, represent the oracles of the law and prophets which were fulfilled in the Lord. . . . The figures of Moses and Elijah embrace all who are finally to reign with the Lord.[33] By Moses, who died and was buried, we can understand those who at the judgment are going to be raised up from death.[34] By Elijah, on the other hand, who has not yet paid the debt of death,[35] we understand those who are going to be found alive in the flesh at the judge's coming. EXPOSITION ON THE GOSPEL OF MARK 1.24.[36]

### 9:5a It Is Well That We Are Here

HOLY CONTEMPLATION. PSEUDO-DIONYSIUS: In most holy contemplation we shall be ever filled with the sight of God shining gloriously around us as once it shone for the disciples at the divine transfiguration.[37] And there we shall be, our minds away from passion and from earth, and we shall have a conceptual gift of light from him and, somehow, in a way we cannot know, we shall be united with him and, our understanding carried away, blessedly happy, we shall be struck by his blazing light. Marvelously, our minds will be like those in the heavens above. THE DIVINE NAMES 1.[38]

### 9:5b Let Us Make Three Booths

AN UNTIMELY PROPOSAL. JEROME: O Peter, even though you have ascended the mountain, even though you see Jesus transfigured, even though his garments are white; nevertheless, because Christ has not yet suffered for you, you are still unable to know the truth. HOMILY 80.[39]

### 9:7a A Cloud Overshadowed Them

THE TENT OF THE SPIRIT. JEROME: It seems to me that this cloud is the grace of the Holy Spirit. Naturally, a tent gives shelter and overshadows those who are within; the cloud, therefore, serves the purpose of the tents. O Peter, you who want to set up three tents, have regard for the one tent of the Holy Spirit who shelters us equally. HOMILY 80.[40]

### 9:7b This Is My Beloved Son; Listen to Him

HIS SONSHIP DECLARED. AMBROSE: In his baptism he identified him, saying: "You are my beloved Son, in whom I am well pleased."[41] He declared him on the mount, saying: "This is my beloved Son, hear him."[42] He declared him in his passion, when the sun hid itself, and sea and earth trembled. He declared him in the centurion, who said: "Truly this was the Son of God."[43] ON THE HOLY SPIRIT 2.6.[44]

TWO SERVANTS, ONE LORD. JEROME: Do not set up tents equally for the Lord and his servants. "This is my beloved Son; hear him,"[45] my Son, not Moses or Elijah. They are ser-

---

[33]Cf. Rev 22:5. [34]Cf. Acts 17:31-32. [35]2 Kings 2:11. [36]Cetedoc 1367, 1.24.144, 151; HOG 1:239*. The transfiguration points symbolically toward the end-time resurrection of the living (Elijah, who did not die but was taken up to heaven) and the dead (Moses, who died on Mt. Nebo). [37]Cf. Mt 17:1-8; Mk 9:2-8. [38]TLG 2798.004, 114.9-115.5; CWS 52-53. Through holy contemplation we receive the fullness of his light and purity. [39]Cetedoc 0594, 6.216; FC 57:166. The time had not yet come for his full glory to be revealed. [40]Cetedoc 0594, 6.231; FC 57:167. The promised coming of the Holy Spirit was anticipated in the cloud. [41]Mt 3:17; Mk 1:11; Lk 3:22. [42]Mt 17:5; Mk 9:7; Lk 9:35. [43]Mt 27:54; Mk 15:39. [44]Cetedoc 0151, 2.6.57.109.88; NPNF 2 10:122*. [45]Mt 17:5; Mk 9:7; Lk 9:35.

vants; this is the Son. This is my Son, of my nature, of my substance, abiding in me, and he is all that I am. This is my beloved Son. They, too, indeed are dear to me, but he is my beloved; hear him, therefore. They proclaim and teach him, but you, hear him. He is the Lord and master, they are companions in service. Moses and Elijah speak of Christ; they are your fellow servants. He is the Lord; hear him. HOMILY 80.[46]

**ONLY ONE IS SON.** AUGUSTINE: Moses was there, and Elijah. The voice did not say: These are my beloved sons. For One only is the Son; others are adopted. It is he that is commended to them: He from whom the law and prophets derive their glory. SERMONS ON NEW TESTAMENT LESSONS.[47]

---

[46]Cetedoc 0594, 6.249; FC 57:166-67.  [47]SSGF 2:63; cf. Cetedoc 0284, 78.38.491.41; NPNF 16 ad loc.

# 9:9-13 THE COMING OF ELIJAH

[9]*And as they were coming down the mountain, he charged them to tell no one what they had seen, until the Son of man should have risen from the dead.* [10]*So they kept the matter to themselves, questioning what the rising from the dead meant.* [11]*And they asked him, "Why do the scribes say that first Elijah must come?"* [12]*And he said to them, "Elijah does come first to restore all things; and how is it written of the Son of man, that he should suffer many things and be treated with contempt?* [13]*But I tell you that Elijah has come, and they did to him whatever they pleased, as it is written of him."*

**OVERVIEW:** John Chrysostom's comments on the text focus upon the relation of Elijah, John the Baptist and Jesus. Christ called John Elijah, because he had fulfilled the ministry of the type of Elijah. The death of Jesus was darkly foreshadowed in this text immediately after the confession of Peter and the transfiguration. In his atonement, the heart of the Father was being restored to sinners by the self-giving of the Son (CHRYSOSTOM).

## 9:9 *Tell No One*

**UNTIL HE SHALL HAVE RISEN.** CHRYSOSTOM: So He bound them to silence. Furthermore he spoke of his passion as though it were the reason why he asked them to be silent. Note that he did not tell them that they must never tell this to anyone. Instead they should not tell it until he had risen from the dead. In this respect he was silent as to what was painful, and spoke only of what was joyful. GOSPEL OF ST. MATTHEW, HOMILY 57.[1]

---

[1]TLG 2062.152, 58.554.27-32; SSGF 2:57-58*.

## 9:12a Elijah Does Come First to Restore All Things

**RESTORING THE HEART OF THE FATHER TO THE SON.** CHRYSOSTOM: Note the extreme accuracy of [the prophetic] expression.[2] He does not say "He will restore the heart of the son to the father," but "of the father to the son."[3] GOSPEL OF ST. MATTHEW, HOMILY 57.1.[4]

## 9:12b The Son of Man Should Suffer Many Things

**THE PREDICTION OF THE PASSION.** CHRYSOSTOM: "Then"—when? When he was confessed to be the Christ, the Son of God. Again on the mountain, when he had shown them the marvelous vision, and the prophets had been discoursing of his glory, he reminded them of his passion. GOSPEL OF ST. MATTHEW, HOMILY 57.2.[5]

## 9:13 Elijah Has Come

**JOHN AND ELIJAH.** CHRYSOSTOM: Christ called John Elijah, not because he was Elijah, but because he was fulfilling the ministry of that prophet. GOSPEL OF ST. MATTHEW, HOMILY 57.1.[6]

---

[2]To which Mk 9:12 is a reference. [3]Mal 4:5-6 (LXX): "And, behold, I will send to you Elijah the Tishbite, before the great and glorious day of the Lord comes; who shall turn again the heart of the father to the son." In the atonement, the cross turns the heart of God the Father to reconcile the lives of sinners whose lives are hid in the Son by faith. [4]TLG 2062.152, 58.559.33-36; NPNF 1 10:352. As the heart of the Father was being restored to the Son by his self-giving, so the hearts of the apostles were being restored to the covenant. [5]TLG 2062.152, 58.560.20-24; NPNF 1 10:353. [6]TLG 2062.152, 58.559.16-19; NPNF 1 10:352*.

---

## 9:14-29 AN EPILEPTIC BOY HEALED

[14]*And when they came to the disciples, they saw a great crowd about them, and scribes arguing with them.* [15]*And immediately all the crowd, when they saw him, were greatly amazed, and ran up to him and greeted him.* [16]*And he asked them, "What are you discussing with them?"* [17]*And one of the crowd answered him, "Teacher, I brought my son to you, for he has a dumb spirit;* [18]*and wherever it seizes him, it dashes him down; and he foams and grinds his teeth and becomes rigid; and I asked your disciples to cast it out, and they were not able."* [19]*And he answered them, "O faithless generation, how long am I to be with you? How long am I to bear with you? Bring him to me."* [20]*And they brought the boy to him; and when the spirit saw him, immediately it convulsed the boy, and he fell on the ground and rolled about, foaming at the mouth.* [21]*And Jesus*[b] *asked his father, "How long has he had this?" And he said, "From*

*childhood.* <sup>22</sup>*And it has often cast him into the fire and into the water, to destroy him; but if you can do anything, have pity on us and help us." <sup>23</sup>And Jesus said to him, "If you can! All things are possible to him who believes." <sup>24</sup>Immediately the father of the child cried out[i] and said, "I believe; help my unbelief!" <sup>25</sup>And when Jesus saw that a crowd came running together, he rebuked the unclean spirit, saying to it, "You dumb and deaf spirit, I command you, come out of him, and never enter him again." <sup>26</sup>And after crying out and convulsing him terribly, it came out, and the boy was like a corpse; so that most of them said, "He is dead." <sup>27</sup>But Jesus took him by the hand and lifted him up, and he arose. <sup>28</sup>And when he had entered the house, his disciples asked him privately, "Why could we not cast it out?" <sup>29</sup>And he said to them, "This kind cannot be driven out by anything but prayer."[j]*

**h** Greek *he*   **i** Other ancient authorities add *with tears*   **j** Other ancient authorities add *and fasting*

**OVERVIEW:** We pray that we may believe and believe that we might pray (AUGUSTINE). No measure of faith is preserved without prayer (JEROME, JOHN CASSIAN). The demonic compulsions are bound up when they come into the presence of the incarnate Lord (TERTULLIAN, PETER CHRYSOLOGUS). We see this in Jesus' simple gesture of taking the child by the hand and lifting him up (BEDE). Those who lack the sustaining power of the Holy Spirit remain vulnerable to demonic systems and powers (TERTULLIAN, MINUCIUS FELIX). Aspects of faith are recognizable as praiseworthy even by those without faith (CAESARIUS OF ARLES).

### 9:18 He Foams and Grinds His Teeth and Becomes Rigid

**THE DEVIL'S BUSINESS: UNDOING OTHERS.**
MINUCIUS FELIX: These spirits therefore, having lost the simplicity of their created being and the primitive fineness of their nature, are now clogged and laden with iniquity. Utterly undone themselves, they make it their whole business to undo others, for companions in misery. Being depraved themselves, they would infuse the same depravity into others. . . .

When we command them by the one true God, the wretches, bitterly against their will, fall into horrible shiverings, and either spring straightaway from the bodies they possess, or vanish by degrees, according to the faith of the patient or the grace of the physician. OCTAVIUS 26-27.[1]

### 9:20 It Convulsed the Boy

**THE USURPING SPIRIT.** PETER CHRYSOLOGUS: Though it was the boy who fell on the ground, it was the devil in him who was in anguish. The possessed boy was merely convulsed, while the usurping spirit was being convicted by the awesome judge. The captive was detained, but the captor was punished. Through the wrenching of the human body, the punishment of the devil was made manifest. SERMONS 51.[2]

### 9:21 "How Long Has He Had This?" And He Said, "From Childhood."

---

[1]PL 3:321-326; *GMI* 204\*\*; cf. ANF 4:190. The business of devils is to undo others in the same way as they themselves have been voluntarily undone.   [2]Cetedoc 0227, 24.51.62; *GMI* 205-6\*.

## THE TAINT OF THE FIRST TRANSGRESSION.

BEDE: Lacking the premise of original sin, what possible cause can be imagined in this youth why he should since childhood have been vexed with this most fierce demonic possession? It seems clear that no actual sin of his own could have elicited this. So let the catholic remember and confess that no one is born into this world free from the taint of the first transgression.[3] Let him implore the grace of God through which he might be "delivered from this body of death through Jesus Christ our Lord."[4] EXPOSITION ON THE GOSPEL OF MARK 3.9.21-22.[5]

### 9:22 If You Can! All Things Are Possible to Him Who Believes

## THE INFIRM FAITH OF THE BOY'S FATHER.

CHRYSOSTOM: The Scripture indicates that this man was extremely weak in faith, as is evident at four points: from Christ's saying that "All things are possible to him that believes;"[6] from the saying of the man himself as he approached, "Help me in my unbelief;"[7] from Christ's commanding the devil to "enter no more into him;"[8] and from the man's saying again to Christ, "If you can."[9] THE GOSPEL OF ST. MATTHEW, HOMILY 57.3.[10]

### 9:24 I Believe; Help My Unbelief

## EMERGENT FAITH SEEKING MATURITY. AU-

GUSTINE: In saying, "When the Son of Man shall come, shall he find faith upon the earth?" our Lord spoke of that faith which is fully matured, which is so seldom found on earth. The church's faith is full, for who would come here if there were no fullness of faith? And whose faith when fully matured would not move mountains?[11] Look at the apostles themselves, who would not have left all they had,

trodden under foot this world's hope, and followed the Lord, if they had not had proportionally great faith. And yet if they had already experienced a completely matured faith, they would have not said to the Lord, "Increase our faith."[12] Rather we find here an emerging faith, which is not yet full faith, in that father who when he had presented to the Lord his son to be cured of an evil spirit and was asked whether he believed, answered, "Lord, I believe, help me in my unbelief."[13] "Lord," says he, "I believe." "I believe": therefore there was faith; but "help me in my unbelief": therefore there was not full faith.[14] SERMONS ON NEW TESTAMENT LESSONS 65.[15]

## PRAY TO BELIEVE, BELIEVE TO PRAY. AUGUS-

TINE: Where faith fails, prayer perishes. For who prays for that in which he does not believe? . . . So then in order that we may pray, let us believe,[16] and let us pray that this same faith by which we pray may not falter. SERMONS ON NEW TESTAMENT LESSONS 65.1.[17]

## GRACE TO ASSIST FAITH. JOHN CASSIAN: See-

ing that his faith was being driven by the waves of unbelief on the rocks which would cause a fearful shipwreck,[18] he asks of the Lord an aid to his faith, saying "Lord, help me in my unbelief."[19] So thoroughly did the apostles and those who live in the gospel realize that everything which is good is brought to completion by the aid of the

---

[3]Cf. Rom 5:12-14. [4]Cf. Rom 7:24. [5]Cetedoc 1355.39.260; CCL 120:548; GMI 206*; cf. HOG 1:240. [6]Mk 9:23. [7]Mk 9:24. [8]Mk 9:25. [9]Mk 9:22. [10]TLG 2062.152, 58.561.10-17; NPNF 1 10:354. [11]Cf. Mt 17:20; 21:21. [12]Lk 17:5. [13]Mk 9:24. [14]Cf. Heb 10:22. [15]Cetedoc 0284, 115.38.665.42; NPNF 1 6:454*; cf. WSA 3 4:199, Sermon 115.1. [16]Cf. Mt 21:22; Mk 11:24. [17]Cetedoc 0284, 115.38.655.19; NPNF 1 6:454*; cf. WSA 3 4:198, Sermon 115.1. When we pray to believe, we pray that the will itself will not waver in faith; in this way prayer and faith are intrinsically linked acts. [18]Cf. 1 Tim 1:19. [19]Mk 9:24.

Lord, and not imagine that they could preserve their faith unharmed by their own strength or free will, that they prayed that it might be helped and granted to them by the Lord.[20] CONFERENCE OF ABBOT PAPHNUTIUS 16.[21]

**EVEN THE FAITHLESS RECOGNIZE THE VALUE OF FAITH.** CAESARIUS OF ARLES: So great is the virtue of faith that even those who refuse to keep it still presume to praise it. Truly deservedly is faith extolled, for without it no good work is ever begun or completed. SERMONS 12.[22]

### 9:27 Jesus Took Him by the Hand

**THE HUMAN HAND OF THE DIVINE LORD.** BEDE: As he revealed himself to him in the reality of his Godhead by his power to save, so he further exhibited to him the reality of his human nature by taking him by the hand. EXPOSITION ON THE GOSPEL OF MARK 3.9.26-27.[23]

### 9:28 Why Could We Not Cast It Out?

**THE WEAPON OF CHOICE.** TERTULLIAN: Fasting is the weapon of choice for battling with the more dreadful demons.[24] Should we be surprised if the expulsion of the spirit of iniquity requires the indwelling of the Holy Spirit? ON FASTING 8.8.[25]

### 9:29 This Kind Cannot Be Driven Out by Anything but Prayer

**THE NECESSITY OF PRAYER.** JEROME: The Lord himself consecrated his baptism by a forty days' fast,[26] and taught us that the more violent devils cannot be overcome except by prayer and fasting. AGAINST JOVINIANUS 2.15.[27]

---

[20]Cf. Lk 17:5. [21]Cetedoc 0512, 3.16.88.22; NPNF 2 11:327. [22]Cetedoc 1008, 103.12.1.8; FC 31:67. [23]Cetedoc 1355, 3.9.316; CCL 120:550; GMI 209*; cf. HOG 1:241. [24]Mt 17:21; Mk 9:29. [25]Cetedoc 0029, 284.3; ANF 4:107**. [26]Cf. Mt 4:2; Lk 4:2-3. [27]Cetedoc 0610, 2.15.323.11; NPNF 2 6:400.

---

## 9:30-32 THE SECOND PREDICTION OF THE PASSION

[30]*They went on from there and passed through Galilee. And he would not have any one know it;* [31]*for he was teaching his disciples, saying to them, "The Son of man will be delivered into the hands of men, and they will kill him; and when he is killed, after three days he will rise."* [32]*But they did not understand the saying, and they were afraid to ask him.*

**OVERVIEW:** John Chrysostom commented on how little the disciples grasped the meaning of the clearly predicted death of the Lord. Even after all these revealing miracles, after this distinct unveiling of Jesus' identity from the voice from above and after the direct prediction of his death and resurrection, they missed the point and were preoccupied with their own anxiety (CHRYSOSTOM).

### 9:32a They Did Not Understand

ON NOT UNDERSTANDING. CHRYSOSTOM: It is remarkable how, when Peter had been rebuked,[1] and Moses and Elijah had discoursed,[2] and had seen the glory of what was coming, and the Father had uttered a voice from above,[3] and so many miracles had been done, and the resurrection was right at the door (for he said, he should by no means abide any long time in death, but should be raised the third day),[4] even after all that they did not fathom what was happening. Rather they were troubled, and not merely troubled, but exceedingly mournful.[5] Now this arose from their being ignorant as yet of the force of his sayings.[6] THE GOSPEL OF ST. MATTHEW, HOMILY 58.1.[7]

THE REASON FOR GRIEF. CHRYSOSTOM: If ignorant, how could they be sorrowful?[8]

Because they were not altogether ignorant. They knew that he was soon to die, for they had continually been told about it. But just what this death might mean, they did not grasp clearly, nor that there would be a speedy recognition of it, from which innumerable blessings would flow. They did not see that there would be a resurrection. This is why they grieved.[9] THE GOSPEL OF ST. MATTHEW, HOMILY 58.[10]

### 9:32b They Were Afraid to Ask

BENT BY PREVIOUS ASSUMPTIONS. ANONYMOUS: They were greatly grieved[11] because they had formed a very different notion previously in their minds and hearts. A TREATISE ON REBAPTISM 9.[12]

---

[1]Cf. Mt 16:23; Mk 8:33. [2]Cf. Mt 17:3; Mk 9:4; Lk 9:30. [3]Cf. Mt 3:17; 17:5; Mk 1:11; 9:7; Lk 3:22. [4]Cf. Jn 2:19-22. [5]Cf. Mt 17:23. [6]Cf. Mk 9:32; Lk 9:45. [7]TLG 2062.152, 58.565.45-53; cf. NPNF 1 10:358 [8]Cf. Mt 17:23; Mk 9:32; Lk 9:45. [9]Cf. Mt 17:23. [10]TLG 2062.152, 58.566.37-43; NPNF 1 10:358**. [11]Cf. Mt 17:23. [12]PL 3:1193A-B; ANF 5 672*.

## 9:33-37 THE DISPUTE ABOUT GREATNESS

[33]And they came to Capernaum; and when he was in the house he asked them, "What were you discussing on the way?" [34]But they were silent; for on the way they had discussed with one another who was the greatest. [35]And he sat down and called the twelve; and he said to them, "If any one would be first, he must be last of all and servant of all." [36]And he took a child, and put him in the midst of them; and taking him in his arms, he said to them, [37]"Whoever receives one such child in my name receives me; and whoever receives me, receives not me but him who sent me."

**OVERVIEW:** The key mark of discipleship is servanthood (GREGORY OF NYSSA). The text teaches that discipleship grows first by a downward, lowly movement, as a tree seeking roots, in order then to reach skyward (AUGUSTINE). Be ready to receive the lowly neighbor as if sent by Christ (TERTULLIAN). The disciplines of humility are most pertinent to those most prone to vanity (CHRYSOSTOM). Childlike innocence is characteristic of those who dwell in the kingdom of God (SHEPHERD OF HERMAS).

### 9:34 They Discussed Who Was the Greatest

**ROOTING BY DOWNWARD MOVEMENT.** AUGUSTINE: Observe a tree, how it first tends downwards, that it may then shoot forth upwards. It fastens its root low in the ground, that it may send forth its top towards heaven. Is it not from humility that it endeavors to rise? But without humility it will not attain to higher things.[1] You are wanting to grow up into the air without a root. Such is not growth, but a collapse. THE GOSPEL OF JOHN, SERMON 38.[2]

### 9:35 If Any One Would Be First, He Must Be Last of All and Servant of All

**GUILELESS COHESION.** GREGORY OF NYSSA: Let vanity be unknown among you. Let simplicity and harmony and a guileless attitude weld the community together. Let each remind himself that he is not only subordinate to the brother at his side, but to all.[3] If he knows this, he will truly be a disciple of Christ. ON THE CHRISTIAN MODE OF LIFE 8.1.[4]

**THE PURSUIT OF MEEKNESS.** CHRYSOSTOM: If you are in love with precedence and the highest honor, pursue the things in last place, pursue being the least valued of all, pursue being the lowliest of all, pursue being the smallest of all, pursue placing yourselves behind others. THE GOSPEL OF ST. MATTHEW, HOMILY 58.[5]

### 9:36 He Put a Child in the Midst of Them

**THE CHILD AS PATTERN.** SHEPHERD OF HERMAS: They are as veritable infants, whose hearts do not invent evil, who hardly know what corruption is, and who have remained childlike forever. People such as these, therefore, undoubtedly dwell in the kingdom of God, because they in no way defile God's commandments, but have continued in innocence all the days of their lives in the same state of mind. SHEPHERD OF HERMAS 3.9.29.[6]

### 9:37 Whoever Receives Me, Receives Not Me but Him Who Sent Me

**RECEIVING AND OFFERING REFRESHMENT.** TERTULLIAN: Do not receive without prayer one who enters your house, especially if that one is a stranger, lest he turn out to be an angelic messenger.[7] Do not offer your earthly refreshments prior to receiving heavenly refreshment. ON PRAYER 26.[8]

---

[1]Cf. Prov 18:12. [2]Cetedoc 0284, 117.38.671.39; GC 1:215*. [3]Cf. Gal 5:13-14. [4]TLG 2014.024, 8.1.70.20-71.3; FC 58:147*. [5]TLG 2062.152, 58.568.60-569.3; NPNF 1 10:360. [6]AF 284*; cf. TLG 1419.001, 106.1.2-3.1. [7]Cf. Heb 13:12. [8]Cetedoc 0007, 26.1; ANF 3:690**.

# 9:38-41 THE MAN WHO CAST OUT DEMONS IN JESUS' NAME

³⁸*John said to him, "Teacher, we saw a man casting out demons in your name,ᵏ and we forbade him, because he was not following us." ³⁹But Jesus said, "Do not forbid him; for no one who does a mighty work in my name will be able soon after to speak evil of me. ⁴⁰For he that is not against us is for us. ⁴¹For truly, I say to you, whoever gives you a cup of water to drink because you bear the name of Christ, will by no means lose his reward."*

k Other ancient authorities add *who does not follow us*

**OVERVIEW:** According to Augustine, this passage teaches that the judgment of God lies heavy upon those who tempt the children of light. As civic virtues may be found apart from the church, so doctrinal corruptions may also be found within the church. Those who do mighty works without full participation in the body of Christ are not to be forbidden. The unbaptized who perform acts of kindness to those who are not yet incorporated into the body of Christ may be more profitable servants than are those in the church who draw others into evil deeds. One may do mighty works in Christ's name and still possess only a crude, preliminary knowledge of his regenerative power. If the balance between rigor and charity is lost in the administration of discipline, the peace of the church is disturbed and disunity increased. Those who separate themselves from the body of Christ do not need to be corrected on all points but only those that involve separation (AUGUSTINE). God never asks what is impossible. God's requirement comes in small measures as grace enables, like giving a cup of cold water in the name of Christ (GREGORY OF NYSSA).

## 9:38a A Man Casting Out Demons in Your Name

**THE MERCIFUL WORKS OF THE UNBAPTIZED.** AUGUSTINE: His situation was in some ways parallel to that of one who, while not yet embracing the sacraments of Christ, nevertheless esteems the Christian name so far as even to welcome Christians and accommodate oneself to their service for this very reason and no other—that they are Christians. This is the type of person of whom it was said that he would not lose his reward.[1] This does not mean, however, that such individuals ought prematurely to imagine themselves quite safe and secure simply on account of this kindness which they cherish toward Christians, while at the same time remaining uncleansed by Christ's baptism, and not thereby incorporated into the unity of his body. Such persons are now already being guided by the mercy of God in such a way that they may also come to receive these loftier gifts, and so depart this present world in safety. Such persons assuredly are more profitable servants even before they

[1]Cf. Mt 10:42; Mk 9:41.

become a part of the body of Christ, than those who, while already bearing the Christian name and partaking in the sacraments, recommend courses of action which are only fitted to drag others along with them into eternal punishment. HARMONY OF THE GOSPELS 4.6.[2]

### 9:38b We Forbade Him, Because He Was Not Following Us

THE BREADTH OF CATHOLICITY. AUGUSTINE: There may be something catholic outside the Church catholic. The name of Christ could exist outside the congregation of Christ, as in the case of the man casting out devils in Christ's name. There may by contrast exist pretenses within the church catholic, as is unquestionably the case of those "who renounce the world[3] in words and not in deeds," and yet the pretense is not catholic. So as there may be found in the church catholic something which is not catholic, so there may be found something which is catholic outside the church catholic. ON BAPTISM, AGAINST THE DONATISTS 7.39 (76).[4]

### 9:39 Do Not Forbid Him

ENCOURAGING GOOD WORKS DONE IN CHRIST'S NAME. AUGUSTINE: We ought not be disturbed because some who do not belong or do not yet belong to this temple, that is, among whom God does not or does not yet dwell, perform some works of power, as happened to the one who cast out devils in the name of Christ.[5] Although he was not a follower of Christ, Christ ordered that he be allowed to continue because it gave a valuable testimony of his name to many. . . . The centurion Cornelius also saw the angel that was sent to him to say that his prayers had been heard and his alms accepted,[6] even before he was incorporated into

this temple by regeneration. LETTER 187, To DARDANUS 36.[7]

JUDGMENTAL EXCESS. AUGUSTINE: Some who are intent on severe disciplinary principles which admonish us to rebuke the restless, not to give what is holy to dogs,[8] to consider a despiser of the church as a heathen, to cut off from the unified structure of the body the member which causes scandal,[9] so disturb the peace of the church that they try to separate the wheat from the chaff before the proper time.[10] Blinded by this error, they are themselves separated instead from the unity of Christ. FAITH AND WORKS 4.6.[11]

### 9:40 He That Is Not Against Us Is for Us

STANDING WITH THE WHOLE CHURCH. AUGUSTINE: Both declarations are true: that "he who is not with me is against me, and he that gathers not with me scatters abroad";[12] and also the injunction, "Forbid him not; for he that is not against you is for you."[13] This means that one fittingly shares in the worshiping community insofar as one stands with the whole church, and not against it. Yet those same individuals must be reproached for separating themselves from the church, wherever their gathering inadvertently becomes a scattering. If then one seeks reconciliation with the church, one does not need to receive what one already possesses,[14] but merely needs to be set aright on those points at which one had gone astray. ON BAPTISM,

---

[2]Cetedoc 0273, 4.6.7.401.20; NPNF 1 6:229**. [3]In baptism; cf. Rom 12:2; 1 Jn 2:15; 5:4. [4]Cetedoc 0332, 7.39.77.363.5; NPNF 1 4:508**. [5]Cf. Mk 9:38; Lk 9:49. [6]Cf. Acts 10:3-4. [7]Cetedoc 0262, 187.57.12.113.20; FC 30:250. [8]Cf. Mt 7:6; 15:26; Mk 7:27. [9]Cf. Mt 5:30; 18:8-9; Mk 9:42-48. [10]Cf. Mt 13:29-30. [11]Cetedoc 0294, 4.6.41.9; FC 27:227*. [12]Mt 12:30; Lk 11:23. [13]Lk 9:50; cf. Mk 9:39-40. [14]The rule of faith, the sacred text, the sacraments.

AGAINST THE DONATISTS 1.7 (9).[15]

**RESISTING SENTIMENTS ADVERSE TO PEACE.**
AUGUSTINE: This is the principle on which the
whole church acts, not condemning common
sacraments among heretics; for in these they
are with us, and they are not against us.[16] But
she condemns and forbids division and separation, or any sentiment adverse to peace and
truth. For in this respect they are against us,
precisely because they are not with us, in the
sense that and due to the fact that in not gathering with us, they are consequently scattering.[17] HARMONY OF THE GOSPELS 4.[18]

## 9:41 A Cup of Water

**SIMPLICITY IN SERVICE.** GREGORY OF NYSSA:

God never asks his servants to do what is
impossible. The love and goodness of his Godhead is revealed as richly available. It is poured
out like water upon all. God furnishes to each
person according to his will the ability to do
something good. None of those seeking to be
saved will be lacking in this ability, given by the
one who said: "whoever gives you a cup of
water to drink because you bear the name of
Christ, will by no means lose his reward."[19] ON
THE CHRISTIAN MODE OF LIFE 8.1.[20]

---

[15]Cetedoc 0332, 1.7.9.155.5; NPNF 1 4:416*. Those who divide
and scatter the body of Christ do not need to be corrected on all
points but only those that involve separation, which offends against
the intrinsic oneness of the church. [16]Cf. Mk 9:39-40; Lk 9:50.
[17]Cf. Mt 12:30; Lk 11:23. [18]Cetedoc 0273, 4.5.6.400.10; NPNF 1
6:228*. [19]Mt 10:42; Mk 9:41. [20]TLG 2017.024, 8.1.87.21-88.7;
FC 58:157*.

# 9:42-50 ON TEMPTATION

[42]"Whoever causes one of these little ones who believe in me to sin,[l] it would be better for
him if a great millstone were hung round his neck and he were thrown into the sea. [43]And if
your hand causes you to sin,[l] cut it off; it is better for you to enter life maimed than with two
hands to go to hell,[m] to the unquenchable fire.[n] [45]And if your foot causes you to sin,[l] cut it off; it
is better for you to enter life lame than with two feet to be thrown into hell.[m] [47]And if your eye
causes you to sin,[l] pluck it out; it is better for you to enter the kingdom of God with one eye
than with two eyes to be thrown into hell,[m] [48]where their worm does not die, and the fire is not
quenched. [49]For every one will be salted with fire.[o] [50]Salt is good; but if the salt has lost its salt-
ness, how will you season it? Have salt in yourselves, and be at peace with one another."

l Greek stumble   m Greek Gehenna   n Verses 44 and 46 (which are identical with verse 48) are omitted by the best ancient authorities   o Other ancient authorities add and every sacrifice will be salted with salt

**OVERVIEW:** The Fathers warn against flat literalism in interpreting this text: To follow literally the command to cut off the hand would be to fail to hear its meaning (CLEMENTINA). We are not referring to earthworms or earthly fires but unending misery over willed sin (GREGORY OF NYSSA). The dynamics of temptation work so elusively as to prevent sinners from awareness even of their own stench and illness, which others can smell easily (CHRYSOSTOM). The eye colludes in causing sin by making an entryway into the heart (SALVIAN THE PRESBYTER). Hell is not merely a rhetorical hyperbole (BASIL). The reader of the Word cannot select out comfortable passages and ignore those that make us uneasy (CHRYSOSTOM). Temporary disciplinary rejection within the church is a minor inconvenience compared with God's final rejection of sin (CAESARIUS OF ARLES). When the sting of judgment falls, it is not to punish but to heal (METHODIUS). Those who finally reject salvation suffer eternally in both body and soul (AUGUSTINE). Our words become salt when they receive the wisdom that flows from the revealed Word, without which our hasty words may inadvertently shatter integrity (GREGORY THE GREAT).

### 9:42 It Would Be Better for Him if a Great Millstone Were Hung Round His Neck and He Were Thrown into the Sea

**A TERRIFYING REPETITION.** AUGUSTINE: He did not shrink from using the same words three times[1] over in one passage. And who is not terrified by this repetition and by the threat of that punishment uttered so vehemently by the lips of the Lord himself? THE CITY OF GOD 21.9.[2]

### 9:43 If Your Hand Causes You to Sin, Cut It Off

**LITERALLY CUT OFF?** CLEMENTINA[3]: Let none of you think, brothers, that the Lord is here commending the cutting off of members. His meaning is that the incentive should be cut off, not the members. The causes which allure to sin are to be cut off, in order that our thought, borne up on the chariot of sight, may push toward the love of God, supported by the bodily senses. So do not give loose reins to the eyes of the flesh as if you were wanton horses, eager to turn their running away from the commandments. Subject the bodily sight to the judgment of the mind. Do not permit these eyes of ours, which God intended to be viewers and witnesses of his work, to become procurers of evil desire.[4] RECOGNITIONS OF CLEMENT 7.1.37.[5]

### 9:45 It Is Better for You to Enter Life Lame Than with Two Feet to Be Thrown into Hell

**HELL IS NOT A HYPERBOLE.** BASIL: Do not think that I am threatening you with false goblins like some mother or nurse, as they are accustomed to do with small children. Whenever the children wail wildly and incessantly, they put the children to silence by means of bogus tales. But these things I am telling you are not a fiction. Rather, they are true reason publicly proclaimed with a straightforward voice. HOMILIES 5, SAYINGS FOR A TIME OF HUNGER AND THIRST 2.[6]

### 9:47 If Your Eye Causes You to Sin

---

[1]Augustine is asking why "it would be better for him" is repeated three times. [2]Cetedoc 0313, 48.21.9.16; NPNF 1 2:461. [3]The *Clementina* is a collection of writings erroneously ascribed to Clement of Rome. [4]Cf. Mt 6:23. [5]GCS 15:215; ANF 8:165*. To follow the command literally would be to deny it. [6]TLG 2040.024, 31.328.27-33.

**THE COLLUSION OF THE EYE WITH SIN.**
SALVIAN THE PRESBYTER: Knowing that the lights of the eyes are like windows to our hearts, and that all corrupt desires enter us through the eyes, as if through a natural crevice, our Lord asks us to veil them from wandering about, in order to resist the spreading of their toxic illusions, so those illusions will not take ever firmer root in our hearts, having first budded in the eye.[7] ON THE GOVERNANCE OF GOD 3.8.[8]

## 9:48a *Their Worm Does Not Die*

**THE SYNDROME OF UNAWARENESS.** CHRYSOSTOM: Christ has killed and buried your former transgressions, like worms. How then is it that you have bred others? For sins that harm the soul are more deadly than worms which harm the body. And they make a more offensive stench.[9] Yet we do not even perceive their rankness, and so we sense no urgency to purge them out. So the drunkard fails to recognize how disgusting stale wine is, while one who is sober perceives the difference easily. So with sins: one who lives soberly sees easily the mire and the stain, but one who gives himself up to wickedness, like one made drowsy with drunkenness, does not even realize that he is ill. This is the worst aspect of evil, that it does not allow those who fall into it even to see the seriousness of their own diseased state, but as they lie in the mire, they think they are enjoying perfumes. So they do not have the slightest inclination to free themselves. And when full of worms they act like those who pride themselves in precious stones, exulting in them. For this reason they not only have no will to kill them, but they even nourish them, and multiply them in themselves, until they send them on to the worms of the age to come. THE EPISTLE TO THE ROMANS, HOMILY 40.[10]

## 9:48b *The Fire Is Not Quenched*

**ORDINARY FIRE AND ETERNAL FIRE.** GREGORY OF NYSSA: Nor, too, does anything which afflicts the senses here equal in torment the future life of sinners. Even if we denote some of those torments by terms familiar to us here, the difference is not slight. When you hear the word "fire," you have been taught to think of it differently from ordinary fire, since a new factor is added. For that fire is not quenched, while experience has devised many ways to quench the fire we know. And there is a great difference between fire which is quenched and that which cannot be put out. They are, therefore, different, and not the same. Then again, when a person hears the word "worm," the analogy must not be misapplied directly from the creature we know to the eternal. For the addition of the phrase "that does not die" suggests the thought that this worm is not simply the creature we know. ADDRESS ON RELIGIOUS INSTRUCTION 40.[11]

**WHY NOT SKIP OVER SUCH PASSAGES?** CHRYSOSTOM: This is no trivial subject of inquiry that we propose, but rather it concerns things most urgent, and about which many inquire: namely, whether hell fire has any end. For that it has no end Christ indeed declared when he said, "Their fire shall not be quenched, and their worm shall not die."[12] Yes, I know a chill comes over you on hearing these things. But what am I to do? For this is God's own command. . . . Ordained as we have been to the ministry of the word, we must cause our hearers discomfort when it is necessary for them to

---

[7]Cf. Sir 14:9. [8]Cetedoc 0485, 3.8.37.64; *GMI* 227*. [9]Chrysostom is puzzled by why sinners so love their sin and have no will to change. [10]NPNF 1 9:413*; TLG 2062.155, 60.490.38-58. [11]LCC 3:325; TLG 2017.046, 40.77-89. [12]Is 66:24.

hear. We do this not arbitrarily but under command. HOMILIES ON FIRST CORINTHIANS 9.1.[13]

**DISCIPLINARY REJECTION—TEMPORARY AND ETERNAL.** CAESARIUS OF ARLES: If today one is cast out of the assembly of this church because of some enormity, in how much grief and tribulation will his soul be?[14] If it causes unbearable pain to be thrown out of this church, where the one who is rejected can eat and drink and speak with others and has the hope of being called back, how much more pain will there be if, because of his sins, one is separated from that church which is in heaven, and eternally separated from the assembly of the angels and the company of all the saints? For such a person it will not be enough punishment for him to be cast away, but in addition he will be shut out into the night, to be consumed by an eternal fire. One whose impenitent behavior has warranted his being finally shut out of that heavenly Jerusalem will not only be deprived of divine fellowship, but will also suffer the flames of hell, "where there is weeping and gnashing of teeth,"[15] where there will be the wailing of lamentation without any remedy, where the worm does not die, and the fire is not extinguished;[16] where death would be sought as an end to torment, and not found. SERMONS 227.4.[17]

### 9:50 Have Salt in Yourselves

**THE MEANING OF SALT.** METHODIUS: According to levitical law,[18] every gift, unless it be seasoned with salt, is forbidden to be offered as an oblation to the Lord God. Now the whole spiritual meditation of the Scriptures is given to us as salt which stings in order to benefit. Without this disinfection, it is impossible for a soul, by means of reason, to be brought to the almighty. THE BANQUET OF THE TEN VIRGINS 1.1.[19]

**A FIT PINCH OF SALT.** EPHREM THE SYRIAN:
Glory be to God on high,
Who mixed his salt in our minds,
His leaven in our souls.
His body became bread,[20]
To quicken our deadness.
HYMNS ON THE NATIVITY 2.[21]

**HAVING SALT IN OUR SPEECH.** GREGORY THE GREAT: When the counselor prepares himself for speaking, let him bear in mind with what diligent caution he ought to speak, lest, if he is too hurried in speaking, the hearts of hearers be struck with the wound of error. Desiring to seem wise, he may unwisely sever the bond of unity. It is for this reason that the One who is truth has said: "Have salt in yourselves, and have peace one with another."[22] Now by salt is denoted the word of wisdom. Let him, therefore, who strives to speak wisely fear greatly, lest by his eloquence the integrity of his hearers be disturbed. PASTORAL CARE 4.12.[23]

---

[13]NPNF 1 12:49*; TLG 2062.156, 61.75.24-31, 32-34. [14]Caesarius is asking how temporary disciplinary rejection within the church is to be compared with God's final rejection of sin. [15]Mt 22:13. [16]Mk 9:48. [17]Cetedoc 1008, 104.227.4.1; FC 66:166*. [18]Lev 2:13; Mk. 9:49-50. [19]PG 18:40; ANF 6:311**. [20]Cf Mt 26:26; Mk 14:22; Lk 22:19. [21]CSCO 186-187:21; NPNF 2 13:237. [22]Mk 9:50. [23]Cetedoc 1712, 2.4.56; NPNF 2 12:12**.

## 10:1-12 ON DIVORCE

¹*And he left there and went to the region of Judea and beyond the Jordan, and crowds gathered to him again; and again, as his custom was, he taught them.*

²*And Pharisees came up and in order to test him asked, "Is it lawful for a man to divorce his wife?" ³He answered them, "What did Moses command you?" ⁴They said, "Moses allowed a man to write a certificate of divorce, and to put her away." ⁵But Jesus said to them, "For your hardness of heart he wrote you this commandment. ⁶But from the beginning of creation, God made them male and female. ⁷For this reason a man shall leave his father and mother and be joined to his wife,ᵖ ⁸and the two shall become one flesh. So they are no longer two but one flesh. ⁹What therefore God has joined together, let not man put asunder."*

¹⁰*And in the house the disciples asked him again about this matter. ¹¹And he said to them, "Whoever divorces his wife and marries another, commits adultery against her; ¹²and if she divorces her husband and marries another, she commits adultery."*

p  Other ancient authorities omit *and be joined to his wife*

**OVERVIEW:** God could have provided an infinite number of partners for Adam but gave him only one. Marriage is no burden when the two become equally one in all things, losing all, sharing all (TERTULLIAN). The mystery of the joining of one man and one woman in one flesh is viewed by analogy to the joining of God and humanity in the incarnation (ORIGEN). The biblical prototype of one flesh is the relation of Christ and the church (AUGUSTINE). Meanwhile, the tempter promotes a permissive view of divorce and remarriage (CLEMENT OF ALEXANDRIA, ATHENAGORAS). The Lord's teaching on divorce applies equally to men and women (BASIL). Fornication evidences the failure of original intent in the marriage. Four adulterers can emerge from the aftermath of one marriage of two previously married spouses (AUGUSTINE). Jesus was not vexed when he was challenged by deceptive questioners who hoped more for a gaffe than an answer (ORIGEN).

### 10:2 To Test Him

**FACING DECEPTIVE INTERROGATION.** ORIGEN: Of those who came to Jesus and interrogated him, some put questions to him simply to trick him. If our glorious Savior was tested in this way, should any of his disciples called to teach be annoyed when questioned by some who probe, not from the desire to know, but from the intent to trip up? COMMENTARY ON MATTHEW 14.16.[1]

### 10:6 God Made Them Male and Female

**THE LAW OF MONOGAMY.** TERTULLIAN: I will call your attention to the law of monogamy. The very origin of the human race sanctions it.[2]

---

[1]TLG 2042.030, 14.16.9-20; cf. ANF 9:505.  [2]Gen 1:27.

It is abundantly clear that God ordained it at the beginning as a pattern for posterity. For after he had made Adam, and had foreseen the necessity of providing a helpmate for him, he borrowed from his loins one alone.[3] One woman only did he design for man. EXHORTATION TO CHASTITY 5.[4]

## 10:8 The Two Shall Become One

**MUTUAL SERVANTS, EQUALLY SERVING.** TERTULLIAN: Where are we to find language adequately to express the happiness of that marriage which the church cements, the oblation confirms, the benediction signs and seals, the angels celebrate, and the Father holds as approved? For all around the earth young people do not rightly and lawfully wed without their parents' consent.[5] What kind of yoke is that of two believers who share one hope, one desire, one discipline, one service?[6] They enjoy kinship in spirit and in flesh. They are mutual servants with no discrepancy of interests. Truly they are "two in one flesh."[7] Where the flesh is one, the spirit is one as well. Together they pray, together bow down, together perform their fasts, mutually teaching, mutually entreating, mutually upholding. In the church of God they hold an equal place.[8] They stand equally at the banquet of God, equally in crises, equally facing persecutions, and equally in refreshments. Neither hides anything from the other. Neither neglects the other. Neither is troublesome to the other.[9] TO HIS WIFE 2.8.[10]

**THE ONE FLESH OF MAN AND WOMAN.** ORIGEN: For the Word of God is to be considered as being more in one flesh with the soul than a man is one flesh with his wife.[11] But to whom is it more becoming to be also one spirit with God, than to this human soul which has so

joined itself to God by love as that it may justly be said to be one spirit with God?[12] ON FIRST PRINCIPLES 2.6.3.[13]

**THE BRIDEGROOM AND THE BRIDE.** JACOB OF SARUG: In his mysterious plans the Father had destined a bride for his only Son and presented her to him under the guise of prophetic images. Moses appeared and with deft hand sketched a picture of bridegroom and bride but immediately drew a veil over it. In his book he wrote that a man should leave father and mother so as to be joined to his wife, that the two might in very truth become one. The prophet Moses spoke of man and woman in this way in order to foretell Christ and his church. With a prophet's penetrating gaze he contemplated Christ becoming one with the church through the mystery of water.[14] He saw Christ even from the virgin's womb drawing the church to himself, and the church in the water of baptism drawing Christ to herself. Bridegroom and bride were thus wholly united in a mystical manner, which is why Moses wrote that the two should become one.... Wives are not united to their husbands as closely as the church is to the Son of God. What husband but our Lord ever died for his wife, and what bride ever chose a crucified man as her husband? Who ever gave his blood as a gift to his

---

[3]Gen 2:21-22. [4]Cetedoc 0020, 5.1; *GMI* 235**; ANF 4:53**. [5]The sacrificial offering of the Son in the Eucharist. [6]Cf. Eph 4:4. [7]Gen 2:24; Mt 19:5; Eph 5:31. [8]Cf. Rom 12:15; 15:6; Gal 3:28; 1 Cor 12:12. [9]Cf. Phil 1:27. The assumption of equality between women and men, their mutual self-disclosure and charity, is clearly expressed in this text. [10]Cetedoc 0012, 2.8.37; ANF 4:48*. [11]Cf. Gen 2:24. [12]Cf. Deut 11:22; Rom 5:5; 1 Jn 2:5; 4:7-16. [13]Cetedoc 0198E(A) 2.6.3; ANF 4:282*. Through faith the human soul joins itself to God by love so as to become one spirit in a unity even more profound than that of husband and wife. The joining of one man and one woman in one flesh is viewed in the light of the Incarnation. [14]Of baptism.

wife except the one who died on the cross and sealed the marriage bond with his wounds? Who was ever seen lying dead at his own wedding banquet with his wife at his side seeking to console herself by embracing him? At what other celebration, at what other feast is the bridegroom's body distributed to the guests in the form of bread? Death separates wives from their husbands, but in this case it is death that unites the bride to her beloved. HOMILIES.[15]

### 10:11 Whoever Divorces and Marries Another Commits Adultery

**WHICH REMARRIED PARTY IS ACCOUNTABLE?** CLEMENT OF ALEXANDRIA: Guilt in this does not attach merely to the man who divorces her. It attaches also to the man who takes her on, since he provides the starting point for the woman's sin. STROMATEIS 2.23.[16]

**VEILED ADULTERY.** ATHENAGORAS: We hold that a man should either remain as he is born or else marry only once. For a second marriage is a veiled adultery. A PLEA REGARDING CHRISTIANS 33.[17]

**EQUAL APPLICATION TO MEN AND WOMEN.** BASIL: This declaration of the Lord applies equally to man and woman. It prohibits departing from marriage except in the case of fornication.[18] LETTER 188, TO AMPHILOCHIUS 9.[19]

**THE DURABILITY OF THE BOND.** AUGUSTINE: "For a woman is bound, as long as her husband is alive."[20] As a consequence, therefore, the husband is also bound, as long as his wife is alive. This bond renders any further union impossible without the implication of adultery. Hence, four adulterers are produced of necessity from the two marriages, if the wife remarries and the husband marries an adulteress. However, a more infamous adultery is imputed to the one who remarries after the dismissal of his wife for other than the cause of fornication. Matthew spoke of this type of adultery.[21] Such a one is not the only one who commits adultery, but, as we read in Mark: "Whoever puts away his wife and marries another, commits adultery against her; and if the wife puts away her husband, and marries another, she commits adultery."[22] ADULTEROUS MARRIAGES 2.9.8.[23]

**WHETHER FORNICATION IS AN EXCEPTION.** AUGUSTINE: God created marriage. As the union is from God, so divorce is from the devil. But one is allowed to divorce a wife in case of fornication for the precise reason that one never originally wished to have a wife who has not preserved conjugal fidelity to her husband. TRACTATE ON JOHN 9.2.2.[24]

---

[15]JF B 122-23; MS 1:78, 80. [16]FC 85:254*; TLG 0555.004, 2.23.146.3.1-2; cf. ANF 2:379. Accountability is broadly shared by all parties in the breaking up a marriage. [17]LCC 1:337. [18]Cf. Mt 5:31-32; 19:9; Mk 10:11-12; Lk 16:18; Rom 7:2-3; 1 Cor 7:10-11. [19]TLG 2040.004, 188.9.1-4; FC 28:19**. [20]1 Cor 7:39. [21]Cf. Mt 19:9. [22]Mk 10:11-12. [23]Cetedoc 0302, 2.9.8.391.12; FC 27:111. [24]Cetedoc 0278, 9.2.9; FC 78:195*.

## 10:13-16 LET THE CHILDREN COME TO ME

[13]*And they were bringing children to him, that he might touch them; and the disciples rebuked them.* [14]*But when Jesus saw it he was indignant, and said to them, " "Let the children come to me, do not hinder them; for to such belongs the kingdom of God.* [15]*Truly, I say to you, whoever does not receive the kingdom of God like a child shall not enter it."* [16]*And he took them in his arms and blessed them, laying his hands upon them.*

**OVERVIEW:** The ancient Christian exegetes repeatedly celebrated the way in which children are welcomed and blessed by the Lord (CYPRIAN, AUGUSTINE). In this way the reception of preparatory or prevening grace begins from infancy (BASIL). Those who come to the Lord who have not yet exercised the use of free will are not yet held accountable for voluntary acts that befit repentance (AUGUSTINE).

### 10:13 They Were Bringing Children to Him, That He Might Touch Them

**WHO IS EXEMPT FROM REPENTENCE?** AUGUSTINE: When any people, you see, who are already of an age to make free decisions of will, approach the sacraments of the faithful, they cannot begin the new life unless they repent of the old. It's only babies that are exempt from this kind of repentance when they are baptized; after all they are not yet capable of making free choices.

However, the faith of those who present them for baptism can avail them for sanctification and the remission of original sin; thus whatever defilement of wrongdoing they may have contracted through others, of whom they have been born, they can be purged of it through the interrogation of these others and the replies they give. SERMON 351.2.[1]

### 10:14 Let the Children Come to Me

**WHETHER REMISSION IS GRANTED TO CHILDREN WHO AFTERWARD BELIEVE.** CYPRIAN: Even to the foulest offenders, when they afterward believe, remission of sin is granted.[2] On this premise no one is prohibited from baptism and grace.[3] How much more should an infant be admitted, who, just born, has not sinned in any respect, except that, being born of the flesh according to Adam, has in his first birth contracted the contagion of the ancient deadly nature.[4] Would not such a child obtain remission of sins with the less difficulty, because not his own actual guilt, but that of another, is to be remitted? Our sentence therefore, dearest brother, in the Council[5] was that none by us should be prohibited from baptism and the grace of God, who is merciful and kind to all.[6] LETTER 58.[7]

**WHEN THE RECEPTION OF GRACE BEGINS.** BASIL: The apostle praised one [Timothy] who

---

[1]Cetedoc 0284, 351.39.1537.13; WSA 3 10:120. In Augustine's days, the baptismal rite included the interrogation of those to be baptized about the faith. When the infants were baptized, their parents or godparents answered the questions for them. [2]Cf. Acts 10:43. [3]Cf. Mk 16:16; 1 Cor 12:13. [4]Cf. Rom 5:12. [5]Council of Carthage, A.D. 254. [6]Acts 2:38-39. [7]Cetedoc 0433, 62A.9.16.7; Ad Fidum 5-6; GMI 239; ANF 5:354.

had known the holy Scripture from infancy.[8] He also instructed that children be reared "in the discipline and correction of the Lord."[9] So we consider every time of life, even the very

earliest, suitable for receiving persons into the community of faith. THE LONG RULES 15.[10]

---

[8]2 Tim 3:15. [9]Eph 6:4. [10]FC 9:264*; TLG 2040.048, 31.952.13-18.

---

## 10:17-22 THE RICH YOUNG MAN

[17]*And as he was setting out on his journey, a man ran up and knelt before him, and asked him, "Good Teacher, what must I do to inherit eternal life?"* [18]*And Jesus said to him, "Why do you call me good? No one is good but God alone.* [19]*You know the commandments: 'Do not kill, Do not commit adultery, Do not steal, Do not bear false witness, Do not defraud, Honor your father and mother.'"* [20]*And he said to him, "Teacher, all these I have observed from my youth."* [21]*And Jesus looking upon him loved him, and said to him, "You lack one thing; go, sell what you have, and give to the poor, and you will have treasure in heaven; and come, follow me."* [22]*At that saying his countenance fell, and he went away sorrowful; for he had great possessions.*

---

**OVERVIEW:** The text portrays Jesus not merely as teacher of the law but as Lord of the law (HILARY OF POITIERS). The proximate goodness of any creature is best grasped in relation to the incomparable goodness of the triune God (ORIGEN). Where the incarnation is misunderstood, the human scales of goodness are likely to be misleading. Jesus would not have rejected the designation of goodness if it had been addressed to him as incarnate Lord. The young man questioned the giver of eternal life on a false premise, that of neglecting that he is indeed God incarnate (HILARY OF POITIERS, JEROME). This skewed assumption of the questioner colored the reply (HILARY OF POITIERS). One who does not receive Christ as Lord is not in any proper position to address him as merely a good teacher (JEROME). He is none other than the source and ground of all good who asks, "Why do you call me, in human terms, 'good'?" (ORIGEN). The term good is here applied absolutely to God and only derivatively to created goods (GREGORY OF NAZIANZUS). God is uniquely good, being good in a way that cannot be diminished (AUGUSTINE). Temporal beings are good only by participation in the eternal goodness of God (BEDE). The wholeness of God's goodness cannot be ascribed directly to some partial good in creation (PSEUDO-DIONYSIUS). The incarnate Lord himself enacts the good in an incomparably complete way by offering himself as veritable mediator of divine goodness to human history (HILARY OF POITIERS). Grace does not coerce the will but cooperates with human willing (CLEMENT OF ALEXANDRIA). Those not yet ready to follow the command to radical responsiveness to grace do well at least to follow the command of the law that is addressed to those struggling at preliminary levels of responsiveness to the divine command (CAESARIUS OF ARLES). The young man went away sad because he remained trapped in his own earthly desires (AUGUSTINE).

### 10:17 *What Must I Do to Inherit Eternal Life?*

**THE FALSE PREMISE OF THE QUESTION.** HILARY OF POITIERS: The young man became arrogant through the observance of the law. He did not recognize that the consummation of the law is Christ.[1] He assumed he could be justified by works.[2] He was not aware that Jesus had come for the lost sheep of the house of Israel,[3] and that the law could not save except through justifying faith.[4] He questioned the Lord of the law and the only begotten God as if he were an ordinary teacher of precepts that were written down in the law. Hence, the Lord rejected this declaration of a spurious faith, because the question was put to him as if he were merely a teacher of the law. He replied: "Why do you call me good?"[5] In order to make known how much he was to be recognized and acknowledged as good, he declared: "No one is good but God only."[6] He would not have rejected the attribute of goodness if it had been attributed to him as God. ON THE TRINITY 9.16.[7]

### 10:18a *Why Do You Call Me Good?*

**ON RIGHTLY NAMING THE GOOD.** EPHREM

THE SYRIAN: The rich man called Jesus "good,"[8] as if he were offering him a favor, just as some favor others with honorary titles. [The Lord] fled from that by which people favored him, so that he might show that he had received this goodness from the Father through nature and generation, and not [merely] in name. "Only one is good,"[9] [he said], and did not remain silent, but added, "the Father," so that he might show that the Son is good in just the way that the Father is good. COMMENTARY ON TATIAN'S DIATESSARON.[10]

**LATER ERRORS ECHO THE SAME FALSE PREMISE.** HILARY OF POITIERS: He who is by nature God of God must possess the nature of his origin, which God possesses. The indistinguishable unity of a living nature cannot be divided by the birth of a living nature.[11] But the troublers of church unity, under cover of the saving confession of the gospel faith, are subversively trying to take captive the truth by undermining it. By forcing their own interpretations on words spoken with other meanings and intentions, they are robbing the Son of his distinctive unity [with the Father].[12] ON THE TRINITY 9.2.[13]

**HOW THE SKEWED PREMISE SHAPES THE REPLY.** HILARY OF POITIERS: A complete understanding of the reply must come from the reason that prompted the question, for the answer will be directed to the matter that led to

---

[1]Cf. Rom 10:4; Gal 3:13. [2]Cf. Rom 4:5; Gal 2:16. [3]Cf. Mt 10:6; 15:24. [4]Cf. Acts 13:39; Rom 3:20; Gal 2:16;. [5]Mk 10:18; Lk 18:19. [6]Mk 10:18; Lk 18:19. [7]Cetedoc 0433, 62A.9.16.7; FC 236-37**. [8]Mk 10:17; Lk 18:18. [9]Mt 19:17; cf. Mk 10:18; Lk 18:19. [10]Leloir 1963:140; JSSS 2:229-30**. [11]Cf. Mt 16:15-16; Jn 1:1-18; Gal 4:4. [12]Cf. 2 Pet 2—3. [13]Cetedoc 0433, 62A.9.2.1; NPNF 2 9:155**. This false premise is analogous to misleading theories of heretics, among them the Arians and the Modalists.

the inquiry. . . . He voiced his objection to the title of "good master" in such a way as to challenge the faith of the questioner rather than the designation of himself as a master or as good. ON THE TRINITY 9.2.[14]

**THE OVERTURNING OF THE PREMISE IN THE QUESTION.** JEROME: The question is something like a priest who, while inwardly despising his bishop, yet continues to address him openly as "bishop." Whereupon the bishop answers, "To you I am not the bishop; you may leave my presence." HOMILY 53.[15]

## 10:18b No One Is Good but God Alone

**THE INCOMPARABLE GOODNESS OF THE SON.** ORIGEN: There is no other secondary goodness existing in the Son than that which is in the Father. So the Savior himself rightly says in the Gospel that "none is good save one, God the Father."[16] The purpose of this statement is to make it understood that the Son is not of some other ancillary "goodness," but of that alone which is in the Father; whose image he is rightly called. For he neither springs from any other source than from original goodness itself (if that were so, there would seem to be a different goodness in the Son from that which is in the Father), nor has the goodness that is in him any dissimilarity or divergence from that of the Father.[17] Accordingly we ought not to imagine that there is some kind of blasphemy in the saying that "none is good save one, God the Father."[18] These words are not to be taken as a denial that either Christ or the Holy Spirit is good. But, as we said before, the original goodness must be believed to reside in God the Father, and from him both the Son and Holy Spirit undoubtedly draw into themselves the nature

of that goodness existing in the font from which the one is born and the other proceeds.[19] If then there are any other things called good in the Scriptures such as an angel,[20] or a man,[21] or a servant,[22] or a treasure,[23] or a good heart,[24] or a good tree,[25] all these are so called by an inexact use of the word, since the goodness contained in them is accidental and not essential. ON FIRST PRINCIPLES 1.2.13.[26]

**DEFINING THE GOOD.** ORIGEN: The good, then, is the same as the one who incomparably is. Over against good is evil or wickedness. Over against the one who incomparably is, is merely that which is not. So it follows that evil and corruption are, finally, that which becomes nothing.[27] This, perhaps, is what has led some to affirm that the devil is not created by God.[28] In respect that he is the devil he is not the work of God, but he who is the devil is a created being, and as a creature nonetheless remains a work of God, since there is nothing created that is not created by God. Think of it this way: A murderer is not a work of God insofar as he murders, while we may still say that insofar as he is a human being, God made him. COMMENTARY ON JOHN 2.7.[29]

---

[14]Cetedoc 0433, 62A.9.15.12 and 62A.9.16.5; FC 25:335**. The motivation of the questioner is what is in question. [15]Cetedoc 0592, 142.66; FC 48:379**. [16]Mk 10:18; Lk 18:19. [17]Cf. Jn 10:30. [18]Mk 10:18; Lk 19:19. [19]Cf. Jn 3:16; 15:16. [20]Cf. Tob 5:21; 2 Macc 11:6; 15:23. [21]Cf. Ps 37:23; 112:5; Prov 12:2; Mt 12:35; Acts 11:24. [22]Cf. Sir 7:21; Lk 19:17. [23]Cf. Tob 4:9; Lk 6:45. [24]Cf. Jdt 8:28; Wis 1:1; Sir 26:4; Lk 8:15. [25]Cf. 2 Kings 3:19; Mt 7:17-19; Lk 6:43. [26]OBP 154-57; OFP 27-28**. [27]In the sense that their evil depends upon something good and is a deprivation of that good. [28]Cf. Eph 3:9. [29]ANF 9:330*; TLG 2042.005, 2.13.96.3-97.7. To view the greatest good, God incarnate, only by the measurements of creaturely goods is to miss the good. The wickedness of the devil must not be linked to his creatureliness as such but to his will to do evil.

**COMPLETE GOODNESS BELONGS TO GOD ALONE.** GREGORY OF NAZIANZUS: The words, "None is good"[30] are a reply to the young ruler who was testing him and had borne witness to his goodness as a human being. Consummate goodness, he meant, belongs to God alone, though the word "good" can be derivatively applied to human beings.[31] ORATION 30, ON THE SON 13.[32]

**GOD'S GOODNESS DISTINGUISHED FROM OTHER GOODS.** AUGUSTINE: God, therefore, is uniquely good, and this he cannot lose. He is good. He is not good by sharing in any other good, because the good by which he is good is himself. But, when a finite human being is good, his goodness derives from God, because he cannot be his own good. All who become good do so through his Spirit. Our nature has been created to attain to him through acts of its own will. If we are to become good, it is important for us to receive and hold what he gives, who is good in himself. LETTER 153, TO MACEDONIUS.[33]

**NO PART IS WHOLLY GOOD.** PSEUDO-DIONYSIUS: It is the entire divine reality which is adored in Scripture, as that absolute goodness defines and reveals itself to be.[34] How else are we to understand the sacred Word of God when it declares that the deity, speaking of itself, had this to say: "Why do you ask me about what is good? No one is good but God alone."[35] I have discussed all this elsewhere, how in Scripture all the names appropriate to God are praised regarding the whole, entire, full, and complete divinity rather than any aspect of it. They all refer indivisibly, absolutely, unreservedly and totally to God in his entirety. THE DIVINE NAMES 2.1.[36]

**GOOD BY PARTICIPATION.** BEDE: It is only by participation in the divine goodness that a rational creature is capable of becoming good.[37] EXPOSITION ON THE GOSPEL OF MARK 11.4.[38]

### 10:19 *You Know the Commandments*

**COMMANDS THAT LEAD TO LIFE.** AUGUSTINE: The rich man asked the good teacher what he should do to gain eternal life.[39] He regarded the good teacher as a man and nothing more (as distinct from the assumption that He is good as God incarnate). Hear the good teacher respond to him: if he wishes to enter into life, he should keep the commandments; that he should remove from himself the bitterness of malice and wickedness; that he should not kill, or commit adultery, or steal, or bear false witness, in order that dry land[40] may appear and bring forth the honor of mother and father and the love of our neighbor.[41] CONFESSIONS 13.19.[42]

---

[30] Mk 10:18; Lk 18:19. [31] Cf. Ps 37:23; 112:5; Prov 31:10-31; Acts 11:24. [32] TLG 2022.010, 13.15-18; FGFR 271*. Good can be derivatively applied to human beings only by primarily being applied to God. [33] Cetedoc 0262, 153.44.5.409.6; FC 20:289*. God is good in a way that cannot be diminished or lost, while human willing participates proximately in God's goodness through divine grace. [34] The issue is whether the term *good* is applied to God according to the wholeness of divine goodness or some particular aspect of it. [35] Mk 10:18; Lk 18:19. [36] TLG 2798.004, 122.1-10; CWS 58*. The wholeness of God's goodness cannot be ascribed directly to some partial good in creation. [37] Cf. Phil 2:13; Heb 13:20-21. [38] Cetedoc 1367, 2.14.233; HOG 2:132. Humans are good by participation in the eternal goodness of God. [39] Cf. Mt 19:16; Mk 10:17; Lk 18:18. [40] The allusion is to the dry land of the exodus (cf. Ex 14:29). Augustine's reference to dry land is illumined by his earlier comment in the *Confessions*: "before the Lord says to us: Wash yourselves clean, spare me the sight of your busy wickedness, of your wrong-doing take farewell [Is 1:16-18], so that the dry land may appear." See Augustine, *Confessions* (New York: Penguin, 1961), 326 (13.19). Cf. Neh 9:11; Ps 66:6; Heb 11:29. [41] Cf. Mt 19:17-19; Mk 10:19; Lk 18:20. [42] Cetedoc 0251, 13.19.6; FC 21:429**.

## 10:20 *All These I Have Observed from My Youth*

**RATIONALIZING OBSERVANCE.** JEROME: He who declared that he had observed all the commandments had already yielded to the power of riches from the very outset. LETTER 118, TO JULIAN.[43]

**FEIGNED RESPONSIVENESS.** AUGUSTINE: But the young man went away sad, so anyone can see how far he kept those commandments of the law. I think he spoke with more pride than truth when he answered that he had kept them. LETTER 157, TO HILARIUS.[44]

## 10:21a *Go, Sell What You Have and Give to the Poor*

**HOW WEALTH OBSTRUCTS DISCIPLESHIP.** JEROME: This is why those who are rich find it hard to enter the kingdom of heaven.[45] For it is a kingdom which desires for its citizens a soul that soars aloft free from all ties and hindrances. "Go your way," the Lord said, "and sell" not a part of your substance but "all that you have, and give to the poor";[46] not to your friends or kinsfolk or relatives, nor to your wife or to your children. . . . When once you have put your hand to the plough, you must not look back.[47] When once you stand on the housetop, you must think no more of your clothes within. To escape your Egyptian mistress,[48] you must abandon the cloak that belongs to this world. Even Elijah, in his quick translation to heaven could not take his mantle with him, but left in the world the garments of the world.[49] LETTER 118, TO JULIAN.[50]

**INWARD INTENT.** AUGUSTINE: I who write this have greatly loved the total devotion of which the Lord spoke when he once said to the rich young man: "Go, sell what you have and give to the poor, and come, follow me."[51] I have so loved it that I have indeed acted upon it myself, not by my own strength but by his assisting grace. The apostles were the first to follow in the practice of this complete self-giving.[52] One who gives up both what one owns and what one desires to own, gives up the whole world. LETTER 157, TO HILARIUS.[53]

**FULL OBEDIENCE.** CAESARIUS OF ARLES: What that man heard, most beloved, we, too, have heard. The gospel of Christ is in heaven, but it does not cease to speak on earth. Let us not be dead to him, for he thunders. Let us not be deaf, for he shouts. If you are unwilling to commit to full obedience, do what you can. But here is the radical divine requirement: "Sell all that you have, and give to the poor; and come, follow me."[54] The lesser road of the law says: You shall not kill, you shall not commit adultery, you shall not seek false witness, you shall not steal, honor your father and mother, and love your neighbor as yourself."[55] SERMONS 153.1.[56]

---

[43]Cetedoc 0620, 118.55.4.439.17; NPNF 2 6:222**. He was not ready to observe the commands he said he observed. [44]Cetedoc 0262, 157.44.4.474.21; FC 20:342. [45]Cf. Mt 19:24; Mk 10:25; Lk 18:25. [46]Mt 19:21; Mk 10:21; Lk 18:22. [47]Lk 9:62. [48]Gen 39:12. [49]2 Kings 2:11, 13. [50]Cetedoc 0620, 118.55.4.439.18; NPNF 2 6:222*. The call to discipleship is simple and unconditional. [51]Mt 19:21; Mk 10:21; Lk 18:22. [52]They had no riches to give up, but the value of their response did not depend quantitatively upon how much wealth they gave up. The quantity of how much one gives up does not determine the worthiness of the act. One who having nothing gives up little is not less worthy than one who having much gives up all. Cf. Mt 4:18-22; Mk 2:14. [53]Cetedoc 0262, 157.44.4.485.15; FC 20:352**. Note that the command is to give up not only what one has but also what one desires to have. [54]Mt 19:21; Mk 10:21; Lk 18:22. [55]Mt 19:18-19; Mk 10:19; Lk 18:20. [56]Cetedoc 1008, 104.153.1.12; FC 47:337**. Greater and lesser commands are distinguishable.

### 10:21b Follow Me

**Performing the Good.** Hilary of Poitiers: He exercises the duties of goodness when he opens the treasures of heaven[57] and becomes himself a guide to them. He abhors whatever is offered to him merely as a man. Yet he makes it clear that he is no stranger to those qualities attributed to God. While recognizing the one God as good, he himself speaks of and performs those very actions which are characteristic of the incomparable power, goodness and nature of God. On the Trinity 9.17.[58]

### 10:22 He Went Away Sorrowful

**God Saves Only the Willing.** Clement of Alexandria: God provides a fairer wind[59] for more willing souls. But if they early abandon their eagerness, the wind which God provides is thereby obstructed. For to save the unwilling is an act of compulsion. But to save the willing is the act of one showing grace. Salvation of the Rich Man 21.[60]

**Whether Jesus Was Harsh Toward Riches.** Tertullian: The rich man followed his own counsel, having rejected the precept of dividing his resources with the needy. He was abandoned by the Lord to his own opinion.[61] There is no justification for applying the term "harshness" on this account to describe Christ. For each individual free will is able to choose to defile itself. "Behold, I have set before you good and evil."[62] Choose that which is good. If you cannot because you will not (for he has shown that you can if you will, because he has proposed each to your free will) you ought to depart from him whose will you elect not to do. On Monogamy 14.[63]

**The Burden of Choice.** Augustine: He did not follow. He just wanted a good teacher, but he questioned who the teacher was, and scorned the identity of the One[64] who was teaching. "He went away sad," bound up in his desires. "He went away sad," carrying a great burden of possessiveness upon his shoulders.[65] Tractate on John 34.8.[66]

---

[57]Cf. Mt 19:21; Lk 18:22. [58]Cetedoc 0433, 62A.9.17.10; FC 25:337**. The incarnate Lord himself enacts the good in an incomparably good way by offering himself as mediator of goodness. [59]Cooperates spiritually. [60]TLG 0555.006, 21.1.2-3.1; cf. ANF 2:597. God's grace is not another form of compulsion. [61]Mt 19:16-22; Mk 10:17-22; Lk 18:18-27. [62]Deut 11:26-28; 30:1, 15, 19; Josh 24:15. [63]Cetedoc 0028, 14.45; ANF 4:71* [64]The uniquely good one. [65]Mt 19:22; Mk 10:22. [66]Cetedoc 0278, 34.8.11; FC 88:66-67**.

## 10:23-31 ON RICHES

[23]And Jesus looked around and said to his disciples, "How hard it will be for those who have riches to enter the kingdom of God!" [24]And the disciples were amazed at his words. But Jesus said to them again, "Children, how hard it is[r] to enter the kingdom of God! [25]It is easier for a

*camel to go through the eye of a needle than for a rich man to enter the kingdom of God."* <sup>26</sup>*And they were exceedingly astonished, and said to him,<sup>s</sup> "Then who can be saved?" <sup>27</sup>Jesus looked at them and said, "With men it is impossible, but not with God; for all things are possible with God." <sup>28</sup>Peter began to say to him, "Lo, we have left everything and followed you." <sup>29</sup>Jesus said, "Truly, I say to you, there is no one who has left house or brothers or sisters or mother or father or children or lands, for my sake and for the gospel, <sup>30</sup>who will not receive a hundredfold now in this time, houses and brothers and sisters and mothers and children and lands, with persecutions, and in the age to come eternal life. <sup>31</sup>But many that are first will be last, and the last first."*

r Other ancient authorities add *for those who trust in riches*    s Other ancient authorities read *to one another*

**OVERVIEW:** By merely having wealth one tends to love it inordinately. Hence the rich find faith exceptionally hard (AUGUSTINE). Yet Christianity does not leave the wealthy in despair (CLEMENT OF ALEXANDRIA). If one is able in the midst of wealth to turn from its powerful mystique so as to exercise self-control, seeking God alone, one may yet remain unwounded by it (CLEMENT OF ALEXANDRIA). The poor do not thereby have an absolutely privileged position over the rich with respect to salvation (CAESARIUS OF ARLES). Richness in virtue is greater than richness in worldly goods (SALVIAN THE PRESBYTER). Just as readiness to give up wealth is required, so is readiness to give up those most dear to us, our family, insofar as they may be an obstacle to our salvation (CLEMENT OF ALEXANDRIA). Those who seek to live the life of faith are blessed with the gift of a worldwide family beyond that natural family from which they came (JOHN CASSIAN). Nothing is impossible to God except that which is contrary to God's nature (THEODORET OF CYR).

### 10:23 For Those Who Have Riches

**THE RICH NEED NOT DESPAIR.** CLEMENT OF ALEXANDRIA: Let this teach the prosperous that they are not to neglect their own salvation, as if they had been already foredoomed, nor, on the other hand, to cast wealth into the sea, or condemn it as a traitor and an enemy to life, but learn in what way and how to use wealth and obtain life. SALVATION OF THE RICH MAN 27.[1]

**WHETHER IN MERELY HAVING WEALTH ONE TENDS TO LOVE IT INORDINATELY.** AUGUSTINE: Such, O my soul, are the miseries that attend on riches. They are gained with toil and kept with fear. They are enjoyed with danger and lost with grief. It is hard to be saved if we have them; and impossible if we love them; and scarcely can we have them, but we shall love them inordinately. Teach us, O Lord, this difficult lesson: to manage conscientiously the goods we possess, and not covetously desire more than you give to us. LETTER 203.[2]

**WHETHER THE POOR HAVE A DECISIVE ADVANTAGE OVER THE RICH.** CAESARIUS OF ARLES: The rich man "went away sad," as you have heard, and the Lord says: "With what difficulty will they who have riches enter the king-

---

[1]ANF 2:599*; TLG 0555.006, 27.1.2-2.1. [2]Cetedoc 0262, 203.57.316.1; GMI 247-48.

dom of God!"[3] At length the disciples became very sad when they heard this and they said: "If this is so, who then can be saved?"[4] Rich and poor, listen to Christ: I am speaking to God's people. Most of you are poor, but you too must listen carefully to understand. And you had best listen even more intently if you glory in your poverty. Beware of pride, lest the humble rich surpass you. Beware of wickedness, lest the pious rich confound you. Beware of drunkenness, lest the sober excel you. SERMONS 153.2.[5]

**THE RICHES MOST TO BE DESIRED.** SALVIAN THE PRESBYTER: Note what kind of riches it is that God loves. Note what wealth does he demand that we should store up for children. Note what possessions he especially orders us to guard: faith, fear of God, modesty, holiness, and discipline. Nothing earthly, nothing base, nothing perishable or transitory. THE FOUR BOOKS OF TIMOTHY TO THE CHURCH 1.4.[6]

## 10:25 Eye of a Needle

**WHETHER THE RICH CAN BE SAVED.** CLEMENT OF ALEXANDRIA: The Savior by no means has excluded the rich on account of wealth itself, and the possession of property, nor fenced off salvation against them, if they are able and willing to submit their life to God's commandments, and prefer them to transitory things. Let them look to the Lord with steady eye, as those who look toward the slightest nod of a good helmsman, what he wishes, what he orders, what he indicates, what signal he gives his mariners, where and when he directs the ship's course. . . . If one is able in the midst of wealth to turn from its mystique, to entertain moderate desires, to exercise self-control, to seek God alone, and to breathe God and walk

with God, such a man submits to the commandments, being free, unsubdued, free of disease, unwounded by wealth. But if not, "sooner shall a camel enter through a needle's eye, than such a rich man reach the kingdom of God."[7] SALVATION OF THE RICH MAN 26.[8]

**ON PASSING WEALTH TO CHILDREN.** SALVIAN THE PRESBYTER: There is no compelling necessity for you to store up large earthly treasures for your children. You would do better to make your offspring treasures of God than make them richer in worldly goods.[9] THE FOUR BOOKS OF TIMOTHY TO THE CHURCH 1.4.[10]

## 10:27 All Things Are Possible with God

**WHETHER ANYTHING IS IMPOSSIBLE FOR GOD.** Theodoret of Cyr:

| | |
|---|---|
| Orthodox | The Lord God wishes nothing inconsistent with his nature, and is able to do all that he wishes, and what he wishes is appropriate and agreeable to his own nature. . . . |
| Eranistes | Nothing is impossible to almighty God. |
| Ortho. | Then according to your definition sin is possible to almighty God? |
| Era. | By no means. |
| Ortho. | Why? |
| Era. | Because he does not wish it. |
| Ortho. | Why does he not wish it? |
| Era. | Because sin is foreign to his nature. |
| Ortho. | Then there are many things which he cannot do, for there are many |

---

[3]Mt 19:22-23; Mk 10:22-23. [4]Mt 19:25; Mk 10:26; Lk 18:26. [5]Cetedoc 1008, 104.153.2.1; FC 47:338*. [6]SC 176:152; FC 3:276**. Richness in virtue is greater than richness in worldly goods. [7]Mt 19:24; Mk 10:25; Lk 18:25. [8]ANF 2:598-99*; TLG 0555.006, 26.2.1-3.1, 6.1-8.1. [9]Cf. Mt 6:19-21. [10]SC 176:154; FC 3:277**. Offering children wealth without salvation is not a good economy.

kinds of transgression.

Era.     Nothing of this kind can be wished
         or done by God.

Ortho.   Nor can those things which are con-
         trary to the divine nature. . . . But
         not to be able in any of these respects
         is proof not of weakness, but of infi-
         nite power, and to be able would cer-
         tainly be proof not of power but of
         impotence.
         DIALOGUE 3.[11]

### 10:29 *There Is No One Who Has Left House or Brothers*

**THE SPIRITUAL SENSE OF LEAVING THE FAM-ILY.** CLEMENT OF ALEXANDRIA: Do not let this passage trouble you. Put it side by side with the still harder saying Jesus delivered in another place in the words, "Whoever hates not father, and mother, and children, and his own life besides, cannot be my disciple."[12] Note that the God of peace, who exhorts us to love our ene-mies, does not arbitrarily require us literally to hate or abandon those dearest to us. But if we are to love our enemies, it must be in accor-dance with right reason that, by analogy we should also love our nearest relatives. . . . But insofar as one's father, or son, or brother, becomes for you a hindrance to faith or an impediment to godly life, one should then not collude with that temptation. Attend to the

spiritual, rather than the fleshly, meaning of the command. SALVATION OF THE RICH MAN 22.[13]

### 10:30 *Receive a Hundredfold*

**BLESSINGS WITHIN OF THE NEW FAMILY OF GOD.** JOHN CASSIAN: For he who for the sake of Christ's name distances himself from his particular beloved father or mother or child, and gives himself over to the purest love of all who serve Christ, will receive a hundred times the measure of brothers and kinsfolk.[14] Instead of but one he will begin to have so many fathers and brothers bound to him by a still more fer-vent and admirable affection. That this is so you can prove by your own experience, since you have each left but one father and mother and home, and as you have done so you have gained without any effort or care countless fathers and mothers and brothers, as well as houses and lands and most faithful servants, in any part of the world to which you go, who receive you as their own family, and welcome, and respect, and take care of you with the utmost attention. CONFERENCES 3.24.26.[15]

---

[11]NPNF 2 3:219*; TLG 4089.002, 194.24-26; 195.10-19; 196.18-20. [12]Lk 14:26; "hate" must be understood spiritually, not literally, in relation to the ordering of one's earthly values so as not to make an idolatry of them. [13]TLG 0555.006, 22.2.1-4.2, 7.1-4; cf. ANF 2:597. Resist whatever is detrimental to salvation even if it means resisting one's natural family. [14]Cf. Mt 19:29; Mk 10:29-30; Lk 18:29-30. [15]Cetedoc 0512, 24.26.707.21; NPNF 2 11:544*.

---

## 10:32-45 THE REQUEST OF JAMES AND JOHN

*[32]And they were on the road, going up to Jerusalem, and Jesus was walking ahead of them; and they were amazed, and those who followed were afraid. And taking the twelve again, he*

began to tell them what was to happen to him, [33]saying, "Behold, we are going up to Jerusalem; and the Son of man will be delivered to the chief priests and the scribes, and they will condemn him to death, and deliver him to the Gentiles; [34]and they will mock him, and spit upon him, and scourge him, and kill him; and after three days he will rise."

[35]And James and John, the sons of Zebedee, came forward to him, and said to him, "Teacher, we want you to do for us whatever we ask of you." [36]And he said to them, "What do you want me to do for you?" [37]And they said to him, "Grant us to sit, one at your right hand and one at your left, in your glory." [38]But Jesus said to them, "You do not know what you are asking. Are you able to drink the cup that I drink, or to be baptized with the baptism with which I am baptized?" [39]And they said to him, "We are able." And Jesus said to them, "The cup that I drink you will drink; and with the baptism with which I am baptized, you will be baptized; [40]but to sit at my right hand or at my left is not mine to grant, but it is for those for whom it has been prepared." [41]And when the ten heard it, they began to be indignant at James and John. [42]And Jesus called them to him and said to them, "You know that those who are supposed to rule over the Gentiles lord it over them, and their great men exercise authority over them. [43]But it shall not be so among you; but whoever would be great among you must be your servant, [44]and whoever would be first among you must be slave of all. [45]For the Son of man also came not to be served but to serve, and to give his life as a ransom for many."

**OVERVIEW:** The text teaches that we are not to ask for privilege in the kingdom without readiness to die for it (CHRYSOSTOM). The sons of Zebedee were not mistaken in recognizing that they were special recipients of his love, but they were mistaken in imagining that this would be without cost (CHRYSOSTOM, BEDE). Only through humbling oneself does one come into the glory of the Lord (AUGUSTINE). The history of the martyrs demonstrates that many have been unreservedly willing to drink this same cup with the Lord, to suffer and die for the truth (POLYCARP). Martyrdom itself is a type of baptism, in which the love of the Father through the Son acts to bury the old life of sin and raise the believer into new life through the Holy Spirit (CHRYSOSTOM). As Christ rose effortlessly from water having been buried in it, so we rise with

him having died to sin. He shared with us our punishment but not our sin (AUGUSTINE). His incomparable righteousness, sanctification, redemption and resurrection all become ours by faith (GREGORY OF NAZIANZUS). Without his incarnate humiliation, only the angels would have known his identity (CHRYSOSTOM).

### 10:33 The Chief Priests Will Condemn Him to Death and Deliver Him to the Gentiles

**UNDER WHAT AUTHORITY HE DIED.** AUGUSTINE: In so speaking the Lord foreshadowed those by whose hand he would die. He does not mean here the death upon the cross as such, but that the Jews would deliver him up to the Gentiles, or, in other words, to the Romans. For Pilate was a Roman, and had been sent by the Romans into Judea as governor. TRACTATE ON JOHN 94.5.[1]

### 10:35a The Sons of Zebedee

THE PLEA FOR PRIVILEGED POSITION. BEDE: They knew that among the disciples they were warmly loved by our Lord, that together with the blessed Peter they had often been informed of hidden mysteries of which the rest were unaware, as the text of the holy gospel frequently indicates.[2] Thus a new name was given to them, just as it was to Peter. As the one who was formerly called Simon was given the name of Peter on account of the strength and firmness of his unassailable faith, so they were called *Boanērges*, that is, sons of thunder,[3] because they heard, along with Peter, the voice of the Father honoring the Lord,[4] and they recognized the secrets of the mysteries more than the rest of the disciples. They sensed that they clung to our Lord with their whole heart and embraced him with the greatest love. So they did not disbelieve that it was possible that they would be sitting closely on either side of him in the kingdom, particularly when they saw that John, for his singular purity of mind and body, was held in such great love that he rested on his breast at supper.[5] EXPOSITION ON THE GOSPEL OF MARK 2.21.[6]

THEIR PLEA TRANSCENDED. BEDE: When the sons of Zebedee were seeking from Jesus seats in his kingdom, he at once called them to drink of his chalice,[7] that is, to pattern themselves after the struggle of his suffering. EXPOSITION ON THE GOSPEL OF MARK 2.21.[8]

### 10:35b Do for Us Whatever We Ask

THE MISTAKEN PREMISE OF THEIR REQUEST. CHRYSOSTOM: They were expecting him to enter into [the kingdom], but not to go to the cross and death. Even though they had heard it ten thousand times, they could not clearly understand. Since they had not gotten a clear and certain knowledge of his teachings, they thought that he was going to this visible kingdom and would rule in Jerusalem. So the sons of Zebedee caught up with him on the road. They thought they had found the opportune moment. They put their request to him. They had broken away from the throng of the disciples and, just as if the whole situation had turned out exactly as they wanted, they asked about the privilege of the first seats and about being first among the others.[9] They asked for this because they assumed that everything was finished and the whole business was over and done with. They made their request because they thought that now was the time for crowns and rewards. ON THE INCOMPREHENSIBLE NATURE OF GOD 8.31.[10]

### 10:37 Grant Us to Sit

THE WAY TO LOFTINESS. AUGUSTINE: Ponder how profound this is. They were conferring with him about glory. He intended to precede loftiness with humility and, only through humility, to ready the way for loftiness itself. For, of course, even those disciples who wanted to sit, the one on his right, the other on his left, were looking to glory.[11] They were on the lookout, but did not see by what way. In order that they might come to their homeland in due order, the Lord called them back to the narrow

---

[1]Cetedoc 0278, 114.5.19; NPNF 1 7:422**. [2]As in the transfiguration narrative. Cf. Mt 17:1-3; Mk 5:37; 9:2-4; 14:33; Lk 8:51; 9:28-30. [3]Mk 3:16-17. [4]Mt 17:5. [5]Jn 13:23. [6]Cetedoc 1367, 2.21.42; HOG 2:212-13*. [7]Cf. Mt 20:22; Mk 10:38. [8]Cetedoc 1367, 2.21.19; HOG 2:212*. [9]Cf. Mk 10:35-37. [10]TLG 2062.016, 48.774.16-29; FC 72:225*. [11]Mt 20:20-23; Mk 10:35-40.

way. For the homeland is on high and the way to it is lowly. The homeland is life in Christ; the way is dying with Christ.[12] The way is suffering with Christ; the goal is abiding with him eternally. Why do you seek the homeland if you are not seeking the way to it? TRACTATE ON JOHN 28.5.2.[13]

## 10:38a You Do Not Know What You Are Asking

AN UNTIMELY REQUEST. CHRYSOSTOM: Do you see? They did not understand what they were asking for when they were talking to him about crowns and rewards and the privilege of the first seats and honors even before the contest had begun. Christ was communicating with them on two levels when he said: "You do not know what you are asking for."[14] One was that they were talking about an earthly kingdom and he had said nothing about this. There had been no announcement or promise about a visible kingdom on earth. The other was that, when they sought at this time the privilege of the first seats and the honors of heaven, when they wished to be seen as more illustrious and splendid than the others, they were not asking for these things at the right time. The timing was precisely wrong. For this was not the right time for crowns or prizes. It was the time for struggles, contests, toils, sweat, wrestling rings and battles. ON THE INCOMPREHENSIBLE NATURE OF GOD 8.32-33.[15]

## 10:38b Are You Able to Drink the Cup That I Drink?

THE WILLINGNESS TO SUFFER FOR THE TRUTH. POLYCARP: I bless you, Lord, because you have deemed me worthy of this day and hour, to take my part in the number of the martyrs, in the cup of your Christ, for "resurrection to eternal life"[16] of soul and body in the immortality of the Holy Spirit; among whom may I be received in your presence this day as a rich and acceptable sacrifice, just as you have prepared and revealed beforehand and fulfilled, O you who are the true God without any falsehood. THE MARTYRDOM OF POLYCARP 14.[17]

THE MEANING OF THE CUP. AUGUSTINE: He meant, of course, the cup of humility and suffering. TRACTATE ON JOHN 28.5.2.[18]

## 10:38c To Be Baptized with the Baptism with Which I Am Baptized

SHARERS WITH ME. CHRYSOSTOM: This he calls a baptism, showing that from it the whole world would receive a great purification. Then they say to him: "We can." In the fervor of their spirit they promise immediately, not knowing what they said, but looking to obtain that which they were asking. . . . He foretold great things for them; that is, you shall be held worthy of martyrdom, you shall suffer the things I have suffered, you shall end your life with a death from violence, and in this also you shall be sharers with me. THE GOSPEL OF ST. MATTHEW, HOMILY 65.[19]

THE GRACE OFFERED IN BAPTISM. CHRYSOSTOM: For when we immerse our heads in the water, the old humanity is buried as in a tomb

---

[12]Cf. Mt 6:25; Mk 8:35; Lk 9:24; 17:33. [13]Cetedoc 0278, 28.5.15; FC 88:6-7**. [14]Mt 20:22; Mk 10:38. [15]TLG 2062.016, 48-774.33-49; FC 72:225-26**. [16]Cf. Jn 5:29; 6:54. [17]TLG 1484.001, 14.2.1-7; LCC 1:154*. The martyrs gave their lives as evidence of the willingness to drink the cup that the Lord himself drank. Polycarp delivered the definitive statement of this willingness. [18]Cetedoc 0278, 28.5.27; FC 88:7. [19]TLG 2062.152, 58.619.53-620.1, 620.3-6; SSGF 1:413; PG 58-617.

below, and wholly sunk forever. Then as we raise them again, the new humanity rises in its place. As it is easy for us to dip and to lift our heads again, so it is easy for God to bury the old humanity, and to lift up and display the new. And this is done three times, that you may learn that the power of the Father, the Son and the Holy Ghost[20] fulfills all this. Homilies on John 25.2.[21]

**Cross as Cup, Death as Baptism.** Chrysostom: Here Christ was calling his crucifixion a cup and his death a baptism.[22] He called his cross a cup because he was coming to it with pleasure. He called his death a baptism because by it he cleansed the world. Not only on this account did he call his death a baptism but also because of the ease with which he would rise again. For just as one who is baptized in water easily rises up because the nature of the water poses no hindrance, so, too, Christ rose with greater ease because he had gone down into death. And this is why he calls his death a baptism. On the Incomprehensible Nature of God 8.35.[23]

### 10:44 Whoever Would Be Great Among You Must Be Slave of All

**What Lowliness Accomplished.** Chrysostom: He erased the curse,[24] he triumphed over death,[25] he opened paradise.[26] He struck down sin, he opened wide the vaults of the sky, he lifted our first fruits[27] to heaven, he filled the whole world with godliness. He drove out error, he led back the truth, he made our firstfruits mount to the royal throne. He accomplished so many good deeds that neither I nor all humanity together could set them before your minds in words.[28] Before he humbled himself, only the angels knew him. After he humbled himself, all

human nature knew him. You see how his humbling of himself did not make him have less but produced countless benefits, countless deeds of virtue, and made his glory shine forth with greater brightness.[29] God wants for nothing and has need of nothing. Yet, when he humbled himself, he produced such great good, increased his household, and extended his kingdom. Why, then, are you afraid that you will become less if you humble yourself? On the Incomprehensible Nature of God 8.46-47.[30]

### 10:45 To Give His Life as a Ransom for Many

**Setting Free Captives.** Gregory of Nazianzus: He is our sanctification, as himself being purity, that the pure may be encompassed by his purity.[31] He is our redemption, because he sets us free who were held captive under sin,[32] giving himself as a ransom for us,[33] the sacrifice to make expiation for the world.[34] He is our resurrection, because he raises up, and brings to life again, those who were slain by sin.[35] Oration 30, On the Son 20.[36]

**The Personal Relevance of His Act of Ransom.** Ambrose: It is profitable to me to know that for my sake Christ bore my infirmities, submitted to the affections of my body,

---

[20]Cf. Mt 28:19. [21]NPNF 1 14:89*; TLG 2062.153, 59.151.14-23. [22]Cf. Mk 10:38. [23]TLG 2062.016, 48.775.4-14; FC 72:226*. [24]Gal 3:10-13. [25]1 Cor 15:55-57; 2 Tim 1:10. [26]Lk 23:43; 2 Cor 12:4. [27]1 Cor 15:20. [28]Cf. Jn 21:25. [29]Cf. Phil 2:6-11. [30]TLG 2062.016, 48.777. 9-778.4; FC 72:231; cf. JF B 127; Homilies Against the Anomeans, OCJC 8.2, 253-54. Without his humiliation, only the angels would have known his identity. Humility produces surprising fruit in unexpected places. [31]Cf. Tit 2:14. [32]Cf. 2 Tim 2:26. [33]Cf. Mt 20:28; Mk 10:45. [34]Cf. Heb 7:26-27; 9:24-26; 10:10-12. [35]Cf. Jn 6:40. [36]LCC 3:192*; TLG 2022.010, 20.36-41. His incomparable righteousness, sanctification, redemption and resurrection are all ours.

that for me and for all he was made sin and a curse, that for me and in me was he humbled and made subject,[37] that for me he is the lamb,[38] the vine,[39] the rock,[40] the servant,[41] the Son of a handmaid,[42] knowing not the day of judgment, for my sake ignorant of the day and the hour.[43] On the Christian Faith 2.92.[44]

**Canceling Sin.** Augustine: He shared with us our punishment, but not our sin. Death is the punishment of sin. The Lord Jesus Christ came to die; he did not come to sin. By sharing with us the penalty without the sin, he canceled both the penalty and the sin.[45] Sermons on the Liturgical Seasons, For the Easter Season, Sermon 231.2.[46]

[37]Cf. Heb 9:24-28. [38]Cf. Jn 1:29, 36. [39]Cf. Jn 15:1-5. [40]Cf. 1 Cor 10:4. [41]Cf. Is 53:11; Mt 12:18; Phil 2:7. [42]Cf. Lk 1:38. [43]Cf. Mt 24:36; Mk 13:32. [44]Cetedoc 0150, 2.11.32; NPNF 2 10:236. [45]Cf. 2 Cor 5:21; Heb 4:15; 9:26-28; 10:1-18. [46]Cetedoc 0284,

## 10:46-52 BLIND BARTIMAEUS RECEIVES HIS SIGHT

[46]*And they came to Jericho; and as he was leaving Jericho with his disciples and a great multitude, Bartimaeus, a blind beggar, the son of Timaeus, was sitting by the roadside. [47]And when he heard that it was Jesus of Nazareth, he began to cry out and say, "Jesus, Son of David, have mercy on me!" [48]And many rebuked him, telling him to be silent; but he cried out all the more, "O Son of David, have mercy on me!" [49]And Jesus stopped and said, "Call him." And they called the blind man, saying to him, "Take heart; rise, he is calling you." [50]And throwing off his mantle he sprang up and came to Jesus. [51]And Jesus said to him, "What do you want me to do for you?" And the blind man said to him, "Master,[t] let me receive my sight." [52]And Jesus said to him, "Go your way; your faith has made you well." And immediately he received his sight and followed him on the way.*

t Or Rabbi

**Overview:** The wretched helplessness of fallen humanity is seen symbolically in the blindness of Bartimaeus (Augustine). Grace calls for responsiveness on our part. God's electing and assuring promise does not coerce our will or preempt free response (Chrysostom). To follow him on the way is to take him as our pattern, receive nourishment from his grace, and let him be our ransom for sins (Augustine).

**10:46 The Son of Timaeus**

**THE FALL FROM LOFTINESS.** AUGUSTINE:
Mark has recorded both the name of Bartimaeus and of his father,[1] a circumstance which scarcely occurs in all the many cases of healing which had been performed by the Lord. . . . Consequently there can be little doubt that this Bartimaeus, the son of Timaeus, had fallen from some position of great prosperity, and was now regarded as an object of the most notorious and the most remarkable wretchedness, because, in addition to being blind, he had also to sit begging. HARMONY OF THE GOSPELS 2.65.[2]

### 10:51 *What Do You Want Me to Do for You?*

**WILLING THE HEALTHY WAY.** CHRYSOSTOM:
He will save assuredly;[3] yet he will do so just in the way he has promised. But in what way has he promised?[4] On our willing it, and on our hearing him. For he does not make a promise to blocks of wood.[5] HOMILY ON 2 THESSALONIANS 3.4.[6]

### 10:52a *And Immediately He Received His Sight*

**ADORATION OF THE LIGHT.** CLEMENT OF ALEXANDRIA: The commandment of the Lord shines clearly, enlightening the eyes. Receive Christ, receive power to see, receive your light, that you may plainly recognize both God and man. More delightful than gold and precious stones, more desirable than honey and the honeycomb is the Word that has enlightened us.[7] How could he not be desirable, who illumined minds buried in darkness, and endowed with clear vision "the light-bearing eyes" of the soul? . . . Sing his praises, then, Lord, and make known to me your Father, who is God. Your Word will save me, your song instruct me. I have gone astray in my search for God; but now that you light my path, Lord, I find God through you, and receive the Father from you, I become co-heir with you, since you were not ashamed to own me as your brother. Let us, then, shake off forgetfulness of truth, shake off the mist of ignorance and darkness that dims our eyes, and contemplate the true God, after first raising this song of praise to him: "All hail, O light!" For upon us buried in darkness, imprisoned in the shadow of death, a heavenly light has shone, a light of a clarity surpassing the sun's, and of a sweetness exceeding any this earthly life can offer. EXHORTATION TO THE GREEKS 11.[8]

---

[1]Cf. Mk 10:46. Augustine is asking about the implication of the curious fact that the father of the blind beggar is named. [2]Cetedoc 0273, 2.65.125.227.17; NPNF 1 6:159. [3]Cf. Ps 145:19; Prov 20:22; Is 25:9; Zeph 3:17. [4]The issue is, Does his electing and assuring promise coerce our will or preempt our free response? [5]Is 1:19-20; Jn 5:40. [6]TLG 2062.163, 62.493.5-9; GMI 263*. [7]Cf. Ps 19:10. [8]TLG 0555.001, 11.113.1.9-3.1; 113.4.4-114.2.1; JF B 128-29*; SC 2, 181-83.

# 11:1-10 THE ENTRY INTO JERUSALEM

¹*And when they drew near to Jerusalem, to Bethphage and Bethany, at the Mount of Olives, he sent two of his disciples, ²and said to them, "Go into the village opposite you, and immediately as you enter it you will find a colt tied, on which no one has ever sat; untie it and bring it. ³If any one says to you, 'Why are you doing this?' say, 'The Lord has need of it and will send it back here immediately.'" ⁴And they went away, and found a colt tied at the door out in the open street; and they untied it. ⁵And those who stood there said to them, "What are you doing, untying the colt?" ⁶And they told them what Jesus had said; and they let them go. ⁷And they brought the colt to Jesus, and threw their garments on it; and he sat upon it. ⁸And many spread their garments on the road, and others spread leafy branches which they had cut from the fields. ⁹And those who went before and those who followed cried out, "Hosanna! Blessed is he who comes in the name of the Lord! ¹⁰Blessed is the kingdom of our father David that is coming! Hosanna in the highest!"*

**OVERVIEW:** Zechariah had prophesied that the messianic king would come from a tiny village (ORIGEN), meekly on a gentle donkey (JUSTIN MARTYR, EPHREM THE SYRIAN, BEDE) as a sign of humility, a condescension of mercy. By this lowly means the king of ages would become the king of our souls. "Hosanna" is a spontaneous expression of amazement at God's saving work. By studying Scripture, the disciples gradually recognized its prophetic fulfillments (AUGUSTINE).

## 11:2a Go into the Village

### COMPARING THE VILLAGE TO THE HEAVENS.
ORIGEN: Note that the place where the ass was found tied was a village, and a village without a name. For in comparison with the great world in heaven, the whole earth is a village. COMMENTARY ON JOHN 18.[1]

## 11:2b Find a Colt

**WHY A COLT?** JUSTIN MARTYR: It was foretold expressly that he would sit upon the foal of an ass and enter Jerusalem.[2] FIRST APOLOGY 35.[3]

**ZECHARIAH'S PROPHESY FULFILLED.** BEDE: Say to the daughter of Zion, "Behold, your king will come to you, gentle, and sitting upon a donkey, and its foal, the offspring of a beast of burden."[4] The daughter of Zion is the church of the faithful, a figure of the heavenly Jerusalem, which is the mother of us all, of which there then existed a sizeable group among the people of Israel.[5] They had a king who was gentle, for it was not God's pleasure to give an earthly kingdom to the powerful, but a heavenly kingdom to the gentle. HOMI-

---

[1]TLG 2042.005, 10.30.189.1-4; ANF 9:397-98**. Viewed in relation to eternity, this little unnamed village, the earth, is being visited by the saving God. [2]Zech 9:9. [3]TLG 0645.001, 35.10.1-3; ANF 1:175. [4]Zech 9:9; cf. Is 62:11; Mt 21:5. [5]The gathered *ekklēsia* in Jerusalem of the first century. Cf. Jn 11:45.

LIES ON THE GOSPELS 2.3.[6]

## 11:2c *On Which No One Has Ever Sat*

**WHY UNSAT UPON?** ORIGEN: Here he seems to me to be hinting at the circumstance of those who afterwards would come to believe, but who as yet had never sat under the authority of the Word prior to Jesus' coming. COMMENTARY ON JOHN 18.[7]

**BEASTS OF BURDEN IN THE MESSIANIC DRAMA.** EPHREM THE SYRIAN: "Untie the donkey and bring it to me."[8] He began with a manger and finished with a donkey, in Bethlehem with a manger, in Jerusalem with a donkey. COMMENTARY ON TATIAN'S DIATESSARON.[9]

## 11:2d *Untie It*

**WHY UNTIE?** ORIGEN: Some interpret the tied-up ass as a reference to believers who come from the circumcision. They were being freed from many bonds by those who instructed them in the word.[10] COMMENTARY ON JOHN 18.[11]

## 11:4 *They Found a Colt Tied at the Door*

**PREFIGURING THE PASSION.** JUSTIN MARTYR: The prophecy, "binding his foal to the vine, and washing his robe in the blood of the grape,"[12] contained symbols of the things that were to happen to Christ, and of what he was to do. For the foal of an ass stood bound to a vine at the entrance of a village, and he ordered his disciples to bring it to him then. When it was brought, he mounted and sat upon it, and rode into Jerusalem, where the stately temple of the Jews was which you

[Romans][13] have razed to the ground. After this he was crucified, in order that the rest of the prophecy be verified. For the words "washing his robe in the blood of the grape," prefigured the passion he was to undergo, purifying with his blood those who believe in him.[14] FIRST APOLOGY 31.[15]

**GRADUAL DISCOVERY OF PROPHETIC CORRELATIONS.** AUGUSTINE: "His disciples did not understand this at first; but when Jesus was glorified, then they remembered that this had been written of him and had been done to him,"[16] that is, when he had manifested the power of his resurrection.... In short, mentally comparing with the contents of Scripture what was accomplished both prior to and in the course of our Lord's passion, they found this also in Scripture, that it was in accordance with the utterance of the prophets that he sat on an ass's colt. TRACTATE ON JOHN 51.6.[17]

## 11:7 *They Brought the Colt to Jesus and He Sat upon It*

**EMBODYING HUMILITY.** AUGUSTINE: The master of humility is Christ who humbled himself and became obedient even to death, even the death of the cross.[18] Thus he does not lose his divinity when he teaches us humility.... What great thing was it to the king of the ages to become the king of humanity? For Christ was not the king of Israel so that he might

---

[6]Cetedoc 1367, 2.3.89; *HOG* 2:26-27*. [7]TLG 2042.005, 10.32.207.2-4; cf. ANF 9:399. [8]Mt 21:2; Mk 11:2. [9]Leloir 1963:204; *JSSS* 2:269. [10]Cf. Acts 10:45. [11]TLG 2042.005 10.29.180.1-4; ANF 9:397-98**. [12]Gen 49:10. [13]The Romans destroyed the second temple in A.D. 70. [14]Cf. Heb 9:14-28. [15]TLG 0645.001, 32.5.1-7.4; *GMI* 266*; cf. FC 6:69; ANF 1:173. [16]Jn 12:16. [17]Cetedoc 0278, 51.6.1; NPNF 1 7:284*. The rememberers discovered some of these prophetic correlations only after the events had occurred. [18]Phil 2:8.

exact a tax or equip an army with weaponry and visibly vanquish an enemy. He was the king of Israel in that he rules minds, in that he gives counsel for eternity, in that he leads into the kingdom of heaven for those who believe, hope, and love. It is a condescension, not an advancement for one who is the Son of God, equal to the Father, the Word through whom all things were made, to become king of Israel. It is an indication of pity, not an increase in power. TRACTATE ON JOHN 51.3-4.[19]

### 11:8a *Many Spread Their Garments on the Road*

**SPREADING THE HEART BEFORE HIM.** METHODIUS: Instead of our garments, let us spread our hearts before him.[20] ORATION ON THE PALMS 1.[21]

### 11:8b *Others Spread Leafy Branches*

**THE TRIBUTE OF THEIR VOICES.** JEROME: And others cut boughs . . . and strewed them in the way. They cut branches from the fruitbearing trees with which the Mount of Olives was planted, and spread them in the way; so as to make the crooked ways straight, and the rough ways smooth, that Christ the conqueror of sin might walk straightly and safely into the hearts of the faithful. . . . And when they had done all that was to be done by their hands, they offered also the tribute of their voices; and going before

and following after they cry, not in a brief and wordless confession, but with all their might: "Hosanna to the son of David. Blessed is he that comes in the name of the Lord." HOMILIES 94.[22]

### 11:9 *Hosanna!*

**WHY HOSANNA?** JEROME: The boys in the Gospel raised aloft their branches as the Savior entered Jerusalem. They kept on crying: "Hosanna." . . . They borrowed these versicles from Psalm 117.[23] Hosanna, moreover, is the Hebrew for "O Lord, grant salvation!" HOMILIES 94.[24]

**THE MEANING OF THE EXCLAMATION.** AUGUSTINE: "Hosanna," however, is a word of supplicating, as some say who know the Hebrew language, more declaring a feeling than signifying something. Just as in the Latin language there are words which we call interjections, as when in sorrow we say, *Heu!* Or when we are delighted, we say, *Vah!* Or when we are amazed, we say, "Oh, what a great thing!" For then *oh* signifies nothing except the feeling of one who is amazed. TRACTATE ON JOHN 51.2.[25]

---

[19]Cetedoc 0278, 51.3.8; NPNF 1 7:284; FC 88:273. [20]Ps 62:8. [21]PG 18:385; ANF 6:394. [22]Cetedoc 0590, 3.122; Mt 21:9; cf. Mk 11:9; Lk 19:38; Jn 12:13. SSGF 2:174; CCL 77:184. [23]Ps 118:25-26 (117:25 LXX). [24]Cetedoc 0604, 65; FC 57:253. [25]Cetedoc 0278, 51.2.9; NPNF 1 7:283; cf. FC 88:272.

# 11:11-14 THE CURSING OF THE FIG TREE

[11]*And he entered Jerusalem, and went into the temple; and when he had looked round at everything, as it was already late, he went out to Bethany with the twelve.*
[12]*On the following day, when they came from Bethany, he was hungry.* [13]*And seeing in the distance a fig tree in leaf, he went to see if he could find anything on it. When he came to it, he found nothing but leaves, for it was not the season for figs.* [14]*And he said to it, "May no one ever eat fruit from you again." And his disciples heard it.*

**OVERVIEW:** The incarnate Lord hungered just as we do, in order to identify himself with our human poverty (HILARY OF POITIERS). As a figure of the law, the tree was cursed at an inopportune time, because the law at an opportune time did not bear fruit (EPHREM THE SYRIAN). The last act of Jesus' ministry, the cursing of the fig leaves, transmuted the first act of human history, the fig leaves of Adam and Eve, who had not borne worthy fruit (CYRIL OF JERUSALEM). Faith is called to bear fruit actively through love (AUGUSTINE, GREGORY THE GREAT). Merely existing without yielding fruit is not the purpose for which human beings are given the gift of life (AUGUSTINE).

## 11:12a On the Following Day

**THE CHRONOLOGY OF DAYS.** AUGUSTINE: Mark, on his side, has recorded in connection with the second day what he had omitted to notice as occurring really on the first—namely, the incident of the expulsion of the sellers and buyers from the temple. On the other hand, Matthew, after mentioning what was done on the second day—namely, the cursing of the fig tree as he was returning in the morning from Bethany into the city—has omitted certain facts which Mark

has inserted, namely, his coming into the city, and his going out of it in the evening, and the astonishment which the disciples expressed at finding the tree dried up as they passed by in the morning; and then to what had taken place on the second day, which was the day on which the tree was cursed, he has attached what really took place on the third day—namely, the amazement of the disciples at seeing the tree's withered condition, and the declaration which they heard from the Lord on the question of the power of faith.[1] HARMONY OF THE GOSPELS 68.132.[2]

## 11:12b He Was Hungry

**THE LORD OF GLORY VULNERABLE TO HUNGER.** HILARY OF POITIERS: As we behold the mystery of his tears,[3] hunger[4] and thirst,[5] let us remember that the one who wept also raised the dead to life, rejoicing for Lazarus. From the very One who thirsted flowed rivers of living water.[6] He who hungered was able to wither the fig tree which offered no fruit for his hun-

---

[1]Cf. Mt 21:12-22; Mk 11:12-25. [2]Cetedoc 0273, 2.68.131.234.10; NPNF 1 6:161-62*. Mark's account does not contradict Matthew's when the time differential is properly understood. [3]Cf. Jn 11:35. [4]Cf. Mk 11:12. [5]Cf. Jn 19:28. [6]Cf. Jn 4:10.

ger. How could this be, that he who was able to strike the green tree dead merely by his word could also have a nature that could hunger?[7] This was the mystery of his hunger, grief, and thirst, that the Word was assuming flesh. His humanity was entirely exposed to our weaknesses, yet even then his glory was not wholly put away as he suffered these indignities. His weeping was not for himself, his thirst was not for water, nor his hunger merely for food. He did not eat or drink or weep just to satisfy his appetites. Rather, in his incarnate humbling he was demonstrating the reality of his own body by hungering, by doing what human nature does. And when he ate and drank, it was not a concession to some necessity external to himself, but to show his full participation in the human condition. On the Trinity 10.24.[8]

### For What Did He Hunger? Augustine:
Did Christ really want physically to relish and consume fruit himself when he sought the fruit of this fig tree? And if he had found it there, would he then even have eaten it? Did he really want to drink water when he said to the woman of Samaria, "Give me a drink"?[9] When he was on the cross saying "I thirst,"[10] was this really all about his physical thirst? For what does Christ hunger more than our good works? For what does Christ thirst more than our faithful response? On the Psalms 35.15.[11]

### 11:13 Nothing but Leaves

### Early, Moist Buds. Ephrem the Syrian:
The nature of the fig tree is such that when it is cut, because of its moisture, it [requires] many months for it to dry up. Our Lord chose it as a symbol, therefore, to make the quality of his power known through it. It is evident that the

fig tree becomes moist and tender before the other trees. Hence our Lord said: "From the fig tree learn this parable. As soon as its branch becomes tender and opens up in the outer covering of its buds, you know that summer is near."[12] You see that he proposes it [as a symbol] because of its abundant moisture and its early buds. Commentary on Tatian's Diatessaron.[13]

### Leaves of Law. Gregory the Great: The
figs which the Lord had sought were the fruit of the synagogue, which had the leaves of the law, but not the fruit of works. For the creator of all things could not be ignorant that the fig tree had no fruit. That was something anyone might know, since it was not the time of figs. Letter 39, To Eulogius.[14]

### 11:13 It Was Not the Season for Figs

### Discerning the Times. Augustine: Some
who witnessed Christ's miracles did not understand what they meant, and how they spoke to those who knew they had special meaning. They wondered only at the miracles themselves. Others both marvelled at the miracles, and attained some preliminary understanding of them. For this we must come to the school of Christ himself. Those fixed only upon the plain sense of Scripture tend to focus merely upon miracle for miracles' sake. Hence they may prematurely conclude that Jesus himself was ignorant of the time of the

---

[7]Cf. Mk 11:14. [8]Cetedoc 0433, 62A.10.24.3; NPNF 2 9:188**. Being in the form of God he humbled himself and hungered with us in servant form, in order to identify himself with our human hunger. [9]Jn 4:7. [10]Jn 19:28. [11]Cetedoc 0283, 38.34.2.4.2; NPNF 1 8:83**. He was hungry for food but more so for faith active in love. [12]Mt 24:32; Mk 13:28; Lk 21:30. [13]Leloir 1963:170, 172; JSSS 2:247*. [14]Cetedoc 1714, 140A.10.21.32; NPNF 2 13:48*. The leaves symbolized the law, which lacked the fruit of good works.

year, something any ordinary farmer could discern. For it was not yet the season for the tree to bear fruit. Nevertheless, since he was hungry, he looked for fruit on the tree.[15] Does this imply that Christ knew less than what every peasant could easily discern? Surely not. Wouldn't you expect the maker of the fig tree to know what the ordinary orchard worker would know in a snap? So when he was hungry he looked for fruit on the tree, but he seemed to be looking for something more from this tree. He noted that the tree had no fruit, but was full of leaves. It was at that point that he cursed it, and it withered away. So what terrible thing had the poor tree done simply in not bearing fruit? Could the tree reasonably be faulted for its fruitlessness? No. But human beings who by their own free will decide not to bear fruit—that is a different matter. Those found wanting in accountability in this case are those who had the benefit of the law, which was meant to bear fruit, but they had no fruit to show for it. They had a full growth of leaves (the law), yet they bore no fruit (works of mercy). SERMONS ON NEW TESTAMENT LESSONS 48.3.[16]

## 11:14 May No One Ever Eat Fruit from You Again

**WITHHOLDING FRUITS. EPHREM THE SYRIAN:** The owner of the fig tree did not obey the law but spurned it. Our Lord came and found that there was [nothing] left on it, so he cursed it, lest its owner eat from it again, since he had left [nothing] for the orphan and widows. . . . He cursed the fig tree and it shriveled up to show them the power of his divinity, so that by means of [this] action near at hand which they could see, they might believe that which was to come. Because [Jerusalem] had not accepted

the law, he cursed [the fig tree], so that there might no longer be fruit on it, according to its law. . . . He sought fruit from the fig tree at an inopportune time, that it might be a symbol of one who had deceitfully withheld the fruits of the law at the opportune time.[17] For, if he had sought fruit from it at the opportune time, no one would have known that there was a figurative meaning embedded here. Instead of the fig tree, therefore, he showed that it was Jerusalem that he was reproaching, for he had sought love in her, but she had despised the fruit of repentance. . . . Why, therefore, did he who was good and gentle, who everywhere revealed great things out of little things, and completion out of imperfection, why did he command the fig tree to dry up? For he healed the sufferings of everyone, changed water to wine, made an abundance from a little bread, opened the eyes of the blind, cleansed lepers and raised the dead to life. But this fig tree alone did he cause to wither. It was because the time of his suffering was near, and, lest it be thought that he was captured because he was unable to free himself, he cursed the fig tree, that it might be a sign for his friends, and a miracle for his enemies. Thus, the disciples would be strengthened by his word, and others would be amazed at his power. Because he did all things well,[18] and [the time] for him to suffer was near, it might be thought, as indeed it was, that he was captured because he possessed no power. He showed in advance, therefore, by means of a living plant which he caused to wither, that he would have been able to destroy his crucifiers with a word. COMMENTARY ON TATIAN'S DIATESSARON.[19]

---

[16]Cetedoc 0284, 98.38.592.39; NPNF 1 6:413-14**; cf. WSA 3 4:44-45. Sermon 98.3. [17]Cf. Mk 11:13. Jerusalem, signifying Israel, is probably intended here. [18]Cf. Mk 7:37. [19]Leloir 1963:164, 168, 170; JSSS 2:243-46*.

**FIG LEAVES.** CYRIL OF JERUSALEM: Remember at the time of the sin of Adam and Eve they clothed themselves—with what? Fig leaves.[20] That was their first act after the fall. So now Jesus is making the same figure of the fig tree the very last of his wondrous signs. Just as he was headed toward the cross, he cursed the fig tree—not every fig tree, but that one alone for its symbolic significance—saying: "May no one ever eat fruit of you again."[21] In this way the curse laid upon Adam and Eve was being reversed. For they had clothed themselves with fig leaves. CATECHETICAL LECTURES 13.18.[22]

---

[20]Cf. Gen 3:7. [21]Mk 11:14. [22]TLG 2110.003, 13.18.5-12; FC 64:16**.

## 11:15-19 THE CLEANSING OF THE TEMPLE

[15]*And they came to Jerusalem. And he entered the temple and began to drive out those who sold and those who bought in the temple, and he overturned the tables of the money-changers and the seats of those who sold pigeons;* [16]*and he would not allow any one to carry anything through the temple.* [17]*And he taught, and said to them, "Is it not written, 'My house shall be called a house of prayer for all the nations'? But you have made it a den of robbers."* [18]*And the chief priests and the scribes heard it and sought a way to destroy him; for they feared him, because all the multitude was astonished at his teaching.* [19]*And when evening came they[u] went out of the city.*

u Other ancient authorities read *he*

---

**OVERVIEW:** Before gloating over the driving out of the traders from the temple, remember that divine judgment on the church in history may be equally severe (BEDE). The textual evidence may indicate that the scourging of the sellers happened on two different occasions (AUGUSTINE).

### 11:15a He Began to Drive Out Those Who Sold and Those Who Bought

**THE TWO REPORTS.** AUGUSTINE: This account of the many sellers who were cast out of the temple was reported by all the Evangelists, including John, but in his case he introduces it in a completely different order. . . . John proceeds to tell us that he went up to Jerusalem at the season of the Jews' passover, and when he had made a scourge of small cords drove out of the temple those who were selling in it. This makes it evident that this act was performed by the Lord not on a single occasion, but twice over. Only in the first instance was it recorded by John, but in the last by the other three.[1] HARMONY OF THE GOSPELS 2.67.[2]

---

[1]Cf. Mt 21:12-13; Mk 11:15-17; Lk 19:45-46; Jn 2:13-17. [2]Cetedoc 0273, 2.67.129.231.15; NPNF 1 6:160**.

**11:15b He Overturned the Tables of the Moneychangers and the Seats of Those Who Sold Pigeons**

**DRIVEN OUT.** BEDE: He scattered the fraudulent traders, and drove them all out, together with the things that had to do with the carrying on of trade. What, my beloved, do you suppose our Lord would do if he should discover people involved in disputes, wasting time gossiping, indulging in unseemly laughter, or engaged in any other sort of wicked actions?

Remember: when he saw traders in the temple buying the sacrificial offerings meant to be made to him, he was prompt in getting rid of them.[3] . . . These things should cause us great perturbation, beloved; we should dread them exceedingly with well-deserved fear, and carefully avoid them with painstaking diligence, lest he come unexpectedly and find something evil in us, as a result of which we should rightly be scourged and cast out of the church. EXPOSITION ON THE GOSPEL OF MARK 2.1.[4]

[3]Cf.Mt 21:12; Mk 11:15; Lk 19:45; Jn 2:15. [4]Cetedoc 1367, 2.1.39; HOG 2:23*. Cf. Jerome *Commentary on Matthew* 21.15 (CCL 77:188).

## 11:20-25 THE MEANING OF THE WITHERED FIG TREE

[20]As they passed by in the morning, they saw the fig tree withered away to its roots. [21]And Peter remembered and said to him, "Master,[v] look! The fig tree which you cursed has withered." [22]And Jesus answered them, "Have faith in God. [23]Truly, I say to you, whoever says to this mountain, 'Be taken up and cast into the sea,' and does not doubt in his heart, but believes that what he says will come to pass, it will be done for him. [24]Therefore I tell you, whatever you ask in prayer, believe that you have received[a] it, and it will be yours. [25]And whenever you stand praying, forgive, if you have anything against any one; so that your Father also who is in heaven may forgive you your trespasses."[w]

v Or *Rabbi*  a Other ancient authorities read *are receiving*  w Other ancient authorities add verse 26, *But if you do not forgive, neither will your Father who is in heaven forgive your trespasses*

**OVERVIEW:** Beware of fruitlessness. It will be cursed (CYRIL OF JERUSALEM). Faith prays without hesitation and in doing so already is obtaining what is rightly asked for according to the divine will (JOHN CASSIAN). In this way prayer participates actively in the power of almighty God (CHRYSOSTOM). The perfect faith required for moving mountains, even if it is unexampled, is not intrinsically impossible (AUGUSTINE). The text teaches us to forgive in the manner in which we would desire to be forgiven (EPISTLE TO LUCIAN).

## 11:21 *The Fig Tree Which You Cursed Has Withered*

**ADMONITION FOR THOSE PREPARING TO BE BAPTIZED.** CYRIL OF JERUSALEM: You are now being joined with the holy vine.[1] If, then, you abide in the vine, you grow into a fruitful branch, but if you do not so abide, you will be burnt in the fire. Let us therefore bring forth worthy fruit. For let it not come about that it should happen to us what happened to the barren fig tree in the Gospel.[2] Let not Jesus come in these days and utter the same curse upon the fruitless. But instead may all of you say, "I am like a green olive tree in the house of God."[3] CATECHETICAL LECTURES 1.4.[4]

## 11:23a *Whoever Does Not Doubt in His Heart but Believes*

**THE POWER OF PRAYER.** CHRYSOSTOM: Prayer is an all-efficient panoply, a treasure undiminished, a mine never exhausted, a sky unobstructed by clouds, a haven unruffled by storm. It is the root, the fountain, and the mother of a thousand blessings. It exceeds a monarch's power. . . . I speak not of the prayer which is cold and feeble and devoid of zeal. I speak of that which proceeds from a mind outstretched, the child of a contrite spirit,[5] the offspring of a soul converted—this is the prayer which mounts to heaven. . . . The power of prayer has subdued the strength of fire, bridled the rage of lions, silenced anarchy, extinguished wars, appeased the elements, expelled demons, burst the chains of death, enlarged the gates of heaven, relieved diseases, averted frauds, rescued cities from destruction, stayed the sun in its course, and arrested the progress of the thunderbolt. In sum, prayer has power to destroy whatever is at enmity with the good. I speak not of the prayer of the lips, but of the prayer that ascends from the inmost recesses of the heart. ON THE INCOMPREHENSIBLE NATURE OF GOD, HOMILY 5.44, 46, 57, 58.[6]

## 11:23b *Believe That You Will Receive It and You Will*

**FULL CONFIDENCE.** JOHN CASSIAN: While we are praying, there should be no hesitation that would intervene or break down the confidence of our petition by any shadow of despair. We know that by pouring forth our prayer we are obtaining already what we are asking for. We have no doubt that our prayers have effectually reached God.[7] For to that degree that one believes that he is regarded by God, and that God can grant it, just so far will one be heard and obtain an answer. CONFERENCES 1.9.32.[8]

## 11:23c *It Will Be Done for Him*

**DIVINE GIVING AND HUMAN WILLING.** AUGUSTINE: Note that Jesus said "for him," not "for me,"[9] and not "for the Father." Yet it is certain that no human being does such a thing without God's gift and workings. Mark well that even if no actual instances of perfect righteousness may be found among humans, that does not rule out perfect righteousness as if it

---

[1]Cf. Jn 15:4-6. [2]Cf. Mt 21:19; Mk 11:20. [3]Cf. Ps 52:8. [4]TLG 2110.003, 1.4.6-14; LCC 4:80*. [5]Cf. Ps 34:18; Is 66:2. [6]TLG 2062.012, 5.430-433, 448-451, 575-583; *GMI* 279-80**; cf. FC 72:156-57, 161-62. [7]Cf. Jas 5:15-16. [8]Cetedoc 0512, 9.32.277.14; NPNF 2 11:398**. [9]The Son.

were formally impossible. For it might have been realized if only sufficient responsive willing had been applied, enough to suffice for so great a deed. ON THE SPIRIT AND THE LETTER 63.[10]

### 11:25 Forgive, If You Have Anything Against Anyone

OVERCOMING PERSONAL ALIENATION. ANONYMOUS:[11] If an injury is done to you, look to Jesus Christ. Even as you desire that he may forgive your sins, just so you must also forgive them theirs. By this you will circumvent ill-will, and bruise the head of that ancient serpent,[12] who is ever on the watch with all subtlety to undo your good works and fruitful aims. Let no day pass by without reading some portion of the sacred Scriptures, whenever you have time, and giving some space to meditation. Never cast off the habit of reading the holy Scriptures. Nothing feeds the soul and enriches the mind so much as those sacred studies.[13] EPISTLE TO LUCIAN 9.[14]

---

[10]Cetedoc 0343, 35.63.223.10; NPNF 1 5:112*. [11]Sometimes attributed to Theonas of Alexandria. [12]Cf. Gen 3:15; Rom 16:20. [13]Cf. Jn 5:39; Acts 17:11; 2 Tim 3:15-16. [14]PG 10:1574. ANF 6:161*.

---

# 11:27-33 THE AUTHORITY OF JESUS QUESTIONED

[27]And they came again to Jerusalem. And as he was walking in the temple, the chief priests and the scribes and the elders came to him, [28]and they said to him, "By what authority are you doing these things, or who gave you this authority to do them?" [29]Jesus said to them, "I will ask you a question; answer me, and I will tell you by what authority I do these things. [30]Was the baptism of John from heaven or from men? Answer me." [31]And they argued with one another, "If we say, 'From heaven,' he will say, 'Why then did you not believe him?' [32]But shall we say, 'From men'?"—they were afraid of the people, for all held that John was a real prophet. [33]So they answered Jesus, "We do not know." And Jesus said to them, "Neither will I tell you by what authority I do these things."

---

OVERVIEW: Readiness to seek the truth affects its disclosure (BEDE). Lacking faith, the legal experts lacked understanding, however much they might know objectively about the law (TERTULLIAN). Since they answered the truth with a lie, Jesus did not force open the doors they themselves had barricaded (AUGUSTINE).

---

## 11:28 By What Authority?

**FEARING THE TRUTH.** AUGUSTINE: Fearing a stoning, but fearing more an admission of the truth, they answered the truth with a lie, reminiscent of the Scripture: "injustice has lied within herself."[1] For they said, "We know not." And because they had shut themselves up against him, by asserting that they did not know what they knew, the Lord did not open up to them because they did not knock. For it has been said, "Knock and it will be opened to you."[2] But they not only had not knocked that it might be opened, but by their denial they barricaded the door itself against themselves. And the Lord said to them, "Neither do I tell you by what authority I do these things."[3] TRACTATE ON JOHN 2.9.[4]

## 11:30 Was the Baptism of John from Heaven or from Men?

**BELIEF AND UNDERSTANDING.** TERTULLIAN: The baptism announced by John formed the subject, even at that time, of a question proposed by the Lord himself to the legal experts. It concerned whether John's baptism was from

heaven or from men.[5] They were unable to give a consistent answer. They did not understand because they did not believe. ON BAPTISM 10.[6]

## 11:33 Neither Will I Tell You

**READINESS TO SEEK TRUTH AFFECTS ITS DISCLOSURE.** BEDE: It is as if Jesus had said: "I will not tell you what I know, since you will not confess what you know."[7] In this way knowledge is hidden from those who wrongly seek it principally for two reasons: first, when the one who seeks it does not have sufficient capacity to understand what he is seeking for, and second, when through contempt for the truth one is unworthy of having the subject of his inquiry explained to him. . . . So these critics were most justly set aback. They retreated in disgrace. EXPOSITION ON THE GOSPELS OF MARK 3.11.33.[8]

---

[1]Ps 27:12 (26:12 LXX). [2]Cf. Mt 7:7; Lk 11:9. [3]Mt 21:27; Mk 11:33; Lk 20:7. [4]Cetedoc 0278, 2.9.12; NPNF 1 7:16; FC 78:68*. [5]Cf. Mt 21:25-26; Mk 11:30-32; Lk 20:4-7. [6]Cetedoc 008, 10.5; ANF 3:372-74**. [7]Mt 21:27; Mk 11:33; Lk 20:8. [8]Cetedoc 1355, 3.11.1589; CCL 120:582-83; GMI 286*; cf. HOG 2:220. Knowledge is hidden from those who seek it wrongly.

---

# 12:1-12 THE PARABLE OF THE WICKED TENANTS

[1]And he began to speak to them in parables. "A man planted a vineyard, and set a hedge around it, and dug a pit for the wine press, and built a tower, and let it out to tenants, and went into another country. [2]When the time came, he sent a servant to the tenants, to get from them some of the fruit of the vineyard. [3]And they took him and beat him, and sent him away

*empty-handed. ⁴Again he sent to them another servant, and they wounded him in the head, and treated him shamefully. ⁵And he sent another, and him they killed; and so with many others, some they beat and some they killed. ⁶He had still one other, a beloved son; finally he sent him to them, saying, 'They will respect my son.' ⁷But those tenants said to one another, 'This is the heir; come, let us kill him, and the inheritance will be ours.' ⁸And they took him and killed him, and cast him out of the vineyard. ⁹What will the owner of the vineyard do? He will come and destroy the tenants, and give the vineyard to others. ¹⁰Have you not read this scripture:*

*'The very stone which the builders rejected*
*has become the head of the corner;*
*¹¹this was the Lord's doing,*
*and it is marvelous in our eyes'?"*

*¹²And they tried to arrest him, but feared the multitude, for they perceived that he had told the parable against them; so they left him and went away.*

---

**OVERVIEW:** The parable vindicates the Lord of the vineyard, who through the resurrection rights the wrongs done by the tenants. Their malice will be disclosed in the resurrection. Both Father and Son appear in the parable not to know under particular historical contingencies what they do know as Godhead (AMBROSE). The outcome of the resurrection shifts the whole premise of the parable, for amid the fury of the oppressors, Jesus looked steadfastly toward the resurrection (AUGUSTINE).

### 12:6 They Will Respect My Son

**LORD OF THE VINEYARD.** AMBROSE: Matthew and Mark say: "He sent his only son, saying 'they will respect my son.'"[1] Luke sounds as though the outcome is in doubt, as though he did not know without doubt.[2] But in Matthew and Mark he says: "they will respect my son," that is, it is declared that respect will be shown. God can neither be in doubt, nor can he be deceived. For one can only be in doubt who is ignorant of the future. One is deceived who has predicted one thing while another

happened. Yet what is plainer than the fact that Scripture states the Father to have said one thing of the Son, and the same Scripture proves another thing to have taken place? The Son was beaten, mocked, crucified, and died. He suffered much worse things in the flesh than those tenants who had been sent to help out. Was the Father deceived, or was he ignorant? Or was he powerless to give help? . . . Neither is the Father deceived nor does the Son deceive. It is the custom of holy Scriptures to speak in these many voices, as I have shown in many examples. In such instances, God feigns not to know what he does know. In this then is shown the unity of Godhead. A unity of character is shown to exist in the Father and the Son. For as God the Father seems to hide what is known to him, so also the Son, who is the image of God,[3] seems to hide what is known to him. ON THE CHRISTIAN FAITH 5.17.214-18.[4]

---

[1]Mt 21:37; Mk 12:6. [2]Lk 20:13. [3]Cf. 2 Cor 4:4; Col 1:15. [4]Cetedoc 0150, 5.17.55; NPNF 2 10:311-12*.

### 12:7 *Come, Let Us Kill Him, and the Inheritance Will Be Ours*

**THE DECEPTION OF THE KILLERS.** AUGUSTINE: But how will you insure that the inheritance will be yours? Merely because you killed him? Hold on! You in fact did kill him, yet the inheritance is still not yours. Do you not recall the Psalm which says: "I lie down and sleep," and then adds, "I wake again"?[5] Did you miss that point? While you were gloating that you had killed him, he was sleeping. The Psalm says: "I slept." Just while they were raging and would kill me, what was I doing? "I slept." And if I had not willed it, I would not even have slept, for "I have power to lay down my life, and I have power to take it up again."[6] So let the oppressors rage. Let the earth even be "given into the hands of the wicked,"[7] let the flesh be left to the hands of persecutors, let them suspend him on wood with nails transfixed, pierced with a spear. The one who lies down and sleeps simply adds: "I rise again."[8] ON PSALM 41: ON THE FEAST OF THE MARTYRS 9.[9]

---

[5]Ps 3:5. [6]Jn 10:17. [7]Job 9:24. [8]Mt 27:63; Mk 8:31; 10:34; Lk 18:33. [9]Cetedoc 0283, 38.40.10.3; NPNF 1 8:130**.

# 12:13-17 THE QUESTION CONCERNING TRIBUTE TO CAESAR

[13]*And they sent to him some of the Pharisees and some of the Herodians, to entrap him in his talk.* [14]*And they came and said to him, "Teacher, we know that you are true, and care for no man; for you do not regard the position of men, but truly teach the way of God. Is it lawful to pay taxes to Caesar, or not?* [15]*Should we pay them, or should we not?" But knowing their hypocrisy, he said to them, "Why put me to the test? Bring me a coin^x, and let me look at it."* [16]*And they brought one. And he said to them, "Whose likeness and inscription is this?" They said to him, "Caesar's."* [17]*Jesus said to them, "Render to Caesar the things that are Caesar's, and to^x God the things that are God's." And they were amazed at him.*

x Greek *a denarius*

---

**OVERVIEW:** In Christ God is reclaiming his own coinage: humanity made in God's image. So we spend ourselves as God's own currency for that which is incomparably valuable (AUGUSTINE). Christian intercession for the health of the state does not depend upon receiving any temporal benefits from the state (JUSTIN MARTYR). The people of God continue guilelessly to intercede for the peace of the society (TERTULLIAN). Unlike the inert and unresponsive physical image of a ruler on a coin, redeemed humans bear the lively image of the living God to whom they belong (AUGUSTINE). One freely gives to God precisely what one must withhold from political authorities: oneself, one's conscience, one's soul (TERTULLIAN). As God freely paid for our freedom from the slavery of sin, so we are called to receive the new life of freedom he gives us, valuing temporal things according to their limited proportional value (ORIGEN). When Jesus' adversaries feigned respect while plotting to trap him (CHRYSOSTOM), he at once broke directly through their deceptions (AUGUSTINE).

## 12:13 To Entrap Him

**FEIGNING RESPECT.** CHRYSOSTOM: They were breathing anger, and straining to plot against him, while they feigned respect. THE GOSPEL OF ST. MATTHEW, HOMILY 70.1.[1]

## 12:14 Is It Lawful to Pay Taxes to Caesar?

**INTERCESSION FOR GOVERNING AUTHORITIES.** JUSTIN MARTYR: So we worship God only, but in temporal matters we gladly serve you, recognizing you as emperors and rulers, and praying that along with your imperial power you may also be found to have a sound mind. Suppose you pay no attention to our prayers and our frank statements about everything. That will not injure us, since we believe, and are convinced without doubt, that everyone will finally experience the restraint of divine judgment in relation to their voluntary actions. Each will be required to give account for the responsibilities which he has been given by God.[2] FIRST APOLOGY 17.[3]

## 12:16 Whose Likeness and Inscription Is This?

**THE COIN'S UNAWARENESS OF THE IMAGE IT BEARS.** AUGUSTINE: The image of the Emperor appears differently in his son and in a piece of coin. The coin has no knowledge of its bearing the image of the prince. But you are the coin of God, and so far highly superior, as possessing mind and even life, so as to know the One whose image you bear.[4] SERMONS ON NEW TESTAMENT LESSONS 43.[5]

## 12:17a Render to Caesar

**MONEY TO CAESAR, SELF TO GOD.** TERTULLIAN: That means render the image of Caesar, which is on the coin, to Caesar, and the image of God, which is imprinted on the person,[6] to God. You give to Caesar only money. But to God, give yourself. ON IDOLATRY 15.[7]

**WE PRAY FROM THE HEART.** TERTULLIAN: We pray for the safety of the emperors to the eternal God, the true, the living God, whom emperors themselves would desire to be benevolent to them, the One who is "above all others who are called gods." We, looking up to heaven with outstretched hands, because we are harmless, with naked heads, because we are not ashamed,[8] without a prompter, because we pray from the heart, constantly pray for all emperors, that they may have a long life, a secure

---

[1]NPNF 1 10:427*; TLG 2062.152, 58.656.14-15. [2]Cf. Rom 14:12. [3]TLG 2062.001, 17.3.1-4.6; cf. LCC 1:253; ANF 1:168. Both subjects and rulers stand under final divine judgment. Christian intercession for political authorities does not hinge on their receiving temporal benefits. [4]Cf. Gen 1:26-27; 2 Cor 3:2-3. [5]Cetedoc 0284, 9.41.351; NPNF 1 6:410-11**; cf. GMI 295. [6]Gen 1:26-27; 9:6; 1 Cor 11:7. [7]Cetedoc 0023, 47.25; ANF 3:70*. Christians do not honor the ruling political powers in the same way they honor God. [8]1 Cor 11:7.

empire, a safe center of governance, adequate defense, a faithful senate, a well-instructed people, a quiet state—whatever Caesar would wish for himself in his public and private capacity.[9] APOLOGY 30.[10]

**GOD'S COINS.** AUGUSTINE: We are God's money. But we are like coins that have wandered away from the treasury. What was once stamped upon us[11] has been worn down by our wandering. The One who restamps his image upon us is the One who first formed us. He himself seeks his own coin, as Caesar sought his coin. It is in this sense that he says, "Render to Caesar the things that are Caesar's, and to God the things that are God's,"[12] to Caesar his coins, to God your very selves. TRACTATE ON JOHN 40.9.[13]

**GOD'S TRIBUTE FOR US.** ORIGEN: For the sake of those who were in captivity, like the bondage of the Hebrews, the Son of God took upon himself the form of a slave,[14] yet doing nothing worldly or servile. As one who came in the form of a slave, he paid tax and tribute for us, in the same way that a restitution would be paid for his blood and that of his disciples. . . .

Therefore, let anyone who possesses the things of Caesar render freely them to Caesar, so that he may be able then to render freely to God the things of God. . . . Just as our Lord paid our debt, not having initiated it, nor expended it, nor acquired it, nor at any time made it his own possession. COMMENTARY ON MATTHEW 13.10.[15]

### 12:17b *They Were Amazed at Him*

**GIVING WHAT IS GOD'S.** AUGUSTINE: Caesar seeks his image; render it. God seeks his image; render it. Do not withhold from Caesar his coin. Do not keep from God his coin. To this they could not think of anything to answer. For they had been sent to slander him. And they went back saying: No one could answer him. Why? Because he had shattered their teeth in their mouth. ON THE PSALMS 58.8.[16]

---

[9]Jer 29:7; Dan 6:21; 1 Tim 2:1-2; 1 Pet 2:13-17. [10]Cetedoc 0003, 30.1; ANF 3:42**; *GMI* 295-96. [11]The image of God. [12]Mt 22:21; Mk 12:17; Lk 20:25. [13]Cetedoc 0278, 40.9.36; NPNF 1 7:228*; FC 88:133*. [14]Phil 2:7. [15]TLG 2042.030, 13.10.21-29, 46-49, 62-65; cf. ANF 9:481. [16]Cetedoc 0283, 39.57.11.49; NPNF 1 8:233*.

---

# 12:18-27 THE QUESTION CONCERNING THE RESURRECTION

[18]*And Sadducees came to him, who say that there is no resurrection; and they asked him a question, saying,* [19]*"Teacher, Moses wrote for us that if a man's brother dies and leaves a wife, but leaves no child, the man*[y] *must take the wife, and raise up children for his brother.* [20]*There were seven brothers; the first took a wife, and when he died left no children;* [21]*and the second took her, and died, leaving no children; and the third likewise;* [22]*and the seven left no children. Last of all*

*the woman also died.* [23]*In the resurrection whose wife will she be? For the seven had her as wife."*

[24]*Jesus said to them, "Is not this why you are wrong, that you know neither the scriptures nor the power of God?* [25]*For when they rise from the dead, they neither marry nor are given in marriage, but are like angels in heaven.* [26]*And as for the dead being raised, have you not read in the book of Moses, in the passage about the bush, how God said to him, 'I am the God of Abraham, and the God of Isaac, and the God of Jacob'?* [27]*He is not God of the dead, but of the living; you are quite wrong."*

y Greek *his brother*

**OVERVIEW:** In arguing an obscure point, the Sadducees lost sight of the power of God to raise the dead. Jesus' own resurrection became final proof of his divine identity (TERTULLIAN). Our resurrected bodies will be like Christ's resurrected body (JOHN OF DAMASCUS). No jealousy will arise in heaven. In the next life God will not separate those he has joined in marriage in this life (TERTULLIAN). The promises he has already fulfilled stand as a credible guarantee of his future promise of the general resurrection (AUGUSTINE).

## 12:18 The Sadducees, Who Say There Is No Resurrection, Came to Him

**CHALLENGING DECEIVERS TO DIVULGE DECEPTIONS.** TERTULLIAN: They put to him the strongest case they could to impair his credibility. They fashioned a contorted argument to pursue the question which they had initiated. Their deceptive inquiry concerned the flesh, whether or not it would be subject to marriage after the resurrection. They assumed the case of a woman who had married seven brothers, so as to make it doubtful as to which of them she should be restored.[1] Now, let the gist both of the question and the answer be kept steadily in view, and the discussion is settled at once in this way: The Sadducees indeed denied the resurrection, while the Lord affirmed it. In affirming it, he

reproached them as being both ignorant of the Scriptures—which declare the resurrection—and disbelieving of the power of God as able to raise the dead. He then spoke without ambiguity of the dead being raised. ON THE RESURRECTION OF THE FLESH 36.[2]

## 12:23 In the Resurrection Whose Wife Will She Be?

**THE END OF JEALOUSY.** TERTULLIAN: To Christians, after their departure from this world, no restoration of the carnal aspect of marriage is promised in the day of the resurrection, translated as they will be into the condition and sanctity of angels.[3] In the day of resurrection no dilemma arising from sexual jealousy will injure any of her so many husbands, even in the case of her whom they chose to represent as having been married to seven brothers successively. To HIS WIFE 1.1.[4]

## 12:24 You Know Neither the Scriptures nor the Power of God

**HOPE OF RESURRECTION.** AUGUSTINE: The

---

[1]Mt 22:23-32; Mk 12:18-27; Lk 20:27-40. [2]Cetedoc 0019, 36.2; ANF 3:571**. [3]Cf. Mt 22:30; Mk 12:25; Lk 20:36. [4]Cetedoc 0012, 1.1.23; ANF 4:39**. There will be no marital jealousy in heaven, where resurrected bodies will be sanctified.

Sadducees do not have our hope for the resurrection, since they "know neither the scriptures nor the power of God,"[5] who is able to restore what is lost, to raise what is dead to life, to revive what has rotted away, to gather together what is corruptible and finite. The Lord promised to do this, and he gives as a guarantee the promises he has already fulfilled. So let your faith speak of this to you, since your hope will not be disappointed even though your love may be put to the test. LETTER 263, TO SAPIDA.[6]

### 12:25 When They Rise from the Dead, They Neither Marry nor Are Given in Marriage, but Are Like Angels

**SPIRITUAL PARTNERSHIP.** TERTULLIAN: All the more we shall be bound to them [our departed spouses], because we are destined to a better estate, destined to rise to a spiritual partnership. We will recognize both our own selves and those to whom we belong. Else how shall we sing thanks to God to eternity, if there shall remain in us no sense and memory of this relationship? Or if we shall be reformed only materially, but not in consciousness? Consequently, we who are together with God shall remain together. . . . In eternal life God will no more separate those whom he has joined together than in this life where he forbids them to be separated. ON MONOGAMY 10.[7]

**NEEDS OF THE RESURRECTED BODY.** JOHN OF DAMASCUS: The body of the Lord after the resurrection was such that it entered through the closed doors without difficulty, and needed neither food, nor sleep, nor drink. "For they shall be," says the Lord, "like the angels of God,"[8] and there shall no longer be marriage or the procreation of children. ORTHODOX FAITH 4.27.[9]

---

[5]Cf. Mt 22:29. [6]Cetedoc 0262, 263.57.4.634.11; FC 32:273**. [7]Cetedoc 0028, 10.35; ANF 4:67. [8]Mk 12:25; Lk 20:36. [9]FC 37:405; TLG 2934.004, 100.98-101.

---

## 12:28-40 THE GREAT COMMANDMENT

[28]And one of the scribes came up and heard them disputing with one another, and seeing that he answered them well, asked him, "Which commandment is the first of all?" [29]Jesus answered, "The first is, 'Hear, O Israel: The Lord our God, the Lord is one; [30]and you shall love the Lord your God with all your heart, and with all your soul, and with all your mind, and with all your strength.' [31]The second is this, 'You shall love your neighbor as yourself.' There is no other commandment greater than these." [32]And the scribe said to him, "You are right, Teacher; you have truly said that he is one, and there is no other but he; [33]and to love

*him with all the heart, and with all the understanding, and with all the strength, and to love one's neighbor as oneself, is much more than all whole burnt offerings and sacrifices." *[34]And when Jesus saw that he answered wisely, he said to him, "You are not far from the kingdom of God." And after that no one dared to ask him any question.*

*[35]And as Jesus taught in the temple, he said, "How can the scribes say that the Christ is the son of David? [36]David himself, inspired by*[z] *the Holy Spirit, declared,*

*'The Lord said to my Lord,*

*Sit at my right hand,*

*till I put thy enemies under thy feet.'*

*[37]David himself calls him Lord; so how is he his son?" And the great throng heard him gladly.*

*[38]And in his teaching he said, "Beware of the scribes, who like to go about in long robes, and to have salutations in the market places [39]and the best seats in the synagogues and the places of honor at feasts, [40]who devour widows' houses and for a pretense make long prayers. They will receive the greater condemnation."*

z Or *himself, in*

---

**OVERVIEW:** To love God truly is to love God with all that you are as body, soul and spirit (GREGORY OF NYSSA). Loving God with the whole heart cannot be split apart into diverse, creaturely loves. The love of God loves all else in relation to the one incomparably lovable. It emerges only through the death of creaturely idolatries (BASIL). To confess the one true God is to renounce all false gods (ORIGEN). If the Lord of all fills all things in heaven and earth, then there is no room left for a second supposed god (ATHANASIUS). The majesty of God is best honored through lowly service to the needy neighbor, not by words alone (CHRYSOSTOM, PSEUDO-CLEMENT). Singlemindedly loving God by showing mercy to the neighbor brings one to a higher level of accountability than do any sacrificial burnt offerings (CALLISTUS). Love of God and neighbor cannot be disjoined so that one is thought more important than the other (BEDE). All virtues—prudence, fortitude, temperance and justice—are encompassed in this twofold command (CHRYSOSTOM, AUGUSTINE). Our common capacity to reason makes us partners with all other human beings (AUGUSTINE). Faith cannot remain silent in response to the Arian charge that because God is one, the Son cannot be God (HILARY OF POITIERS). He is son of David according to his humanity and Lord of David according to his divinity (AUGUSTINE). To the extent that the incarnate identity of the giver of the command remained unrecognized, the questioner would remain unready to grasp the depths of the great commandment, even if the formal scope of the command is understood (HEGEMONIUS, HILARY OF POITIERS, PSEUDO-JEROME).

### 12:29 The Lord Is One

**GOD FILLS ALL THINGS.** ATHANASIUS: Since God is one,[1] it is ridiculous to suppose that

---

[1]Cf. Deut 6:4.

there could be still another "Lord" of heaven and earth in addition to the Lord who is one. There is simply no room for a second Lord of all, if the one true God fills all things in the compass of heaven and earth. AGAINST THE HEATHEN 6.4.[2]

**THE ONE GOD.** HILARY OF POITIERS: If sacred truth, when challenged by blasphemy, is met by silence, even that silence may be falsely construed as consent. This is what has happened in the case of the Arian assertion that because God is one, therefore his Son is not God. . . . The same one who authorizes us to confess the Son of God as God justifies us in proclaiming the one God. ON THE TRINITY 5.1-2.[3]

### 12:30a *You Shall Love the Lord Your God*

**SPENDING THE POWER OF LOVE ON WHAT IS UNWORTHY.** BASIL: It is not the privilege of any chance person to go forward to the perfection of love and to learn to know him who is truly beloved, but of him who has already "put off the old man, which is being corrupted through its deceptive lusts, and has put on the new man,"[4] which is being renewed that it may be recognized as an image of the creator. Moreover, he who loves money and is aroused by the corruptible beauty of the body and esteems exceedingly this little glory here, since he has expended the power of loving on what is not proper, he is quite blind in regard to the contemplation of him who is truly beloved. EXEGETIC HOMILIES, HOMILY 17.[5]

### 12:30b *With All Your Heart*

**RENOUNCING OTHER GODS.** ORIGEN: When you decide to keep the command of this precept and reject all other gods and lords and

have no god or lord except the one God and Lord, you have declared war on all others without treaty. When, therefore, we come to the grace of baptism, renouncing all other gods and lords, we confess the only God, Father, Son and Holy Spirit.[6] ON EXODUS, HOMILY 8.4.[7]

**NO DIVISION INTO PARTS.** BASIL: The expression, "with the whole," admits of no division into parts. As much love as you shall have squandered on lower objects, that much will necessarily be lacking to you from the whole. EXEGETIC HOMILIES, HOMILY 17.[8]

### 12:30c *With All Your Soul, Mind and Strength*

**THREEFOLD UNITY IN LOVING WITH ONE'S WHOLE SELF.** GREGORY OF NYSSA: Human life consists in a threefold unity. We are taught similarly by the apostle in what he says to the Ephesians, praying for them that the complete grace of their "body and soul and spirit" may be preserved at the coming of the Lord. We use the word "body," for the nutritive part, the word for the vital, "soul," and the word "spirit" for the intellective dimension. In just this way the Lord instructs the writer of the Gospel that he should set before every commandment that love to God which is exercised with all the heart and soul and mind.[9] This single phrase

---

[2]NPNF 2 4:7**; TLG 2035.001, 6.22-25. By definition, there can only be one Lord of all. [3]Cetedoc 0433, 62.5.1.5; NPNF 2 9:85**; cf. FC 25:135. God the Son is truly God, even as God the Father is truly God. [4]Eph 4:22, 24. [5]TLG 2040.018, 29.392.14-24; FC 46:278-79. The perfect love of God is learned only through the costly death of idolatries. [6]Cf. Mt 28:19. [7]FC 71:322-23. If with all your heart you love God, other proximate, temporal loves must take their place within this framework. [8]TLG 2040.018.29.392.27-30; FC 46:279. Love for God with a pure heart cannot be divided or apportioned into various loves for various creatures. [9]Mt 22:37; Mk 12:30; Lk 10:27.

embraces the human whole: the corporeal heart, the mind as the higher intellectual and mental nature, and the soul as their mediator. ON THE MAKING OF MAN 8.5.[10]

## 12:31a *Love Your Neighbor as Yourself*

**CONFESSING THROUGH ACTIONS.** PSEUDO-CLEMENT: So then, brothers, let us acknowledge him in our actions by loving one another,[11] by not committing adultery[12] or slandering one another[13] or being jealous,[14] but by being self-controlled, compassionate and kind.[15] And we ought to have sympathy for one another, and not be avaricious. By these actions let us acknowledge him, and not by their opposites. 2 CLEMENT 3.4.[16]

**THE SUMMIT OF VIRTUE.** CHRYSOSTOM: This is the summit of virtue, the foundation of all God's commandments: to the love of God is joined also love of neighbor.[17] One who loves God does not neglect his brother, nor esteem money more than a limb of his own, but shows him great generosity, mindful of him who has said, "Whoever did it to the least of my brothers did it to me."[18] He is aware that the Lord of all considers as done to himself what is done in generosity to the poor in giving relief. He does not take into consideration the lowly appearance of the poor, but the greatness of the One who has promised to accept as done to himself what is given to the poor.[19] HOMILIES ON GENESIS, HOMILY 55.12.[20]

**LOVING GOD THROUGH NEIGHBORS.** BEDE: Neither of these two kinds of love is expressed with full maturity without the other, because God cannot be loved apart from our neighbor, nor our neighbor apart from God.[21] Hence as many times as Peter was asked by our Lord if he loved

him, and attested his love, the Lord added at the end of each inquiry, "Feed my sheep," or "feed my lambs,"[22] as if he were clearly saying: "There is only one adequate confirmation of whole-hearted love of God—laboring steadily for the needy in your midst, exercising continuing care of them." EXPOSITION ON THE GOSPEL OF MARK 2.22.[23]

## 12:31b *No Other Commandment*

**NOTHING ELSE REQUIRED.** CHRYSOSTOM: Christ looks for nothing else from you, in fact, Scripture says, than loving him with all your heart and carrying out his commands. I mean, obviously the person who loves him in the way he ought to love is also ready to carry out his commands. You see, when one is kindly disposed to another, he takes pains to do everything able to attract the loved one to love for him. So, we too, if we sincerely love the Lord, will manage to discharge his commands and do nothing capable of angering our loved one. This is the kingdom of heaven; this, the enjoyment of goods; this, blessings beyond number, being found worthy to love him sincerely and in the manner he deserves. Our love for him will be genuine if we give evidence of great love for our fellow servants as well as for him.[24] HOMILIES ON GENESIS, HOMILY 55.11.[25]

**LOVING WHAT IS WORTHY OF LOVE.** AUGUSTINE: This virtue consists in nothing else but in loving what is worthy of love; it is prudence

---

[10]TLG 2017.079, 145.40-148.1; NPNF 2 5:394**. [11]Cf. Jn 13:35; 15:12; 1 Jn 3:11. [12]Cf. Ex 20:14; Gal 5:19. [13]Cf. Prov 10:18. [14]Cf. Prov 6:34. [15]Cf. Eph 4:32; 1 Pet 3:8. [16]AF 69-70; cf. FC 1:67; TLG 1271.002, 4.3.1-4.2. [17]Cf. Mt 22:39; Mk 12:31; Lk 10:27. [18]Mt 25:40. [19]Cf. Mt 25:31-46. [20]FC 87:113*; TLG 2062.112, 54.483.19-34. [21]Mt 22:37-39; Mk 12:30-31; Lk 10:27. [22]Jn 21:15-17. [23]Cetedoc 1367, 2.22.4; HOG 2:220**. [24]1 Jn 4:19-21. [25]TLG 2062.112, 54.482.61-483.14; FC 87:112-13.

to choose this, fortitude to be turned from it by no obstacles, temperance to be enticed by no allurements, justice to be diverted by no pride. Why do we choose what we exclusively love, except that we find nothing better? But this is God, and if we prefer or equate any creature with God, we know nothing about loving ourselves. We are made better by approaching closer to him than whom nothing is better. We go to him not by walking, but by loving. We will have him more present to us in proportion as we are able to purify the love by which we draw near to him, for he is not spread through or confined by corporeal space; he is everywhere present and everywhere wholly present,[26] and we go to him not by the motion of our feet but by our conduct. Conduct is not usually discerned by what one knows but by what one loves; good or bad love makes good or bad conduct. LETTER 155, TO MACEDONIUS.[27]

## 12:32 You Are Right, Teacher

ABOVE BURNT OFFERINGS. HILARY OF POITIERS: The answer of the scribe seems to accord with the words of the Lord, for he too acknowledges the inmost love of one God, and professes the love of one's neighbor as real as the love of self, and places love of God and love of one's neighbor above all the burnt offerings of sacrifices. ON THE TRINITY 9.24.[28]

## 12:33 More Than All Whole Burnt Offerings

MERCY IS BETTER. CALLISTUS: My brothers, shun not only the holding, but even the hearing, of the judgment that bans mercy. For mercy is better than all whole burnt offerings and sacrifices.[29] THE SECOND EPISTLE TO ALL THE BISHOPS OF GAUL 6.[30]

## 12:34 Not Far from the Kingdom

STILL AT SOME DISTANCE. PSEUDO-JEROME: To say "you are not far from" suggests that the scribe was still at some distance from the reign of God. COMMENTARY ON MARK.[31]

## 12:36 The Lord Said to My Lord

LOVE ABOVE ALL. HILARY OF POITIERS: The scribe, therefore, is not far from the kingdom of God when he acknowledges the one God who is to be loved above all things. But he is admonished by his own confession in that he does not fully grasp the mystery of the law as being fulfilled in Christ. . . . The scribe only recognized him according to the flesh and the birth from Mary, who was descended from David,[32] rather than as David's Lord.[33] ON THE TRINITY 9.26.[34]

## 12:37 David Himself Calls Him Lord, So How Is He His Son?

LORD AS SON. GREGORY OF NAZIANZUS: What is lofty you are to apply to the Godhead, and to that nature in him which is superior to sufferings and incorporeal; but all that is lowly to the composite condition of him who for your sakes made himself of no reputation and was incarnate. ORATION 29, ON THE SON 18.[35]

SON OF DAVID AND LORD OF DAVID. AUGUS-

---

[26]Cf. Ps 139. [27]Cetedoc 0262, 155.44.4.443.7; FC 20:314-15*. [28]Cetedoc 0433, 62A.9.24.24; NPNF 2 9:163*. [29]1 Sam 15:22; Hos 6:6. [30]PG 10:152; ANF 8:618*. In PG 10 the author is listed as Asterius Urbanus. [31]Cetedoc 0632, 12.54.47; CG 1:431. To the extent that the giver of the command remained unrecognized, the scribe remained at a distance. [32]Cf. Mt 1:20; Lk 1:27. [33]Cf. Ps 110:1; Mt 22:41-46; Mk 12:35-37; Lk 20:41-44. [34]Cetedoc 0433, 62A.9.26.8; FC 25:346-47**. The scribe did not grasp the identity of the incarnate one who was giving the command. [35]TLG 2022.009, 18.17-20; LCC 3:173.

TINE: For that through which Mary had been made was not dying, but that which was made from Mary was dying. The eternity of [his] divinity was not dying, but the weakness of [his] flesh was dying. Therefore he made that reply, distinguishing in the faith of believers the one who came from the one through whom he came. For he, God and Lord of heaven and earth, came through a woman as his mother. In regard to the fact that he was Lord of the world, Lord of heaven and earth, he was also, of course, Lord of Mary; and in regard to the fact that he was creator of the world, creator of heaven and earth, he was also the creator of Mary. But insofar as it was said, "made of a woman, made under the law,"[36] he was the son of Mary. He was the Lord of Mary, he was the son of Mary; he was the creator of Mary, he was created from Mary. Do not be amazed that he is both son and Lord. For as he was [the son] of Mary, so, also, he was said to be the son of David; indeed the son of David precisely because the son of Mary. Hear the apostle speaking clearly: "who was born of the seed of David, according to the flesh."[37] Hear that he was also the Lord of David; and let David himself say this: "The Lord said to my Lord, 'Sit at my right hand.' "[38] And Jesus himself proposed this to the Jews, and by it refuted them.[39] Therefore just as he was both the son and the Lord of David, the son of David according to the flesh, the Lord of David according to [his] divinity, so he was the son of Mary according to the flesh and the Lord of Mary according to [his] majesty. Because, therefore, she was not the mother of [his] divinity and what she sought would be a miracle through [his] divinity, he answered her, "What is it to me and to you, woman?"[40] But that you may not think that I am denying you as my mother, "My hour has not yet come."[41] For there shall I acknowl-

edge you when the weakness of which you are the mother has begun to hang on the cross. TRACTATE ON JOHN 8.9.[42]

**INSTRUCTION ON HIS AUTHORITY.** AUGUSTINE: He spoke in the hearing of those whom he wished profitably to instruct on his authority, and to turn away from the teaching of the scribes, whose knowledge of Christ amounted then only to this, that he was made of the seed of David according to the flesh. They did not understand that he was God, and on that ground also the Lord even of David. HARMONY OF THE GOSPELS 2.74.[43]

## 12:38 Beware of the Scribes, Who Devour Widows

**WHY BEWARE?** HEGEMONIUS: The Pharisees looked to the "tithing of anise and cummin, and left undone the weightier matters of the law."[44] While devoting great care to the things which were external, they overlooked those which bore upon salvation of the soul. For they also paid much attention to "greetings in the marketplace,"[45] and to the "uppermost seats at feasts."[46] To them the Lord Jesus, knowing their perdition, made this declaration: that they attended to those things only which were external, and despised as strange those things which were within, and did not understand that he who made the body made also the soul. THE DISPUTATION WITH MANES 21.[47]

---

[36]Gal 4:4. [37]Rom 1:3. [38]Ps 110:1. [39]Cf. Mt 22:41-46; Mk 12:35-37; Lk 20:41-44. [40]Jn 2:4. [41]Jn 2:4. [42]Cetedoc 0278, 8.9.22; FC 78:189-90. [43]Cetedoc 0273, 2.74.143.246.16; NPNF 1 6:167*. [44]Mt 23:23; Lk 11:42. [45]Mt 23:6; Mk 12:38; Lk 20:46. [46]Mt 23:6-7; Mk 12:38-39; Lk 20:46. [47]PG 10:1462; ANF 6:194*; PG 10, 1429, sometimes attributed to Archelaus. The religious professionals were attentive to outward observances but not those inward things upon which salvation depends.

## 12:41-44 THE WIDOW'S GIFT

[41]*And he sat down opposite the treasury, and watched the multitude putting money into the treasury. Many rich people put in large sums.* [42]*And a poor widow came, and put in two copper coins, which make a penny.* [43]*And he called his disciples to him, and said to them, "Truly, I say to you, this poor widow has put in more than all those who are contributing to the treasury.* [44]*For they all contributed out of their abundance; but she out of her poverty has put in everything she had, her whole living."*

**OVERVIEW:** The widow's gift was measured not by its weight but by the goodwill by which it was offered. The quantity of possessions does not count in the kingdom's audits (JEROME). A good will alone suffices for readiness for the kingdom (CAESARIUS OF ARLES). The Lord paid no attention to the amount of her money but only to the abundance of her generosity. When those of limited means respond faithfully to the full extent of their means, they express deeper faith than do those of greater means who respond only in part (CHRYSOSTOM). To the scribe's lack of responsiveness to grace Mark contrasts the widow's simple unconditional responsiveness. Those who have nothing may possess all, while those who have much may lack the condition of truly possessing anything (JEROME). Small beginnings are better than rich fantasies (EVAGRIUS). Readiness for the kingdom may require treasures for the rich or a widow's penny for the poor (AUGUSTINE). While Moses received gifts from those who had, Jesus received gifts even from those who had not (HEGEMONIUS).

### 12:42 She Put In Two Copper Coins

**THE KINGDOM NOT FOR SALE. CHRYSOSTOM:** Do not despair. One cannot buy heavenly things with money. . . . If money could pur-

chase such things, then the woman who deposited the two small copper coins would have received nothing very large. But since it was not money but rather her intention that prevailed, that woman received everything because she demonstrated firm conviction. Therefore, let us not say that the kingdom may be bought with money. It is not bought with money, but rather with an unsullied intention that may demonstrate itself by means of money. Therefore, one answers, is there no need for money? There is no need for money, but for a Christian disposition. If you have this, you will even be able to buy heaven with two small copper coins. Without this disposition, one will not be able to do with ten thousand talents of gold the very thing that the two coins can do. Why? Because whenever you have many things and deposit a lesser amount, you have given alms, but not the same kind of alms that the widow gave. For you were not depositing it with the same kind of eagerness that she did. For she robbed herself of everything, or rather did not rob but gave to herself a free gift. HOMILIES ON PHILIPPIANS.[1]

---

[1]TLG 2062.160, 62.291.13-14, 17-33; cf. NPNF 1 5:251. Her intention prevailed, not her money. Money cannot buy blessedness in the kingdom.

**MEASURING THE VALUE OF GIFTS.** JEROME:
The poor widow cast only two pennies into the
treasury; yet because she gave all she had it is
said of her that she surpassed all the rich in
offering gifts to God.[2] Such gifts are valued not
by their weight but by the good will with which
they are made. LETTER 118, TO JULIAN 5.[3]

**THE SONG OF SERAPHIM.** JEROME: I pass on to
the widow in the Gospel who though she was
but a poor widow was yet richer than all the
people of Israel.[4] She had but a grain of mustard seed, but she put her leaven in the measures of flour; and, tempering her confession of
the Father and of the Son with the grace of the
Holy Spirit, cast her two pennies into the treasury. All the substance that she had, all her
possessions she offered in the two testaments
of her faith. These are like the two seraphim
which glorify the trinity with threefold song[5]
and are stored among the treasures of the
church. They are like the two legs of the tongs
by which live coal is caught up to cleanse the
sinner's lips.[6] LETTER 54, TO FURIA 17.[7]

### 12:43 More Than All Those

**ALL WITHIN YOUR POWER.** CHRYSOSTOM:
When alms are given, we attend to nothing else
except the disposition required. And if you say
that money is needed, and houses and clothes
and shoes, read those words of Christ, which
he spoke concerning the widow,[8] and stop
being anxious. For even if you are extremely
poor, and among those that beg, if you cast in
your two small coins, you have done all in your
power. Though you offer only a barley cake,
having only this, you will have arrived at the
heart of the matter. THE GOSPEL OF ST.
MATTHEW, HOMILY 52.5.[9]

**THE SHARE OF THE POOR IN THE KINGDOM.**
AUGUSTINE: But what, brethren, is more
mighty than that not only Zacchaeus should
acquire the kingdom of heaven by the half of
his goods,[10] but even the widow for two pennies,[11] and that each should possess an equal
share there? What is greater than that the same
kingdom should be worth treasures to the rich
man, and a cup of cold water to the poor?[12] ON
THE PSALMS 112.3.[13]

**A GOOD WILL ALONE IS SUFFICIENT.** CAE-
SARIUS OF ARLES: Therefore, those who possess good will have everything. This alone can
be sufficient if there are no other things, but if
it alone is lacking, whatever they possess profits nothing. If it is present, it alone suffices, but
everything else avails nothing if charity alone is
lacking.[14] SERMONS 182.3.[15]

**THAT WHICH MAKES A GOOD DEED GOOD.**
BEDE: The treasure in one's heart is the intention of the thought, from which the searcher of
hearts judges the outcome. Hence it quite frequently occurs that some persons perform good
deeds of lesser importance with a greater reward
of heavenly grace. This is because of the intention in their hearts to accomplish greater good if
they could. Others, though they display greater
works of virtue, are allotted smaller rewards by
the Lord on account of the indifference in their
lukewarm hearts. The deed of the widow who

---

[2]Mk 12:43-44. [3]Cetedoc 0620, 118.55.5.442.4; NPNF 2 6:223*.
[4]Mk 12:43; Lk 21:3-4. [5]Is 6:2-3. [6]Is 6:6-7. [7]Jerome *Letters* 263*
(LCL); Cetedoc 0620, 54.54.17.484.18; cf. NPNF 2 6:108. [8]Mk
12:43; Lk 21:3-4. [9]NPNF 1 10:324*; TLG 2062.152, 58.523.22-30.
The mighty who give much respond less faithfully than do the poor
who give all. [10]Lk 19:8. [11]Mk 12:42. [12]Cf. Mt 10:42. [13]Cetedoc
0283, 40.111.3.5; NPNF 1 8:547. The poor who give their all share
the kingdom with the rich who give only a part. [14]Cf. Eph 6:7.
[15]Cetedoc 1008, 104.182.3.42; FC 47:470*. If one has nothing but a
good will, that alone is sufficient.

contributed two copper coins to the temple was preferred to the large contributions of those who were rich by the One who weighs what is within our hearts.[16] HOMILIES ON THE GOSPELS 2.25.[17]

### 12:44a *They All Contributed out of Their Abundance*

**WHAT THE MISER LACKS.** JEROME: There is an old saying that a tightwad lacks as much what he has as what he has not. One may have a whole world of wealth, another not a single scrap. Let each one live "as having nothing and yet possessing all."[18] LETTER 53, TO PAULINUS 11.[19]

**TRAVELING STEP BY STEP.** EVAGRIUS: It is better to begin from one's feeble state and end up strong, to progress from small things to larger, than to set your heart from the very first on the perfect way of life, then only to abandon it later—or keep to it solely out of habit, because of what others will think—in which case all this labor will be in vain. It is the same with people who travel: if they tire themselves out on the very first day by rushing along, they will end up wasting many days as a result of sickness. But if they start out walking at a gentle pace until they have gotten accustomed to walking, in the end they will not get tired, even though they walk great distances. Likewise anyone who wishes to embark on the labors of the virtuous life should train himself gently, until he gradually reaches the full extent of his abilities. Do not be perplexed by the many paths walked by our fathers of old, each different from the other. Do not overzealously try to imitate them all—this would only upset your way of life. Rather, choose a way of life that suits your feeble state; travel on that, and you will live, for your Lord is merciful and he will receive you, not because of your achievements, but because of your inten-

tion, just as he received the destitute woman's gift.[20] ADMONITION ON PRAYER.[21]

### 12:44b *She Out of Her Poverty*

**INVEST WITH THE LORD WHAT HE HAS GIVEN.** PAULINUS OF NOLA: We have been entrusted with the administration and use of temporal wealth for the common good, not with the everlasting ownership of private property. If you accept the fact that ownership on earth is only for a time, you can earn eternal possessions in heaven. Call to mind the widow who forgot herself in her concern for the poor and, thinking only of the life to come, gave away all her means of subsistence, as the judge himself bears witness. Others, he says, have given of their superfluous wealth; but she, possessed of only two small coins and more needy perhaps than many of the poor—though in spiritual riches she surpassed all the wealthy—she thought only of the world to come, and had such a longing for heavenly treasure that she gave away, all at once, whatever she had that was derived from the earth and destined to return there. Let us then invest with the Lord what he has given us, for we have nothing that does not come from him: we are dependent upon him for our very existence. . . . So let us give back to the Lord the gifts he has given us. Let us give to him who receives in the person of every poor man or woman. Let us give gladly, I say, and great joy will be ours when we receive his promised reward. LETTERS 34, 2-4.[22]

---

[16]Mk 12:42-44; Lk 2:1-4. [17]Cetedoc 1367, 2.25.121; HOG 2:259*. Some perform good deeds of less importance yet with purer intent and hence receive greater divine approval. [18]2 Cor 6:10. [19]Cetedoc 0620, 53.54.11.464.17; NPNF 2 6:102**. [20]Cf. 2 Chron 6:14; 30:9; Neh 1:5; Ps 25:10; Dan 9:4; Jas 5:11. [21]CS 101:66-67*. [22]Cetedoc 0202, 29.74.2.305.3; JF B 132-33; 2-4; CSEL 29:305-6.

**BEYOND WHAT MOSES PRESCRIBED.** HEGEMO-
NIUS: In that offering truly something is exhibited that goes beyond what Moses prescribed
on the subject of the receipt of moneys. For he
received gifts from those who had; but Jesus
receives them even from those who have not.
THE DISPUTATION WITH MANES 42.[23]

**GENEROSITY SEEN IN THE LIGHT OF INTEN-
TION.** CHRYSOSTOM: When the widow put into
the collection box only two small coins,[24] the
master did not give her a recompense worth

only two coins. Why was that? Because he paid
no attention to the amount of the money. What
he did heed was the wealth of her soul. If you
calculate by the value of her money, her poverty
is great. If you bring her intention into the
light, you will see that her store of generosity
defies description. ON THE INCOMPREHENSI-
BLE NATURE OF GOD 6.12.[25]

---

[23]PG 10:1498; ANF 6:217 (Pseudo-Archelaus). The widow transcended the requirements of Mosaic law.   [24]Cf. Mk 12:41-44; Lk
2:1-4.   [25]TLG 2062.014, 48.750.49-50; FC 72:168-69.

---

## 13:1-8 THE SIGNS OF THE PAROUSIA

[1]*And as he came out of the temple, one of his disciples said to him, "Look, Teacher, what wonderful stones and what wonderful buildings!"* [2]*And Jesus said to him, "Do you see these great
buildings? There will not be left here one stone upon another, that will not be thrown down."*

[3]*And as he sat on the Mount of Olives opposite the temple, Peter and James and John and
Andrew asked him privately,* [4]*"Tell us, when will this be, and what will be the sign when these
things are all to be accomplished?"* [5]*And Jesus began to say to them, "Take heed that no one
leads you astray.* [6]*Many will come in my name, saying, 'I am he!' and they will lead many
astray.* [7]*And when you hear of wars and rumors of wars, do not be alarmed; this must take
place, but the end is not yet.* [8]*For nation will rise against nation, and kingdom against kingdom; there will be earthquakes in various places, there will be famines; this is but the beginning of the birth pangs."*

---

**OVERVIEW:** The death of trees, contaminated
air and the pollution of the fruits of the
earth—all these are signs of the final judgment
(ORIGEN). The Gospels offer a cohesive account of history when they are compared text
by text to seek the sense of the whole. Not

merely wars between nations but also the final
conflict between the kingdom of Christ and Satan will be resolved in the end (AUGUSTINE).
Antichrist falsifies the truth, mimicking the
goodness of Christ (ORIGEN). The ruin of the
edifice of Christian teaching, as of temples and

buildings, does not happen instantly but gradually (ORIGEN). As long as some portions of the temple still remain intact, it would be improper to say that the Antichrist had already come (CYRIL OF JERUSALEM).

## 13:1 What Wonderful Stones and What Wonderful Buildings

**BELIEVER AS TEMPLE.** ORIGEN: The temple was not overthrown all at once, but gradually as time went by. Similarly, every one who welcomes the Word of God into himself is something like a temple. If, after committing sin he does not completely fall away from the Word of God, but still partially preserves in himself traces of faith and accountability to God's commands, he is a temple partly destroyed, partly standing. But he who after sinning has no care for himself but is always prone to depart from faith and from life according to the gospel, till he completely departs from the living God, he is a temple in which no stone of doctrine is left upon any stone and not thrown down. COMMENTARY ON MATTHEW 29.[1]

## 13:2 Not One Stone upon Another

**THE TEMPLE IN RUINS.** CYRIL OF JERUSALEM: Antichrist[2] will come at such a time as there shall not be left of the temple of the Jews "one stone upon another," to quote the sentence pronounced by the Savior.[3] For it is not until all the stones are overthrown, whether by the decay of age, or through being pulled down for building material or in consequence of this or that other happening, and I do not mean merely the stones of the outer walls, but the floor of the inner temple where the cherubim were,[4] that Antichrist will come "with all signs and lying wonders"[5] treating all the idols with

disdain. CATECHETICAL LECTURES 15.15.[6]

## 13:3-4 They Asked Him Privately, "Tell Us, When Will This Be?"

**READING THE SIGNS.** AUGUSTINE: There is no discrepancy in the Gospels as to facts of the end time,[7] although one may supply details which another may pass over or describe differently. Rather, they supplement each other when compared, and thus give direction to the mind of the reader.[8] LETTER 199, TO HESYCHIUS 25.[9]

## 13:6 Many Will Come in My Name, Saying, "I Am He!"

**EXPERTS AT IMPERSONATION.** ORIGEN: Christ is truth. Antichrist falsifies truth. Christ is wisdom. Antichrist deftly simulates wisdom. All genuine excellences have a correspondence with Christ. All pretended virtues correspond with Antichrist. For each variety of good which Christ embodies in himself to build up the faithful, the demonic will find a way of mimicking in appearance to deceive the faithful.[10] COMMENTARY ON MATTHEW 32.[11]

---

[1]PG 13:1640; AEG 5:113-14*. [2]Cf. 1 Jn 2:18-22; 4:3; 2 Jn 7. [3]Mk 13:2. [4]Cf. 1 Kings 6:27; 8:6. [5]2 Thess 2:9; cf. Mt 24:24; Mk 13:22. [6]TLG 2110.003, 15.15.12-9; LCC 4:159. This passage is made more interesting and historically weighty in the light of the fact that it was written in Jerusalem and taught in catechetical lectures at the site of the present Church of the Holy Sepulchre in the mid-fourth century, three centuries before the Muslim conquest and seven centuries before the Crusaders. It may indicate that the outer walls were already pulled down but the floor of the inner temple was still intact. One can assume that Cyril was familiar with the site as it appeared in his day. Since in his view the antichrist had not yet come, he understood himself in between the times of the basic destruction of the temple in A.D. 70 and the final destruction of the temple. [7]Augustine is asking how the reader is to reason about apparently conflicting accounts of last things. [8]Cf. Mt 24:3-8; Mk 13:3-8; Lk 21:7-11. [9]Cetedoc 0262, 199.57.9.265.15; FC 30:376**. [10]Cf. Mt 24:24; Mk 13:22. [11]PG 13:1644-45; AEG 5:117-18*.

**THE COMMON CONDITION OF NATIONS.**
AUGUSTINE: As to wars, when has the earth
not been scourged by them at different periods
and places? To pass over remote history, when
the barbarians were everywhere invading
Roman provinces in the reign of Gallienus,[12]
how many of our brothers who were then alive
do we think could have believed that the end
was near, since this happened long after the
ascension of the Lord! Thus, we do not know
what the nature of those signs will be when the
end is really near at hand, if these present ones
have not been so foretold that they should at
least be understood in the church. Certainly,
there are two nations and two kingdoms,
namely, one of Christ, the other of the devil.
LETTER 199, TO HESYCHIUS 35.[13]

### 13:8 There Will Be Earthquakes, There Will Be Famines

**ECOLOGICAL CRISIS.** ORIGEN: Just as bodies
become sick before their death if they do not
suffer violence from without, and in all cases
the way of separation of soul from body comes
through weakness, so it happens with the
whole course of the world creation. When the
creation begins to decay, having as it has both
beginning and end, it must grow weak before
its dissolution. At this point the earth may be
frequently shaken with earthquakes. The air
having received some diseased contagion may
become overrun with pestilence.[14] Moreover
the vital energies of the earth itself may suddenly fail and strangle its fruits. These destruc-
tive forces may pollute the regenerative
capacity of all trees. COMMENTARY ON MAT-
THEW 34.[15]

---

[12]Emperor from 260 to 268. [13]Cetedoc 0262, 199.57.10.274.8; FC
30:384. [14]Cf. Lk 21:10-11. [15]PG 13:1649; AEG 5:122*.

---

## 13:9-23 THE DESOLATING SACRILEGE

[9]"But take heed to yourselves; for they will deliver you up to councils; and you will be
beaten in synagogues; and you will stand before governors and kings for my sake, to bear testimony before them. [10]And the gospel must first be preached to all nations. [11]And when they
bring you to trial and deliver you up, do not be anxious beforehand what you are to say; but
say whatever is given you in that hour, for it is not you who speak, but the Holy Spirit. [12]And
brother will deliver up brother to death, and the father his child, and children will rise against
parents and have them put to death; [13]and you will be hated by all for my name's sake. But he
who endures to the end will be saved."

[14]"But when you see the desolating sacrilege set up where it ought not to be (let the reader
understand), then let those who are in Judea flee to the mountains; [15]let him who is on the
housetop not go down, nor enter his house, to take anything away; [16]and let him who is in the

*field not turn back to take his mantle.* [17]*And alas for those who are with child and for those who give suck in those days!* [18]*Pray that it may not happen in winter.* [19]*For in those days there will be such tribulation as has not been from the beginning of the creation which God created until now, and never will be.* [20]*And if the Lord had not shortened the days, no human being would be saved; but for the sake of the elect, whom he chose, he shortened the days.* [21]*And then if any one says to you, 'Look, here is the Christ!' or 'Look, there he is!' do not believe it.* [22]*False Christs and false prophets will arise and show signs and wonders, to lead astray, if possible, the elect.* [23]*But take heed; I have told you all things beforehand."*

**OVERVIEW:** Far from being nothingness, the final end for the faithful is the most complete conceivable fullness of being (HILARY OF POITIERS). Origen argued that the consummation would not occur until crucial prophecies are fulfilled and not before the gospel is preached to the whole world. Since there are still a number of known nations to whom the gospel had not yet been preached, it could not be argued that the end has yet come. Hippolytus thought that the reference to flight in winter was not merely to a literal winter but to an unexpectedly harsh spiritual challenge. On that final day, however, those lacking faith will not be saved, even if they seem to be abiding within the faithful community and its sacraments (CYPRIAN, AUGUSTINE). The Antichrist will personify many seemingly plausible teachings (ORIGEN).

### 13:10 The Gospel Must First Be Preached to All Nations

**WHETHER THIS HAS ALREADY OCCURRED.** ORIGEN: It is evident that the gospel of the kingdom has not yet been preached in all the world. It is not reported to have been preached among all the Ethiopians, especially among those beyond the river,[1] nor among the Serae,[2] nor in the East. What are we to say of the Britons, or of the Germans along the ocean,[3] or of the barbarians, Dacians,[4] Samaritans and Scythians,[5] the greatest part of whom have not yet[6] heard the word of the gospel, but who will certainly hear it by the time of the end? If any one is minded to say rashly that the gospel of the kingdom has already been preached in all the world as a testimony to all nations, he will consequently be constrained to say that the end has already come![7] That would be a most rash statement indicating a lack of understanding. COMMENTARY ON MATTHEW 39.[8]

### 13:13 He Who Endures to the End

**PROMISE OF BLESSEDNESS.** HILARY OF POITIERS: Therefore the Lord exhorts us to wait with patient and reverent faith until the end comes, for "Blessed is he that endures to the end."[9] It is neither a blessed nothingness that awaits us, nor is nonexistence the fruit, nor annihilation the appointed reward of faith. Rather the end is the final attainment of the promised blessedness. They are blessed who endure until the goal of perfect happiness is reached, when the expectation of faith reaches toward complete fulfill-

---

[1]Nile. [2]Beyond Parthia. [3]North Sea. [4]Transylvania on the Danube. [5]Both Scythians and Samaritans were in the region now known as Bulgaria and northwest of the Black Sea. [6]Ca. A.D. 230. [7]Origen here anticipates and meets the arguments that would later become known as "realized eschatology." [8]PG 13:1655; AEG 5:126-27*. [9]Mt 10:22; 24:13; Mk 13:13; Lk 21:19.

ment. Their end is to abide with unbroken rest in that condition toward which they are presently pressing.[10] On the Trinity 11.28.[11]

### 13:14a Set Up Where It Ought Not Be

THE PLACE OF SACRILEGE. ORIGEN: By the holy place is to be understood every saying of divine Scripture spoken by the prophets from Moses onwards, and by the Evangelists and apostles. In this holy place of all the Scriptures, Antichrist, the false Word, has often stood. This is the abomination of desolation.[12] COMMENTARY ON MATTHEW 42.[13]

### 13:14b Let Those Who Are in Judea Flee to the Mountains

WHEN AND WHERE TO FLEE. ORIGEN: He who flees ought to know the place to which he ought to flee, and also to pray that he may not flee in the time which is opposed to flight. COMMENTARY ON MATTHEW 41.[14]

### 13:15 Let Him Who Is on the Housetop Not Go Down, nor Enter His House, to Take Anything Away

WHAT TOP OF WHAT HOUSE? ORIGEN: The housetop in this case suggests a lofty and exalted mind. We are commanded not to descend down from this housetop. Let one who flees in persecution not fail to go up to this housetop, but also from this housetop let him not come down to scramble for the things down below, in his house. HOMILIES ON JEREMIAH 12.13 (18).[15]

### 13:17 Alas for Those Who Give Suck in Those Days!

PROVIDING FOR WHAT ONE HAS ACQUIRED.

AUGUSTINE: This is said figuratively, distinguishing those with child from those who give suck. Those who are with child are the souls whose hope is in the world. Those who have acquired what they hoped for are "those who give suck." Suppose someone yearns to buy a country estate. She is with child, for her object is not gained as yet. The womb swells in hope. She buys it. When she has given birth, she now gives suck to what she has bought. Woe to those who put their hope in the world. Woe also to those who cling to those things which they brought forth through hope in the world. ON THE PSALMS 96.14.[16]

### 13:18 Pray That It May Not Happen in Winter

WHEN SLUGGISH IN RIGHTEOUSNESS. HIPPOLYTUS: When the elect pray that their flight not be on the Sabbath or in the winter, this means that God asks us not to let ourselves be surprised by the things which meet us unexpectedly when we might be sluggish in righteousness (neglecting the Sabbath or caught in worldly preoccupations). AGAINST GAIUS 5.[17]

KEEP ON PRAYING. EPHREM THE SYRIAN: Winter is without fruit and sabbath without labor.[18] Do not let it be you who might be led away captive under such circumstances—when you have neither fruit nor work. Pray that captivity does not come either of some external necessity, such as the winter, or during a time

---

[10]Cf. 2 Thess 1:5-7. [11]Cetedoc 0433, 62A.11.28.11; NPNF 2 9:211**. [12]Cf. Dan 9:27; 11:31; 12:11; 1 Macc 1:54; Mt 24:15. [13]PG 13:1660; AEG 5:131*. [14]PG 13:1664; AEG 5:135*. [15]TLG 2042.021, 19.13.22-26; AEG 5:133. [16]Cetedoc 0283, 39.95.14.7; NPNF 1 8:474*. Idolatry toward worldly goods may come in the form of expecting fulfillment in the worldly or in living with the strains of the achievement of what had been hoped for in the worldly. [17]CSCO 101:17; AEG 5:138*. [18]Cf. Mt 24:20, which has "sabbath."

of inattentiveness such as the sabbath. This means that neither the constraint of others nor the relaxation of your own will should be the occasion to take you away from the work of the Lord your God.... It is true that distress will come and that you will have to flee. But keep on praying lest this calamity come upon you in the winter, or surprise you on the sabbath when you are resting.... Winter is the time of repose from all the work of the summer, just as the sabbath is the time of repose, the seventh day, when work is not done. COMMENTARY ON TATIAN'S DIATESSARON.[19]

### 13:19 For in Those Days There Will Be Such Tribulation As Has Not Been from the Beginning

**THE LAST TRIBULATION.** GREGORY THE GREAT: Let us keep in mind that these present afflictions are as far below the last tribulations, as is the person of the herald below the majesty of the judge he precedes. Reflect with all your mind upon this day, my dearest ones. Remedy what is now defective in your present life. Amend your ways. Overcome evil temptations by standing firm against them. Repent with tears of the sins you have committed. For the more you make ready against the severity of his justice by serving him in fear, the more serenely shall you behold the coming of that eternal judge, who with the Father and the Holy Spirit lives and reigns, world without end. Amen. ON THE GOSPEL, HOMILY 1.[20]

### 13:22a False Christs Will Lead Astray, If Possible, the Elect

**THE PRETENSE OF TRUTH.** ORIGEN: While Antichrist is generically one, there may be many species of him. It is as if one would say that falsehood is generically one, but according to the differences of false doctrines there are found many specific falsehoods.... "If possible" is a hyperbole. For he did not suggest or indicate that even the elect are to be thrown into error, but wishes to show that often the words of the heretics are exceedingly plausible and have power to move even those who hear them wisely. Every word professing to be truth while not the truth, whether among gentiles or barbarians, is in a sense Antichrist, seeking to mislead as though the truth, and to separate from the One who said, "I am the truth."[21] COMMENTARY ON MATTHEW 46.[22]

### 13:22b I Have Told You All Things Beforehand

**BEWARE OF THE ADVERSARY.** CYPRIAN: The more the Adversary rages, the more error deceives. Senselessness makes its pretenses, envy inflames, covetousness makes blind, impiety depraves, pride puffs up, discord exasperates, anger hurries headlong.... Let the brethren beware of these things, for "I have told you all things beforehand."[23] Avoid such people. Drive them away from your side and your ears, as if their mischievous conversation were the contagion of death.... It is an enemy of the altar, a rebel against Christ's sacrifice, who offers the faithful faithlessness, who is a disobedient servant, an impious son, a hostile brother, who despises bishops, who forsakes the elders, who dares to set up another altar to make another prayer with prohibited words, to profane the truth of the Lord's offering. TREATISES, ON THE UNITY OF THE CHURCH 16-17.[24]

---

[19]CSCO 137:261-262; JSSS 2:277-78**. [20]Cetedoc 1711, 1.1.6.33; SSGF 1:20*; Migne PL 76, 1077-81, Homily 1. [21]Jn 14:6. [22]PG 13:1668-9; AEG 5:143-44*. [23]Mt 24:25; Mk 13:22. [24]Cetedoc 0041, 16.410; ANF 5:426-27*. Avoid the purveyors of error.

## 13:24-27 THE PAROUSIA OF THE SON OF MAN

[24]*"But in those days, after that tribulation, the sun will be darkened, and the moon will not give its light,* [25]*and the stars will be falling from heaven, and the powers in the heavens will be shaken.* [26]*And then they will see the Son of man coming in clouds with great power and glory.* [27]*And then he will send out the angels, and gather his elect from the four winds, from the ends of the earth to the ends of heaven."*

**OVERVIEW:** The various inspired texts on the final judgment must be read for their meaning rather than for a specific chronology (VICTORINUS OF PETOVIUM). The final coming of light will overwhelm the light of the stars (BEDE). When the pillars of heaven shake, everything in creation becomes vulnerable (GREGORY THAUMATURGUS, BEDE). Even the most faithful will be shaken in the tribulation (AMBROSE). Even amid this calamity, God is restoring the brokenness of humanity, broken in Adam's fall, by gathering from the whole world the new humanity in Christ. If we resist his first coming, we will tremble at his second (AUGUSTINE). The coming Son of Man will judge the nations and fulfill the longings of the saints (TERTULLIAN). He will come with power in his own body and in the risen bodies of the faithful (AUGUSTINE).

### 13:24a After That Tribulation

**No Specific Chronology.** VICTORINUS OF PETOVIUM: We must not inordinately fix upon the chronology of what is said in Scripture, because frequently the Holy Spirit,[1] having spoken of the end of the last times, then returns again to address a previous time, and fills up what had before been left unsaid. Nor must we look for a specific chronology in apocalyptic visions,[2] but rather follow the meaning of those things which are prophesied. COMMENTARY ON THE APOCALYPSE 7.[3]

### 13:24b The Moon Will Not Give Its Light

**As Persecution Mounts.** AMBROSE: As in its monthly eclipse, the moon, by reason of the earth coming between it and the sun, disappears from view, so likewise the holy church, when the vices of the flesh stand in the way of the celestial light, can no longer borrow the splendor of its divine light from the sun of Christ.... Also the stars, that is, leaders surrounded by the praise of their fellow Christians, shall fall, as the bitterness of persecution mounts up. COMMENTARY ON LUKE 10.[4]

### 13:25a The Stars Will Be Falling

**The Faithful Shaken.** AUGUSTINE: When impious persecutors rage beyond measure, and when the fortune of this world seems to smile upon them and fear leaves them and they say:

---

[1]In inspiring the sacred text. [2]Cf. Mt 24:36; Mk 13:32. [3]PL 5:331; ANF 7:352*. [4]Cetedoc 0143, 10.358; SSGF 1:4.

"Peace and security," then the stars shall fall from heaven and the powers of heaven shall be moved, when many who seemed to shine brilliantly with grace will yield to the persecutors and will fall, and even the strongest of the faithful will be shaken. LETTER 199, To HESYCHIUS 39.[5]

**WHEN THE TRUE LIGHT MAKES STARS SEEM DARK.** BEDE: The stars at the day of judgment will seem to be dark, not by any failure of their own luster, but in consequence of the increase of the true light throwing them into the shade. EXPOSITION ON THE GOSPEL OF MARK 4.13.24.[6]

### 13:25b *The Powers in the Heavens Will Be Shaken*

**THE COMING OF THE SON.** TERTULLIAN: If you examine this whole passage of Scripture from the inquiry of the disciples down to the parable of the fig tree,[7] you will find that it makes sense at every point in connection with the coming of the Son of Man. He will bring both sorrow and joy. The Son of Man is coming in the midst of both calamities and promises, both the grief of nations and the longing of the saints. He is the common element in both. He who is common to both will end the one by inflicting judgment on the nations, and will commence the other by fulfilling the longings of the saints. AGAINST MARCION 4.39.[8]

**FLIGHT INTO DARKNESS.** GREGORY THAUMATURGUS: The powers above—the angels guarding the universe—will be put into action in that storm and tumult of all things. Powerful men will stop. Laboring women will also stop and flee into the dark places of their houses. ON ECCLESIASTES 12.[9]

**THE PILLARS SHAKE.** BEDE: What wonder is

it, that human beings should be troubled at this judgment, the sight of which makes the very angelic powers tremble? What will the upper parts of the house do when the pillars underneath begin to shake? EXPOSITION ON THE GOSPEL OF MARK 4.13.25.[10]

### 13:26 *Son of Man Coming in the Clouds*

**WITH GREAT MAJESTY.** AUGUSTINE: This could be taken in two ways: one, that he will come in the church as in a cloud, as he continues to come now according to his word: "Hereafter you shall see the Son of man sitting on the right hand of the power of God, and coming in the clouds of heaven."[11] He comes with great power and majesty because his greater power and majesty will appear in the saints to whom he will give great power, so that they may not be overcome by such persecution. The other way in which he will come will be in his body in which he sits at the right hand of the Father,[12] in which, also, he died and rose again and ascended into heaven. LETTER 199, To HESYCHIUS 41.[13]

**TREMBLING AT HIS SECOND COMING.** AUGUSTINE: In his last advent he will come in the clouds to judge the quick and the dead,[14] just as he preached of clouds in his first voice which sounded forth in the gospel: "They will see the Son of man coming in clouds with great power

---

[5]Cetedoc 0262, 199.57.11.278.7; FC 30:388. [6]Cetedoc 1355, 4.13.211; CCL 120:600; *GMI* 338.[7]Mk 13:3-31. [8]AEG 5:147-48**; Cetedoc 0014, 4.556.23; cf. ANF 3:416. The coming of the Son of Man stands at the juncture of historical catastrophe and intense joy, judging the nations and fulfilling the longings of the saints. [9]TLG 2063.006, 1016.34-39; Gregory Thaumaturgus, *Gregory's Ecclesiastes*, ed. J. Jarick (Atlanta, Ga.: Scholars Press, 1990), p. 291*. [10]Cetedoc 1355, 4.13.211; *GMI* 338*. [11]Mt 26:64. [12]Mk 16:19; Rom 8:34; Col 3:1. [13]Cetedoc 0262, 199.57.11.279.15; FC 30:389. [14]Cf. Acts 10:42; 2 Tim 4:1; 1 Pet 4:5.

and glory."[15] What is "then"? Will not the Lord come again in later times, when all the peoples of the earth shall lament? He came first in preaching, and filled the whole wide world. Let us not resist his first coming, that we may not tremble at his second. ON THE PSALMS 96.14.[16]

### 13:27 He Will Gather His Elect from the Four Winds

THE GATHERING OF ALL THE ELECT FROM THE WHOLE WORLD. AUGUSTINE: That he will gather his elect from the four winds means from the whole world.[17] For Adam himself, as I have shown, signifies in Greek the whole world, with the four letters (A, D, A, M). As the Greeks think of these matters, the four quarters of the world have these initial letters, Anatole (east), Dysis (west), Arktos (north), and Mesembria (south). Adam after the fall has been scattered over the whole world.[18] He was

in one place, but fell, and as if crushed in tiny pieces, his progeny filled the whole world. But the mercy of God is gathering together the fragments from every side and is forging them together by the fire of love, and making one what was pulverized. That incomparable artist knew just how to do this. So let no one despair. This indeed is a great work of art. But reflect upon who the artist is. The very one who made shall restore. The one who formed shall reform. Where finally shall we come to know righteousness and truth? He will gather together his elect with him to the judgment, and the rest will be separated out.[19] ON THE PSALMS 96.15.[20]

---

[15]Mt 24:30; Mk 13:26; Lk 21:27. [16]Cetedoc 0283, 39.95.14.7; NPNF 1 8:474. [17]Cf. Mt 24:31; Mk 13:27. [18]Cf. Gen 3:1-24. [19]Cf. Mt 25:32. [20]Cetedoc 0283, 39.95.15.4; NPNF 1 8:474-75**; cf. Tractate on John 10.12.2; FC 78:223.

---

# 13:28-31 THE LESSON OF THE FIG TREE

[28]"From the fig tree learn its lesson: as soon as its branch becomes tender and puts forth its leaves, you know that summer is near. [29]So also, when you see these things taking place, you know that he is near, at the very gates. [30]Truly, I say to you, this generation will not pass away before all these things take place. [31]Heaven and earth will pass away, but my words will not pass away."

OVERVIEW: Summer is symbolic of endings and gatherings (HIPPOLYTUS). God, knowing the future as if it were present, knows already the whole of history that is yet to be (AMBROSE). Great world conflicts signify for faith the prom-

ised coming of the kingdom of God (TERTULLIAN). The Word of God does not pass away, even if all earthly things pass away (ORIGEN). The passing away or destruction of the old in Scripture points to the passing forward to a fuller expression of the divine glory (Methodius). Nothing is more passing than speech in this world, but nothing is more durable in this world than God's speech (Gregory the Great).

### 13:28 You Know That Summer Is Near

**Sproutings of Summer.** Tertullian: As the sproutings of small trees afford a sign of the approach of summer time, so do the great conflicts of the world point toward the kingdom by preceding it.[1] Both sign and thing signified belong to the same One who orders all. So if conflicts are signs of the kingdom, as sproutings are of summer, then the kingdom also is the creator's, to whom the conflicts are ascribed, which are the signs of the coming kingdom. Against Marcion 4.39.[2]

**The Gathering of Fruit.** Hippolytus: The summer signifies the end of the world, because at that time fruits are gathered up and stored. On Matthew.[3]

### 13:31a Although Heaven and Earth Will Pass Away

**What Is Meant By "Pass Away"?** Methodius: It is usual for the Scriptures to call the change of the world from its present dire condition to a better and more glorious one by the idiom of "destruction." For its earlier form is thereby lost in the change of all things to a state of greater splendor. This is not a contradiction or absurdity. Paul says that it is not the world as such but the "fashion of this world"[4] that passes away. So it is Scripture's habit to call the passing from worse to better as "destruction." Think of a child who passes from a childish stage to amore mature stage. We sometimes express this as an undoing of outmoded pat-

terns. On the Resurrection 9.[5]

### 13:31b My Words Will Not Pass Away

**The Word Will Not Come to Nothing.** Origen: Although heaven and earth, and the things that are in them, may pass away, yet his divine speech regarding each individual thing, whether viewed as parts of a whole or species of a genus, shall by no means pass away.[6] The utterances of God the Word, who was in the beginning with God, will not come to nothing. Against Celsus 5.22.[7]

**Durability of Matter and Speech.** Gregory the Great: Nothing of this world is more durable than the heavens and the earth, and nothing in the order of nature passes away more quickly than speech. Words, as long as they are incomplete, are not yet words. Once completed they cease utterly to be. In fact they cannot be perfected except by their own passing away. Therefore he says: "Heaven and earth shall pass away, but my words shall not pass." As if he were openly to say: all that seems to you enduring and unchangeable is not enduring and without change in eternity. And everything of mine that seems to pass away is enduring and without change. My speech, that seems to pass away, utters thoughts (*sententiae manentes*) which endure forever. Homilies 1.[8]

**God's Making of Things Future.** Ambrose: For just as he calls the things that are

---

[1]Mt 24:32-33; Mk 13:28-29; Lk 21:29-31. [2]Cetedoc 0014, 4.557.20; AEG 5:156**; cf. ANF 3:417. [3]CA 215; AEG 5:156*; loc. cit. *On Matthew* 13.28. [4]1 Cor 7:31. [5]PG 18:276; ANF 6:366**; cf. AEG 5:161. [6]Cf. Mt 24:35; Mk 13:31; Lk 21:33. [7]TLG 2042.001, 5.22.16-20; cf. ANF 4:553. The divine speech that creates each particular thing will not pass away. [8]Cetedoc 1711, 1.1.4.5; SSGF 1:19*; PL 76, 1077-81, Homily 1.

not as though they were,[9] so he has made things future as though they were. It cannot come to pass that they should not be. Those things that he has directed to be necessarily will be. Therefore he who has made the things that are to be, knows them already in the way in which they are to be. ON THE CHRISTIAN FAITH 5.4.192.[10]

---

[9]Rom 4:17. [10]Cetedoc 0150, 5.16.86; NPNF 2 10:309**. God has a different relation to time than we do. God exists in eternal simultaneity with all times and hence knows the future as now.

---

## 13:32-37 THE NECESSITY OF WATCHFULNESS

[32]*"But of that day or that hour no one knows, not even the angels in heaven, nor the Son, but only the Father.* [33]*Take heed, watch;[a] for you do not know when the time will come.* [34]*It is like a man going on a journey, when he leaves home and puts his servants in charge, each with his work, and commands the doorkeeper to be on the watch.* [35]*Watch therefore, for you do not know when the master of the house will come, in the evening, or at midnight, or at cockcrow, or in the morning,* [36]*lest he come suddenly and find you asleep.* [37]*And what I say to you I say to all: Watch."*

a Other ancient authorities add *and pray*

---

**OVERVIEW:** Augustine's comment on this passage focused upon the perplexing question of the Son's not knowing the final day. When the Son is said not to know the final day, it is not because he is ignorant of it but because he causes it not to be known by them for whom it is not expedient to know it. He does not show it to them, and they will not learn it from him. It would not have been for our good to have known everything that was known to him. He spoke of knowing something by analogy, in the sense of knowing that which was fitting that hearers should know from him. The fullness of time is not yet humanly known as present but only as future. Christ "knew not that day" with no other meaning than that he, by concealing it, caused others not to know it. It is according to a common form of speech that the Son is said not to know what he does not teach; hence he is said not to know what he causes us not to know (AUGUSTINE).

Insofar as he truly assumes and participates in our ordinary humanity, the Son shares our human limitations of not seeing into the future (ATHANASIUS). The not knowing is attributed to the humanity of the incarnate Lord, not to the Godhead (GREGORY OF NAZIANZUS). It is not a defect in the truly human Son of God that he does not know the final hour but that it is not yet the time to speak or within the divine plan to act (HILARY OF POITIERS). Jesus knew the hour of judgment in the nature of his humanity but not from the nature of his humanity (GREGORY THE GREAT). Faith watches for the day of which it remains ignorant and trembles daily for that for which it daily hopes (TERTULLIAN). Watchfulness for final judgment is not occasional but belongs to the continuing response of believers (APOSTOLIC CONSTITUTIONS). If we knew the future, we would easily be tempted to postpone all human seriousness and delay all decision making (ATHANASIUS). The pride that pretends one knows something one does not know is a greater moral danger than awareness of limited knowledge (AUGUSTINE). Since everything is not yet revealed, the text calls us to humility (IRENAEUS).

### 13:32a That Hour No One Knows, Not Even the Son

**IGNORANCE OF THE FUTURE IS OUR ORDINARY HUMAN CONDITION.** ATHANASIUS: When his disciples asked him about the end, he said with precision: Of that day or that hour no one knows, not even he himself[1]—that is, when viewed according to the flesh, because he too, as human, lives within the limits of the human condition. He said this to show that, viewed as an ordinary man, he does not know the future, for ignorance of the future is characteristic of the human condition. Insofar as he is viewed according to his divinity as the Word who is to come, to judge, to be bridegroom, however, he knows when and in what hour he will come.... For as upon becoming human he hungers, thirsts and suffers,[2] along with all human beings, similarly as human he does not see the future. But viewed according to his divinity as the Word and wisdom of the Father, he knows, and there is nothing which he does

not know. FOUR DISCOURSES AGAINST THE ARIANS 3.46.[3]

**WHETHER THE SON IS DEFICIENT IN KNOWLEDGE.** HILARY OF POITIERS: It is sometimes turned into a reproach against the only begotten God that he did not know the day and the hour. It is said that, though God, born of God, he is not in the perfection of divine nature, since he is subjected to the limitation of ignorance, namely, to an external force stronger than himself, triumphing, as it were, over his weakness. The heretics in their frenzy would try to drive us to this blasphemous interpretation: that he is thus captive to this external limitation, which makes such a confession inevitable. The words are those of the Lord himself. What could be more unholy, we ask, than to corrupt his express assertion by our attempt to explain it away? But, before we investigate the meaning and occasion of these words, let us first appeal to the judgment of common sense. Is it credible, that he, who stands to all things as the author[4] of their present and future, should not know all things? ... All that is derives from God alone its origin, and has in him alone the efficient cause of its present state and future development. Can anything be beyond the reach of his nature, through which is effected, and in which is contained, all that is and shall be? Jesus Christ knows the thoughts of the mind, as it is now, stirred by present motives, and as it will be tomorrow, aroused by the impulse of future desires.... Whenever God says that he does not know, he professes ignorance indeed, but is not under the defect of ignorance. It is not because of the infirmity of ignorance that he does not know, but

---

[1]Cf. Mt 24:36; Mk 13:32. [2]Cf. Mt 4:2; Mk 8:31; Lk 24:46; Jn 19:28. [3]NPNF 2 4:419*; TLG 2035.042, 26.420.29-38, 421.1-5. The God-man according to his humanity shares with us our ordinary human condition of ignorance of the future. [4]Cf. Heb 12:2.

because it is not yet the time to speak, or in the divine plan to act.... This knowledge is not, therefore, a change from ignorance, but the coming of a fullness of time. He waits still to know, but we cannot suppose that he does not know. Therefore his not knowing what he knows, and his knowing what he does not know, is nothing else than a divine economy in word and deed. ON THE TRINITY 9.58-62.[5]

**WHETHER THE SON KNOWS ALL THAT THE FATHER KNOWS.** AUGUSTINE: According to "the form of God"[6] everything that the Father has belongs to the Son: for "All things that are mine are yours, and yours are mine."[7] According to the form of a slave,[8] however, his teaching is not his own, but of the One who sent him. Hence "Of that day or hour no one knows, neither the angels in heaven, nor the Son, but the Father only."[9] He is ignorant of this in the special sense of making others ignorant. He did not "know it" in their presence in such a way as to be prepared to reveal it to them at that time. Recall that in a similar way it was said to Abraham: "Now I know that you fear God,"[10] in the sense that now I am taking you through a continuing journey to know yourself, because Abraham came to know himself only after he had been tried in adversity.... Jesus was "ignorant" in this sense, so to speak, among his disciples, of that which they were not yet able to know from him. He only said that which was seasonally fitting for them to know. Among those with mature wisdom he knew in a different way than among babes.[11] ON THE TRINITY 1.12.23.[12]

**FIGURATIVE SPEECH CONCERNING WHAT THE SON DOES NOT WILL TO KNOW.** AUGUSTINE: I am by no means of the opinion that a figurative mode of expression can be rightly termed a

falsehood. For it is no falsehood to call a day joyous because it makes people joyous. A lupine seed is not sad because it lengthens the face of the eater because of its bitter taste. So also we say that God "knows" something when he makes his hearers know it (an instance quoted by yourself in the words of God to Abraham, "Now I know that you fear God"[13]). These are by no means false statements, as you yourself readily see. Accordingly, the blessed Hilary threw light on an obscure point by this kind of figurative expression, showing how we ought to understand the words that "he did not know the day,"[14] with no other meaning than this: In proportion as he had made others ignorant by concealing his meaning, he spoke of it figuratively as his own lack of knowledge. So by concealing it, he so to speak caused others not to know it. He did not by this explanation condone lying, but he proved that it was not lying to use the common figures, including metaphors, as a form of speech available to all, a mode of expression entirely familiar to all in daily conversation. Would anyone call it a lie to say that vines are jeweled with buds, or that a grainfield waves, or that a young man is in the flower of his youth, because he sees in these objects neither waves nor precious stones, nor grass, nor trees to which these expressions would literally apply? LETTER 180, TO OCEANUS 3.[15]

---

[5]Cetedoc 0433, 62A.9.58.4; NPNF 2 9:175-77**. The hour referred to is the fullness of time, which is not yet known as present but is known as future. It is not a defect in the Son of God that he does not know, but it is not yet the time to speak. [6]Cf. Phil 2:6. [7]Jn 17:10. [8]Cf. Phil 2:7. [9]Mt 24:36; Mk 13:32. [10]Cf. Gen 22:12. [11]Cf. 1 Cor 3:1. [12]Cetedoc 0329, 50.1.11.31; FC 45:34-35**. [13]Gen 22:12. [14]Cf. Mt 24:36; Mk 13:32. [15]Cetedoc 0262, 180.44.3.698.26; NPNF 1:547-48**; cf. FC 30:119. This is a true statement figuratively understood, for Christ knew not that day with no other meaning than that he, by concealing it, caused others not to know it.

**THE TIME NOT DISCLOSED TO FLESH.** AUGUSTINE: No one should arrogate to oneself the knowledge of that time by any computation of years. For if that day is to come after seven thousand years, everyone could learn its advent simply by adding up years. What comes then of the Son's even "not knowing" this? This is said with this meaning, that his hearers do not learn this from the Son, not that he by himself does not know it. It is to be understood according to that form of speech by which "The Lord your God tries you that he may know,"[16] which means, that he may make you know. Again, the phrase "arise, O Lord"[17] means make us arise. Thus when the Son is said not to know this day, it is not because he is ignorant of it, but because he causes those to know it not for whom it is not yet expedient to know it, for he does not show it to them. ON THE PSALMS 6.1.[18]

### 13:32b Only the Father

**WHETHER EVERYTHING IS ALREADY REVEALED.** IRENAEUS: The gnostics presumptuously assume acquaintance with the unspeakable mysteries of God. Remember that even the Lord, the very Son of God, allowed that the Father alone knows the very day and hour of judgment.... If then the Son was not ashamed to ascribe the knowledge of that day to the Father only, but declared what was true regarding the matter, neither let us be ashamed to reserve for God those enigmatic questions which come our way. AGAINST HERESIES 2.28.6.[19]

**THE ALL-KNOWING GOD.** GREGORY OF NAZIANZUS: The last day and hour no one knows, not even the Son himself, but the Father.[20] Yet how can the source of wisdom be ignorant of anything—that is, wisdom who made the world, who perfects all, who remodels all, who is the limit of all things that were made, who knows the things of God and the spirit of a person, knowing the things that lie deep within?[21] For what can be more perfect than this knowledge? How then can you say that all things before that hour he knows accurately, and all things that are to happen about the time of the end, but of the hour itself he is ignorant? For such a thing would be like a riddle. It is as if one were to say that he knew accurately all that was in front of the wall, but did not know the wall itself. Or that, knowing the end of the day, he did not know the beginning of the night. Yet knowledge of the one necessarily implies the other. Thus everyone must see that the Son knows as God, and knows not as man (if we may for the purposes of argument distinguish that which is discerned by sight from that which is discerned by thought alone). For the absolute and unconditioned use of the name "the Son" in this passage, without the addition of whose Son,[22] leads us to conclude: We are to understand the ignorance in the most reverent sense, by attributing it to his human nature, and not to the Godhead. ORATION 30, ON THE SON, SECOND ORATION 15.[23]

**NOT FOR OUR GOOD TO KNOW ALL.** AUGUSTINE: It was not part of his office as our master that through him the day should become known to us.[24] It remains true that the Father knows nothing that the Son does not know, since his Son, the Word, is his wisdom, and his

---

[16]Deut 13:3. [17]Ps 3:7. [18]Cetedoc 0283, 38.6.1.9; NPNF 1 8:15**. When the Son is said not to know this day, it is not because he is ignorant of it but because he does not disclose its time to those for whom this knowledge would not be helpful. [19]AHR 1:355; ANF 1:401*. The text calls us to humility. [20]Mt 24:36; Mk 13:32. [21]1 Cor 2:2. [22]Whether the reference is to the son of Mary or Son of God. [23]TLG 2022.010, 15.1-17; NPNF 2 7:315**. [24]Augustine is asking whether it would have been for our good to have known everything that was known to God.

wisdom is to know. But it was not for our good to know everything which was known to him who came to teach us. He surely did not come to teach us that which it was not good for us to know. As master he both taught some things and left other things untaught. He knew both how to teach us what was good for us to know, and not to teach us what was not for our good to know. It is according to this common form of speech that the Son is said "not to know" what he does not choose to teach. We are in the daily habit of speaking in this way. Accordingly he is said "not to know" what he causes us not to know. ON THE PSALMS 37.1.[25]

**THE SON'S DISCERNMENT OF THE FUTURE.**
GREGORY THE GREAT: When we speak of a glad day, we do not mean that the day itself is glad, but that it makes us glad. So also the Almighty Son says that he does not know the day which he causes not to be known. It is not that he himself does not know it, but that he does not allow it to be known. Only the Father is said to know the future in this same way.[26] The Son, who according to his divinity is of the same essential nature with the Father, has knowledge of that which the angels are ignorant. The only begotten, being incarnate and made for us a perfect man, knew indeed *in* the nature of his incarnate humanity the day and hour of the judgment, but still it was not *from* the nature of his humanity as such that he knew it. What then he knew in his humanity he knew not from it. EPISTLE 41, TO EULOGIUS.[27]

## 13:33a *Take Heed, Watch*

**THE COMING JUDGMENT.** TERTULLIAN: How useless is the advice of those simplistic moralists who teach that after death rewards and punishments fall with lighter weight! That is, if

any judgment at all awaits the soul! Rather it ought to be assumed that judgment will be weightier at the end of life than during it. For nothing is more telling and complete than that which comes at the very end. So no judgment could be more complete than God's. Accordingly, God's judgment will be incomparably radical and comprehensive, because it will be pronounced at the very last, in an eternal irrevocable sentence, both of punishment and of consolation. Then souls will not conveniently dissolve into senselessness, but will return into their own proper bodies. All this occurs once for all, on "that day, too, of which the Father only knows,"[28] in order that a full trial be made of faith, and of faith's concerned sincerity which awaits in trembling expectation, keeping her gaze ever fixed on that day, in her perpetual ignorance of when it will arrive, daily trembling at that for which she yet daily hopes. ON THE SOUL 33.[29]

**DAILY READINESS.** ATHANASIUS: The end of all things is concealed from us. For in the end of all is the end of each, and in the end of each is the end of all [on the last day]. Whereas this time is uncertain and always in prospect, we may advance day by day as if summoned, reaching forward to the things before us and forgetting the things behind.[30] For who, if they knew the day of the end, would not disregard the

---

[25]Cetedoc 0283, 38.36.1.1.5; NPNF 1 8:91**. It is according to a common form of speech that the Son is said not to know what he does not teach; hence he is said not to know what he causes us not to know. [26]Similarly we say the Father alone knows, not so as to imply that it is known only by the Father and not the Son. The eternal Son knows what the eternal Father knows. [27]Cetedoc 1714, 10.21.47; NPNF 2 13:48** (italics added). [28]Mt 24:36; Mk 13:32. [29]Cetedoc 0017, 33.72; ANF 3:215**; cf. AEG 5:164. Faith remains calm in watching for the day of which it remains ignorant and confident even in trembling daily for that for which it daily hopes. [30]Phil 3:13.

interval? But if ignorant, would they not be more ready day by day? It was on this account that the Savior said: "Watch; for you do not know when the time will come."[31] FOUR DISCOURSES AGAINST THE ARIANS 3.49.[32]

### 13:33b You Do Not Know When the Time Will Come

**THE PRETENSE OF KNOWING SOMETHING UNKNOWN.** AUGUSTINE: A person does not go wrong when he knows that he does not know something, but only when he thinks he knows something which he does not know. LETTER 199, TO HESYCHIUS 52.[33]

### 13:35 You Do Not Know When the Master of the House Will Come

**SOBER HEARTS.** PRUDENTIUS:
"Away," he cries, "with dull repose,
The sleep of death and sinful sloth;
With hearts now sober, just and pure,
Keep watch, for I am very near."
A HYMN FOR COCK-CROW.[34]

### 13:37 What I Say to You, I Say to All: Watch

**FORMER GOOD DEEDS UNPROFITABLE.** APOSTOLIC CONSTITUTIONS: Watch therefore, and pray, that you do not sleep unto death.[35] For your former good deeds will not profit you if in the end of your life you go astray from the true faith.[36] CONSTITUTIONS OF THE HOLY APOSTLES 7.2.31.[37]

**HIS SECOND COMING.** AUGUSTINE: The first coming of Christ the Lord, God's Son and our God, was in obscurity. The second will be in sight of the whole world. When he came in obscurity, no one recognized him but his own servants. When he comes openly, he will be known by both the good and the bad. When he came in obscurity, it was to be judged. When he comes openly, it will be to judge. He was silent at his trial, as the prophet foretold. . . . Silent when accused, he will not be silent as judge. Even now he does not keep silent, if there is anyone to listen. But it says he will not keep silent then, because his voice will be acknowledged even by those who despise it. SERMONS 18.1-2.[38]

**COMING SUDDENLY TO THOSE UNPREPARED.** AUGUSTINE: Who are the "all" to whom he says this if not his elect and his beloved, the members of his body which is the church?[39] Therefore, he said this not only to those who then heard him speaking, but also to those who came after them and before us, as well as to us and to those who will come after us until his final coming. Is that day going to encounter only those currently living, or is anyone likely to say that these words are also addressed to the dead, when he says: "Watch, lest he comes suddenly and finds you asleep?"[40] Why, then, does he say to all what concerns only those who will then be living? For that day will come to every single one, when the day comes for him to leave this life, such as it is, to be judged on the last day.[41] For this reason, every Christian ought to watch lest the coming of the Lord find him unprepared. But the last day will find unprepared anyone whom this day will find unprepared.[42] This at least

---

[31]Mt 25:13; Mk 13:33. [32]NPNF 2 4:420-21*; TLG 2035.042, 26.428.14-26. [33]Cetedoc 0262, 199.57.13.289.16; FC 30:398-99*. [34]Cetedoc 1438, 1.5; FC 43:3. [35]Cf. Lk 21:36. [36]Cf. Ezek 18:24; 33:13; 1 Tim 1:18-19. [37]PG 1:1021; ANF 7:471. [38]Cetedoc 0284, 18.41.7; JF B 10; PL 38, 128-29; cf. WSA 3 1:373, Sermon 18.1-2. [39]Col 1:18, 24. [40]Mk 13:35-36. [41]Cf. Jn 12:48. [42]Cf. Mt 25:1-13.

was certainly clear to the apostles. Even if the Lord did not come in their times, while they were still living here in the flesh, yet who would doubt that they watched most carefully and observed what he said to all, lest coming suddenly he might find them unprepared? LETTER 199, TO HESYCHIUS 3.[43]

---

[43]Cetedoc 0262, 199.57.1.246.13; FC 30:359*. We the living are also called to watch for his coming, as did the apostles.

---

## 14:1-9 THE ANOINTING AT BETHANY

[1]*It was now two days before the Passover and the feast of Unleavened Bread. And the chief priests and the scribes were seeking how to arrest him by stealth, and kill him;* [2]*for they said, "Not during the feast, lest there be a tumult of the people."*

[3]*And while he was at Bethany in the house of Simon the leper, as he sat at table, a woman came with an alabaster flask of ointment of pure nard, very costly, and she broke the flask and poured it over his head.* [4]*But there were some who said to themselves indignantly, "Why was the ointment thus wasted?* [5]*For this ointment might have been sold for more than three hundred denarii,[b] and given to the poor." And they reproached her.* [6]*But Jesus said, "Let her alone; why do you trouble her? She has done a beautiful thing to me.* [7]*For you always have the poor with you, and whenever you will, you can do good to them; but you will not always have me.* [8]*She has done what she could; she has anointed my body beforehand for burying.* [9]*And truly, I say to you, wherever the gospel is preached in the whole world, what she has done will be told in memory of her."*

b The denarius was a day's wage for a laborer

---

**OVERVIEW:** This simple, beautiful act of a guileless Judean woman is even now being remembered the world over (CHRYSOSTOM). The woman understood that Jesus was about to die and was anointing him for his burial (BEDE). The broken vessel was a reminder that the destruction of death precedes resurrection to life. The perfume is better released to all the world than sealed up. In baptism believers are anointed with oil by analogy to his anointing (JEROME). The faithful are called nard because they share by faith in this costly, unsullied anointing, which points to the Lord's messianic Sonship. Early exegetes thought it likely that the woman who poured ointment on Jesus' head, as reported in Mark, was the same as she who poured ointment on his feet, as reported in Luke. Jesus was with the church bodily for

---

only a short time, whereas the poor will always be bodily present to welcome our care (BEDE). Those who hypocritically champion the cause of the poor while pilfering the church's funds for the poor choose the part of Judas (ORIGEN). The Passover was the Mosaic type of Jesus' sacrifice as paschal lamb (BEDE).

## 14:1 Before the Passover

**THE PASCHAL LAMB.** BEDE: Having observed up to that point the observances of the old Passover, he brought them to perfection, and he handed over the new sacraments to his disciples to be observed henceforth.[1] . . . Our Lord is the counterpart of the paschal lamb. Five days before he entered upon his suffering, he came to the place of his passion to teach that he was the one Isaiah[2] had predicted. EXPOSITION ON THE GOSPEL OF MARK 2.3.[3]

## 14:3a A Woman Came with an Alabaster Jar of Ointment

**WHICH WOMAN?** BEDE: We should not doubt that this was that same woman, once a sinner, who, as the Evangelist Luke reports, came to our Lord with an alabaster vase of ointment "and, standing behind him at his feet, began to bathe his feet with her tears, and she wiped them with the hair of her head, and kissed his feet and anointed them with ointment."[4] This is the same woman, but there, she bent over and anointed only our Lord's feet, and she did this amid her tears of repentance. Here amid the joy of her righteous action she did not hesitate both to anoint his feet and to stand up to anoint his head also. EXPOSITION ON THE GOSPEL OF MARK 2.4.[5]

## 14:3b Of Pure Nard, Very Costly

**WHY NARD?** JEROME: This woman is outside the temple and carries with her a jar of ointment containing nard, genuine nard, from which she has prepared the ointment.[6] This is why the faithful are called "genuine" or pure nard. The church, gathered from the nations, is offering the Savior the abounding faith of believers. The alabaster jar which had been sealed[7] is broken that all may receive its perfume. HOMILIES OF SAINT JEROME, HOMILY 84.[8]

**THE MEANING OF NARD.** BEDE: It was compounded from spikenard which was pure (that is, untainted and unadulterated with other different kinds), and which was precious, to imply the chastity of perfect faith and action. EXPOSITION ON THE GOSPEL OF MARK 2.4.[9]

**HEAD AND FEET ANOINTED.** BEDE: His head, which Mary anointed, represents the sublimity of his deity. His feet indicate the lowliness of his incarnation.[10] We too anoint his feet when we proclaim with due praise the mystery of the incarnation which he took upon himself. We too anoint his head when we venerate the loftiness of his divinity with a consent fitting to him. EXPOSITION ON THE GOSPEL OF MARK 2.4.[11]

---

[1]Cf. Lk 22:14-20. [2]Is 53. [3]Cetedoc 1367, 2.3.10; HOG 2:24*. Jesus was the paschal lamb sacrificed once for all. [4]Lk 7:37-38; cf. Jn 12:3. [5]Cetedoc 1367, 2.4.9; HOG 2:36-37. [6]Cf. Mt 26:7; Mk 14:3; Lk 7:37. [7]The fulfillment of Hebrew prophecy had until now been sealed. [8]Cetedoc 0594, 10.78; FC 57:189**. [9]Cetedoc 1367, 2.4.102; HOG 2:37. [10]Cf. Jn 12:3. [11]Cetedoc 1367, 2.4.105; HOG 2:37**. Hence, by their praise of the mystery of the incarnation and consent to Christ's lordship, the faithful continue to take part in his anointing.

### 14:3c *She Broke the Jar*

**WITHOUT BREAKING, THE FRAGRANCE IS HELD WITHIN.** JEROME: Just as the grain of wheat, unless it falls into the ground and dies, does not bring forth any fruit,[12] so, also, unless the alabaster jar be broken, we cannot spread its fragrance.[13] HOMILIES OF ST. JEROME, HOMILY 84.[14]

**PROPHETIC TESTIMONY FULFILLED.** BEDE: What is accomplished here is what the bride glorifies in the canticle of love, "While the king was resting [on his couch], my spikenard gave forth its fragrance."[15] Here it is clearly shown that what Mary once did as a type,[16] the entire church and every perfect soul should do always. EXPOSITION ON THE GOSPEL OF MARK 2.4.[17]

### 14:3d *She Poured It over His Head*

**BAPTISMAL ANOINTING ANTICIPATED.** JEROME: This woman has a very special message for you who are about to be baptized. She broke her alabaster jar that Christ may make you "christs," his anointed. Hear what it says in the Canticle of Canticles: "Your name spoken is a spreading perfume, therefore the maidens love you. We will follow you eagerly in the fragrance of your perfume!"[18] HOMILIES OF ST. JEROME, HOMILY 84.[19]

**WE SHARE IN HIS ANOINTING.** BEDE: We anoint our Lord's head when we cherish the glory of his divinity, along with that of his humanity, with the worthy sweetness of faith, hope and charity,[20] [and] when we spread the praise of his name by living uprightly. We anoint our Lord's feet when we renew his poor by a word of consolation, so that they may not lose hope when they are under duress. We wipe

[the feet of] these same ones with our hair when we share some of what is superfluous to us [to alleviate] the wants of the needy.[21] EXPOSITION ON THE GOSPEL OF MARK 2.4.[22]

### 14:4 *Why Wasted?*

**SHARING THE PERFUME WITH THE WHOLE WORLD.** JEROME: To him [Judas], it seemed to be wasting the ointment because the jar is broken, but, for us, it was a great good because the perfume spread throughout the world. Why are you indignant, Judas, because the alabaster jar is broken? God, who made you and all the nations, is blessing us with that precious perfume. You wanted to keep the perfume sealed up so that it would not reach others. HOMILIES OF SAINT JEROME, HOMILY 84.[23]

### 14:5 *It Might Have Been Sold and Given to the Poor*

**IN DEFENSE OF THE POOR.** ORIGEN: The traitor Judas, who in appearance championed the cause of the poor, said with indignation, "This ointment might have been sold for more than three hundred denarii, and the money given to the poor."[24] But in reality he "was a thief, and as he had the money box he used to take what was put into it."[25] If, then, any one in our time who has the money box of the church speaks

---

[12]Cf. Jn 12:24. [13]Mk 14:3. [14]Cetedoc 0594.10.86; FC 57:189. The destruction of death precedes the resurrection to life. [15]Song 1:12. [16]Jn 12:3. [17]Cetedoc 1367, 2.4.129; HOG 2:38. Mary's anointing is anticipatory of the church's abiding praise of his lordship. [18]Song 1:3-4. [19]Cetedoc 0594, 10.50; FC 57:188. The anointing of the believer with oil recalls the Lord's own messianic anointing. [20]Cf. 1 Cor 13:13. [21]Cf. Deut 15:11; Prov 31:9; Lk 14:13; Gal 2:10. [22]Cetedoc 1367, 2.4.118; HOG 2:37-38. [23]Cetedoc 0594, 10.111; FC 57:190*. Those who freely receive the fragrance of grace perceive its value differently than did the miserly betrayer who wanted to save it. [24]Jn 12:5. [25]Jn 12:6.

like Judas as if speaking for the poor, but steals what is placed there, let there be assigned to him the same portion along with Judas. COMMENTARY ON MATTHEW 11.9.[26]

## 14:6 A Beautiful Thing

BETWEEN BEAUTY AND NEED. JEROME: When the apostles[27] pleaded that the ointment was being wasted, they were rebuked by the voice of the Lord. Christ did not need the ointment, nor do martyrs need the light of candles. Yet that woman freely poured out the ointment in honor of Christ, and her heart's devotion was accepted. . . . Hence throughout the whole Eastern Church, even when there are no relics of the martyrs, whenever the gospel is to be read the candles are lighted although the dawn may be reddening the sky, not of course to scatter the darkness, but by way of evidencing our joy. AGAINST VIGILANTIUS 7.[28]

## 14:7 You Always Have the Poor with You, and Whenever You Will, You Can Do Good to Them

HIS VISITATION BRIEF. BEDE: [Jesus] was going to remain bodily with the church for but a brief while, whereas the poor, for whom alms could be provided, were always to be found in it. EXPOSITION ON THE GOSPEL OF MARK 2.4.[29]

## 14:8 Anointed My Body Beforehand for Burying

WHAT SHE UNDERSTOOD. BEDE: As though Judas was asking an innocent question, our Lord simply and gently explained the mystery of what Mary's action meant, namely that he himself was about to die, and that he was to be anointed for his burial with the spices. . . . This is to say clearly, "She will not be able to touch my body once I am dead; she has done what she was able to do; she has anticipated, while I am still alive, the performance of the duty of burying me." EXPOSITION ON THE GOSPEL OF MARK 2.4.[30]

## 14:9 In Memory of Her

WHO REMEMBERS HER? CHRYSOSTOM: The Persians, the Indians, Scythians, Thracians, Samaratians, the race of the Moors and the inhabitants of the British isles celebrate a deed, performed in a private family in Judea by a woman who had been a sinner. THE GOSPEL OF ST. MATTHEW, HOMILY 80.2.[31]

---

[26]ANF 9:438; TLG 2042.030, 11.9.81-89. [27]Cf. Mt 26:8. [28]Cetedoc 0611, 7.361.11; NPNF 2 6:420**. [29]Cetedoc 1367, 2.4.169; HOG 2:39. Jesus could not be bodily always with his disciples, whom he had to die to save. Yet under the continuing conditions of sin in history, the poor will always be there to receive our gifts. [30]Cetedoc 1367, 2.4.156; HOG 2:39. [31]TLG 2062.152, 57.725.53-57; NPNF 1 10:481; GMI 355.

## 14:10-11 THE BETRAYAL BY JUDAS

[10]*Then Judas Iscariot, who was one of the twelve, went to the chief priests in order to betray him to them.* [11]*And when they heard it they were glad, and promised to give him money. And he sought an opportunity to betray him.*

**OVERVIEW:** As Jesus was sold, the salvation of humanity was bought (GREGORY OF NAZIANZUS). Note that the chronology after the betrayal of Judas is able to be tracked almost hourly (DIDASCALIA).

### 14:11a They Promised to Give Him Money

**WHAT WAS SOLD AND WHAT BOUGHT.** GREGORY OF NAZIANZUS: He is sold, and cheap was the price—thirty pieces of silver;[1] yet he buys back the world at the mighty cost of his own blood.[2] A sheep, he is led to the slaughter[3]—yet he shepherds Israel[4] and now the whole world as well.[5] ORATION 29, ON THE SON 20.[6]

### 14:11b He Sought an Opportunity to Betray Him

**THE CHRONOLOGY OF THE PASSION WEEK.** DIDASCALIA: And Judas Iscariot, who was one of us, rose up and went his way to betray him.[7] And Judas came with the scribes and with the priests of the people, and betrayed our Lord Jesus.

Now this was done on the fourth day of the week. And in the night they seized our Lord Jesus. And the next day, which was the fourth of the week, he remained in ward in the house of Caiaphas the high priest. And on the same day the chiefs of the people were assembled and took counsel against him. And on the next day again, which was the fifth of the week, they brought him to Pilate the governor. And he remained again in the ward with Pilate the night after the fifth day of the week. But when it drew on (towards day) on the Friday, they accused him much before Pilate; and they could show nothing that was true, but gave false witness against him. And they asked him of Pilate to be put to death; and they crucified him on the same Friday.

He suffered, then, at the sixth hour on Friday. And these hours wherein our Lord was crucified were reckoned a day. And afterwards, again, there was darkness for three hours; and it was reckoned a night. And again, from the ninth hour until evening, three hours, (reckoned) a day. And afterwards again (there was) the night of the Sabbath of the Passion. DIDASCALIA APOSTOLORUM 21.[8]

---

[1]Cf. Mt 26:15. [2]Cf. 1 Cor 6:20; 1 Pet 1:19. [3]Cf. Acts 8:32; Is 53:7. [4]Cf. Ps 80:1. [5]Cf. Jn 10:11, 16. [6]FGFR 259; TLG 2022.010, 20.18-21. [7]Cf. Mt 26:14; Mk 14:10; Lk 22:4. [8]DA 181-2.

## 14:12-16 PREPARATION FOR THE PASSOVER

[12]*And on the first day of Unleavened Bread, when they sacrificed the passover lamb, his disciples said to him, "Where will you have us go and prepare for you to eat the passover?"* [13]*And he sent two of his disciples, and said to them, "Go into the city, and a man carrying a jar of water will meet you; follow him,* [14]*and wherever he enters, say to the householder, 'The Teacher says, Where is my guest room, where I am to eat the passover with my disciples?'* [15]*And he will show you a large upper room furnished and ready; there prepare for us."* [16]*And the disciples set out and went to the city, and found it as he had told them; and they prepared the passover.*

**OVERVIEW:** For those being baptized into the Lord's passion, Easter is an especially fitting day for baptism. The metaphor of water suggests the anticipation of baptism in the passion narrative (TERTULLIAN).

### 14:12 *When They Sacrificed the Passover Lamb*

**EASTER AND BAPTISM.** TERTULLIAN: The Passover affords a more than usually solemn day for baptism. For that is the day when in effect the Lord's passion, into which we are baptized, was completed. ON BAPTISM 19.[1]

### 14:13 *A Man Carrying a Jar of Water Will Meet You*

**THE SIGN OF WATER.** TERTULLIAN: Nor will it be incongruous to interpret figuratively the fact that, when the Lord was about to celebrate the last Passover, he told the disciples who were sent to make preparation that they would meet a man bearing water.[2] He thus points out the place for celebrating the Passover by the sign of water. ON BAPTISM 19.[3]

---

[1]Cetedoc 0008, 19.1; ANF 3:678*. [2]Cf. Mk 14:13; Lk 22:10. [3]Cetedoc 0008, 19.2; ANF 3:678*; cf. AEG 5:201-2. In this way baptism is figuratively embedded already in the passion story.

## 14:17-21 THE TRAITOR

[17]*And when it was evening he came with the twelve.* [18]*And as they were at table eating, Jesus said, "Truly, I say to you, one of you will betray me, one who is eating with me."* [19]*They began to be sorrowful, and to say to him one after another, "Is it I?"* [20]*He said to them, "It is one of the twelve, one who is dipping bread into the dish with me.* [21]*For the Son of man goes as*

*it is written of him, but woe to that man by whom the Son of man is betrayed! It would have been better for that man if he had not been born."*

**OVERVIEW:** Jesus is portrayed as exceedingly patient in the face of his betrayer (CYPRIAN). Judas was cursed by his own freely willed choice. God did not make a mistake in giving Judas life but brought to judgment the evil that Judas's own will had acquired by his own choice (ORIGEN, JOHN OF DAMASCUS). Origen noted that Jesus' way of confronting his betrayer was subtle, by quoting a psalm on duplicity. The "woe" is addressed also to the devil and to all who with Judas betray Christ. Having been taught to be self-critical, each disciple questioned his own conscience about whether he could have betrayed the Lord. It was for the disciples' own good that Jesus tested their consciences by not pointing out the betrayer directly (ORIGEN).

### 14:18a As They Were at the Table Eating

**JESUS' UNIQUE RELATION WITH HIS BETRAYER.** CYPRIAN: His wonderful patience is seen in the way he dealt with his disciples. He was even able to tolerate Judas to the end with enduring patience. He could eat calmly with his betrayer. He could patiently be aware of his enemy at his own table and not let on. He did not even refuse the kiss of the traitor.[1] THE GOOD OF PATIENCE 6.[2]

### 14:18b One of You Will Betray Me

**CHARACTER TESTED.** ORIGEN: While he might have at once specially pointed out the betrayer, he did not do so, but said generally, "One of you will betray me,"[3] so the character of each might be tested by the witness of his astonished heart. This underscored the good-

ness of the disciples who believed Christ's words more than their own consciousness, and the wickedness of Judas because he did not believe the One who knew his plans. He embraced the obscurity by lying through his own teeth. COMMENTARY ON MATTHEW 50.[4]

### 14:19 They Began to Be Sorrowful

**TENDERNESS OF CONSCIENCE.** ORIGEN: If the eleven apostles were of good conscience, having not in any way betrayed their teacher, why were they grieved, as though it might have been that he was speaking of one of them? I think that each of them knew from Jesus' teaching that human freedom is infinitely changeable and may easily be turned toward evil. It may happen, in the struggle against principalities and powers and rulers of this world of darkness, that one may fall quite unexpectedly into evil, either being deceived or overcome by demonic powers. Thus, each disciple feared lest it might be he who was foreknown as betrayer. COMMENTARY ON MATTHEW 50.[5]

### 14:20 One Who Is Dipping Bread into the Dish with Me

**THE BETRAYER CHALLENGED.** ORIGEN: Seeing that the disciples were disturbed, Jesus called the betrayer to accountability by poignantly recalling the prophetic words of the psalmist:

---

[1]Cf. Mt 26:48-49; Lk 22:47-48. [2]Cetedoc 0048, 6.118; FC 36:269**. [3]Mt 26:21; Mk 14:18; Jn 13:21. [4]PG 13:1730; AEG 5:235-6*. [5]PG 13:1730; AEG 5:236*. The disciples had by this time been prepared to be intensely self-critical amid the temptations of spiritual warfare.

"Even my bosom friend in whom I trusted, who ate of my bread, has lifted up his heel against me."[6] This corresponds to the Evangelist's report of him saying: "It is one of the twelve, one who is dipping bread into the dish with me."[7] Judas the betrayer was thrusting his hand into the very same dish along with Jesus as they were eating the passover meal. This highlighted Judas' shamelessness. The very one who was being generously received to a common table betrayed Jesus who had embraced him with such great affection. He betrayed the bestower of these good gifts for the promise of thirty pieces of silver.[8] Isn't this especially characteristic of extremely malevolent persons—to plot against those with whom they have shared bread and salt, who would in no way injure them? COMMENTARY ON MATTHEW 50.[9]

### 14:21a Woe to That Man by Whom the Son of Man Is Betrayed!

WOE TO ALL BETRAYERS. ORIGEN: There was another by whom he was betrayed, namely, the devil, of whom Judas was the instrument. The "woe" is not only for Judas, but for all who betray Christ. COMMENTARY ON MATTHEW 50.[10]

### 14:21b It Would Have Been Better if He Had Not Been Born

WHETHER GOD MADE A MISTAKE IN CREATING FREEDOM. JOHN OF DAMASCUS: Knowledge is of what exists and foreknowledge is of what will surely exist in the future.[11] For simple being comes first and then good or evil being. But if the very existence of those, who through the goodness of God are in the future to exist, were to be prevented by the fact that they were to become evil of their own choice, evil would have prevailed over the goodness of God. In this way God makes all his works good, but each becomes of its own choice good or evil. Although, then, the Lord said, "Good were it for that man that he had never been born,"[12] he said it in condemnation not of his own creation but of the evil which his own creature had acquired by his own choice and through his own heedlessness. EXPOSITION OF THE ORTHODOX FAITH 4.21.[13]

---

[6]Ps 41:9 (40:9 LXX). [7]Mk 14:20. [8]Mt 26:15. [9]PG 13:1731-32; AEG 5:237-38*. [10]PG 13:1732; AEG 5:239*. [11]To know something is to know that it now exists. To foreknow something is to know that it will exist. [12]Mt 26:24; Mk 14:21. [13]NPNF 2 9:94; TLG 2934.004, 94.5-14. God makes all his works good, but each becomes of its own choice good or evil.

---

## 14:22-25 THE LAST SUPPER

[22]*And as they were eating, he took bread, and blessed, and broke it, and gave it to them, and said, "Take; this is my body." [23]And he took a cup, and when he had given thanks he gave it to them, and they all drank of it. [24]And he said to them, "This is my blood of the[c] covenant, which is poured out for many. [25]Truly, I say to you, I shall not drink again of the fruit of the*

*vine until that day when I drink it new in the kingdom of God."*

c Other ancient authorities insert *new*

**OVERVIEW:** Like the wheat that is scattered over the hills and is gathered together to become one, so does the community of faith, gathered from the ends of the earth, become one in the Eucharist (DIDACHE). As the bread and wine are consecrated according to Christ's institution, they become his body broken for us and his redeeming blood that offers salvation (AMBROSE). It is not the visible bread alone that has saving efficacy but the word of the mystery of the Lord's broken body and not the visible wine alone but the word of the mystery of the Lord's blood poured out on the cross that saves (ORIGEN). As the new birth is by both water and Spirit, so the bread of the new covenant is both common bread and his body broken for us, so as to correspond with Adam's compound nature ( JOHN OF DAMASCUS). Marcion's theory of the phantom body of Jesus offers no adequate premise for developing the figure of bread as body (TERTULLIAN). All around the world by these ordinary creaturely elements the faithful offer to God the first fruits of his creatures, and God offers to the faithful eternal life (IRENAEUS). The consecrated bread and wine are offered to those who have repented and believe ( JUSTIN MARTYR).

## 14:22a He Took Bread and Blessed and Broke It

**AN EARLY EUCHARISTIC PRAYER.** DIDACHE: We thank you, our Father, for the holy vine of David your servant;[1] to you be glory forever. And concerning the broken bread: We thank you, our Father, for the life and knowledge which you made known to us through Jesus your servant; to you be the glory for ever. Even as this broken bread was scattered over the hills, and was gathered together and became one, so let your church be gathered together from the ends of the earth into your kingdom. DIDACHE 9.[2]

**HOW THE BREAD IS BROKEN.** JUSTIN MARTYR: When the president has given thanks and the whole congregation has assented, those whom we call deacons give to each of those present a portion of the consecrated bread and wine and water. They then take it to those absent. This food we call Eucharist, of which no one is allowed to partake except one who believes that the things we teach are true, and has received the washing for forgiveness of sins and for rebirth, and who lives according to the way Christ handed down to us.[3] For we do not receive these things as common bread or common drink; but as Jesus Christ our Savior being incarnate by God's Word took flesh and blood for our salvation, so also we have been taught that the food consecrated by the word of prayer which comes from him, from which our flesh and blood are nourished by transformation, is the flesh and blood of that incarnate Jesus. For the apostles in the memoirs composed by them, which are called Gospels, thus handed down what was commanded them: that Jesus, taking bread and having given thanks, said, "Do this in remembrance of me. This is my body"; and similarly taking the cup and giving thanks he said, "This is my blood"; and gave it to them alone.[4] FIRST APOLOGY 65-66.[5]

---

[1]Cf. Mt 26:29; Mk 14:25; Jn 15:1. [2]TLG 1311.001, 9.2.2-4.3; cf. ANF 7:380. [3]Cf. 1 Cor 11:27-29. [4]Cf. Mt 26:26-28; Mk 14:22-24; Lk 22:19-20; 1 Cor 11:23-25. [5]LCC 1:286; TLG 0645.001, 65.5.1—66.3.6.

### 14:22b *Take, This Is My Body*

**CREATURELY ELEMENTS CONSECRATED.** IRENAEUS: Giving directions to his disciples to offer to God the first fruits of his creatures—not as if he stood in need of them, but that they might be themselves neither unfruitful nor ungrateful—he took that created thing, bread, and gave thanks, and said, "This is my body." And the cup likewise, which is part of the creation to which we belong, he confessed to be his blood,[6] and taught the new offering of the new covenant. This is what the church has received from the apostles and throughout the whole world offers to God, who affords us nourishment as the first fruits of his gifts in the New Testament. AGAINST HERESIES 4.17.5.[7]

**THE BODY OF JESUS.** TERTULLIAN: Then having taken the bread and given it to his disciples, he made it his own body by saying "This is my body,"[8] that is, the figure of my body. A figure, however, there could not have been, unless there had first been a palpable body. A phantom or mere void is not capable of embodying a figure. But Marcion would claim that Jesus only pretended that the bread was his body because he presumably had no bodily substance, so in the absence of his body he gives us bread. It wouldn't change his theory of a phantom body much if we stretched the point to say that the bread was crucified! But in that case why would we need to call his body bread? Why not rather come up with some more interesting edible thing, like a melon, which maybe Marcion had in place of a heart! AGAINST MARCION 4.40.[9]

**THE BREAD AND ITS MYSTERY.** ORIGEN: That bread which God the Word confesses to be his own body is the Word that nourishes souls, the Word proceeding from God, the very bread that comes from the living bread which is set out upon our table of which was written: "Thou preparest a table before me in the presence of my enemies."[10] That drink which God the Word confesses to be his blood is the Word that gives refreshment and exhilarates the heart.... This drink is the fruit of the true vine,[11] the blood of that grape cast in the winepress of the passion. So also the bread is the word of Christ made from that corn which, falling onto the good ground, brought forth much fruit.[12] He was not speaking of the visible bread alone which he was holding in his hands as he called it his body. It is the word in the mystery of which that bread was to be broken. Nor did he call that visible drink as such his blood, but the word in the mystery of which that drink was to be poured out. For to what else could the body and blood of the Lord refer other than the atoning Word that nourishes and gladdens the heart? Why did he not say, "This is my bread of the New Testament" just as he said, "This is my blood of the New Testament?"[13] Because the bread is the word of righteousness, by the eating of which souls are nourished. The drink is the word of knowledge of Christ according to the mystery of his birth and passion. COMMENTARY ON MATTHEW 85.[14]

**THE BREAD CONSECRATED.** AMBROSE: Do you wish to know how it is consecrated with heavenly words? Accept what the words are. The priest speaks. He says: "Perform for us this oblation[15] written, reasonable, acceptable,

---

[6]Cf. Mt 26:26-28; Mk 14:22-24; Lk 22:19-20; 1 Cor 11:23-25. [7]AHR 2:197-99; ANF 1:484*; cf. AEG 5:260. [8]Mt 26:26; Mk 14:22; Lk 22:19; 1 Cor 11:24. [9]Cetedoc 0014, 4.559.22; ANF 3:418**. [10]Ps 23:5. [11]Cf. Mk 14:25; Jn 15:1. [12]Mt 13:8; Mk 4:8; Lk 8:8. [13]Mt 26:28; Mk 14:24; Lk 22:20; 1 Cor 11:25. [14]PG 13:1734-35; AEG 5:263-64**. [15]Perform this offering just as it is promised in the written word.

which is a figure of the body and blood of our Lord Jesus Christ. On the day before he suffered he took bread in his holy hands, looked toward heaven, toward you, holy Father omnipotent, eternal God, giving thanks, blessed, broke, and having broken it gave it to the apostles and his disciples," saying: "Take and eat of this, all of you; for this is my body, which shall be broken for many."[16] Take note. Before it is consecrated, it is bread; but when Christ's words have been added, it is the body of Christ. THE SACRAMENTS 4.5.[17]

### HOW DOES OUR HUMAN NATURE CORRESPOND WITH THE SPIRITUAL BREAD GIVEN IN REGENERATION? JOHN OF DAMASCUS: Human beings have a compound nature: body and spirit. So it is fitting that the new birth should correspond to that compound nature, and also that the food of faith be compound. We were therefore given a birth both by water and by the Spirit,[18] that is, in holy baptism, and with it food that is the very bread of life, even our Lord Jesus Christ, who came down from heaven.[19] For when he was about to take on himself a voluntary death for our sakes, on the night on which he gave himself up, he offered a new covenant to his holy disciples and apostles,[20] and through them to all who believe on him. In an upper chamber, then, on holy and glorious Zion, after he had eaten the ancient Passover with his disciples and had fulfilled the ancient covenant, he washed his disciples' feet[21] in token of the holy baptism. Then having broken bread he gave it to them saying, "Take, eat, this is my body broken for you for the remission of sins."[22] EXPOSITION OF THE ORTHODOX FAITH 4.13.[23]

### 14:23 He Took a Cup

**WINE, WORD AND BLOOD.** AMBROSE: Before the words of Christ, the chalice is full of wine and water; when the words of Christ have been added, then the blood in effect redeems the people. So behold in what great respects the expression of Christ is able to change all things. Then the Lord Jesus himself testified to us that we receive his body and blood. Should we doubt at all about his faith and testimony? THE SACRAMENTS 4.23.[24]

### 14:24 This Is My Blood of the Covenant, Which Is Poured Out for Many

**WHY BLOOD?** CLEMENT OF ALEXANDRIA: He blessed wine, saying: "Take, drink, this is my blood." He used the "blood of the vine"[25] as a figure of the Word who "was shed for us for the remission of sins,"[26] a stream of gladness. CHRIST THE EDUCATOR 2.32.[27]

**CONSECRATION OF THE WINE.** AMBROSE: Jesus himself speaks of his blood. Before the consecration it is mentioned as something else; after the consecration it is called blood. And you say "Amen," that is, "It is true." Let the mind within confess what the mouth speaks. Let the heart feel what the words utter. ON THE MYSTERIES I.[28]

---

[16]1 Cor 11:24. [17]Cetedoc 0154 (M), 4.5.21.55.1; FC 44:304-5. In the eucharistic prayer, which asks God to accomplish what was promised in the Last Supper, as the bread is consecrated according to Christ's institution it becomes the body of Christ. Medieval speculations on the substance of the eucharistic bread were to come much later. It is best not to read these or sixteenth-century controversies into Ambrose's intention. [18]Cf. Jn 3:5. [19]Jn 6:35, 48, 51. [20]Cf. Lk 22:20. [21]Jn 13:4-12. [22]Mt 26:26. [23]NPNF 2 9:82*; TLG 2934.004, 86.40-53. [24]Cetedoc 0154 (M), 4.5.23.56.22; FC 44:305*. By Christ's institution the wine and water in the cup become for us the redeeming blood that offers salvation. [25]Cf. Gen 49:11; Sir 50:15-16. [26]Mt 26:28. [27]FC 23:121-22; TLG 0555.002, 2.2.32.2.5-3.1. The blood of the vine is a figure for the incarnate Word who suffered for our sins. [28]Cetedoc 0155, 9.54.113.57; FC 44:26*.

## 14:26-37 THE WAY TO GETHSEMANE

<sup>26</sup>*And when they had sung a hymn, they went out to the Mount of Olives.* <sup>27</sup>*And Jesus said to them, "You will all fall away; for it is written, 'I will strike the shepherd, and the sheep will be scattered.'* <sup>28</sup>*But after I am raised up, I will go before you to Galilee."* <sup>29</sup>*Peter said to him, "Even though they all fall away, I will not."* <sup>30</sup>*And Jesus said to him, "Truly, I say to you, this very night, before the cock crows twice, you will deny me three times."* <sup>31</sup>*But he said vehemently, "If I must die with you, I will not deny you." And they all said the same.*

<sup>32</sup>*And they went to a place which was called Gethsemane; and he said to his disciples, "Sit here, while I pray."* <sup>33</sup>*And he took with him Peter and James and John, and began to be greatly distressed and troubled.* <sup>34</sup>*And he said to them, "My soul is very sorrowful, even to death; remain here, and watch."* <sup>35</sup>*And going a little farther, he fell on the ground and prayed that, if it were possible, the hour might pass from him.* <sup>36</sup>*And he said, "Abba, Father, all things are possible to thee; remove this cup from me; yet not what I will, but what thou wilt."* <sup>37</sup>*And he came and found them sleeping, and he said to Peter, "Simon, are you asleep? Could you not watch one hour?"*

**OVERVIEW:** Jesus' human vulnerability is the focus of patristic comment. This is clearly portrayed in his ordeal in Gethsemane, yet without diminishing his deity (ORIGEN). He is speaking here in his fully human voice, which naturally shrinks from death, as does ours (CHRYSOSTOM). Jesus treaded the winepress of suffering alone (JEROME). The cup of suffering does not pass away simply by being avoided. His freely chosen obedience demonstrates by its unpretentiousness the eternal mystery of his humiliation (HILARY OF POITIERS). Jesus taught patience in suffering by himself becoming patient in suffering (AUGUSTINE). He felt the anguish of death (EPHREM THE SYRIAN). His sadness was not caused by death as such but was finished and removed by death, and in this sense he was "sorrowful unto death." We with our temporally bound minds cannot

grasp or measure his almighty power that stooped to suffer for us (HILARY OF POITIERS).

### 14:30 Before the Cock Crows Twice

**PETER DID NOT KNOW HIS WEAKNESS.**
AUGUSTINE: God knows in us even what we ourselves do not know in ourselves. For Peter did not know his weakness when he heard from the Lord that he would deny him three times.[1] TRACTATE ON JOHN 32.5.[2]

### 14:31 I Will Not Deny You

**THE FLIGHT OF PETER.** JEROME: One of twelve deserted; eleven remained loyal. The cross came; they fled; one remained—Peter, one with

---

[1]Cf. Mt 26:33-35; Mk 14:29-31; Lk 22:31-34; Jn 13:36-38.
[2]Cetedoc 0278, 32.5.19; FC 88:44.

One. This one himself fled, and would that he had! He denied Christ. We may say, then, that the entire human race was lost. Because it had perished, the complaint of the Lord crucified is: "The wine press I have trodden alone, and of my people there was no one with me."[3] Then was the Psalm fulfilled: "Help, O Lord! For no one now is dutiful."[4] "There is none who does good, no not even one."[5] He who has promised: "Even if I should have to die with thee, or be imprisoned, I will not deny thee,"[6] denied him. ON THE PSALMS, HOMILY 54.[7]

### 14:34 My Soul Is Very Sorrowful Even unto Death

**HIS DEITY DID NOT CANCEL OUT HIS HUMANITY.** ORIGEN: He was troubled, as we are told, in the hour of death, as he himself confesses when he says, "My soul is sorrowful even unto death."[8] He was finally led to that death which is considered the most shameful of all. On the third day he rose again.[9] When, therefore, we see in him some things so human that they appear in no way to differ from the common frailty of mortals, and some things so divine that they are appropriate to nothing else but the primal and ineffable nature of deity, the human understanding with its own narrow limits is baffled, and struck with amazement at so mighty a wonder. It does not know which way to turn, what to hold to, or how to establish itself. ON FIRST PRINCIPLES 2.6.2.[10]

**THE CAUSE OF HIS SADNESS.** HILARY OF POITIERS: What is meant by "sorrowful even unto death?"[11] It cannot mean the same as "to be sorrowful because of death"; for where there is sorrow because of death, it is the death that is the cause of the sadness. But a sadness even

unto death implies that death is the completion, not the cause, of the sadness. ON THE TRINITY 10.36.[12]

### 14:35a He Fell to the Ground

**HIS HUMAN AFFECTIONS.** AMBROSE: He has fully taken upon himself the flesh of humanity, and with it human affections. So you read in Scripture that "going a little farther, he fell on the ground and prayed that, if it were possible, the hour might pass from him."[13] Here he speaks not in the voice of God but as fully human. For how could God be ignorant of the possibility or impossibility of anything? Or is anything beyond God's ability, when as Scripture itself says: "For you nothing is impossible?"[14] ON THE CHRISTIAN FAITH 2.5.42.[15]

### 14:35b If It Were Possible

**THE WEAKNESS THAT BELONGS TO HUMAN NATURE.** CHRYSOSTOM: How is it, then, that in his prayer he says: "If it be possible?"[16] He is showing the weakness that belongs to a human nature. Human nature would prefer not to be torn from the present life. It would draw back and shrink from death. Why? Because God has implanted in human nature a love for the life of this world. ON THE INCOMPREHENSIBLE NATURE OF GOD 7.46.[17]

---

[3]Is 63:3. [4]Ps 12:1-2. [5]Ps 14:1-3; Rom 3:12. [6]Mt 26:35; Mk 14:31. [7]Cetedoc 0592, 143.270; FC 48:390. [8]Mt 26:38; Mk 14:34. [9]Cf. Mt 28:6; Mk 16:6; Lk 24:5; 1 Cor 15:4. [10]OBP 358; OFP 109. [11]Mt 26:38; Mk 14:34. [12]Cetedoc 0433, SL 62A, 10.36.4; NPNF 2 9:191. [13]Mk 14:35. [14]Cf. Lk 1:37. [15]Cetedoc 015, 2.5.17; NPNF 2 10:228*. [16]Mt 26:39. [17]TLG 2062.015, 48.765.3-8; FC 72:204. God gave Jesus the same human nature as we have, a nature that shrinks from death.

## 14:36a *Abba, Father, All Things Are Possible to Thee*

**WHETHER ALL THINGS ARE POSSIBLE TO GOD.** HILARY OF POITIERS: The Father from whom every nature has derived its laws is not subject to the laws of nature. The Father who transcends every measure of power is not limited in anything, either by deficiency or by changeability in his nature. As the Son said: "Father, all things are possible to thee."[18] So much so that the human mind cannot grasp as much as lies within his power. ON THE TRINITY 9.72.[19]

## 14:36b *Remove This Cup from Me*

**PERSEVERING IN PRAYER THROUGH TEMPTATION.** EPHREM THE SYRIAN: He knew what he was saying to his Father, and was well aware that this chalice could pass from him. But he had come to drink it for everyone, in order to acquit, through this chalice, the debt of everyone, [a debt] which the prophets and martyrs could not pay with their death. . . . He assumed flesh. He clothed himself with weakness, eating when hungry, becoming tired after working, being overcome by sleep when weary. It was necessary, when the time for his death arrived, that all things that have to do with the flesh would be fulfilled then. The anguish of death in fact invaded him, to manifest his nature as a son of Adam, over whom death reigns,[20] according to the word of the apostle. . . . Or alternatively, in this hour of his corporeal death, he gave to the body that which belonged to it, saying that all the sufferings of [his] body would show to the heretics and schismatics that his body was [real]. Did not this body of his appear to them, just as it was visible to everyone else? Just as he was hungry and thirsty, tired and had need of

sleep, so too, he was afraid. Or, [he said that], so that it would be difficult for people in the world to say that it was without suffering and toil that our debts were remitted by him. Or [it was] to teach his disciples to confide their life and death to God. If he, who is wise on account of the wisdom of God, asked for what was fitting for him, how much more [should] ordinary people surrender their will to the One who knows all things. . . . If he who is fearless was afraid [of death], and asked to be delivered from it, although he knew that it was impossible, how much more should others persevere in prayer before temptation, so that, in time of temptation, they may be delivered from it. COMMENTARY ON TATIAN'S DIATESSARON.[21]

**HE PRAYS IN A HUMAN MANNER.** HILARY OF POITIERS: Though with God nothing is impossible, yet for human nature it is impossible to ignore the fear of suffering. Only by trial can faith be proved.[22] Thus as a human being he prays in a human manner that the cup may pass away, but as God from God, his will is in unison with the Father's effectual will. ON THE TRINITY 10.38.[23]

**WHAT PASSES AWAY?** HILARY OF POITIERS: He does not pray that the cup may pass around him. He prays that the cup may pass away from him, but it cannot pass away unless he drinks it. To pass away does not mean to depart from its place, but not to exist at all.[24] And this is indeed the very meaning that the apostles have

---

[18]Mk 14:36. [19]Cetedoc 0433, SL 62A, 10 9.72.18; FC 25:394**; cf. NPNF 2 9:180. [20]Cf. Rom 5:14, 17. [21]CSCO 137:280, 282, 284; JSSS 2:292-96*. [22]1 Pet 1:7. [23]NPNF 2 9:192*. As son of Mary he shrinks from suffering; as God the Son his will remains in unity with that of God the Father. [24]If the cup is to pass away finally, it must be drunk. It does not pass away by being avoided. If the cup passes around him and still exists for someone else to deal with, the cup has not fully passed away.

in mind when they say: "Heaven and earth will pass away, but my words will not pass away."[25] ON THE TRINITY 10.42.[26]

### 14:36c Yet Not What I Will but What Thou Wilt

**WITHIN TIME FOR ETERNITY.** HILARY OF POITIERS: Although he was obedient, it was a voluntary obedience. The only begotten Son humbled himself, and obeyed his Father even to the death of the cross. But was it as human or as God that he was subjected to the Father? His subjection is that of one to whom all things have been subjected.[27] This subjection is not a sign merely of a temporal obedience, for his allegiance is eternal. Rather it was an instance in time of the dispensation of the eternal mystery of his humbling. His actual humbling occurred within time.[28] Yet in its very unpretentiousness it displays the eternal mystery of his humiliation. ON THE TRINITY 11.30.[29]

**EMBODYING OBEDIENCE.** AUGUSTINE: To show sufferers that they need not despair, the true Savior became the good teacher by himself epitomizing the truth in his own person. He participated in our suffering in an empathic way,[30] knowing that through human frailty sorrow might steal in upon our hearts amid afflictions, and knowing that we would overcome it if we yield to God's will above our own, mindful that God knows best those whose well-being he superintends.[31] HARMONY OF THE GOSPELS 3.4.14.[32]

---

[25]Mt 24:35; Mk 13:31; Lk 21:33. [26]Cetedoc 0433, SL 62A, 10.42.12; FC 25:430**. [27]Cf. 1 Cor 15:27-28. [28]As a series of events within time. Cf. Phil 2:6-8. [29]Cetedoc 9433, SL 62A, 11.30.21; NPNF 2 9:212**. [30]Cf. Heb 2:9, 18; 4:15. [31]Cf. 2 Pet 2:9; Jas 1:12. [32]Cetedoc 9273, 3.4.14.285.11; NPNF 1 6:184**.

---

## 14:38-42 THE WEAKNESS OF THE FLESH

[38]"Watch[d] and pray that you may not enter into temptation; the spirit indeed is willing, but the flesh is weak." [39]And again he went away and prayed, saying the same words. [40]And again he came and found them sleeping, for their eyes were very heavy; and they did not know what to answer him. [41]And he came the third time, and said to them, "Are you still sleeping and taking your rest? It is enough; the hour has come; the Son of man is betrayed into the hands of sinners. [42]Rise, let us be going; see, my betrayer is at hand."

d Or keep awake

---

**OVERVIEW:** We pray for grace that we neither evade the challenges of temptation nor be encompassed by them (ORIGEN). If the will itself sufficed to protect us from temptation, we would not have to pray for grace to face temptation. Thus we watch and pray for grace lest we enter into temptation, not praying for what our nature already possesses by our own strength (Augustine). To pray that we not enter into temptation is preparatory for the more radical prayer: "not as I will but thou" (Dionysius of Alexandria). Rather than make excuses for the weakness of the flesh, the faithful are called to rely on the strength of the spirit. Flesh is called to take strength from spirit, as weaker to stronger. Faith does not focus inordinately on the weakness of the flesh, as if the weaker were without the stronger (Tertullian).

### 14:38a Watch and Pray That You May Not Enter into Temptation

**Prayer to Not Be Encompassed by Temptation.** Origen: We do not pray that we will never be tempted at all. For that is impossible.[1] We pray rather that we not be encompassed by temptation.[2] On Prayer 29.11.[3]

**Prayer to Not Enter Voluntarily into the Arena of Temptation.** Dionysius of Alexandria: This is the first form of not falling into temptation, when he counsels the weak to pray not to enter into temptation. The temptation to come, for offenses must come, will require that they pray that they enter not into temptation. But the more perfect way of not entering into temptation is what he asks for the second time: "not as I will but as thou."[4] For God cannot be tempted, but wills to give above what we ask or think.[5] Fragments.[6]

**Can We Do by Ourselves What We Pray For?** Augustine: The Lord has commanded us to watch and pray that we enter not into temptation. Obviously, if we could endow ourselves

with this gift merely by willing it, we would not be asking it in prayer. If the will itself sufficed to protect us from temptation, we would not have to pray for it. But if we were not given a will at all, we would be unable to pray. Grant, then, that we may will it freely, praying that we may be made able by grace to do what we have willed, when by mercy we have attained to wise discernment. Letter 218, To Palatinus.[7]

**We Ask Not for What We Already by Nature Possess.** Augustine: For, if these things are placed in our power through the capability of nature and the freedom of the will,[8] anyone can see that it would be useless to ask them of the Lord, and even deceitful to pray, if we ask in prayer for what our nature so constituted already possesses by our own strength. Then, the Lord Jesus would not have said: "Watch and pray,"[9] but only "Watch, lest you enter into temptation." He would not have said to the blessed chief of the apostles: "I have prayed for you," but simply: "I warn you, or command you, or enjoin you that your faith should not fail."[10] Letter 175, To Pope Innocent.[11]

### 14:38b The Spirit Indeed Is Willing, but the Flesh Is Weak

**The Strength of the Spirit Amid the Weakness of the Flesh.** Tertullian: He clearly acknowledged that his "soul was sorrow-

---

[1]To be forever untempted is to never test the strength of freedom. Even Christ faced temptation. Cf. Sir 2:1. [2]Cf. Lk 22:40; 1 Cor 10:13. [3]TLG 2042.008, 29.11.1-2; cf. CWS 156. [4]Mt 26:37; Mk 14:36; Lk 22:42. [5]Cf. Eph 3:20. [6]PG 10:1597; C. L. Feltoe, ed., *St. Dionysius of Alexandria* (London: SPCK, 1918), p. 232; cf. AEG 5:326*. [7]Cetedoc 0262, 218.57.3.427.1; FC 32:98**. [8]Augustine's issue: Would it be deceitful to pray for what our nature already possesses by our own strength? [9]Mt 26:41; Mk 14:38. [10]Lk 22:32. [11]Cetedoc 0262, 175.44.4.659.3; FC 30:88-89**.

ful, even unto death,"[12] and his flesh weak. His intention was to show, from his troubled soul and weak flesh, that both his soul and body were fully human. For some have wrongly asserted that either the flesh or soul of Christ might be entirely different from ours. He sought by an extraordinary exhibition of the body-soul interaction, to show that neither body nor soul has any power at all of itself apart from the spirit. This is why he states first that the spirit is willing, so that you may understand that you have within you the spirit's strength and not merely the weakness of the flesh. From this it is hoped that you may learn what to do under challenge, by what means to do it, and how to order priorities. The weak must be brought under the strong—the flesh under the spirit. This will help you avoid making excuses, as you are now prone to do, for the weakness of your flesh while failing to understand the strength of the spirit.[13] ON FLIGHT AMID PERSECUTION 8.[14]

**MAKING EXCUSES FOR THE WEAKNESS OF THE FLESH.** TERTULLIAN: Let us, however, not take premature comfort in the Lord's acknowledgment of the weakness of the flesh. For note that he declared first of all that the spirit is willing. He wanted to show which one ought to be subject to the other: the flesh is called to be submissive to the spirit, the weaker to the stronger, so that the flesh may draw strength from the spirit. Let the spirit converse with the flesh on their common salvation. Do not despair over the hardships of prison. Rather think about the eventual outcome of the contest. To THE MARTYRS 4.1-2.[15]

## 14:39 Again He Went Away and Prayed

**FOR WHOM DID HE PRAY?** HILARY OF POITIERS: Is the cause of this sadness and this prayer any longer doubtful? He bids them to watch and pray with him for this purpose, that they may not enter into temptation; "for the spirit indeed is willing, but the flesh is weak."[16] If they had remained firm under the promise to faithful souls, they would not have violated their trust. Yet through the weakness of the flesh, they did fall away. It is not, therefore, for himself that the Lord is sorrowing and prays. It is for those whom he exhorts to watchfulness and prayer, lest the cup of suffering should be their lot, lest that cup which he prays may pass away from him should rest with them. ON THE TRINITY 10.37.[17]

## 14:40 He Found Them Sleeping

**THE MEANING OF THEIR SLEEPING.** TERTULLIAN: Susceptibilities to weakness and sloth are footprints of the devil. When God commanded Abraham to sacrifice his only son, it was not for the purpose of seducing him toward evil, but of proving his faith.[18] Through Abraham God sought to offer a pattern of one who followed the precept that he should hold no pledge of affection dearer than God.[19] Later when the Lord asked his disciples to "pray that you may not enter into temptation,"[20] the same pledge was required. Yet they were tempted. They deserted their Lord by giving way to sleep rather than persevering in prayer. ON PRAYER 8.[21]

---

[12]Mt 26:37; Mk 14:34. [13]Cf. Mt 26:41; Mk 14:38. [14]Cetedoc 0025, 8.5; ANF 4:120-21**. [15]Cetedoc 0001, 6.4.11; FC 40:24**. [16]Mt 26:41; Mk 14:38. [17]Cetedoc 0433, SL 62A, 10.37.36; NPNF 2 9:192*. His prayer is not for himself but for his disciples, to whom the cup of suffering may come, lest the cup that he prays may pass away from him should rest with them. [18]Cf. Gen 22:1-18. [19]Cf. Deut 13:6-10; 33:9; Mt 10:37; Lk 14:26. [20]Mt 26:41; Mk 14:38; Lk 22:40. [21]Cetedoc 0007, 8.6; ANF 3:684*. The disciples, by sleeping rather than praying, succumbed to temptation at the crucial moment.

## 14:43-52 JESUS TAKEN CAPTIVE

[43]*And immediately, while he was still speaking, Judas came, one of the twelve, and with him a crowd with swords and clubs, from the chief priests and the scribes and the elders.* [44]*Now the betrayer had given them a sign, saying, "The one I shall kiss is the man; seize him and lead him away under guard."* [45]*And when he came, he went up to him at once, and said, "Master!"* [e] *And he kissed him.* [46]*And they laid hands on him and seized him.* [47]*But one of those who stood by drew his sword, and struck the slave of the high priest and cut off his ear.* [48]*And Jesus said to them, "Have you come out as against a robber, with swords and clubs to capture me?* [49]*Day after day I was with you in the temple teaching, and you did not seize me. But let the scriptures be fulfilled."* [50]*And they all forsook him, and fled.*

[51]*And a young man followed him, with nothing but a linen cloth about his body; and they seized him,* [52]*but he left the linen cloth and ran away naked.*

**e** Or *Rabbi*

**OVERVIEW:** The timing of Jesus' betrayal fell between the Passover, when he instituted the holy supper, and when he himself was sacrificed as a lamb (BEDE). Jesus was patient even with his betrayer (DIONYSIUS OF ALEXANDRIA). Judas lost everything—his money, soul and life (CHRYSOSTOM)—and thereby became an instance of teaching (EPHREM THE SYRIAN).

### 14:43 Judas Came and with Him a Crowd with Swords and Clubs

**THE TYRANNY OF COVETOUSNESS.** CHRYSOSTOM: Consider what befell him, how he simultaneously lost the money, committed the sin, and destroyed his own soul. Such is the tyranny of covetousness. He did not even enjoy the money in this life nor did he have any benefits in the life to come. He lost everything at once and, branded as a bad character even by his co-conspirators, hanged himself.[1] THE

GOSPEL OF ST. MATTHEW 85.2.[2]

### 14:44 The One I Shall Kiss Is the Man; Seize Him

**JESUS' RESPONSE WAS SOFTER THAN A KISS.** DIONYSIUS OF ALEXANDRIA: How magnificent is the endurance of evil by the Lord who even kissed his own traitor, and then spoke words even softer than a kiss! For he did not say, O you abominable one, or traitor, is this what you do in return for great kindnesses? He simply says "Judas," using his first name.[3] This is in the voice of one commiserating with another or who wished another to come back to him, not the voice of anger. EXEGETICAL FRAGMENTS.[4]

---

[1]Cf. Mt 27:3-10. [2]NPNF 1 10:508; TLG 2062.152, 58.760.11-17. [3]Cf. Lk 22:48. [4]PG 10:1596; ANF 6:116*.

### 14:46 They Seized Him

**WHEN WAS HE SEIZED?** BEDE: At last, after five days, having observed up to that point the sacraments of the old Passover, he brought them to perfection, and handed over the new sacraments to his disciples to be observed from that time forward. Then, having gone out to the Mount of Olives, he was seized by the Jews and crucified the next morning. He redeemed us from the sway of the devil on that very day when the ancient people of the Hebrews remembered casting aside the yoke of slavery under the Egyptians by the immolation of a lamb.[5] HOMILIES ON THE GOSPELS 2.3.[6]

**WHAT JESUS TAUGHT THROUGH JUDAS.** EPHREM THE SYRIAN: Why did he choose [Judas], and . . . make him steward? To show his perfect love and his mercy. [It was] also that our Lord might teach his church that, even if there are false teachers in it, it is nevertheless the true seat [of authority]. For the seat of Judas did not come to naught with the traitor himself. It was also [to teach] that, even if there are evil stewards, the stewardship itself is true. He therefore washed his feet,[7] [those very feet] by means of which he had arisen and gone to [Jesus'] slayers. Jesus kissed the mouth of him who, by means of it, gave the signal for death to those who apprehended him.[8] He reached out and gave bread into that hand that reached out and took his price, and sold him unto slaughter. COMMENTARY ON TATIAN'S DIATESSERON.[9]

---

[5]Cf. Ex 12:1-30. [6]Cetedoc 1367, 2.3.10; HOG 2:24. [7]Cf. Jn 13:5. [8]Cf. Mt 26:48-49; Mk 14:44-45; Lk 22:47-48. [9]Leloir 1963:124; JSSS 2:219*.

## 14:53-65 JESUS BEFORE THE SANHEDRIN

[53]And they led Jesus to the high priest; and all the chief priests and the elders and the scribes were assembled. [54]And Peter had followed him at a distance, right into the courtyard of the high priest; and he was sitting with the guards, and warming himself at the fire. [55]Now the chief priests and the whole council sought testimony against Jesus to put him to death; but they found none. [56]For many bore false witness against him, and their witness did not agree. [57]And some stood up and bore false witness against him, saying, [58]"We heard him say, 'I will destroy this temple that is made with hands, and in three days I will build another, not made with hands.'" [59]Yet not even so did their testimony agree. [60]And the high priest stood up in the midst, and asked Jesus, "Have you no answer to make? What is it that these men testify against you?" [61]But he was silent and made no answer. Again the high priest asked him, "Are you the Christ, the Son of the Blessed?" [62]And Jesus said, "I am; and you will see the Son of man seated at the right hand of Power, and coming with the clouds of heaven." [63]And the high

*priest tore his garments, and said, "Why do we still need witnesses?* [64]*You have heard his blasphemy. What is your decision?" And they all condemned him as deserving death.* [65]*And some began to spit on him, and to cover his face, and to strike him, saying to him, "Prophesy!" And the guards received him with blows.*

**OVERVIEW:** Jesus' silence fulfilled messianic prophecy even on the silence of the lamb (AUGUSTINE). He remained silent even when spat upon, but will not be silent in the final judgment (CYPRIAN). The fallen temple attests the vulnerability of all our best artistic efforts (PRUDENTIUS). The temple to be rebuilt was his body that would be resurrected in three days (ORIGEN). The priests did not dispute the messianic premise that the true Christ must be the Son of God but only asked whether he indeed was the Christ, the Son of God (HILARY OF POITIERS). The spitting occurred in the high priest's house (AUGUSTINE). Death dissolved the body born of woman that the eternal Father might restore the same body in the resurrection (PRUDENTIUS). His first coming was in humility; his second will be in glory (JUSTIN MARTYR).

## 14:58a I Will Destroy This Temple

**THE LORD BOUND IN THE TEMPLE.** Prudentius:

> Lo, the house of the wicked blasphemer,
>     Caiaphas, has fallen,
> Where the sacred face of the Christ
>     was cruelly smitten.[1]
> This destruction will be the lot
>     of all reprobate sinners,
> For their life will lie buried
>     in crumbling ruins forever.
> In this house the Lord stood upright,
>     bound and tied to a pillar,
> And submitted his back as a slave

> to the pitiless scourging.
> Worthy of reverence, this pillar still
>     stands,[2] supporting a temple,
> And instructing us how to lead our lives
>     free from all scourges.

SCENES FROM SACRED HISTORY 40, 41.[3]

**THE TEMPLE BUILT BY HANDS.** PRUDENTIUS:

> Do not the quarried stones of Solomon
> Now lie in ruins, that temple built by hand?[4]
> Why so? The mortal hand of mason
>     wrought
> That short-lived work. It rightly lies in
>     ruins,
> Since every work of art returns to nought.
> All that is made is doomed one day to fall.
> Learn what our temple is, if you would
>     know;[5]
> It is one that no artisan has built,
> A structure not of riven fir or pine,
> Nor reared with blocks of quarried marble
>     fair.
> Its massive weight no columns high support
> Beneath the arches of a gilded vault.
> By God's Word it was formed, not by his
>     voice,
> But by the everlasting Word, the Word
>     made flesh.[6]
> This temple is eternal, without end,

---

[1]Cf. Mt 26:57-67; Mk 14:53-65. [2]Prudentius, writing at the end of the fourth century, knew the Jerusalem pilgrims' tradition that the pillar "still stands" on the Via Dolorosa. [3]Cetedoc 1444, 40.157; FC 52:192. Centuries later only the pillar still stands in Jerusalem where he was scourged, instructing us how to be free from the final scourging. [4]Cf. Acts 7:47-48. [5]Cf. Heb 8:1-2. [6]Cf. Jn 1:14.

This you attacked with scourge and cross
and gall.
This temple was destroyed by bitter pains.[7]
Its form was fragile from the mother's
womb,
But when brief death the mother's part
dissolved,
The Father's might restored it in three days.
THE DIVINITY OF CHRIST.[8]

## 14:58b *In Three Days I Will Build Another Not Made with Hands*

WHICH TEMPLE WOULD BE REBUILT? ORIGEN: The accusations they brought against our Lord Jesus Christ appear to have reference to this utterance of his, "Destroy this temple, and I will build it up in three days."[9] Though he was speaking of the temple of his body, they supposed his words to refer to the temple of stone. COMMENTARY ON JOHN 10.21.[10]

## 14:61a *But He Was Silent and Made No Answer*

HIS MEEKNESS. AUGUSTINE: It was not in vain that the prophecy had preceded him: "As a lamb before its shearer is dumb, so he opened not his mouth."[11] When he did not open his mouth, it was reminiscent of the figure of a lamb. It was not as one of bad conscience convicted of sins, but as one who in his meekness was being sacrificed for the sins of others. TRACTATES ON JOHN 116.4.[12]

## 14:61b *The High Priest Asked Him, "Are You the Christ, the Son of the Blessed?"*

LEARNING FROM CHRIST'S TORMENTERS. HILARY OF POITIERS: If you will not learn who Christ is from those who received him, at least learn from those who rejected him. The ironic confession his adversaries were inadvertently forced to make stands as reproof of their very mockery. His accusers did not recognize Christ when he came bodily. Yet they had grasped firmly that the true Christ must be the Son of God. Thus, when the false witnesses whom they had hired against him did not score any blows, the priest interrogated him: "Are you the Christ, the Son of the most high God."[13] They did not realize that the mystery was already being fulfilled in him. But they did, ironically, recognize that the divine nature was the condition of its fulfillment. They did not question the assumption that Christ would be the Son of God. They only asked whether he indeed was the Christ, the Son of God. They were mistaken about the person, but not about the Son of God. They had no doubt that Christ would be the Son of God. So while they asked whether he indeed was the Christ, they did so without denying that the Christ is the Son of God. ON THE TRINITY 6.50.[14]

## 14:62 *You Will See the Son of Man Coming with the Clouds of Heaven*

TWO COMINGS FORETOLD. JUSTIN MARTYR: In reference to his coming from heaven with glory, recall what was spoken to this effect through the prophet: "Behold how the Son of Man comes on the clouds of heaven."[15] . . . For the prophets foretold two comings of

---

[7]Cf. Mk 14:58; Jn 2:19-21. [8]Cetedoc 1439, 512; FC 52:22-23. [9]Jn 2:19. [10]ANF 9:402*; TLG 2042.005, 10.37.251.3-252.3. His resurrection, the resurrection of the temple of his body, would occur within three days. [11]Is 53:7. [12]Cetedoc 0278, 116.4.4; NPNF 1 7:426*. [13]Mt 26:63; Mk 14:61. [14]Cetedoc 0433, SL 62, 6.50.1; NPNF 2 9:116**; cf. FC 25:219. [15]Dan 7:13; cf. Jer 4:13; Mt 24:30; 26:64.

Christ—one, which has already happened, when he comes in the form of a dishonored and dying man, and the second, when as has been foretold he will come from heaven in glory.[16] FIRST APOLOGY 51, 52.[17]

### 14:65 *Some Began to Spit on Him and to Cover His Face*

HIS RESPONSE TO ABASEMENT. CYPRIAN: Who is this strange one who says that he had been silent before, but would not always be silent? Who is he who was led as a sheep to the slaughter and who, like a lamb without making a sound before its shearer, did not open his mouth?[18] Who is he who did not cry out and whose voice was not heard in the streets? Surely it was he who was not stubborn and who did not murmur when he offered his back to the scourges and his cheeks to blows. He did not turn his face away from their filthy spittle.[19] When accused by the priests and elders, he answered nothing[20] and, to the amazement of Pilate, kept a most patient silence.[21] THE GOOD OF PATIENCE 23.[22]

---

[16]Cf. Hag 2:7; Mt 16:27; 25:31; Lk 9:26. [17]LCC 1:275*; TLG 0645.001, 58.8.1-9.3, 52.3.1-3. [18]Is 53:7. [19]Is 50:5-6; Mt 26:67; Mk 14:65; Lk 22:63. [20]Mt 26:63; Mk 14:61. [21]Mt 27:14; Mk 15:5. [22]Cetedoc 0048, 23.454; FC 36:286**.

## 14:66-72 PETER'S DENIAL

[66]*And as Peter was below in the courtyard, one of the maids of the high priest came;* [67]*and seeing Peter warming himself, she looked at him, and said, "You also were with the Nazarene, Jesus."* [68]*But he denied it, saying, "I neither know nor understand what you mean." And he went out into the gateway.[f]* [69]*And the maid saw him, and began again to say to the bystanders, "This man is one of them."* [70]*But again he denied it. And after a little while again the bystanders said to Peter, "Certainly you are one of them; for you are a Galilean."* [71]*But he began to invoke a curse on himself and to swear, "I do not know this man of whom you speak."* [72]*And immediately the cock crowed a second time. And Peter remembered how Jesus had said to him, "Before the cock crows twice, you will deny me three times." And he broke down and wept.*

f Or *fore-court.* Other ancient authorities add *and the cock crowed*

---

OVERVIEW: Peter, who had shuddered at the voice of a maid, would later be made courageous before princes by the power of the resurrected Lord ( JEROME). With his sword Peter had resisted captors, but only with his mouth could he withstand the judgment of the lowly maidservant. This passage reinforces the reasons Mark was designated as Peter's disciple—because he more fully disclosed the faults and repentance of Peter (CHRYSOSTOM). That the disciples had an exceptionally high standard of truth telling is evident from their reporting their own behavior, warts and all (EUSEBIUS). As the penitent David retained his kingship after sinning, so did the penitent Peter remain an apostle (AUGUSTINE). In the denial of Peter the prophecy of Psalm 88:8 was being fulfilled (JEROME). The denial led to an oath that led to cursing (ORIGEN).

## 14:66 I Neither Know nor Understand What You Mean

**THE CRINGING DENIER.** CHRYSOSTOM: O what strange and remarkable turns occur in these ironic events! When Peter merely saw his master seized, he was so ardent as both to draw his sword and to whack off the servant's ear![1] But—alas, then when it might have been even more plausible for him to be even more indignant, and to be inflamed and to burn, upon hearing such revilings against his Lord, then he became a cringing denier . . . and that in the presence of a lowly and diminutive maidservant, and not only once but a second and third time.[2] THE GOSPEL OF ST. MATTHEW, HOMILY 85.1.[3]

## 14:70 But Again He Denied It

**PSALM 88 RECALLED.** JEROME: "You have taken my friends away from me."[4] In the passion of the cross, even my apostles fled from me; so completely did they shun me that Peter himself said: "I do not know this man."[5] HOMILIES OF SAINT JEROME, HOMILY 65.[6]

## 14:71 He Began to Invoke a Curse on Himself and to Swear

**THE MOMENTUM OF CURSING.** ORIGEN: The second time he denied not simply but with an oath, the third time also with cursing. By this we are instructed never to promise without consideration anything above our human ability. COMMENTARY ON MATTHEW 86.[7]

## 14:72a The Cock Crowed a Second Time

**INTERNAL EVIDENCE OF THE RELIABILITY OF MARK'S ACCOUNT.** EUSEBIUS: Mark writes these things, and through him Peter bears witness, for the whole of Mark is said to be a record of Peter's teaching. Note how scrupulously the disciples refused to record those things that might have given the impression of their fame. Note how they handed down in writing numerous charges against themselves to unforgetting ages, and accusations of sins, which no one in later years would ever have known about unless hearing it from their own voice. By thus honestly reporting their own faults, it is reasonable to view them as relatively void of false speaking and egoism. This habit gives plain and clear proof of their truth-loving disposition. As for such critics who imagine they invented and lied, and try to slander them as deceivers, should they not to be regarded as absurd? Aren't they thereby being convicted as friends of envy and malice, and foes of truth itself? For have they not taken those who have exhibited in their own words good proof of their integrity, and their straightforward and

---

[1]Cf. Jn 18:10. [2]Cf. Mt 26:69-75; Mk 14:66-72; Lk 22:55-60; Jn 18:17-27. [3]NPNF 1 10:507; TLG 2062.030, 58.758.32-37, 40-42. [4]Ps 88:8 (87:9 LXX); 88:18. [5]Mt 26:72; Lk 22:57. [6]Cetedoc 0593, 87.79; GMI 401*. [7]PG 13:1738; AEG 5:271.

sincere character, and suggested that they are rascals and clever sophists who invent what never took place, and ascribe gratuitously to their own master what he never did? This is why I think it has been rightly said that "One must put complete confidence in the disciples of Jesus, or none at all." And if we are to distrust them, we must also distrust all writers on the same principle, any who at any time have compiled, either in Greece or anywhere, lives and histories and records of persons of their own times, celebrating their noble achievements. Otherwise we would be considering it reasonable to believe others, and to disbelieve the evangelists only. And this would be clearly invidious. How could it be that these supposed liars would falsify the account of his death? What would be their motive in writing down deeds he never did? They candidly report his be-trayal by one of his disciples,[8] explicit accusations by dubious witnesses,[9] insults and blows to his face,[10] the scourging of his back, the crown of acanthus set on his head in a demeaning way,[11] and finally his carrying of his own cross, and his being nailed to it![12] They report his hands and feet being pierced,[13] his being given vinegar to drink, struck on the cheek with a reed, and reviled by those who looked upon him.[14] Were these things and all else like them in the Gospels simply invented out of whole cloth by the disciples? Highly unlikely. Or must we doubt only the more glorious and lofty parts of the narrative? How could they do so and doubt these candid reports of ignominious actions? How could they reasonably support such an unreasonable conclusion—that the same witnesses spoke the truth and at the same time lied. That would be to predict contraries about the same people at the same time. How then are we to disprove their assertions? If it was their aim to deceive,

and to adorn their master with false words, they would never have written these demeaning accounts of his pain and agony and that he was disturbed in spirit, that they themselves forsook him and fled, or that Peter the apostle and disciple who was chief of the apostles denied him three times, unless they had an extraordinarily high standard of truth-telling. Proof of the Gospel 3.5.[15]

## 14:72b *And He Broke Down and Wept*

**On Not Hiding Peter's Faults.** Chrysostom: In this respect we most marvel at Mark, because not only did he refuse to hide Peter's fault, but wrote the account of it in greater detail than the others. And it is for this very reason that he is called Peter's disciple.[16] The Gospel of St. Matthew 85.1.[17]

**The Weeping Apostle.** Augustine: As holy David repented for his deadly crimes and still retained his kingship,[18] so the blessed Peter earnestly repented, having denied the Lord, and shed such bitter tears, yet remained an apostle.[19] Letter 185, To Boniface.[20]

**Learning Compassion.** Gregory the Great: And here we must ask ourselves, why did almighty God permit the one he had placed over the whole church to be frightened by the voice of a maidservant, and even to deny Christ himself?[21] This we know was a great dispensa-

---

[8]Cf. Mk 14:44-45. [9]Cf. Mt 26:59-60; Mk 14:55-56. [10]Cf. Mt 26:67; Mk 14:65. [11]Cf. Mt 27:26-31; Mk 15:15-19. [12]Cf. Mt 27:31-35; Mk 15:20-24; Lk 23:26-33; Jn 19:17-18. [13]Cf. Jn 20:25-27. [14]Cf. Mt 27:48; Mk 15:36; Lk 23:36; Jn 19:29. [15]TLG 2018.005, 3.5.95.1-97.2; POG 1:140-41. [16]Mk 14:66-72. [17]NPNF 1 10:507*; TLG 2062.152, 58.758.56-59; cf. AEG 5:438. [18]Cf. 2 Sam 12:1-20; 24:17. [19]Cf. Mt 26:69-75; Mk 14:66-72; Lk 22:55-62. [20]Cetedoc 0262, 185.57.10.39.13; FC 30:184**. [21]Cf. Mk 14:66-72.

tion of the divine mercy, so that he who was to be the shepherd of the church might learn through his own fall to have compassion on others. God therefore first shows him to himself, and then places him over others: to learn through his own weakness how to bear mercifully with the weakness of others. Homilies on the Gospels 21.[22]

---

[22]Cetedoc 1711, 2.21.4.15; SSGF 2:243.

## 15:1-5 THE TRIAL BEFORE PILATE

[1]And as soon as it was morning the chief priests, with the elders and scribes, and the whole council held a consultation; and they bound Jesus and led him away and delivered him to Pilate. [2]And Pilate asked him, "Are you the King of the Jews?" And he answered him, "You have said so." [3]And the chief priests accused him of many things. [4]And Pilate again asked him, "Have you no answer to make? See how many charges they bring against you." [5]But Jesus made no further answer, so that Pilate wondered.

**Overview:** Jesus' silence attests his innocence, as sacrificial lamb (Augustine, Ephrem the Syrian). So we are called to be patient with others when we are oppressed. The Lord's patience does not extend interminably but looks toward the decisive verdict on the day of final judgment (Cyprian). Out of his human silence, woundedness and death come divine speech, healing and life (Gregory of Nazianzus).

### 15:4 Have You No Answer? See How Many Charges They Bring Against You

**Practice of Patience Amid Persecution.** Cyprian: What great patience this is that he who is adored in heaven is not yet avenged on earth! Let us think of his patience, beloved brothers and sisters, in our persecutions and sufferings. Let us show forth the full obedience that is inspired by our expectation of his coming. Let us not hasten with the impious and shameless haste of a servant to defend ourselves before the Lord. Let us rather persevere and let us labor, and be watchful with all our heart and steadfast even to total resignation. Let us guard the precepts of the Lord, so that when the day of wrath and vengeance comes,[1] we may not be punished with the impious and sinners but may be honored with the just and those who fear God. The Good of Patience 24.[2]

**Silent Before His Oppressors.** Gregory of Nazianzus: A lamb, he is silent[3]—yet he is "word,"[4] proclaimed by "the voice of one crying

---

[1]Ezek 7:19; Zeph 1:14-18; Rev 6:17. [2]Cetedoc 0048, 24.475; FC 36:287*. As God is patient with us in our rebelliousness, we are to be patient with others under conditions of trial and harassment, according to the pattern of Jesus under trial. [3]Is 53:7. [4]Cf. Jn 1:1.

in the wilderness."[5] He is weakened, wounded[6]—yet he cures every disease and every weakness.[7] He is brought up to the tree[8] and nailed to it[9]—yet by the tree of life he restores us.[10] ORATION 29, ON THE SON 20.[11]

### 15:5 Jesus Made No Further Answer

VICTORY THROUGH SILENCE. EPHREM THE SYRIAN: The Lord became the defender of truth, and came in silence before Pilate, on behalf of truth which had been oppressed.[12] Others gain victory through making defenses, but our Lord gained victory through his silence, because the recompense of his death through divine silence was the victory of true teaching. He spoke in order to teach, but kept silent in the tribunal. He was not silent over that which was exalting us, but he did not struggle against those who were provoking him. The words of his calumniators, like a crown on his head, were a source of redemption. He kept silent so that his silence would make them shout even louder, and so that his crown would be made more beautiful through all this clamor. COMMENTARY ON TATIAN'S DIATESSARON.[13]

THE LIMITS OF SILENCE. CYPRIAN: He is the One who, although he was silent in his passion, will not be silent finally in the day of reckoning. He is our God, even if unrecognized. He is already known among the faithful and all who believe. When he comes manifesting himself in his second coming, he will not be silent. For although he was formerly hidden in humility, he will come manifested in power.[14] THE GOOD OF PATIENCE 23.[15]

HIS MEEKNESS FULFILLED MESSIANIC PROPHECY. AUGUSTINE: This silence of our Lord Jesus Christ took place more than once. It occurred before the chief priest, and before Herod, and before Pilate himself.[16] So it was not in vain that the prophecy regarding him had preceded: "As the lamb before its shearer was dumb, so he opened not his mouth,"[17] especially on those occasions when he did not answer his questioners. Usually he replied to questions addressed to him, but in this case he declined to make any reply. The metaphor of the lamb is used to indicate that his silence does not imply guilt but innocence. When he did not open his mouth as he passed through the process of judgment, it was in the character of a lamb that he did so; that is, not as one with an evil conscience who was convicted of his sins, but as one who in his meekness was sacrificed for the sins of others. TRACTATES ON JOHN 116.4.[18]

---

[5]Cf. Mt 3:3; Mk 1:3; Lk 3:4; Jn 1:23. [6]Cf. Is 53:5. [7]Cf. Mt 9:35. [8]Cf. 1 Pet 2:24. [9]Cf. Jn 19:17-18. [10]Cf. Gen 2:9; 3:22; Rev 2:7. [11]FGFR 259*; TLG 2022.009, 20.21-25. [12]Cf. Jn 18:37-38. [13]CSCO 137:291; JSSS 2:301*. [14]Cf. Mt 16:27; 5:31; 1 Thess 4:13-18; Rev 1:7; 14:7. [15]Cetedoc 0048, 23.462; FC 36:286**. He who was humble in his passion will come in his glory with power. [16]Cf. Mt 26:63; 27:14; Mk 14:61; 15:5; Lk 23:7-9; Jn 19:9. [17]Is 53:7. [18]Cetedoc 1278, 116.4.4; NPNF 1 7:426. His silence attests his innocence, in the manner of a sinless sacrificial lamb.

# 15:6-15 THE SENTENCE OF DEATH

*⁶Now at the feast he used to release for them one prisoner for whom they asked. ⁷And among the rebels in prison, who had committed murder in the insurrection, there was a man called Barabbas. ⁸And the crowd came up and began to ask Pilate to do as he was wont to do for them. ⁹And he answered them, "Do you want me to release for you the King of the Jews?" ¹⁰For he perceived that it was out of envy that the chief priests had delivered him up. ¹¹But the chief priests stirred up the crowd to have him release for them Barabbas instead. ¹²And Pilate again said to them, "Then what shall I do with the man whom you call the King of the Jews?" ¹³And they cried out again, "Crucify him." ¹⁴And Pilate said to them, "Why, what evil has he done?" But they shouted all the more, "Crucify him." ¹⁵So Pilate, wishing to satisfy the crowd, released for them Barabbas; and having scourged Jesus, he delivered him to be crucified.*

**OVERVIEW:** While the guilty were receiving pardon, the pardoner was being pronounced guilty. The civic justice that failed in fair judgment in the presence of the final judge will be corrected on the last day (AUGUSTINE). The classic exegetes found the trial full of poignant ironies: He who now crowns martyrs with garlands was himself once crowned with thorns (CYPRIAN). The incarnate Lord did not remain aloof from sin but identified himself with sinners, taking their sins upon himself. The violent crowd who voluntarily sent him to death was even more culpable than the soldiers who involuntarily carried out the orders of others (AUGUSTINE). Jerusalem repaid him with evil for the immensity of his grace (EPHREM THE SYRIAN).

## 15:12 Crucify Him!

**WHO CRUCIFIED JESUS?** AUGUSTINE: Those who cried out that he should be crucified were the Lord's real crucifiers, rather than those who simply discharged their service to their chief according to their duty. HAR-MONY OF THE GOSPELS 3.13.49.[1]

## 15:13 Why, What Evil Has He Done?

**PILATE'S ASSUMPTION OF JESUS' INNOCENCE.** AUGUSTINE: Mark, who studies brevity more than any of the Evangelists, has given a concise indication of Pilate's desire and of his efforts to save the Lord's life. For, after giving us the statement, "And they cried again, 'Crucify him'" (which makes it clear that they had cried out before for Barabbas to be released), he has appended these words: "Then Pilate continued to say[2] to them, "Why, what evil has he done?"[3] Thus by one short sentence he has given us an idea of matters which took a long time for their transaction. HARMONY OF THE GOSPELS 3.13.47.[4]

---

[1]Cetedoc 0273, 3.13.49.335.19; NPNF 1 6:202**.  [2]In what follows, Augustine argues that Pilate continued to ask what evil Jesus had done. Time is telescoped into one short phrase. [3]Mt 27:22-23; Mk 15:13-14; Lk 23:21-22. [4]Cetedoc 0273, 3.13.47.332.18; NPNF 1 6:201*. Mark, who may have been addressing a Roman audience, pointedly indicated that Pilate made repeated efforts to provide a fair trial.

### 15:15a He Released for Them Barabbas

**THE IRONY OF JESUS' CONDEMNATION COMPOUNDED.** AUGUSTINE: The criminal escaped; Christ was condemned.[5] The one guilty of many crimes received a pardon; he who had remitted the crimes of all who confess was condemned. And yet the cross itself also, if you reflect upon it, was a courtroom. In the middle of it stood the final judge. TRACTATES ON JOHN 31.11.[6]

### 15:15b Having Scourged Jesus

**HIS SCOURGING VINDICATED.** CYPRIAN: He himself suffered the lash, in whose name his servants now scourge the devil and his angels.[7] He who now crowns the martyrs with eternal garlands was himself crowned with thorns.[8] THE GOOD OF PATIENCE 7.[9]

### 15:15c He Delivered Him to Be Crucified

**JERUSALEM'S TREATMENT OF JESUS.** EPHREM THE SYRIAN: [The daughter of Zion] repaid him with evil for the immensity of his grace. The Father had washed her from her blood, but she defiled his Son with her spitting.[10] The Father had clothed her with fine linen and purple, but she clothed him with garments of mockery.[11] He had placed a crown of glory on her head, but she plaited a crown of thorns for him.[12] He had nourished her with choicest food[13] and honey, but she gave him gall.[14] He had given her pure wine, but she offered him vinegar in a sponge.[15] The One who had introduced her into cities, she drove out into the desert. The One who had put shoes on her feet, she made hasten barefoot towards Golgotha.[16] The One who had girded her loins with sapphire, she pierced in the side with a lance.[17] When she had outraged the servants [of God] and killed the prophets, she was led into captivity to Babylon, and when the time of her punishment was completed, her return [from captivity] took place. COMMENTARY ON TATIAN'S DIATESSARON.[18]

**JUDGED WITH THE UNGODLY.** AUGUSTINE: For Christ was not separated from the ungodly, but was judged with the ungodly; for it was said about him, "He was counted among the wicked."[19] TRACTATES ON JOHN 31.11.[20]

---

[5]Cf. Mt 27:26; Mk 15:15. [6]Cetedoc 0278, 31.11.34; FC 88:40*. The one being judged is the final judge. [7]Cf. Mt 27:26; Mk 15:15; Jn 19:1. [8]Cf. Mt 27:29; Mk 15:17; Jn 19:2. [9]Cetedoc 0048, 7.132; FC 36:270. Justice is reversed: the whipped becomes the judge, garlands replace thorns. [10]Cf. Ezek 16:9; Mt 26:67; Mk 14:65. [11]Cf. Ezek 16:10, 13; Mt 27:28; Mk 15:17. [12]Cf. Ezek 16:12; Mt 27:29; Mk 15:17; Jn 19:2. [13]Literally, "with fat." [14]Cf. Ezek 16:13; Mt 27:34. [15]Cf. Jn 19:29. [16]Cf. Ezek 16:10; Mt 27:33; Mk 15:22; Jn 19:17. [17]Cf. Ezek 16:10-11; Jn 19:34. [18]Leloir 1963:204; JSSS 2:269. [19]Is 53:12. [20]Cetedoc 0278, 31.11.32; FC 88:40.

---

## 15:16-20 THE MOCKING BY THE SOLDIERS

[16]*And the soldiers led him away inside the palace (that is, the praetorium); and they called together the whole battalion.* [17]*And they clothed him in a purple cloak, and plaiting a crown of*

*thorns they put it on him. [18]And they began to salute him, "Hail, King of the Jews!" [19]And they struck his head with a reed, and spat upon him, and they knelt down in homage to him. [20]And when they had mocked him, they stripped him of the purple cloak, and put his own clothes on him. And they led him out to crucify him.*

**OVERVIEW:** Ironies abound: The giver of the cloak of righteousness that hides our sin was himself stripped of his earthly clothing. His face is covered with spittle, who cured with spittle the eyes of the blind (CYPRIAN). Even their mockery obliquely served to reveal the revealer, to crown the humbled Lord of glory (CYRIL OF JERUSALEM). A conclusive reversal was being consummated in human history through his mock crowning. The judge is judged; the Word is silent (CYPRIAN).

### 15:17 A Purple Cloak and a Crown of Thorns

**THE REVERSAL IN THE FORM OF MOCKERY.** CYPRIAN: He who now gives true palms to the victors was beaten in the face with hostile palms;[1] he who clothes all others with the garment of immortality was stripped of his earthly garment.[2] THE GOOD OF PATIENCE 7.[3]

**HOW THE MOCKERY ECHOED PROPHECY.** CYRIL OF JERUSALEM: When they "clothed him in purple,"[4] it was in mockery, yet ironically it was a fulfillment of prophecy, for he indeed was a king, so even their parody indirectly served divine revelation. Even though they did it in a spirit of derision, still they did it, and his regal dignity was by that symbolically heralded. So, likewise, though it was with thorns they crowned him, it was still a crown.[5] SERMON ON THE PARALYTIC 12.[6]

### 15:19 They Spat upon Him

**THE SPITTLE OF HIS REVILERS AND THE SPITTLE BY WHICH HE HEALED.** CYPRIAN: In that very hour of his passion and cross, before they had come to the cruel act of his slaughter and the shedding of his blood, what violent abuses he listened to with patience, and what shameful insults he endured! He was even covered with the spittle of his revilers,[7] when, but a short time before, with his own spittle he had cured the eyes of the blind man.[8] THE GOOD OF PATIENCE 7.[9]

### 15:20 They Led Him Out to Crucify Him

**THE PARADOX OF HIS BEING "LED OUT."** CYPRIAN: He who has given the food of heaven was fed with gall;[10] he who has offered us the cup of salvation was given vinegar to drink.[11] He the innocent, he the just, nay rather, innocence itself and justice itself is counted among criminals,[12] and truth is concealed by false testimonies. He who is to judge is judged and the Word of God, silent, is led to the cross. The elements are disturbed, the earth trembles, night blots out the day,[13] "the sun withdraws both its rays"[14] and its eyes lest it be forced to

---

[1]Cf. Mt 26:67; Mk 14:65; Lk 22:63; Jn 19:3. [2]Cf. Mt 27:35; Mk 15:24; Lk 23:34; Jn 19:23. [3]Cetedoc 0278, 31.11.32; FC 36:270. [4]Cf. Mt 27:28; Mk 15:17; Jn 19:2. [5]Cf. Mt 27:29; Mk 15:17; Jn 19:2. [6]TLG 2110.006, 12.1-6; FC 64:217**. [7]Cf. Mt 26:67; 27:30; Mk 10:34; 14:65; 15:19. [8]Cf. Mk 8:23; Jn 9:6. [9]Cetedoc 0048, 7.132; FC 36:269-70. [10]Cf. Mt 27:34. [11]Cf. Mt 27:48; Mk 15:36; Lk 23:36. [12]Cf. Mt 27:38; Mk 15:27; Lk 23:33; Jn 19:18. [13]Cf. Mt 27:45, 51; Mk 15:33; Lk 23:44. [14]Mt 27:45.

gaze upon the crime of the people.[15] Though the stars are confounded at the crucifixion of the Lord, he does not speak, nor is he moved, nor does he proclaim his majesty, even during the suffering itself. He endures all things even to the end with constant perseverance so that

in Christ a full and perfect patience may find its realization. THE GOOD OF PATIENCE 7.[16]

---

[15]Those particular Jews who called for his crucifixion. [16]Cetedoc 0048, 7.132; FC 36:270*.

## 15:21-32 THE CRUCIFIXION

[21]*And they compelled a passer-by, Simon of Cyrene, who was coming in from the country, the father of Alexander and Rufus, to carry his cross.* [22]*And they brought him to the place called Golgotha (which means the place of a skull).* [23]*And they offered him wine mingled with myrrh; but he did not take it.* [24]*And they crucified him, and divided his garments among them, casting lots for them, to decide what each should take.* [25]*And it was the third hour, when they crucified him.* [26]*And the inscription of the charge against him read, "The King of the Jews."* [27]*And with him they crucified two robbers, one on his right and one on his left.*[g] [29]*And those who passed by derided him, wagging their heads, and saying, "Aha! You who would destroy the temple and build it in three days,* [30]*save yourself, and come down from the cross!"* [31]*So also the chief priests mocked him to one another with the scribes, saying, "He saved others; he cannot save himself.* [32]*Let the Christ, the King of Israel, come down now from the cross, that we may see and believe." Those who were crucified with him also reviled him.*

g Other ancient authorities insert verse 28, *And the Scripture was fulfilled which says "He was reckoned with the transgressors"*

**OVERVIEW:** No death is more shameful than the public horror of crucifixion (EUSEBIUS). Its ironies continue to compound: Prophecy was being fulfilled even by his tormentors. He who had turned water into sweet wine is offered vinegar and gall (CYRIL OF JERUSALEM, GREGORY OF NAZIANZUS). The incomparably innocent one tasted the extreme bitterness of the degrading death of a criminal, spurning supposed comforts (AUGUSTINE, PRUDENTIUS). His deity was expressed through his humilia-tion (AUGUSTINE). He did not become king of glory without first being mocked on the cross as king of the Jews (TERTULLIAN). Derided by those who passed by and mocked by the chief priests, he was reviled even by one of those crucified by his side (CYRIL OF JERUSALEM). What they did with their tongues on the third hour they did with their hands on the sixth hour (AUGUSTINE). The penitent faithful even today pray on the third, sixth and ninth hour to recall and once again participate in his trial, crucifixion and death (Apostolic Constitutions). The ultimate sentence came not at the trial but at the cross. There the final judge was placed with one criminal on his right and one on his left, as if to anticipate final judgment. He did not cease being Son of God on the cross. He who was able not to die unless he willed it did die because he willed it (Augustine, John of Damascus).

## 15:21 They Compelled a Passer-by, Simon of Cyrene

**Why Simon Was Compelled to Carry The Cross.** The Gospel of Nicodemus:[1] From the many blows and the weight of the cross he was unable to walk. . . . They gave the cross, then, to Simon of the city of Cyrene, who had also two sons by the name of Alexander and Rufus.[2] They did this not because they pitied Jesus, and wished to lighten his load, but because they ever more eagerly wanted to put him to death speedily. The Gospel of Nicodemus 10.1.[3]

**The Burden Shifted.** Chrysostom: When they went out of the Praetorium, Christ was carrying it: but as they proceeded Simon took it from him and bore it. Homily on the Paralytic Let Down Through the Roof 3.[4]

## 15:22 The Place Called Golgotha

**Twice Dawned One Day.** Anonymous:
Already robed as king, he must sustain
Blows from rough palms.
With spit his face is covered.
A thorn-inwoven crown pierces his head,
While to the tree he is fixed.
Wine drugged with myrrh is drunk,
And gall is mixed with vinegar.
His robe is parted and on it lots are cast.

Each one keeps for himself what he has
seized.
In this murky gloom,
God silently outbreathed his soul from
fleshly body.
The trembling day took refuge with the sun.
Twice dawned one day.
Five Books in Reply to Marcion 5.227.[5]

## 15:23a Wine Mingled with Myrrh

**Why Wine and Myrrh?** Cyril of Jerusalem: What sort of gall did they put in my mouth? "They gave him," it says, "wine mixed with myrrh."[6] Myrrh is like gall in taste, and very bitter. "Is the Lord to be thus repaid by you?"[7] Are these the offerings you make to your master, O vine? Catechetical Lectures 13.28.[8]

**The Taste of Bitterness.** Gregory of Nazianzus: He is given vinegar to drink[9] and gall to eat[10]—and who is he? Why, One who turned water into wine,[11] who took away the taste of bitterness,[12] who is all sweetness and desire.[13] Oration 29, On the Son 20.[14]

**Exceedingly Bitter.** Augustine: The gall is mentioned with a view to express the bitterness of the potion. And wine mingled with myrrh[15] is remarkable for its bitterness. The fact may

---

[1]An apocryphal Gospel probably redacted in the fifth century. Cf. Quast. 1.116. [2]Cf. Mt 27:32; Mk 15:21; Lk 23:26. [3]EA 302-303; ANF 8:429**. [4]NPNF 1 9:214; TLG 2062.063, 51.53.56-58. A pilgrim at Passover from distant Africa, later known to the apostles, assisted him in his travail. [5]Cetedoc 2036, 5.165; An anonymous poetic attempt to epitomize Tertullian's *Five Books Against Marcion*. The date and author are uncertain. ANF 4:164; cf. Mt 27:28-50; Mk 15:17-37; Lk 23:26-46; Jn 19:16-30. [6]Cf. Mt 27:34; Mk 15:23. [7]Deut 32:6. [8]TLG 2110.003, 13.29.11-14; FC 64:23. [9]Cf. Mt 27:48; Mk 15:36; Lk 23:36; Jn 19:29. [10]Cf. Mt 27:34. [11]Cf. Jn 2:7-9. [12]Cf. Ex 15:25. [13]Cf. Song 5:16. [14]FGFR 260; TLG 2022.009, 20.26-28. [15]A sedative.

also be that gall and myrrh together made the wine exceedingly bitter. Again, when Mark says that "he did not receive it," we understand the phrase to denote that he did not receive it so as actually to drink it. He did taste it. Harmony of the Gospels 3.11.[16]

## 15:23b He Did Not Take It

**The Sedative Rejected.** Augustine: Be cautious and receive the words of our adversaries in order to spit them out, not to gulp them down and ingest them. Do in this instance what the Lord did when they offered him a bitter drink; he tasted it, and spat it out.[17] So also should you, taste and spit. Tractate on John 6.11.[18]

**Spurning the Cup.** Prudentius:
Thus did Christ in the hour of crucifixion
Spurn the cup that was offered when he
thirsted,[19]
And refusing to drink, prolonged his
anguish.
Hymn 6.[20]

## 15:24 They Crucified Him

**His Manner of Death.** Eusebius: What death is more shameful than to be crucified? What death worse than this condemnation is conceivable? Even now he remains a reproach among all who have not yet received faith in him! Proof of the Gospel 10.9.[21]

**What Happened on the Cross.** John of Damascus: By nothing else except the cross of our Lord Jesus Christ has death been brought low:
The sin of our first parent destroyed,
hell plundered,
resurrection bestowed,

the power given us to despise the things
of this world,
even death itself,
the road back to the former blessedness
made smooth,
the gates of paradise opened,
our nature seated at the right hand of God,
and we made children and heirs of God.
By the cross all these things have been set
aright. . . .
It is a seal that the destroyer may not strike
us,
a raising up of those who lie fallen,
a support for those who stand,
a staff for the infirm,
a crook for the shepherded,
a guide for the wandering,
a perfecting of the advanced,
salvation for soul and body,
a deflector of all evils,
a cause of all goods,
a destruction of sin,
a plant of resurrection,
and a tree of eternal life.
Orthodox Faith 4.[22]

## 15:25a It Was the Third Hour

**Worshiping at Set Hours.** Apostolic Constitutions: Let your prayers be made at "the third hour";[23] for then it was that Pilate gave sentence upon our Lord and savior to have him crucified. . . . Let your prayers be made

---

[16]Cetedoc 0273, 3.11.38. 322.15; NPNF 6:197-98. [17]Cf. Mt 27:34; Mk 15:23. [18]Cetedoc 0278, 6.11.6; FC 78:139*. As he spurned the supposed comforts of adversaries, so does the church reject the pseudo-comforting words of false teachers. [19]Cf. Mk 15:23. [20]Cetedoc 1443, 6.58; FC 43:171. [21]POG 224*; TLG 2018.005, 10.8.55.4-9. Crucifixion is the most shameful reproach conceivable. [22]FC 37:350*, spaces added to present in poetic stanzas; TLG 2934.004, 84.21-29, 43-48. By the cross all manner of wrongs have been set right. [23]Cf. Mk 15:25.

also at the sixth hour; for at that time he was crucified.... We observe also "the ninth hour" of prayer; for at that time the sun was darkened and the earth shaken with horror, as being not able to look upon those bitter cruelties.[24] CONSTITUTIONS OF THE HOLY APOSTLES 8.34.[25]

THIRD OR SIXTH HOUR? AUGUSTINE: One Evangelist says that the Lord was crucified at the sixth hour,[26] and another at the third hour.[27] Unless we understand it, we are left wondering. When the sixth hour was already beginning, Pilate is said to have sat on the judgment seat. In reality when the Lord was lifted up upon the tree, it was the sixth hour.... They had killed him already at the time when they were crying out. The government officials at the sixth hour crucified, the transgressors of the law at the third hour cried out. That which some did with hands at the sixth hour, others did with tongue at the third hour. More guilty are they that with crying out were raging, than they that in obedience were serving. PSALMS 64.5.[28]

### 15:25b When They Crucified Him

HE DIED VOLUNTARILY. AUGUSTINE: He who was able not to die unless he willed it, did die because he willed it. So he made a show of principalities and powers, openly triumphing over them in himself. By his death the one and most real sacrifice was offered up for us. Whatever were the charges by which the principalities and powers held us under bondage, he cleansed, abolished, extinguished.[29] ON THE TRINITY 4.13.17.[30]

### 15:26 The King of the Jews

KING OF GLORY. TERTULLIAN: He was not hailed as the king of glory by the angels until he had been censured on the cross as "King of the Jews."[31] ... You owe your life to him as a debt for these favors. So try as best you can to be accountable to him in the same way that he became accountable for you. Or, be not crowned with flowers at all if you cannot bear the thorns,[32] because with flowers you cannot be crowned. THE CHAPLET 14.[33]

### 15:27a With Him They Crucified Two Robbers

THE DIFFERENCE BETWEEN THE TWO THIEVES. CYRIL OF JERUSALEM: Of the robbers crucified with him, it was said: "He was reckoned among the wicked."[34] Up to this time both were wicked, but one of them was wicked no longer. For one was wicked to the end, yielding not to salvation, and, though his hands were fastened, he struck blasphemously with his tongue. CATECHETICAL LECTURES 13.30.[35]

### 15:27b One on His Right and One on His Left

THE COMING JUDGMENT. AUGUSTINE: Amid the courtroom of the cross, one robber who believed was freed, the other who insulted him was condemned.[36] He was then signifying in advance what he would do concerning the living and the dead, putting some on his right and

---

[24]Cf. Mt 27:24, 51; Mk 15:33; Lk 23:44-45; Acts 3:1; 10:3, 9, 30. [25]PG 1:1135; GMI 423*. [26]Cf. Jn 19:14. [27]Cf. Mk 15:25. [28]Cetedoc 0283, 39.63.5.1; NPNF 1 8:264*. Cf. an alternative interpretation in HOG 3.13, NPNF 1 6:203. [29]Cf. Eph 6:11-12. [30]Cetedoc 0329, 50.4.13.49; NPNF 1 3:78. [31]Mt 27:37; Mk 15:26; Lk 23:38; Jn 19:19. [32]Cf. Mt 27:29; Mk 15:17; Jn 17:2. [33]Cetedoc 0021, 14.27; FC 40:266*. [34]Is 53:12; Mk 15:28. [35]TLG 2110.003, 13.30.1-5; FC 64:24. One was wicked and redeemed, the other wicked and unredeemed. [36]Cf. Lk 23:39-43.

some on his left.[37] The one robber was like to those who would be on the left; the other, to those who would be on the right. He who was being judged was anticipating final judgment. Tractates on John 31.11.[38]

### 15:29 Those Who Passed By Derided Him

**The Psalm Remembered.** Cyril of Jerusalem: Those who passed by wagged their heads, mocking the crucified, fulfilling the Scripture: "When they see me, they shake their heads."[39] Catechetical Lectures 13.30.[40]

### 15:31 The Chief Priests Mocked Him

**Without Comeliness.** Augustine: Such he appeared on the cross, such when crowned with thorns did he exhibit himself, disfigured, and without comeliness, as if he had lost his power, as if not the Son of God. Such did he seem to the blind.[41] Sermons on the Gospels 138.6.[42]

### 15:32 They Who Were Crucified with Him Also Reviled Him

**One Was Penitent.** Chrysostom: In the case of the robbers, one Evangelist says that the two blasphemed,[43] another that one of them reproved him who was reviling the Lord.[44] Yet in this again there is no contradiction. Both things took place, and at the beginning both the men behaved badly. Afterwards when signs occurred, when the earth shook and the rocks were torn apart, and the sun was darkened, one of them was penitent, became more chastened, recognized the crucified One and acknowledged his kingdom. The Paralytic Let Down Through the Roof 3.[45]

---

[37]Cf. Mt 25:31-33. [38]Cetedoc 0278, 31.11.37; FC 88:40*. [39]Ps 109:25. [40]TLG 2110.003, 13.30.5-7; FC 64:24. [41]Cf. Is 53:2. [42]Cetedoc 0284, 138.38.766.2.1; NPNF 1 6:524; cf. WSA 3 4:388, Sermon 138.6. [43]Cf. Mt 27:44; Mk 15:32. [44]Cf. Lk 23:40. [45]TLG 2062.063, 51.53.59-54.9; NPNF 1 9:214*. Two blasphemed, one repented.

---

## 15:33-41 THE DEATH ON THE CROSS

[33]*And when the sixth hour had come, there was darkness over the whole land[h] until the ninth hour.* [34]*And at the ninth hour Jesus cried with a loud voice, "Elo-i, Elo-i, lama sabach-thani?" which means, "My God, my God, why hast thou forsaken me?"* [35]*And some of the bystanders hearing it said, "Behold, he is calling Elijah."* [36]*And one ran and, filling a sponge full of vinegar, put it on a reed and gave it to him to drink, saying, "Wait, let us see whether Elijah will come to take him down."* [37]*And Jesus uttered a loud cry, and breathed his last.* [38]*And the curtain of the temple was torn in two, from top to bottom.* [39]*And when the centurion, who stood facing him, saw that he thus[i] breathed his last, he said, "Truly this man was the Son[x] of God!"*

⁴⁰*There were also women looking on from afar, among whom were Mary Magdalene, and Mary the mother of James the younger and of Joses, and Salome, ⁴¹who, when he was in Galilee, followed him, and ministered to him; and also many other women who came up with him to Jerusalem.*

h Or *earth*    i Other ancient authorities insert *cried out and*    x Or *a son*

**OVERVIEW:** In repeating the psalm that begins with "My God, my God, why have you forsaken me?" Christ took on the speech of our human infirmity. By appropriating the psalmist's voice to himself, his full humanity was evidenced by his longing to retain his life. His complete identification with our vulnerable humanity is seen in his experience of forsakenness (AUGUSTINE). As fully human, the affections of his soul were feeling the full weight and terror of forsakenness and so were bearing our terrors. Yet according to his divinity the incarnate Lord remained serenely faithful (AMBROSE). The hour was dark not only in the literal sense but also in the spiritual sense in reference to darkened hearts and minds (EUSEBIUS). With his last words all that had been prophesied of him was brought to completion. He breathed his last not under necessity but voluntarily. His freedom to die demonstrated his power, not his weakness (AUGUSTINE). He received and accepted the temporal ministries of women so the harvest of salvation might abound to their honor eternally (CHRYSOSTOM). Onlookers beheld the incomparable compassion of Christ on the cross (AUGUSTINE). The temple curtain and the rocks were split apart (EPHREM THE SYRIAN), the tombs opened and Jesus was recognized even by the Roman centurion as "Son of God" (GREGORY OF NAZIANZUS).

### 15:33a *When the Sixth Hour Had Come*

**THE SIXTH HOUR RATIFIED THE VERDICT OF THE THIRD HOUR.** AUGUSTINE: The Lord was crucified at the third hour by the tongues of the populace,[1] at the sixth hour by the hands of the soldiers.[2] When Pilate took his seat before the tribunal, it was "about the sixth hour," or early in the sixth hour. When Jesus was nailed to the tree between two thieves, it was the end of the sixth hour. It was between the sixth and ninth hour that the sun was obscured and the darkness prevailed, as we have it jointly attested on the authority of the three Evangelists Matthew, Mark and Luke.[3] TRACTATES ON JOHN 117.1.[4]

### 15:33b *Darkness over the Whole Land Until the Ninth Hour*

**THEIR UNDERSTANDING WAS DARKENED.** EUSEBIUS: Note how clearly was fulfilled the prophecy of our Savior's passion. It was to be a day in which "there shall be no light."[5] "From the sixth hour to the ninth hour there was darkness over all the earth."[6] . . . This was also fulfilled figuratively by his priestly persecutors, for among them came darkness, cold and ice, following upon their indignities to the anointed One. Their understanding also was darkened, so that the light of the gospel did not shine in their hearts, and their love to God grew cold. Then in the evening the light

---

[1]Cf. Mk 15:25. [2]Jn 19:14. [3]Mt 27:45; Mk 15:33; Lk 23:44. [4]NPNF 1 7:428**. The testimony of the Evangelists is not contradictory. [5]Eusebius is quoting from Symmachus commenting on Mt 27:45. [6]Mt 27:45; Mk 15:33; Lk 23:44.

of the knowledge of the Christ arose, so that they who sat in darkness and the shadow of death saw a great light.[7] PROOF OF THE GOSPEL 10.7.[8]

## 15:34 *Why Hast Thou Forsaken Me?*

HIS RECOLLECTION OF PSALM 22. AMBROSE: As human he doubts. He experiences amazement. It is not his divinity that doubts, but his human soul. He had no difficulty being amazed because he had taken humanity fully to himself. In taking upon himself a human soul, he also took upon himself the affections of a soul. As God he was not distressed, but as a human he was capable of being distressed. It was not as God he died, but as man. It was in human voice that he cried: "My God, My God, why have you forsaken me?"[9] As human, therefore, he speaks on the cross, bearing with him our terrors. For amid dangers it is a very human response to think ourself abandoned. As human, therefore, he is distressed, weeps, and is crucified. ON THE CHRISTIAN FAITH 2.7.56.[10]

APPROPRIATING THE PSALMIST'S VOICE TO HIMSELF. AUGUSTINE: Out of the voice of the psalmist, which our Lord then transferred to himself, in the voice of this infirmity of ours, he spoke these words: "My God, my God, why have you forsaken me?"[11] He is doubtless forsaken in the sense that his plea was not directly granted. Jesus appropriated the psalmist's voice to himself, the voice of human weakness. The benefits of the old covenant had to be refused in order that we might learn to pray and hope for the benefits of the new covenant. Among those goods of the old covenant which belonged to the old Adam there is a special appetite for the prolonging of this temporal life. But this appetite itself is not interminable, for we all know that the day of death will come. Yet all of us, or nearly all, strive to postpone it, even those who believe that their life after death will be a happier one. Such force has the sweet partnership of flesh and soul.[12] LETTER 140, TO HONORATUS 6.[13]

IDENTIFICATION WITH OUR INFIRMITIES. AUGUSTINE: In his most compassionate humanity and through his servant form we may now learn what is to be despised in this life and what is to be hoped for in eternity.[14] In that very passion in which his proud enemies seemed most triumphant, he took on the speech of our infirmity, in which "our sinful nature was crucified with him"[15] that the body of sin might be destroyed, and said: "My God, my God, why have you forsaken me?"[16] ... Thus the Psalm begins, which was sung so long ago, in prophecy of his passion and the revelation of the grace which he brought to raise up his faithful and set them free. LETTER 140, TO HONORATUS 5.[17]

## 15:36 *Filling a Sponge Full of Vinegar*

PSALM 69 RECALLED. AUGUSTINE: Among the other things prophesied about him, it was also written, "They gave me poison for food, and for my thirst they gave me vinegar to

---

[7]Cf. Is 9:2; Mt 4:16. [8]TLG 2018.005, 6.18. 44-47, 47.1-7; POG 2:214-15**. [9]Ps 22:1; Mt 27:46; Mk 15:34. [10]Cetedoc 0150, 2.7.25; NPNF 2 10:230**. In the affections of his soul he felt the full terror of forsakenness and so bore our terrors, yet as God-man he serenely bore our forsakenness. [11]Ps 22:1. [12]Eph 5:29. [13]Cetedoc 0262, 140.44.6.166.11; FC 20:69**. [14]Augustine is asking how this messianic psalm anticipated his full identification with our death-resisting human infirmity. [15]Rom 6:6. [16]Ps 22:1; Mt 27:46; Mk 15:34. [17]Cetedoc 0262, 140.44.5.165.16; FC 20:68**.

drink."[18] We know in the gospel how these things happened. First, they gave him gall. He took it, tasted it, and spit it out. Later while hanging on the cross, that all prophecies might be fulfilled, he said, "I thirst."[19] They took a sponge full of vinegar, fastened it on a reed, and offered it to him as he hung there. He took it and said, "It is finished."[20] What does "It is finished" mean? All that had been prophesied before my passion has been fulfilled. What then is there still for me to do? TRACTATES ON JOHN 37.9.[21]

### 15:37 He Breathed His Last

**A SIGN OF POWER, NOT NECESSITY.** AUGUSTINE: Those robbers crucified next to him, did they breathe their last when they wanted to?[22] They were held fast by the chains of the flesh because they were not the creators of the flesh. Fastened by nails, they were tormented for a long time because they were not masters of their infirmity.[23] But the Lord took on flesh in the virgin's womb when he wished it. He came forth to humanity when he wished it. He lived in history as long as he wished it. He departed from the flesh when he wished it. This is a sign of power, not of necessity. TRACTATES ON JOHN 37.9.[24]

**HIS POWER OF DYING.** AUGUSTINE: He departed by his [own] power; for he had not come by necessity. And so some marveled more at his power of dying than at his power of performing miracles. TRACTATES ON JOHN 31.6.[25]

### 15:38 The Curtain of the Temple Was Torn in Two

**ALTERNATIVE INTERPRETATIONS.** EPHREM THE SYRIAN: The curtain was torn. [This was] to show that [the Lord] had taken the kingdom away from them and had given it to others who would bear fruit.[26] An alternative interpretation is: By the analogy of the torn curtain, the temple would be destroyed because his Spirit had gone away from it. Since the high priest had wrongfully torn his robe, the Spirit tore the curtain to proclaim the audacity of the pride [of the Jews], by means of an action on the level of created beings. Because [the high priest] had torn his priesthood and had cast it from him, [the Spirit] also split the curtain apart.[27] Or [alternatively], just as the temple in which Judas had thrown down the gold[28] was dissolved and rejected, so too [the Lord] pulled down and rent asunder the curtain of the door through which [Judas] had entered. Or, [it was] because they had stripped him of his garments that he rent the curtain in two. For the heart of the rock was burst asunder,[29] but their own hearts did not repent. COMMENTARY ON TATIAN'S DIATESSARON.[30]

**HIS DEATH AS AN UNVEILING.** GREGORY OF NAZIANZUS: He surrenders his life, yet he has power to take it again.[31] Yes, the veil is torn, for things of heaven are being revealed, rocks split, and dead men have an earlier awakening.[32] ORATION 29, ON THE SON 20.[33]

[18]Ps 69:21. [19]Jn 19:28. [20]Jn 19:30. [21]Cetedoc 0278, 37.9.6; FC 88:102-3*. [22]The issue is, did Jesus breathe his last out of necessity or voluntarily? [23]Cf. Jn 19:32-33. [24]Cetedoc 0278, 37.9.17; FC 88:103. [25]Cetedoc 0278, 31.6.12; FC 88:35. [26]Cf. Mt 21:43. [27]Cf. Mt 27:51. [28]Cf. Mt 27:5. [29]Cf. Mt 27:51. [30]CSCO 137:314; JSSS 2:319*. [31]Cf. Jn 10:17-18. [32]Cf. Mt 27:51-53. [33]FGFR 260; TLG 2022.009, 20.29-31.

### 15:39 *Truly This Man Was the Son of God!*

**A Few Drops of Blood Renew the Whole World.** Gregory of Nazianzus: Many indeed are the wondrous happenings of that time: God hanging from a cross, the sun made dark and again flaming out; for it was fitting that creation should mourn with its creator. The temple veil rent, blood and water flowing from his side: the one as from a man, the other as from what was above man; the earth shaken, the rocks shattered because of the rock; the dead risen to bear witness to the final and universal resurrection of the dead. The happenings at the sepulcher and after the sepulcher, who can fittingly recount them? Yet no one of them can be compared to the miracle of my salvation. A few drops of blood renew the whole world, and do for all men what the rennet does for the milk: joining us and binding us together. On the Holy Pasch, Oration 45.1.[34]

### 15:40a *Women Looking On from Afar*

**What We Behold on the Cross.** Augustine: As they were "looking on,"[35] so we too gaze on his wounds as he hangs. We see his blood as he dies. We see the price offered by the redeemer, touch the scars of his resurrection. He bows his head, as if to kiss you. His heart is made bare open, as it were, in love to you. His arms are extended that he may embrace you. His whole body is displayed for your redemption. Ponder how great these things are. Let all this be rightly weighed in your mind: as he was once fixed to the cross in every part of his body for you, so he may now be fixed in every part of your soul.[36] On Virginity.[37]

**Where the Women Were Standing.** Augustine: How can we understand the same Mary Magdalene both to have stood afar off along with other women as the accounts of Matthew and Mark bear,[38] and to have been by the cross, as John tells us?[39] It could have been the case that these women were at such a distance as made it quite natural to say at once that they were near because they were at hand there in the sight of him, and yet afar off in comparison with the crowd of people who were standing round about in closer vicinity along with the centurion and the soldiers. It is open for us, then, to suppose that those women who were present at the scene along with the Lord's mother, after he commended her to the disciple,[40] began then to retire with the view of extricating themselves from the dense mass of people, and from a greater distance looking on at what remained to be done. Harmony of the Gospels 3.21.58.[41]

### 15:40b *Mary, the Mother of James the Younger*

**Which James?** Bede: How could it be said that the brother of the Lord was not the apostle, but a third James, since Paul also gives him the name of an apostle, saying, "I saw none of the other apostles except James, the brother of the Lord";[42] and the evangelist Mark names the same man, not a third, but one of the two Jameses, saying, "There were women also watching from a distance, among whom were Mary Magdalene and Mary the mother of the James the younger and of Joseph and Salome?"[43] Now "greater and lesser" are customarily used to

---

[34]TLG 2022.052, 36.661.42-664.5; SSGF 2:261. [35]Cf. Mt 27:55; Mk 15:40. [36]Cf. Gal 2:20; 6:17; Phil 3:10. [37]Cetedoc 0300, 54.55.300.12; GMI 428*. [38]Cf. Mt 27:55-56; Mk 15:40. [39]Cf. Jn 19:25. [40]Cf. Jn 19:26-27. [41]Cetedoc 0273, 3.21.58.348.4; NPNF 1 6:207-8. As they withdrew, the women who were once near may have then viewed the horrible scene from farther away. [42]Gal 1:19. [43]Mk 15:40.

establish a difference not among three, but between two. Hence the lesser James is named "of Alphaeus," in distinction from the greater, who was the son of Zebedee. COMMENTARY ON ACTS 1.13.[44]

### 15:41 The Women, When He Was in Galilee, Followed Him and Ministered unto Him, and Also Many Other Women

RECEIVING THE SUPPORT OF WOMEN. CHRYSOSTOM: For what reason then was he being supported by women?[45] For women, it is said, followed him and ministered to him.[46] It was to teach us from the first that he is ready to

receive those who do the good. Could not Paul, who supported others by his own hands, have maintained himself without assistance from others? But you see him receiving and requesting aid. Now hear the reason for it. "Not because I want a gift," he says, "but I want fruit that may abound to your account."[47] HOMILIES ON TITUS 6.[48]

---

[44]Cetedoc 1357, 1.139; CAA 15*. There were not three but two Jameses, the younger of whom is James, the son of Alphaeus, whose mother stood afar with the women. Cf. Mt 10:3; 27:56; Mk 3:18; Lk 6:15; Acts 1:13. [45]Why did Jesus accept substantial support from those least able to offer support? [46]Cf. Mk 15:41. [47]Phil 4:17. [48]TLG 2062.166, 62.697.50-58; cf. NPNF 1 13:541.

---

## 15:42-47 THE BURIAL OF JESUS

[42]And when evening had come, since it was the day of Preparation, that is, the day before the sabbath, [43]Joseph of Arimathea, a respected member of the council, who was also himself looking for the kingdom of God, took courage and went to Pilate, and asked for the body of Jesus. [44]And Pilate wondered if he were already dead; and summoning the centurion, he asked him whether he was already dead.[j] [45]And when he learned from the centurion that he was dead, he granted the body to Joseph. [46]And he bought a linen shroud, and taking him down, wrapped him in the linen shroud, and laid him in a tomb which had been hewn out of the rock; and he rolled a stone against the door of the tomb. [47]Mary Magdalene and Mary the mother of Joses saw where he was laid.

j Other ancient authorities read whether he had been some time dead

---

OVERVIEW: Jesus was placed in a tomb made for someone else to demonstrate that death did not belong to this one (AUGUSTINE). The Lord of glory was buried with utter simplicity, without the accouterments of richness (BEDE). The three days are counted in this way: He died on the first day, was in the grave the whole of the second day and arose on the morning of the third day (IGNATIUS, AUGUSTINE). We can be sure that Jesus died because his death was validated to Pilate by a centurion's inspection (AUGUSTINE). The incarnate Word was not the body as such but was the Word embodied. The Word was not changed into bones and flesh but took upon itself flesh. Jesus descended into the nether world while his body remained in the tomb (ATHANASIUS). Joseph of Arimathea's concealed discipleship became revealed in his courageous act of devotion (CHRYSOSTOM).

### 15:42 The Day Before the Sabbath

**YESTERDAY HE WAS SLAIN.** GREGORY OF NAZIANZUS: Yesterday the lamb was slain, and the door posts sprinkled with his blood, while Egypt mourned for her firstborn. But the destroying angel and his sacrificial knife, fearful and terrifying, passed over us,[1] for we were protected by the precious blood. This day we have wholly departed from Egypt, and from Pharaoh, its cruel tyrant, and his oppressive overseers. We are freed from laboring with bricks and straw,[2] and no one forbids us celebrate the festival of our passing over, our pasch, and to celebrate not with the leaven of malice and wickedness but with the unleavened bread of sincerity and truth.[3] . . . Yesterday I was crucified with Christ; today I am glorified with him. Yesterday I died with him; today I am given life with him. Yesterday I was buried with him; today I rise again with him. ON THE HOLY PASCH AND HIS OWN RELUCTANCE.[4]

**REVIEWING THE CHRONOLOGY OF THE THREE DAYS.** AUGUSTINE: Scripture again witnesses that the space of those three days did not imply whole days in their entirety. Rather the first day is counted as whole from its last part, and the third day is itself also counted as a whole

from its first part; but the intervening day, i.e., the second day, was absolutely whole with its twenty-four hours, twelve of the day and twelve of the night. For he was crucified first by the voices of the Jews in the third hour, when it was the sixth day of the week. Then he hung on the cross itself at the sixth hour, and yielded up his spirit at the ninth hour.[5] ON THE TRINITY 4.6, 10.[6]

### 15:43 Joseph of Arimathea Went to Pilate and Asked for the Body of Jesus

**THE SEQUENCE OF EVENTS.** IGNATIUS: At the sixth hour he was crucified. At the ninth hour he yielded up his spirit. Before sunset he was buried. During the sabbath he continued under the earth in the tomb in which Joseph of Arimathea had laid him.[7] TO THE TRALLIANS 9.[8]

**THE BOLDNESS OF JOSEPH.** CHRYSOSTOM: This was Joseph, who had been concealing his discipleship. Now he became very bold, after the death of Christ. For neither was he an obscure person nor unnoticed. He was one of the council, and highly distinguished, and as we see, courageous.[9] For he exposed himself to death, taking upon himself the enmity of all by his affection to Jesus. He begged for the body and did not desist until he obtained it. Not only that, but by laying it in his own new tomb, he actively demonstrated his love and courage.[10] THE GOSPEL OF ST. MATTHEW, HOMILY 88.[11]

---

[1]Cf. Ex 12. [2]Cf. Ex 5. [3]Cf. 1 Cor 5:8. [4]TLG 2022.015, 35.397.6-16, 18-20; SSGF 2:220. [5]Cf. Mt 27:23-50. [6]NPNF 1 3:74. [7]Cf. Mt 27:57-60; Mk 15:42-47; Lk 23:50-53; Jn 19:38-42. [8]ANF 1:70; TLG 1443.001, 2.9.5.3-5. [9]Cf. Mk 15:43; Lk 23:50. [10]Cf. Mt 27:60; Mk 15:46; Lk 23:53. [11]NPNF 1 10:522*; TLG 2062.152, 58.778.5-15.

### 15:44 Summoning the Centurion, Pilate Asked Whether He Was Already Dead

**WHETHER WE CAN BE SURE THAT JESUS DIED.** AUGUSTINE: As the Gospel declares, those who were present particularly marveled at this: After the lament in which he expressed the figure of sin, he immediately gave up his spirit. For those who were suspended on the cross were tortured by a lingering death. Consequently, the legs of the thieves were broken, in order that they might quickly die and be taken down from the cross before the Sabbath.[12] But that he was found to be already dead was a cause for amazement. And we read that Pilate also wondered at this, when the body of the Lord was asked of him for burial.[13] ON THE TRINITY 4.13.16.[14]

### 15:46a A Linen Shroud

**BURIED WITH UTTER SIMPLICITY.** BEDE: The vanity of the rich, who even in their graves cannot do without their riches, receives its condemnation from the simple and unassuming interment of the Lord. Hence indeed the custom of the church was derived, that the sacrifice of the altar should not be commemorated by wrapping the elements in silk, or any colored cloth, but in linen; as the body of the Lord was buried in clean fine linen.[15] EXPOSITION ON THE GOSPEL OF MARK 4.15.46.[16]

### 15:46b They Laid Him in a Tomb

**WHETHER HIS BODY REMAINED IN THE TOMB WHEN HE DESCENDED INTO THE NETHER WORLD.** ATHANASIUS: This above all shows the foolishness of those who say that the Word was changed into bones and flesh. For if this had been so, there would have been no need of a tomb. For the body would have gone by itself to preach to the spirits in Hades. But as it was, he himself went to preach, while the body that Joseph wrapped in a linen cloth laid away at Golgotha.[17] And so it is demonstrated to all that the body was not the Word, but body of the Word. LETTER 59, TO EPICTETUS 6.[18]

---

[12]Cf. Jn 19:31-32. [13]Cf. Mk 15:43-44. [14]Cetedoc 0329, 50.4.13.13; FC 45:151; cf. NPNF 1:78. [15]Cf. Mt 27:59; Mk 15:46; Lk 23:53; Jn 19:40. [16]Cetedoc 1355, 4.15.1668; CCL 120:638; *GMI* 434; cf. HOG, loc. cit. [17]Cf. Mt 27:59-60; Mk 15:46; Lk 23:53; Jn 19:40-41. [18]TLG 2035.110, 6.1-6; NPNF 2 4:572. It was not the Word laid in the tomb but the body of the Word. The Word was not changed into bones and flesh but assumed bones and flesh. Jesus descended into the nether world while his body remained in the tomb.

## 16:1-8 THE EMPTY TOMB

*[1]And when the sabbath was past, Mary Magdalene, and Mary the mother of James, and Salome, bought spices, so that they might go and anoint him. [2]And very early on the first day of the week they went to the tomb when the sun had risen. [3]And they were saying to one another, "Who will roll away the stone for us from the door of the tomb?" [4]And looking up,*

*they saw that the stone was rolled back; it was very large. [5]And entering the tomb, they saw a young man sitting on the right side, dressed in a white robe; and they were amazed. [6]And he said to them, "Do not be amazed; you seek Jesus of Nazareth, who was crucified. He has risen, he is not here; see the place where they laid him. [7]But go, tell his disciples and Peter that he is going before you to Galilee; there you will see him, as he told you." [8]And they went out and fled from the tomb; for trembling and astonishment had come upon them; and they said nothing to any one, for they were afraid.*

**OVERVIEW:** To behold the resurrection, the stone must be rolled away from our own hearts. The women at the tomb were the first to honor the risen Christ. The apostles were the first to suffer for him (PETER CHRYSOLOGUS). The daily transformation of the early morning from darkness to dawn is forever hallowed by the resurrection (AUGUSTINE). The resurrection was revealed gradually, respecting the frailty of beholders to grasp its significance. The apex moment of the diffusion of darkness is the time of the resurrection (BEDE). The holy sabbath gleams even brighter under the new covenant as the weekly celebration of the resurrection (ATHANASIUS). As the virgin's womb had been sealed and yet he entered life, so also the sepulcher was firmly sealed and yet he was raised to new life (PRUDENTIUS, BEDE). The resurrection is announced by a youth as an allusion that the resurrected body would be developed in full strength (ISIDORE OF SEVILLE). Christ is present where the sign of the cross is rightly exalted—not the material cross itself as a piece of wood but the crucified one who now lives (JOHN OF DAMASCUS). Between Jesus' resurrection and the general resurrection, death is, for those who have faith, in effect dead and lacking in power, as a lion slain (AUGUSTINE). God does not lack power to raise us also (APOSTOLIC CONSTITUTIONS). Christian pilgrims

to Jerusalem in antiquity wrote specifically and in detail of what they thought was the sepulcher reported in Mark (BEDE).

### 16:1a *When the Sabbath Was Past*

**SABBATH AND RESURRECTION.** ATHANASIUS: In the time of the old covenant, the sabbath was highly revered. Now under the gospel the sabbath has been recast, now viewed as the Lord's resurrection day. The sabbath formerly had pertained to the pedagogy and rudiments of the law. When the great master himself came and fulfilled them all for us, all that had prefigured his coming was transformed. The old sabbath was like a candle lit in the night before the rising and appearing of the sun.[1] HOMILIES.[2]

### 16:1b *They Brought Spices*

**WOMEN FIRST TO HONOR THE RISEN CHRIST.** PETER CHRYSOLOGUS: The women were first to honor the risen Christ, the apostles first to suffer for him. The women were ready with spices; the apostles prepared for scourges. The women entered the tomb; the apostles would soon enter the dungeon. The women hastened to express their eulogy; the apostles embraced chains for

---

[1]Cf. Jn 20:26; Heb 8:13; Rev 1:10. [2]TLG 2035.069, 28.148.18.29; *GMI* 435**.

his sake. The women poured oils; the apostles poured out their blood. SERMON 79.[3]

## 16:2a Very Early on the First Day of the Week

**THE DAWN.** AUGUSTINE: All the Gospels refer to the period when the heavens were just beginning to brighten in the east.[4] This, of course, does not take place until the sunrise is at hand. For it is the brightness which is diffused by the rising sun that is familiarly designated by the name of the dawn. Mark does not contradict the other Evangelist who uses the phrase, "When it was yet dark."[5] For as the day breaks, what remains of the darkness passes away just in proportion as the sun continues to rise. HARMONY OF THE GOSPELS 3.24.65.[6]

**THE MEANING OF THE EARLY HOUR.** BEDE: Upon this most sacred early morning hour is bestowed great dignity from the glory of the Lord's victory over death. For it was in the earliest inception of that day that the women became attentive in doing their service to their Lord. Speaking mystically, the night was already beginning to grow toward an emerging dawn.[7] He who is the author and superintendent of time rose from the dead during the final part of the night. The whole of the emerging day is thus made a festival, brightened by the light of his resurrection. EXPOSITION ON THE GOSPEL OF MARK 2.7.[8]

## 16:2b They Went to the Tomb

**THE SEQUENCE OF BURIAL EVENTS.** BEDE: As to its being said in the gospel reading that holy women came to see the sepulcher "on the evening which was growing on toward the dawn of Sunday," we should understand this thus: they

started to come during the evening, but reached the sepulcher as the morning of Sunday was dawning; that is, they prepared the spices with which they wanted to anoint our Lord's body on [Saturday] evening, but brought the spices that they had prepared in the evening to the sepulcher in the morning. Matthew, for the sake of brevity, wrote this more obscurely;[9] but the other evangelists[10] show more distinctly the order in which it was done. After our Lord had been buried on Friday, the women went away from the tomb and prepared spices and ointments for as long as it was permitted them to work. They then refrained from activity on the sabbath, in accord with they commandment,[11] as Luke clearly reports.[12] When the sabbath was over, as evening was coming on, the time for working had returned. Being resolute in their devotion, they bought the spices that they had not prepared [earlier] (as Mark records it) so that they might come and anoint him.[13] EXPOSITION ON THE GOSPEL OF MARK 2.7.[14]

## 16:3 Who Will Roll Away the Stone for Us?

**THE DOOR OF THE HEART.** PETER CHRYSOLOGUS: Is it from the door of the sepulcher, or of your own hearts? From the tomb, or from your own eyes? You whose heart is shut, whose eyes are closed, are unable to discover the glory of the open grave. Pour then your oil, if you wish to see that glory, not on the body of the Lord,

---

[3]Cetedoc 0227+, 24A.79.37; GMI 436. In this way both sexes participated in the earliest celebration of the Lord's death and resurrection. [4]Cf. Mt 28:1; Mk 16:2; Lk 24:1; Jn 20:1. [5]Jn 20:1. [6]Cetedoc 0273, 3.24.65.354.8; NPNF 1 6:210**. [7]Cf. Mt 28:1; Mk 16:2; Lk 24:1. [8]Cetedoc 1367, 2.7.47; HOG 2:60**. [9]Cf. Mt 28:1. [10]Mk 16:1-2; Lk 24:1. [11]Cf. Ex 12:16; 20:8-10. [12]Cf. Lk 23:56. [13]Cf. Mk 16:1. [14]Cetedoc 1367, 2.7.26; HOG 2:59-60. The women who were present on the day before the sabbath returned on the day after the sabbath.

but on the eyes of your hearts. By the light of faith you will then see that which through the deficiency of faith now lies hidden in darkness.[15] SERMON 82.[16]

**THE FRAILTY OF BEHOLDERS AND THEIR GRADUAL RECOGNITION.** BEDE: Our Lord and redeemer revealed the glory of his resurrection to his disciples gradually and over a period of time, undoubtedly because so great was the virtue of the miracle that the weak hearts of mortals could not grasp [the significance of] this all at once. Thus, he had regard for the frailty of those seeking him. To those who came first to the tomb, both the women who were aflame with love for him and the men, he showed the stone rolled back.[17] Since his body had been carried away, he showed them the linen cloths[18] in which it had been wrapped lying there alone. Then, to the women who were searching eagerly, who were confused in their minds about what they had found out about him, he showed a vision of angels[19] who disclosed evidences of the fact that he had risen again. Thus, with the report of his resurrection already accomplished, going ahead of him, the Lord of hosts and the king of glory[20] himself at length appeared and made clear with what great might he had overcome the death he had temporarily tasted. EXPOSITION ON THE GOSPEL OF MARK 2.9.[21]

## 16:4 The Stone Was Rolled Back

**THE STONE COULD NOT HOLD HIM.** PRUDENTIUS:

> Neither the stone nor the bolts of the
> tomb could hold Christ a captive;
> Death lies conquered by him, he has
> trampled on hell's fiery chasm.
> With him a throng of saints ascended to
> heavenly regions,

And to many he showed himself, letting them see and touch him.[22] SCENES FROM SACRED HISTORY 43, THE SEPULCHER OF CHRIST.[23]

**THE STONE AS EVIDENCE.** BEDE: [The angel] rolled back the stone not to throw open a way for our Lord to come forth, but to provide evidence to people that he had already come forth. As the virgin's womb was closed, so the sepulcher was closed, yet he entered the world through her closed womb, and so he left the world through the closed sepulcher. EXPOSITION ON THE GOSPEL OF MARK 2.7.[24]

## 16:5a Entering the Tomb

**WHETHER TWO ANGELS OR ONE.** AUGUSTINE: Mark tells us that the women entered the sepulcher, and there saw a young man sitting on the right side, covered with a long white garment, and that they were frightened.[25] In Matthew's version, the stone was already rolled away from the sepulcher and the angel was sitting upon it.[26] The explanation may be that Matthew has simply said nothing about the angel whom they saw when they entered into the sepulcher, and that Mark has said nothing about the one whom they saw sitting outside upon the stone. In this way they would have seen two angels, and have assumed two separate angelic reports. HARMONY OF THE GOSPELS 3.24.63.[27]

---

[15]Cf. Rev 3:18. [16]Cetedoc 0227+, 42a.82.23; *GMI* 438*. [17]Cf. Mt 28:2; Mk 16:4; Lk 24:2; Jn 20:1. [18]Cf. Lk 24:12; Jn 20:3-7. [19]Cf. Mt 28:1-5; Mk 16:1-6; Lk 24:1-10. [20]Cf. Ps 24:10. [21]Cetedoc 1367, 2.9.1; *HOG* 2:78. [22]Cf. Mt 27:52-53; 28:1-10; Lk 24:39-40; Jn 20:27; Acts 1:3. [23]FC 52:193. [24]Cetedoc 1367, 2.7.91; *HOG* 2:61**. The womb's opening at his birth is viewed as an analogy to the tomb's opening at his resurrection. [25]Cf. Mk 16:5. [26]The issue: Did the witnesses see two angels or one at different times? Cf. Mt 28:2. [27]Cetedoc 0273, 3.24.63.352.15; NPNF 1 6:209**. The reports of the two Evangelists are not contradictory.

**THE PILGRIMS' DESCRIPTION OF THE TOMB.**
BEDE: What we have learned about this,
according to a description related by those of
our contemporaries who have been in Jerusalem who, upon their return, left a written
record for us of what they saw there: It was a
vaulted chamber, hollowed out of rock. Its
height was such that a person standing in the
middle could touch the summit with his hand.
Its entrance faced east, and the great stone
about which the gospel tells us was placed over
it. To the right as one enters was the place that
was specially prepared as a resting place for the
Lord's body, seven feet in length, about two
feet above the rest of the floor. The opening
was not made like that of ordinary sepulchers,
from above, but entirely from the side, from
which the body could be placed inside. EXPOSI-
TION ON THE GOSPEL OF MARK 2.10.[28]

### 16:5b *They Saw a Young Man*

**WHY A YOUTH?** ISIDORE OF SEVILLE: Why a
"young man"?[29] The resurrection of the dead, as
the apostle declares, will be "unto the fullness
of the measure of the stature of Christ,"[30] that
is, in the season of youth, which needs no further development and which is free from all
defect, complete in every respect, having fullness of strength. SENTENCES 1.29.[31]

### 16:5c *Sitting on the Right Side, Dressed in a White Robe*

**THE WORD OF ETERNAL LIFE.** GREGORY THE
GREAT: And let us also take note of what it
means that the angel is seen sitting on the
right side. For what does the left side mean
but this present life; and the right hand side, if
not life eternal? . . . And so, since our
redeemer has now passed over beyond the

mortality of this present life, rightly does the
angel, who had come to announce his entry
into eternal life, sit at the right side. And he
came clothed in white: for he was announcing
the joy of this our present solemnity. HOMI-
LIES 21.[32]

**ANGELIC POSTURES PREFIGURED HIS
PRIESTLY AND REGAL OFFICE.** BEDE: It was fitting that the herald of his resurrection is
reported to have been sitting,[33] so that by sitting he might prefigure him who, having triumphed over the author of death, would
ascend to his seat in his everlasting kingdom.
. . . Sitting on a throne is the act of a king, and
standing at a place of sacrifice is that of a high
priest. Because our redeemer deigned to
become for us at the same time both a king and
a priest—a priest to cleanse us thoroughly
from our sins by being a sacrificial offering in
his passion, a king to bestow on us an everlasting kingdom. The angels who proclaim his resurrection appeared while sitting in order to
signify that he had gone to seek his seat[34] in the
heavenly kingdom after having overcome death.
They appeared also standing[35] to show that he
also intercedes for us in the mysteries of his
Father as a high priest. EXPOSITION ON THE
GOSPEL OF MARK 2.7, 10.[36]

---

[28]Cetedoc 1367, 2.10.182; *HOG* 2:95*. [29]Cf. Mk 16:5. [30]Eph 4:13.
[31]Cetedoc 1199, 1.594.15; *GMI* 439**. [32]Cetedoc 1711, 2.21.2.16;
*SSGF* 2:242. [33]Cf. Mt 28:2; Mk 16:5. The issue is why Mark
reports the young man as sitting while in Luke two men are
standing. [34]Cf. Mk 16:5. [35]Lk 24:4: "two men stood by them in
dazzling apparel." [36]Cetedoc 1367, 2.7.100; 2.10.116; *HOG* 2:62,
92. Since our Redeemer was both priest and king, the angels who
proclaimed his resurrection appeared in the posture of both priest
(standing, as in Luke) and king (sitting, as in Mark). "Standing is
appropriate to one fighting, sitting to one ruling. It was fitting that
the angel who proclaimed the coming of our Lord into the world
appeared standing, that by his standing [position] he might express
the fact that the one he was proclaiming was coming to do battle
with the prince of this world," *HOG* 2:62.

## 16:6a *You Seek Jesus of Nazareth, Who Was Crucified*

**The Tree as Sign.** John of Damascus: When we worship the likeness of the priceless and life-giving cross, we know that it is made out of a tree. We are not honoring the tree as such (God forbid), but the likeness as a symbol of Christ. For he said to his disciples, admonishing them, "Then shall appear the sign of the Son of Man in Heaven,"[37] meaning the cross. And so also the angel of the resurrection said to the woman, "You seek Jesus of Nazareth who was crucified."[38] And the apostle said, "We preach Christ crucified."[39] For there are many named Jesus and many who may claim to be the Christ, but we worship the one crucified. He does not say pierced but crucified. It behooves us, then, to worship the sign of Christ. For wherever the sign may be, there also will he be. But it does not behoove us to worship the material of which the image of the cross is composed, even though it is gold or precious stones. The Orthodox Faith 4.11.[40]

## 16:6b *He Has Risen*

**The Quickening Power of His Resurrection.** Apostolic Constitutions: The resurrection in which we believe is that which has already been demonstrated in the resurrection of our Lord. For it is he that raised Lazarus after he had been in the grave four days,[41] and Jairus' daughter,[42] and the widow's son.[43] It is he that raised himself by the command of the Father in the space of three days, who is the pledge of our resurrection. For he says: "I am the resurrection and the life."[44] Now the very One who brought Jonah[45] alive and unhurt out of the belly of the whale in the space of three days, and who brought the three children out of the furnace of Babylon and Daniel out of the mouth of the lions,[46] does not lack power to raise us up also. Constitutions of the Holy Apostles 5.7.[47]

**The Death of Death.** Augustine: He died, but he vanquished death; in himself he put an end to what we feared; he took it upon himself and he vanquished it, as a mighty hunter he captured and slew the lion.[48] Where is death? Seek it in Christ, for it exists no longer; but it did exist and now it is dead. O life, O death of death! Be of good heart; it will die in us, also. What has taken place in our head will take place in his members; death will die in us also. But when? At the end of the world, at the resurrection of the dead in which we believe and concerning which we do not doubt. Sermon 233.3-4.[49]

**His Resurrection Recapitulated in Our Baptism.** Basil of Seleucia: Christ descended into hell to liberate its captives. In one instant he destroyed all record of our ancient debt incurred under the law, in order to lead us to heaven where there is no death but only eternal life and righteousness. By the baptism which you, the newly enlightened, have just received, you now share in these blessings. Your initiation into the life of grace is the pledge of your resurrection. Your baptism is the promise of the life of heaven. By your immersion you imitated the burial of the Lord, but

---

[37]Mt 24:30. [38]Mt 28:5; Mk 16:6. [39]1 Cor 1:23. [40]TLG 2934.004, 84.61-71; NPNF 2 9:80*; cf. FC 37:351. [41]Cf. Jn 11:1-44. [42]Cf. Mk 5:21-43. [43]Cf. Lk 7:11-15. [44]Jn 11:25. [45]Cf. Jon 2:1-10. [46]Cf. Dan 3:1-30; 6:1-28. [47]PG 1:844; ANF 7:440*. The power of his resurrection is the premise of ours. We are being raised to new life because of his resurrection, which demonstrates that God does not lack power to raise us also. [48]Cf. 1 Sam 17:34-36. [49]Cetedoc 0284, 233.38.1114.27; FC 38:221.

when you came out of the water you were conscious only of the reality of the resurrection.... The grace of the Spirit works in a mysterious way in the font, and the outward appearance must not obscure the wonder of it. Although water serves as the instrument, it is grace which gives rebirth. Grace transforms all who are placed in the font as the seed is transformed in the womb. It refashions all who go down into the water as metal is recast in a furnace. It reveals to them the mysteries of immortality; it seals them with the pledge of resurrection. These wonderful mysteries are symbolized for you, the newly enlightened, even in the garments you wear. See how you are clothed in the outward signs of these blessings. The radiant brightness of your robe stands for incorrupt-ibility. The white band encircling your head like a diadem proclaims your liberty. In your hand you hold the sign of your victory over the devil. Christ is showing you that you have risen from the dead. He does this now in a symbolic way, but soon he will reveal the full reality if we keep the garment of faith undefiled and do not let sin extinguish the lamp of grace. If we preserve the crown of the Spirit, the Lord will call from heaven in a voice of tremendous majesty, yet full of tenderness: Come, blessed of my Father, take possession of the kingdom prepared for you since the beginning of the world. To him be glory and power for ever, through endless ages, amen. EASTER HOMILY.[50]

---

[50]TLG 2800.003, 28.1080.23-42; JF B 46-47.

## 16:9-13 RESURRECTION

[9]Now when he rose early on the first day of the week, he appeared first to Mary Magdalene, from whom he had cast out seven demons. [10]She went and told those who had been with him, as they mourned and wept. [11]But when they heard that he was alive and had been seen by her, they would not believe it.

[12]After this he appeared in another form to two of them, as they were walking into the country. [13]And they went back and told the rest, but they did not believe them.

---

OVERVIEW: The disciples did not recognize the risen Lord, even when he was visibly walking with them on the way, because they had forgotten his promises. Until the breaking of bread their eyes were obstructed not by the risen Lord but by their own lack of perception (AUGUSTINE). Resurrection day, the first day of the week, is set apart as the mark of new beginnings, analogous to the first day of creation (ISIDORE OF SEVILLE). As a woman (Eve) was first to taste death, so a woman (Mary Magdalene) was first to taste life. As a woman was prescient in the fall, so a woman was prescient in beholding the dawning of redemption, thus reversing the curse upon Eve. The first to testify to the risen Lord was a woman from whom he had cast out seven demons (BEDE).

## 16:9a He Rose Early on the First Day of the Week

**THE THREE DAYS.** IGNATIUS: The day of preparation, then, comprises the suffering death, the Sabbath embraces the burial, the Lord's day contains the resurrection. TO THE TRALLIANS 9.[1]

**ON KEEPING EASTER.** UNKNOWN GREEK AUTHOR OF THE FIFTH CENTURY: This is the day which the Lord has made: let us keep it with gladness and rejoicing.[2] Why should we do so? Because the sun is no longer darkened; instead everything is bathed in light. Because the veil of the temple is no longer rent; instead the Church is recognized. Because we no longer hold palm branches; instead we carry the newly enlightened. . . . This is the day in the truest sense: the day of triumph, the day custom consecrates to the resurrection, the day on which we adorn ourselves with grace, the day on which we partake of the spiritual lamb. This is the day on which milk is given to those born again, and on which God's plan for the poor is realized. Let us keep it with gladness and rejoicing, not by running off to the taverns, but by hastening to the martyrs' shrines; not by esteeming drunkenness, but by loving temperance; not by dancing in the marketplace, but by singing psalms at home. . . . This is the day on which Adam was set free and Eve delivered from her affliction. It is the day on which cruel death shuddered, the strength of hard stones was shattered and destroyed, the bars of tombs were broken and set aside. It is the day on which the bodies of people long dead were restored to their former life and the laws of the underworld, hitherto ever power-

ful and immutable, were repealed. It is the day on which the heavens were opened at the rising of Christ the Lord, and on which, for the good of the human race, the flourishing and fruitful tree of the resurrection sent forth branches all over the world, as if the world were a garden. It is the day on which the lilies of the newly enlightened sprang up, the streams that sustained sinners ran dry, the strength of the devil drained away and demonic armies were scattered. EASTER HOMILIES 51.1-3.[3]

**WHY THE FIRST DAY OF THE WEEK IS SET APART.** ISIDORE OF SEVILLE: The sacredness of the Lord's Day is apparent from the holy Scripture. This was the first day of the world. On this day the elements of the creation were formed. On this day the angels were created. On this day Christ rose from the dead. On this day the Holy Ghost came down from heaven on the apostles. On this same day the manna in the wilderness was first given. ON THE ORIGIN OF ECCLESIASTICAL OFFICES 1.24.[4]

## 16:9b He First Appeared to Mary Magdalene, from Whom He Had Cast Out Seven Demons

**THE FALLEN WOMAN FIRST TO SEE THE RISEN LORD.** BEDE: A woman[5] first tasted death, but in Magdalene woman first saw the resurrection, that woman might not bear the perpetual guilt of transgression among men. EXPOSI-

---

[1]TLG 1443.002, 2.9.6.1-2; ANF 1:70. The first day of the week is the day after the Passover sabbath. In this way there were three days. [2]Cf. Ps 118:24. [3]JF B 88-89; SC 187, 318-22. [4]Cetedoc 1207, 1.25..6; GMI 444-45. Thus resurrection day, the first day of the week, is set apart, according to the Christian sanctification of time, as the time of new beginnings comparable to the first day of creation, the day of Pentecost and the receiving of bread from heaven by the people of the exodus. [5]Eve.

TION ON THE GOSPEL OF MARK 4.16.9-10.[6]

### THE FIRST ANNOUNCEMENT COMES BY WOMAN.

BEDE: It was also a woman who first announced to the disciples that the Lord had come forth from the confinement of the grave,[7] so that "where sin abounded grace might more abound."[8] COMMENTARY ON ACTS 12.13.[9]

### 16:12a *As They Were Walking into the Country He Appeared in Another Form to Two of Them*

**THEIR IMPEDED RECOGNITION.** AUGUSTINE: It seems as if some impediment to recognition had been effected in the eyes of those who beheld him; and when it is plainly said elsewhere: "He appeared to them in another shape"[10]—obviously in his own body with another appearance—some effect was produced which acted as an impediment to prevent them, that is, their eyes were subjected to a delay in recognition. LETTER 149, TO PAULINUS.[11]

### 16:12b *They Did Not Believe Him*

**THE DIMNESS OF THEIR PERCEPTION.** AUGUSTINE: Their eyes were obstructed, that they should not recognize him until the breaking of the bread. And thus, in accordance with the state of their minds, which were still ignorant

of the truth (that the Christ would die and rise again), their eyes were similarly hindered. It was not that the truth himself was misleading them, but rather that they were themselves unable to perceive the truth.[12] HARMONY OF THE GOSPELS 3.25.72.[13]

**WHY RECOGNITION CAME HARD.** AUGUSTINE: Jesus appeared; he was visible to their eyes, yet he was not recognized. The master walked with them on the way; in fact, he was the way on which they were not yet walking; but he found that they had wandered some distance from the way. For when he was with them before his passion, he had foretold all—that he would suffer, that he would die, that he would rise again on the third day—he had predicted all; but his death was as a loss of memory for them. They were so disturbed when they saw him hanging on the cross that they forgot his teaching, did not look for his resurrection, and failed to keep his promises in mind. SERMON 235.1.[14]

---

[6]Cetedoc 1355, 4.16.1860; CCL 120:643; GC 1:443. Woman was first to taste the fall and first to behold the resurrection. [7]Cf. Mk 16:10; Jn 20:18. [8]Cf. Rom 5:20. [9]Cetedoc 1357, 12.52; CAA 113. Eve was first to taste death; Mary Magdalene was the first to taste life. [10]Mk 16:12; Lk 24:16. [11]Cetedoc 0262, 149.44.3.377.2; FC 20:263. An inward obstruction of their vision may have delayed their external recognition. [12]Cf. Lk 24:13-32. [13]Cetedoc 0273, 3.25.72.371.21; NPNF 1 6:217*. [14]Cetedoc 0284, 235.67.138.19; FC 38:228.

# 16:14-18 THE COMMISSION
# TO THE APOSTOLATE

*⁴Afterward he appeared to the eleven themselves as they sat at table; and he upbraided them for their unbelief and hardness of heart, because they had not believed those who saw him after he had risen. ¹⁵And he said to them, "Go into all the world and preach the gospel to the whole creation. ¹⁶He who believes and is baptized will be saved; but he who does not believe will be condemned. ¹⁷And these signs will accompany those who believe: in my name they will cast out demons; they will speak in new tongues; ¹⁸they will pick up serpents, and if they drink any deadly thing, it will not hurt them; they will lay their hands on the sick, and they will recover."*

**OVERVIEW:** Jerome was aware of textual difficulties associated with the longer ending of Mark ( JEROME). Early exegetes of this concluding passage in Mark focused largely upon the ironies of the text: Those who at first did not believe became fathers of the faith for all who would later believe (AUGUSTINE). What the apostles themselves had seen and not believed, the Gentiles would later believe without seeing. Thus the reproof of the apostles was justified and was required before their commissioning (AUGUSTINE, NOVATIAN). The unity of the whole body of Christ derives from its continuity with the teaching of the apostles (TERTULLIAN). The gifts of speaking in tongues and casting out demons were given not exclusively to the first apostolic generation but also to the continuing apostolate (AMBROSE, GREGORY THE GREAT). The command to witness is addressed to the apostles and the continuing apostolate that follows after them (AUGUSTINE). Those who hold fast to the faith of the apostles themselves participate in the gifts of the apostolate, whose signs and wonders may convict unbelievers even when words fail (APOSTOLIC CONSTITUTIONS). God the creator, whose guiding providence is running its course throughout all nations, seeks to be known as loving Father ( JUSTIN MARTYR, NOVATIAN). Each believer receives gifts from the Father and Son through the Spirit according to each one's capacity to receive (AMBROSE). Those who study Scripture with good judgment may read and even memorize poisonous, heretical texts without harm provided they remain faithful to the rule of faith learned at their baptism (AUGUSTINE).

## 16:14a *Afterward He Appeared to the Eleven Themselves As They Sat at Table*

**IN SOME COPIES.** JEROME: In some copies, and especially in the Greek codices, it is written according to Mark at the end of his Gospel: "At length Jesus appeared to the eleven as they were at table."[1] AGAINST THE PELAGIANS 2.15.[2]

---

[1]Mk 16:14. [2]Cetedoc 0615, 2.15.1; FC 53:317. Jerome's phrase "in some copies" shows that by the end of the fourth century Christian scholars were aware of textual difficulties associated with the ending of Mark.

**No Eating Without Teeth.** Jerome: As he showed them real hands and a real side,[3] so he really ate with his disciples;[4] really walked with Cleophas;[5] conversed with men with a real tongue;[6] really reclined at supper;[7] with real hands took bread, blessed and broke it, and was offering it to them.[8] . . . Do not put the power of the Lord on a level with the tricks of magicians, so that he may appear to have been what he was not, and may be thought to have eaten without teeth, walked without feet, broken bread without hands, spoken without a tongue, and showed a side which had no ribs. To Pammachius Against John of Jerusalem 34.[9]

**His Presence in the Breaking of Bread.** Bede: He appeared in the breaking of bread to those who, supposing that he was a stranger, invited him to share their table.[10] He will also be present to us when we willingly bestow whatever goods we can on strangers and poor people.[11] And he will be present to us in the breaking of bread, when we partake with a chaste and simple conscience in the sacrament of his body, the living bread.[12] Exposition on the Gospel of Mark 2.8.[13]

## 16:14b He Upbraided Them for Their Unbelief and Hardness of Heart

**Why He Chided Them.** Augustine: The Lord Jesus himself chided his disciples, his earliest followers who remained close to him, because they did not believe that he was now alive, but grieved over him as dead.[14] They were the fathers of the faith, but they were not yet fully believers. They did not yet believe, although they were made teachers so that the whole world might believe what they were destined to preach and what they were going to die for. They did not yet believe that he, whom

they had seen raising others from the dead, had himself arisen. Deservedly, then, were they rebuked. Sermon 231.1.[15]

**The Great Commission.** Augustine: He also showed himself on one final occasion to the eleven as they sat at table together[16]—that is, on the fortieth day itself. He was now on the point of leaving them and ascending into heaven.[17] He was minded on that memorable day especially to reprove them for their refusal to believe those who had seen him after he had risen, until they had seen him themselves. For when they would preach the gospel after his ascension, the nations themselves would be ready to believe what they did not see. . . . If, therefore, they were charged to preach that those who do not believe will be condemned, when they themselves had not believed what they had just seen, was it not fitting that they should themselves first be thus reproved for their own refusal to believe those to whom the Lord had shown himself at an earlier stage until they should have seen him with their own eyes? Harmony of the Gospels 3.25.76.[18]

## 16:15a Go into All the World

**Common Men Who Testified of the Uncommon Grace of God.** Justin Martyr: A band of twelve men went forth from Jerusalem, and they were common men, not trained in

---

[3]Cf. Jn 20:27. [4]Cf. Mk 16:14. [5]Cf. Lk 24:13-35. [6]Cf. Lk 24:17-27. [7]Cf. Mk 16:14. [8]Cf. Lk 24:30. [9]Cetedoc 0612, 34.404.27; NPNF 2 6:442*. There is no magic here. He rose from the dead, with his actual teeth and with no false ribs. [10]Cf. Lk 24:29. [11]Cf. Mt 25:31-46. [12]Cf. Jn 6:51. [13]Cetedoc 1367, 2.8.173; HOG 2:75. Whenever we offer bread to the poor or care for the stranger, the risen Lord is present. [14]Cf. Mk 16:14. [15]Cetedoc 0284, 231.116.244.3; FC 38:203-4*. [16]Cf. Mt 28:16-20; Mk 16:14-15. [17]Cf. Mk 16:19-20; Lk 24:51; Acts 1:9; Eph 4:8-10. [18]Cetedoc 0273, 3.25.76.379.24; NPNF 1 6:220*.

speaking, but by the power of God they testified to every race of humankind. First Apology 39.[19]

**The Church Remains One in Its Countless Cultural Expressions.** Tertullian: Then in this same way the apostles went out to found churches in every city possible. It is from these apostolic churches that all the subsequent churches, one after the other, derived the rule of faith and the seeds of doctrine. Even to today they continue to derive from the apostles that which is necessary in order that they be churches. Indeed, it is for this reason only that they are able to deem themselves as apostolic, as being the offspring of apostolic churches. As in science, every genus reverts to its original for its classification, so with the apostolic church. However many or great these churches may be, they comprise but one primitive church, founded by the apostles, from which they all spring. In this way all are primitive. All are apostolic. They all are one, by means of their unbroken unity, peaceful communion, title of descent, and bond of hospitality. These are privileges that no other rule directs than the one tradition of the same mystery. Prescription Against Heretics 20.[20]

### 16:15b Preach the Gospel to the Whole Creation

**The Gospel Proclaimed to All Creation.** Novatian: He willed that the apostles as spiritual progenitors of the new humanity would be sent by his Son into the entire world,[21] so that all human sufferers might come to the knowledge of their creator. Insofar as any choose to follow him, they have One whom they now address in their prayers as Father,[22] instead of God. His providence has run and at present runs its course not only among individuals but also through whole cities and states, whose overthrow he predicted by the words of the prophets. His providence indeed runs its course through the whole cosmos itself. The Trinity 8.[23]

**The Uttermost Parts of the Earth.** Augustine: The command to the apostles to be witnesses to him in Jerusalem, Judea, Samaria, and even to the uttermost parts of the earth[24] was not addressed exclusively to those to whom it was immediately spoken. They alone would not be the only ones who would carry such an enormous task to completion. Similarly he seems to be speaking to the apostles very personally when he says: "Behold I am with you even to the end of the world,"[25] yet who does not know that he made this promise to the universal church which will last from now even to the consummation of the world by successive births and deaths? Letter 199, To Hesychius 49.[26]

### 16:16 He Who Believes and Is Baptized Shall Be Saved

**Why the Catechetical Précis of Baptismal Faith Is So Brief.** Augustine: The ecumenically received faith is taught in the creed and committed to memory in a form of the utmost possible brevity, so as to frame an expression in few words of that which was intended to be explained at large afterwards to persons in a state of formation and advancement in knowledge of God. Of Faith and the Creed 1.[27]

---

[19]TLG 0645.001, 39.3.1-4; LCC 1:266. [20]Cetedoc 0005, 20.18; ANF 3:252**. [21]Cf. Mt 28:19; Mk 16:15; Eph 4:11-12. [22]Cf. Mt 6:9; Lk 11:2; Rom 8:15. [23]Cetedoc 0071, 8.24; ANF 5:617**; cf. FC 67:39. [24]Cf. Acts 1:8. [25]Mt 28:20. [26]Cetedoc 0262, 199.57.12.287.14; FC 30:396-97**. [27]Cetedoc 0293, 1.1.3.13; GMI 450*. The rule of faith provided at baptism summarizes the faith.

**WHETHER BAPTISMAL FAITH ASSURES SALVATION.** AUGUSTINE: We know that the dead who die in the Lord are blessed,[28] and they have no concern with what they would have done if they had lived a longer time.[29] We know that those who believe in the Lord from their own heart do this of their own will and free choice. We who now believe act rightly when we pray to God for those who refuse to believe, and pray that they themselves may in time freely will to believe. LETTER 217, TO VITALIS.[30]

### 16:17a These Signs Will Accompany Those Who Believe

**THE CHURCH CONTINUES TO EMBODY THESE GIFTS.** GREGORY THE GREAT: Is it, my brethren, because we do not have these signs that you do not believe? These were needed at the church's beginning. The new faith needed to be nourished by miracles to grow. When we plant a vineyard, we must water the plants till we see they have begun to grow in the earth, and when they have once taken root we cease to water them constantly.... But true life cannot be obtained by means of these outward signs by those who perform them. For although corporeal works of this kind sometimes do proclaim an inner holiness of life, they do not bring it about. HOMILIES ON THE GOSPELS 29.[31]

**THE PURPOSE OF ACCOMPANYING SIGNS.** APOSTOLIC CONSTITUTIONS: With good reason did he say to all of us together, when we became fully aware of those gifts that were given from him by the Spirit: "And these signs will accompany those who believe; in my name they will cast out demons; they will speak in new tongues; they will pick up serpents, and if they drink any deadly thing, it will not hurt them; they will lay their hands on the sick, and they will recover."[32]

These gifts were first bestowed on us the apostles when we were about to preach the gospel to every creature. Later they of necessity were afforded to others who had by the apostles come to believe. These gifts were not given for the advantage of those who perform them, but for the conviction of the unbelievers, that those whom the word did not persuade, the power of signs might put to shame. CONSTITUTIONS OF THE HOLY APOSTLES 8.1.1.[33]

### 16:17b And They Will Speak in New Tongues

**WHETHER ALL APOSTOLIC GIFTS ARE RECEIVED BY ALL BELIEVERS.** AMBROSE: See, God sent apostles, and sent prophets and teachers, gave the gift of healings, which as we have found are given by the Holy Spirit, and God gave many kinds of tongues. But yet all are not apostles, all are not prophets, all are not teachers. Not all, says he, have the gift of healings, nor do all, says he, speak with tongues.[34] For the whole range of divine gifts cannot exist in each particular individual. Each, according to his capacity, receives that which he either desires or deserves. ON THE HOLY SPIRIT 2.13.150.[35]

**THE FATHER AND SON AS GIVER OF CHARISMATA.** AMBROSE: As the Father gives the gift

---

[28]Cf. Rev 14:13. [29]It is a speculative question about which the faithful need not fret as to whether if they had lived longer they would have continued in faith. [30]Cetedoc 0262, 217.57.5.416.1; FC 32:87**. Those living in faith are right to pray for unbelievers that they themselves may freely choose to believe. [31]Cetedoc 1711, 2.29.4, 5, 4.39; SSGF 2:428*; PL 76. [32]Mk 16:17-18. [33]PG 1:1061; ANF 7:479*. Those who hold fast to the faith of the apostles themselves participate in the gifts of the apostolate, whose signs of exorcism, healing and tongues may convict unbelievers even when words may fail. [34]Cf. 1 Cor 12:30. [35]Cetedoc 0151, 2.13.150.146.67; NPNF 2 10:134*. Each believer receives not all but some gifts according to his or her capacity to receive.

of healings, so too does the Son give; as the Father gives the gift of tongues, so too has the Son also granted it. On the Holy Spirit 2.13.151.[36]

**How These Gifts Are Distributed in the Church Today.** Gregory the Great: There is something to be said of these signs and powers of a more veiled nature.[37] The holy church is even now doing spiritually, every day, what she then did through the apostles corporately. For when priests, by the grace of exorcism, lay hands on believers and forbid evil spirits to inhabit their minds, what are they doing but "casting out demons"? And any believers whatever who henceforth abandon the profanity of the old life, and utter holy mysteries, and rehearse, as best they can, the praise and power of their maker, what are they doing but "speaking in new tongues?" Moreover, when by their good exhortations they remove evil from the hearts of others, are they not "taking up serpents"? Aren't these miracles the greater because they are spiritual, because they are the means not of raising up bodies but souls? These signs then, beloved, you do if you will.[38] Homilies 29.[39]

## 16:18 If They Drink Any Deadly Thing, It Will Not Hurt Them

**Whether the Faithful May Safely Read the Writings of Heretics.** Augustine: For what else are hearing, reading and copiously depositing things in the memory, than several stages of drinking in thoughts? The Lord, however, foretold concerning his faithful followers, that even "if they should drink any deadly thing, it will not hurt them."[40] And thus it happens that they who read with judgment, and bestow their approval on whatever is commendable according to the rule of faith,[41] and disapprove of things which ought to be repudiated, even if they commit to their memory heretical statements which are declared to be worthy of disapproval, they receive no harm from the poisonous and depraved nature of these sentences. On the Soul and Its Origin 2.23.[42]

---

[36]Cetedoc 0151, 2.13.151.146.85; NPNF 2 10:134. [37]He is poised to raise the question: In what sense do believers today speak in tongues and cast out demons? [38]Cf. Ps 91:13; Jn 14:12-14; 1 Cor 13. [39]Cetedoc 1711, 2.29.4.14; GMI 455*; [40]Mk 16:18. [41]The baptismal confession taught to catechumens. [42]Cetedoc 0345, 2.17.23.358.17; NPNF 1 5:342*.

## 16:19-20 THE ASCENSION

[19]*So then the Lord Jesus, after he had spoken to them, was taken up into heaven, and sat down at the right hand of God.* [20]*And they went forth and preached everywhere, while the Lord worked with them and confirmed the message by the signs that attended it. Amen.*[k]

k Some of the most ancient authorities bring the book to a close at the end of verse 8. One authority concludes the book by adding after verse 8 the following: *But they reported briefly to Peter and those with him all that they had been told. And after this, Jesus himself sent out by means of them, from east to west, the sacred and imperishable proclamation of eternal salvation.* Other authorities include the preceding passage and continue with verses 9-20. In most authorities verses 9-20 follow immediately after verse 8; a few authorities insert additional material after verse 14.

**OVERVIEW:** The ascension confirms what the resurrection evidences demonstrate: that Jesus is the one Lord and creator who rises from the dead and ascends to receive his kingdom (IRENAEUS). The same Son who descended also ascends to heaven (TERTULLIAN). The heavenly span transcends earthly categories of space (AUGUSTINE). The God-man abides with us in our hearts on earth, even as he abides with the Father in heaven (BEDE). As God he is omnipresent, while as man the ascended Lord now dwells bodily in heaven in the same form of flesh in which he lived (AUGUSTINE). Our poor human nature is taken up to heaven with him above angels to the throne of God (GREGORY OF NAZIANZUS, LEO THE GREAT). Healing, comforting, feeding, giving drink, delivering captives—these are continuing works of the ascended Lord (APHRAHAT).

### 16:19a *Taken Up into Heaven*

**WHAT THE ASCENSION CONFIRMS.** IRENAEUS: As he finishes his Gospel, Mark[1] concludes: "So then the Lord Jesus, after he had spoken to them, was taken up into heaven, and sat down at the right hand of God."[2] The ascension confirms what had been spoken by the prophet: "The Lord said to my Lord, Sit thou on my right hand, until I make thy foes thy footstool."[3] Thus God who was announced by the prophets is truly one and the same as God who is celebrated in the true gospel, whom we Christians worship and love with the whole heart as the maker of heaven and earth, and of all things within it. AGAINST HERESIES 3.10.5.[4]

**WE ASCEND WITH HIM.** GREGORY OF NAZIANZUS: He dies,[5] but he makes alive[6] and by

death destroys death.[7] He is buried,[8] yet he rises again.[9] He goes down to Hades, yet he leads souls up,[10] ascends to heaven,[11] and will come to judge the living and the dead,[12] and to probe discussions like these. ORATION 29, ON THE SON 20.[13]

**OUR HUMAN NATURE IS CARRIED UP.** LEO THE GREAT: And so while at Easter it was the Lord's resurrection which was the cause of our joy, our present rejoicing is due to his ascension into heaven. With all due solemnity we are commemorating that day on which our poor human nature was carried up in Christ above all the hosts of heaven, above all the ranks of angels, beyond those heavenly powers to the very throne of God the Father. It is upon this ordered structure of divine acts that we have been firmly established, so that the grace of God may show itself still more marvelous when, in spite of the withdrawal from our sight of everything that is rightly felt to command our reverence, faith does not fail, hope is not shaken, charity does not grow cold. . . . It was in order that we might be capable of such blessedness that on the fortieth day after his resurrection, after he had made careful provision for everything concerning the preaching of the gospel and the mysteries of the new covenant, our Lord Jesus Christ was taken up to heaven before the eyes of his disciples, and so his bodily presence among them came to an end. From that time onward he was to remain at the

---

[1]This passage, often thought to be a later addition to Mark, was regarded by Irenaeus as the received Markan text in the late second century. [2]Mk 16:19. [3]Ps 110:1. [4]AHR 2:39-40; ANF 1:426. [5]Cf. Mt 27:50; Mk 15:37; Lk 23:46; Jn 19:30. [6]Cf. Jn 5:21. [7]Cf. 2 Tim 1:10; Heb 2:14. [8]Cf. Mt 27:60; Mk 15:46; Lk 23:53; Jn 19:41-42; 1 Cor 15:4. [9]Cf. Mt 28:6; Mk 16:6; Lk 24:6; Jn 20:8-9; 1 Cor 15:4. [10]Cf. Eph 4:8-9; Ps 68:18. [11]Cf. Mk 16:19; Lk 24:51; Acts 1:10-11. [12]Cf. 2 Tim 4:1; 1 Pet 4:5. [13]TLG 2022.009, 20.31-34; FGFR 260*.

Father's right hand until the completion of the period ordained by God for the church's children to increase and multiply, after which, in the same body with which he ascended, he will come again to judge the living and the dead. And so our redeemer's visible presence has passed into the sacraments. Our faith is nobler and stronger because empirical sight has been replaced by a reliable teaching whose authority is accepted by believing hearts, enlightened from on high. SERMON 74.1-2.[14]

## 16:19b He Sat Down at the Right Hand of God

**STEPHEN'S VISION.** TERTULLIAN: It is the Son, too, who ascends to the heights of heaven,[15] and also descends to the inner parts of the earth.[16] "He sits at the Father's right hand"[17] —not the Father at his own.[18] He is seen by Stephen at his martyrdom by stoning, still sitting at the right hand of God,[19] where he will continue to sit, until the Father shall make his enemies his footstool.[20] He will come again on the clouds of heaven, just as he appeared when he ascended into heaven.[21] AGAINST PRAXEAS 30.[22]

**WHETHER RIGHT HAND IS A LITERAL REFERENCE.** AUGUSTINE: While such things are mystifying if we take them in a carnal sense, we may be warned thereby to think of them as ineffably spiritual. For this reason, even if we think of the Lord's body, which was raised from the tomb and ascended into heaven, only as having a human appearance and parts, we are not to think that he sits at the right hand of the Father[23] in such a way that the Father should seem to sit [literally] at his left hand. Indeed, in that bliss which surpasses human understanding, the only right hand and the same right hand is a name for that same bliss. LETTER 120, TO CONSENTIUS.[24]

**WHILE SITTING IN HEAVEN, HE IS OMNIPRESENT.** AUGUSTINE: Do not doubt, then, that the man Christ Jesus is now there whence he shall come again. Cherish in your memory and hold faithfully to the profession of your Christian faith that he rose from the dead, ascended into heaven, sits at the right hand of the Father,[25] and will come from no other place but there to judge the living and the dead. He will so come, on the testimony of the angel's voice, as he was seen going into heaven,[26] that is, in the same form and substance of flesh to which, it is true, he gave immortality, but did not take away its nature. According to this fleshly form, we are not to think that he is everywhere present. We must beware of so stressing the divinity of the man that we destroy the reality of his body. It does not follow that what is in God is in him so as to be everywhere as God is. The Scripture says, with perfect truth: "In him we live and move and are,"[27] yet we are not everywhere present as he is, but man is in God after one manner, while God is in man quite differently, in his own unique manner. God and man in him are one person, and both are the one Jesus Christ who is everywhere as God, but in heaven as man. LETTER 187, TO DARDANUS 10.[28]

---

[14]Cetedoc 1657, 138A.74.13; JF B 60-61*; CCL 138A, 455-57. [15]Cf. Jn 3:13. [16]Cf. Eph 4:9. [17]Cf. Mk 16:19; Rev 3:21. [18]As an expression of his eternal sonship. [19]Cf. Acts 7:55-56. [20]Cf. Ps 110:1. [21]Cf. Acts 1:9-11; Lk 24:51. [22]Cetedoc 0026, 30.17; ANF 3:627*. [23]Cf. Mk 16:19. [24]Cetedoc 0262, 1201.34.2.3.717.7; FC 18:312*. Heaven's directionality transcends our categories of space. Our language always falls short of its reality. [25]Cf. Mk 16:19; Col 3:1; Heb 1:3; 10:12. If Jesus is bodily in heaven in the same form of flesh in which he lived, how can he be everywhere? [26]Cf. Acts 1:10-11; 2 Tim 4:1. [27]Acts 17:28. [28]Cetedoc 0262, 187.57.3.89.6; FC 30:228-29*.

**DEATH HAS NO DOMINION.** AUGUSTINE: Having vanquished the devil by the resurrection, he sits at the right hand of the Father,[29] where he dies no more, and death no longer over him shall have dominion.[30] ON THE PSALMS 72.8.[31]

**ASCENDED LORD, COMING LORD.** PRUDENTIUS:

Hail! Thou king of all the living;
Hail! Thou judge of all the dead,[32]
At the right hand of thy Father,
Thou art throned in highest power,[33]
And from thence just judge of sinners,
Thou shalt one day come again.
HYMN 9, A HYMN FOR EVERY HOUR.[34]

**PRESENT ON EARTH WHILE AT THE FATHER'S RIGHT HAND.** BEDE: Because he who was taken up into heaven is both God and a human being, he remains on earth with the saints in the humanity which he took from the earth, but in the divinity with which he fills earth and heaven equally he remains "all days, even to the consummation of the world." From this it is understood that even up to the end, the world will not lack those in whom there will be divine abiding and indwelling. Nor should we doubt that those struggling in this world will deserve to have Christ abiding in their hearts as a guest, and will abide with Christ in his kingdom after the contests of this world. Nevertheless we should note that the divine majesty, while existing everywhere, is present in one way to the elect, in another to the condemned. It is present for the condemned in the power of [God's] incomprehensible nature, by which he knows everything, the most recent happenings and the former ones, understands [human] thoughts from afar, and foresees all the ways of each one.[35] It is present for the elect in the grace of his benevolent protection, by which he draws them, guiding each one individually by his present gifts and chastisements to the possession of their future inheritance as a father guides his children. EXPOSITION ON THE GOSPEL OF MARK 2.8.[36]

### 16:20 *The Lord Confirmed the Message by the Signs That Attended It*

**CONTINUING SIGNS ACCOMPANYING FAITH.** APHRAHAT: Let us draw near, then, my beloved, to faith, since its powers are so many. For faith raised up [Enoch] to the heavens,[37] and overcame the deluge.[38] It caused the barren to bring forth.[39] It delivered from the sword.[40] Faith raised up from the pit.[41] It enriched the poor.[42] It released the captives.[43] It delivered the persecuted.[44] It brought down the fire.[45] It divided the sea.[46] Faith cleft the rock and gave to the thirsty water to drink.[47] It satisfied the hungry.[48] It raised the dead and brought them up from Sheol.[49] It stilled the billows.[50] It healed the sick.[51] DEMONSTRATION 1.18.[52]

---

[29]Cf. Mk 16:19. [30]Cf. Rom 6:9. [31]Cetedoc 0283, 39.71.8.37; NPNF 1 8:329. [32]Cf. Acts 10:42. [33]Cf. Mk 16:19. [34]Cetedoc 1438, 9.106; FC 43:68. [35]Cf. Ps 139:2-4. [36]Cetedoc 1367, 2.8.99; HOG 2:72-73*. [37]Cf. Gen 5:24; Heb 11:5. [38]Cf. Gen 7:1—8.22. [39]Cf. Gen 21:1-3; Heb 11:11-12. [40]Cf. Gen 22:1-9; Heb 11:17, 34. [41]Cf. Gen 37:28. [42]Cf. Mk 12:42-44. [43]Cf. Heb 11:27-29. [44]Cf. Heb 11:27-29. [45]Cf. 1 Kings 18:38. [46]Cf. Ex 14:21. [47]Cf. Ex 17:6. [48]Cf. Ex 16:15. [49]Cf. Heb 11:35. [50]Cf. Mt 8:26. [51]Cf. Mt 9:2, 22; Mk 2:5. [52]PS 1/1:41-43; NPNF 2 13:351*. Healing, comforting, feeding, giving drink, delivering captives—these are continuing evidences of the work of the ascended Lord.

# APPENDIX

## Method of Investigation
## into the Early Exegesis of Mark

We wish to offer an explicit account of how we approached the task of selecting the patristic comments found in this volume. Our procedures were as follows:

1. By using Boolean[1] word search techniques, we searched for Greek and Latin words in all the ancient Christian writers that correlate with a particular phrase or comment in Greek or Latin from the Gospel of Mark. We also sought to identify Markan passages in the patristic texts that could not have been referring to another Evangelist because they use Greek word sequences or phrases found only in Mark and not in Matthew, Luke and John. Where pertinent, we hand-searched in the Greek Septuagint and in the Old Latin and Vulgate versions, using textual variants wherever required. Our Drew Project searching staff, under the guidance of Joel Scandrett and Susan Kipper, executed these extensive computer searches, which would have been unthinkable prior to the advent of computer technology. Serving ably on the Gospel of Mark search team were Vincent Bacote, Edward Blain, Thomas Buchan, Joel Elowsky, Jeffrey Finch, Peter Gilbert, Michael Glerup, Allen Kerkeslager, Michael Kipper, Sergey Kozin, Michael Monos, Wesley Tink, Bernie Van De Walle and Colleen Van De Walle. Thanks are also due to Denise Ratcliffe for editorial work conducted at Eastern College. We are deeply indebted to them for this demanding, time-consuming and selfless service. This procedure yielded approximately three thousand paragraphs of text in Latin and four thousand paragraphs of text in Greek. These were stored on our project's digital database, from which we then selected the best material according to our editorial guidelines.

2. We then identified and photocopied all references to Mark in all English editions[2] of patristic writings.[3] These extractions were sorted and arranged verse by verse and then organized into files

---

[1] Specifying this and/or that selection of words, but excluding others.

[2] Not only in the Fathers of the Church series, the Ancient Christian Writers series, the Library of Christian Classics and the Loeb Library, but also in public domain texts like the ANF/NPNF, the older Oxford texts and numerous independent editions not related to any series. We acknowledge our thanks to the Speer Library at Princeton Theological Seminary, the libraries at Catholic University of America and the Drew Library for many kindnesses, hospitalities and other forms of assistance.

[3] All this labor was accomplished, unfortunately, before the Church Fathers CD-ROM was available from the Electronic Bible Society and Logos Research Systems. If we had been searching with that database, we would have saved a great deal of time by doing these searches digitally in the English text. Our project helped significantly to fund the entry, digitalization and tagging of the texts of all thirty-eight volumes of the Ante-Nicene and Nicene and Post-Nicene Fathers, joining them with the search engine of Logos Research Systems.

according to pericopes. This yielded approximately three thousand short texts of photocopied material. We then examined all this material to make a preliminary sort, selecting those passages we thought had some possibility of being included in the final commentary. We then began building up manuscript drafts on the basis of all of these extracts from all language sources. Then we examined all these texts, rating them according to our editorial objectives and criteria.[4]

3. Having identified second-round selections, we proceeded to translate untranslated texts or to dearchaize those texts that needed further attention.[5] Where longer homilies or parts of extended commentaries were discovered and found acceptable, we entered them in whole or in part into our database, correlated them with our pericope files and selected circumspectly from among them, usually correlating them with specific verses.[6] The above procedures yielded an abundance of material in most searches, so much so that a large percentage of the gross material normally had to be set aside. We then searched out Syriac and Coptic sources with the intent of achieving a fitting balance from all exegetical traditions of ancient Christianity.

4. We then proceeded to append explanatory and clarifying footnotes, to make topical headings according to our editorial criteria, and to cite biblical and other references as needed.

It is important to note that in executing our computer searches, we had many "hits" on Markan texts that by discriminating search techniques and by Greek synoptic harmony comparisons could be shown to be specifically referencing Mark and not the other Evangelists, regardless of where they might have appeared in the author's corpus of writings. Hence some of the most important comments on Mark are found embedded in Origen's, Chrysostom's or Augustine's commentaries or homilies on Matthew or John and not just on Mark. If these sources had been arbitrarily ruled out, we would have been deprived of some of the richest source material on Mark.[7]

We candidly invite others to follow similar procedures on a given text and compare how their selections might correspond with or differ from ours. By this means we could be suitably admonished if we

---

[4]Although we eliminated a large percentage of the material as lacking in some way according to our editorial criteria, we saved all these extracts on disk in order to build eventually a usable raw, digitalized database of all these passages.

[5]The ANF/NPNF translations were made in a late nineteenth-century Victorian-Edwardian linguistic ethos in a period of rather sturdy patristic scholarship, but unfortunately of somewhat wooden sentence construction, often with too literal a reading and with phrases tediously strung together with semicolons. In making the reading of ancient texts smoother and more accessible to modern readers, we have dearchaized these texts by mercifully taking out most of the *thous, thines, begats, whences* and *slaineths*, making shorter sentences easier for readers to navigate, smoothing out transitions and using ellipses where inconsequential material was skipped and brackets where some assistance is needed. In some cases where we were already dearchaizing an antiquated translation, in order to simplify reading we have omitted distracting ellipses and bracketing at the beginning or end of sentences.

[6]Many of the items turned up in the Latin and Greek searches we also discovered to be duplicated in the English editions search. Where this was the case, we compared the best extant English translation with the received Latin or Greek text. Where we felt the best extant English translation had in it anything that was lacking, we translated it afresh or corrected or improved the translation accordingly, indicating that we had made amendments.

[7]The ancient Christian writers often freely blended comments and observations on Mark with comments on other Evangelists. This is why we quote patristic commentaries on Matthew and John in this volume on Mark.

unconsciously biased the selections. We solicit such counsel. We are not defensive about our selections, which were made according to our express criteria in volume editors' guidelines. We acknowledge that other criteria would have produced a different selection. We welcome the admonition of others to see how any of our choices might have been better made according to dissimilar criteria. We have repeatedly asked ourselves: Would it be edifying to hear this patristic voice within a service of common worship as an exposition of a Scripture text? We have ruled out many texts on this basis. If it is not something we ourselves would wish to hear referred to in the task of spiritual formation, then we have been less inclined to include it. This simple intuitive test has significantly shaped our selection process.

We were duly forewarned by some that this volume on Mark probably could or should not be attempted. It was thought by some to be lacking in sufficient primary sources, with not enough commentary material available for Mark to justify the effort, and that the attempt to do such a volume on Mark might result in a nonsequential patchwork of miscellaneous quotations that would not significantly explicate the text. Some argued that this series might do better to confine itself to those biblical books where substantial numbers of line-by-line commentaries are available: Genesis, Isaiah, Song of Solomon, Matthew, John and Romans. This volume is a demonstration that Mark has an ample history of commentary to be presented in the form and tradition of a catena. As general editor of this series, I have accepted this volume assignment as a challenge precisely because it was deemed to be the least feasible among the four Gospels.

## The Genesis of the ACCS

This series, the Ancient Christian Commentary on Scripture, convened its first meeting as a "feasibility consultation" in Washington, D.C., which gathered at the invitation of Drew University in November of 1993. In April of 1994, shortly after the feasibility study had signaled affirmatively that the ACCS project should be undertaken, Drew University announced the reception of a generous grant from an anonymous donor to fund the nine-year project. At that time no other project of this sort was underway.

ACCS has been from the outset decisively committed to producing a commentary on *the whole of Scripture for pastoral use and for a general lay audience*. Why the whole? (1) Because various lectionary approaches to patristic collections already exist; (2) because pastors preach on many different texts in the course of a year, far broader than those in the lectionary or in a few books of Scripture; and (3) because the whole of Scripture is commented on by the ancient Christian writers. We are finding an abundance of commentary material on virtually every text or pericope we have looked at thus far.

The original and continuing ACCS vision of the task has been to use newly available computer search technology to look for *all references in all types of patristic literature—letters, sermons, hymns, doctrinal writings*, as well as specifically exegetical works, eschewing the much easier procedure of working more intensively with fewer texts or preferring complete printed texts to extensive digital searches.

ACCS has preferred from the outset to seek to enlist an *international* team of volume editors whose lives are lived out within both the university and the church, and often within its seminaries. The choice of volume editors expresses a strong concern for ecumenical balance, seeking editors whose judgment would prove trustworthy to all communions East and West—Eastern Orthodox, mainline and evangelical Protestant, and Roman Catholic. ACCS has intentionally selected volume editors who have already proven themselves capable of working significantly in the whole history of exegesis in both Eastern and Western traditions. The alternative approach would have been to distribute its editorial workload on a committee basis by assigning teams of scholarly specialists to meet together and make editorial decisions based on the complementarity of various professional specializations.

We readily concede that there may be various alternative visions of a patristic commentary on the Bible: a commentary on the whole Bible versus an undertaking that comments on selected portions of Scripture; searches embracing all genres of patristic writings versus selections primarily from line-by-line commentaries; central versus ancillary use of computer technology; utilization versus non-utilization of available English translations; service to an international audience of clergy and laity versus service primarily to American historical specialists. In each case, we have chosen the former.

## A Labor of Love

Virtually all those involved in this project have indicated personally that they have grown spiritually through engaging in this precise, laborious, complex task. Without slackening academic rigor, this exercise has been far more than a matter of mere historical curiosity. That it has been a joyful task does not make it any less a demanding intellectual puzzle and a lengthy struggle of heart and mind. It has not been easy to locate the texts, to select them properly, to translate them suitably and to edit them with fitting transitions and footnotes that will help contemporary readers make good sense of them, but the struggle has been a labor of love. This sort of work requires an enormous amount of disciplined solitude and quiet meditation on ancient writings. One must have sustained commitment even to enter this arena. It is not simply a matter of mechanically punching out buttons on a computer, but of thinking through the complex meaning of ancient texts written in different historical periods and languages.

On average perhaps ten out of a hundred digital search attempts have proved to be worth considering, and of those only one out of a hundred was selected. So the rare discoveries have been exciting when they have occurred. Sometimes we have felt like explorers, and often like foreigners in an alien land. We have at times felt chagrined to be forced to extract from a lengthy passage, just taking the heart of it and leaving the rest behind. But such is the poignant work of the catenist, or of any anthologist or compiler of a compendium for general use.

Often we would have liked to write extended footnotes on the context, philology, etymology, social circumstance or location, and historical uncertainties of a particular text. But when faced with the breadth and range of the task at hand, we have had to limit our purpose to the specific task of presenting the most salient ancient comment on a given text of Scripture.

See the volume *Commentary Index and Resources* for a collection of supplemental ACCS material, including a comprehensive Scripture index and authors/writings index.